WOMAN

According to Saint Bonaventure

by

Sister Emma Thérèse Healy
of
The Congregation of the Sisters of Saint Joseph
Erie, Pennsylvania
Villa Maria College
Erie, Pennsylvania

1956

NIHIL OBSTAT:

RT. REV. MSGR. A. H. WIERSBINSKI, P.A., V.G., LL.D.
Censor Librorum
August 16, 1955

IMPRIMATUR:

✠ JOHN MARK GANNON, D.D., D.C.L., LL.D.
Archbishop—Bishop of Erie
August 19, 1955
Erie, Pennsylvania

PRINTED IN THE UNITED STATES OF AMERICA
BY THE GEORGIAN PRESS INC., 175 VARICK STREET, NEW YORK 14, N. Y. 1955

TABLE OF CONTENTS

PAGE

Foreword i
Preface v
Introduction vii

PART ONE

WOMAN IN NATURE

CHAPTER

I. Woman's Equality with Man 1
II. Her Physical Nature 6
III. Her Psychological Nature 16
IV. Her Part in the Fall 27
V. Her Punishment 41
VI. St. Bonaventure's Attitude 46
VII. The Attitude of Christ 52

PART TWO

WOMAN IN GRACE

Introduction 69

WOMAN IN CHRISTIAN MARRIAGE

I. Christian Marriage: Its Symbolism 79
II. Its Nature and Threefold Purpose 87
III. Its Threefold Blessing 100
IV. Its Reciprocal Obligations 104
V. Its Spheres of Activity 109

WOMAN IN THE VIRGINAL LIFE

I. Virginity: Its Three Aspects 119
II. Its Excellence 129
III. Its Reward 135
IV. The Lily of Christ 138

PART THREE

Woman in Glory

I. The Ideal Woman: Virgin and Mother 157

II. The Virgin Mother of God 169

Mary's Physical Motherhood 173

Mary's Physical Virginity 180

III. The Bride Mother of Christ 203

Mary's Spiritual Virginity 207

Mary's Spiritual Motherhood 233

IV. Queen of Heaven and Earth 245

Conclusion 269

Bibliography 271

Index 273

FOREWORD

FOR SEVERAL YEARS PAST the late and lamented Father Philotheus Boehner, Director of the Franciscan Institute at St. Bonaventure, N. Y., had been looking around for a person who would have the courage, the scholarly attainments, and above all the interest and love to assemble in one volume all that the Seraphic Doctor has to say on the theme before us—*Woman according to St. Bonaventure*. Being an ardent and devoted student of Bonaventurian writings, he knew that whoever attempted this arduous task would find "a pearl of great price." The writer was found in the person of the author of this book. Humanly speaking, it is regrettable that the Angel of Death had called Father Philotheus just before he could give final approval to the unearthed "pearl of great price" in its present finished form.

The author is not a novice in the field of Bonaventurian literature. Her doctoral dissertation "St. Bonaventure's *De Reductione Artium ad Theologiam*—A Commentary with an Introduction and Translation" (1939), which was the first book written under the auspices of the Franciscan Institute, has merited high and universal praise. It is now available in its second, revised edition.[1]

In the work before us St. Bonaventure appears in a new role. Previously known to us as the Seraphic Doctor, a leading figure among the great Schoolmen of the Thirteenth Century, the "Prince of Mystics" in the words of Leo XIII, the Re-organizer and eighth Minister General of the Order of Friars Minor, the Patron of the Franciscan School, the peerless orator of his day, a voluminous writer, an inspiring teacher at Paris, the guiding spirit at the Second Council of Lyons, Cardinal and Doctor of the Church,—he now stands before us, on the pages of this book, as the genial, understanding, eloquent, and inspired Champion of Christian Womanhood. Needless to say, the casual or even attentive reader of the frequently intricate and involved Latin text of this erudite medieval professor and bookman will be both amazed and gratified to see him, on the pages of this book, suddenly emerge from his philosophical and theological argumentation and speculation, as a genuinely normal human being with flesh and blood; as a friar and priest who, though groomed and trained in monastic life, knew the world and human nature in every phase and detail and who manifested a sound evalu-

(1) By Sister Emma Thérèse Healy, C. S. J. The book is now republished, under the same title, by the Franciscan Institute, St. Bonaventure, N. Y.

ation as well as a keen appreciation of those endowments with which nature has invested "the devout feminine sex." On these pages St. Bonaventure reveals himself as the gallant knight of Womanhood. A spirit of high-minded chivalry carries his every word and sentence as he champions, defends, and raises to perhaps unprecedented nobility and charm the station, function, and dignity of our race's weaker sex.

One might ask: "Whence did the Seraphic Doctor draw the doctrine, attitude, and inspiration here in evidence?" The obvious answer lies in the fact that he proved himself as a docile pupil. In his own inimitable way he carries forward and enriches the teachings of his Master, Alexander of Hales. His views on woman's part in human generation had been the tradition of the Franciscan School from the beginning and were later on propounded with consummate skill by the Subtle Doctor, John Duns Scotus. Undoubtedly this position has given strength and color to other Franciscan tenets, especially in the field of Mariology.

It may not be entirely amiss to seek at least a contributory motivation for the Saint's reverence for womanhood in the recollection of his own mother. For who would deny that the atmosphere of a true Catholic home, and especially the presence of a devout mother, moulds a man's whole life and destiny? Now we know that Bonaventure's mother, the pious Donna Ritella of Bagnoreo saved her child's life through the intercession of St. Francis of Assisi, and we wonder not that the mother's blessing and the fond recollection of her should accompany the youth to Paris where his Master Alexander was wont to say of him: "It appears that in his youth Adam has not sinned."

Be that as it may, undoubtedly the most powerful formative influence upon the Seraphic Doctor's studies and teachings was the glorious heritage he had received and fully imbibed from Assisi's seraphic Poverello. To the latter the Work of Creation and the Book of Revelation were felicitously blended in God's infinite love. His great son had caught this burning flame and subsequently worked out and built up this as well as other themes in his lectures and writings with a scholar's skill and mystic intuition. He recognized in the Word of God on the pages of Holy Writ a lucid commentary or, as he put it, a poetic composition which gave harmony, beauty, and color to God's work in nature. In the latter he saw vestiges of God's love and divine attributes, all set in focus by the brilliant light of Sacred Scripture, and by the same light he perceived, not merely vestiges, but the very image of God in nature's masterpiece—the human soul. But the soul of woman—no matter what restrictions or inhibitions philosophers might offer—is the perfect equal of the soul of man. And hence, woman is man's equal in nature, grace, and glory. Having thus set his sails, the Seraphic Doctor launched forth upon his theme and braved all obstacles in the conviction that he had the support of sound Catholic belief. No one has ever questioned the soundness of St.

Bonaventure's theological teachings, and if any doubt should arise as to his philosophical knowledge and acumen, the present volume will give a ready answer.

We have spoken of his earthly mother, but much more should be said of his spiritual mother,—Mary, the Mother of God, the Virgin most holy and immaculate. The deep-rooted, unwavering, and childlike devotion to the Mother of God that has been the sacred heritage in the Franciscan Order from the very first comes to full bloom and flowering in the writings of the Seraphic Doctor. To him Mary was the Valiant Woman, the Ideal Woman, and as the present volume beautifully conveys, Mary is the "Woman in glory" and from her seem to radiate all the distinction and dignity accorded by the Creator and Saviour to the Woman in Grace and the Woman in Nature. While the author of this present volume follows St. Bonaventure's line of argument consistently from nature to grace, to glory, we may well surmise that in the consciousness of the Seraphic Doctor, Mary stood reversely at the beginning of the line, and that she was the guiding star, "the pattern" on the holy mountain (Num. 8:4) that inspired and fashioned all his teachings on the present theme.

Whereas we admire the consistency and thoroughness with which the Saint carries forward his thesis throughout all his varied and numerous writings, we cannot but commend the painstaking and penetrating thoroughness of which the present volume gives convincing evidence. It was no easy task to wade through the ten voluminous tomes of St. Bonaventure's *Opera Omnia* and to assemble, analyze, and set in succinct and clear-cut order the vast material set forth either magisterially or, as is frequently the case, hidden away in the Master's peculiar phraseology of medieval Latinity. But what may be called the most distinctive merit of this book is the fact that the author has tried sedulously, if not scrupulously to give us, not her own, but St. Bonaventure's doctrine and opinions throughout.

The division of the book has an additional interest and merit. It shows that a docile pupil will not only accept the Master's doctrine, but will assimilate his approach, method, and style as well as the unction which is the unmistakable mark of St. Bonaventure's seraphic pen. Thus the Saint's symbolic approach is well exemplified on these pages. One is reminded of his "Triplex Via," his "Itinerarium," his "Breviloquium," as one follows the threefold division of Nature, Grace, and Glory. And each of these divisions affords ample opportunity for a generous display of Bonaventurian thought and teaching. In the first part the search light of his philosophical investigation is focused with rare clarity on nature's foremost creature—the human soul, which bears the image of the Triune God. He distinguishes with startling effect between the biblical image and likeness, for while the former may be considered as nature's endowment, the latter stands in the realm of grace.

By the aid of grace man must produce in his soul a likeness to the image. And Divine Grace is St. Bonaventure's favorite and most delightful topic. Somehow we behold womanhood being led from the Purgative to the Illuminative Way, until it finally reaches its true destiny with Mary, the Crown of womanhood in glory, on the Unitive Way with God.

FR. THOMAS PLASSMANN, O. F. M.

PREFACE

SINCE THE GATES OF PARADISE LOST clanged behind her and her hapless spouse, Woman has been the most controversial figure in the history of the world,—the perennial theme of poets, philosophers, and theologians. To some she is an angel in the flesh; to others, the only mistake God ever made. It was at the suggestion of the late Reverend Philotheus Boehner, a fervent son of St. Francis, and now, we trust, associated with him in heaven, that I have attempted to set forth in this book the Seraphic Doctor's ideas about this most revered and most reviled of God's creatures. To Father Philotheus I am indebted not only for directing my attention to the subject but also for valuable suggestions as to the present text. When the sudden death of Ockham's learned expositor left the Franciscan Order mourning and me without the stamp of approval on my efforts, I instinctively turned to the Very Reverend Thomas Plassmann, the well-known Franciscan scholar and writer, and he did not fail me. Not only did the distinguished Rector of Christ the King Seminary graciously read the manuscript, as I knew he would, but he took time out of a busy day to grace the book with his Foreword. To Father Thomas, my heartfelt thanks and appreciation.

Now, to get back to *Woman*. Actually, the status of Woman in any age is a concrete expression of the philosophy which dominates the age in which she lives. Though the prejudice of the past has in some respect obscured the teachings of God's Word concerning the status of Woman and her rightful place in the divine plan, women themselves are not without blame in furthering the low esteem to which they have fallen. No longer the victim of an animal philosophy which looks upon her as a toy, a domestic instrument, or a necessary nuisance, but the exponent rather of a romantic philosophy of life which glorifies her youth and beauty, modern woman herself, by flaunting and glamourizing her physical attractions to the utter disregard of spiritual qualities, has given no little justification to Rudyard Kipling's evaluation of her as "a rag, a bone, and a hank of hair." Utterly unmindful of the designs of God in the essential and radical dissimilarities between the two sexes and attempting, in the words of Tennyson, "to lift woman's fallen divinity upon an equal pedestal with man," Woman herself has stepped down from the divine plane where she belongs as a daughter of the Mother of God and a member of the Mystical Body of Christ.

This is the Age of Mary,—an appropriate time for Woman to recapture her lost glory and to re-establish herself on the pedestal of man's respect and reverence. With the glorious Virgin enthroned in heaven and on earth, with the Mother of God offering her Divine Child for the adoration of the ages, it is impossible for womankind to remain despised and degraded. Mindful, then, of their eternal destiny and the supreme dignity which is theirs by reason of the Incarnation of the Son of God, let women the world over prove themselves worthy daughters of a worthy mother, the blessed Mother of God, the glorious Queen in whom the dignity of every maiden, wife, and mother is consecrated and enthroned forever.

SISTER EMMA THERESE

Villa Maria College
Erie, Pennsylvania
Feast of Our Lady's Assumption, 1955

INTRODUCTION

THE DOCTRINE contained in the authentic words of the Master, or implied in His ways and deeds, stands as irrefragable truth, the infallible rule of faith and conduct for all Christian men and women. In the transmission and interpretation of revealed truth, the Catholic Church, sent by Christ to teach all nations, and endowed by Him with infallible authority, is the divinely qualified messenger to whose teachings every Catholic conscious of his faith owes reverence, loyalty, and intelligent obedience. This submission extends to all points regulating faith and morals as well as to dogmas pertaining to the nature and to the supernatural destinies of the human person without distinction of sex.

Due importance, too, should be attached to the interpretations of the Sacred Text given by the Fathers of the Church whose self-imposed task it was to scan the utterances of Sacred Scripture and to extract from them every particle of knowledge they might contain either directly or by implication. And what a variety of comments, explanations, and deductions! On many matters a wide variance of opinion might exist within the compass of orthodoxy, for Catholicism does not forbid men to value secular knowledge, providing they do not adhere to opinions contradicting Christian verity. When Fathers or Theologians morally agree in setting forth a particular interpretation of some text as belonging to the Faith, we are again in the presence of an indication of the Mind of the Church, and must therefore acquiesce. But where the Fathers differ, and where an interpretation is given simply as an individual expression of opinion, we are at liberty to adopt any view we wish, subject, of course, to the Church's right to decide as to its tenability.

Without philosophy many matters of Faith cannot be discussed intelligently, and the great philosophers of the past are proofs of the fact that mere human reason, subject to countless influences of pride and other passions, is liable to go astray.[1] Hence sometimes misinterpretations and misunderstandings as to the true meaning and import of patristic statements on the

(1) Referring to the doctrines of the pagan philosophers and particularly to those of Aristotle concerning punishment and glory, the eternity of the world, and the unity of the intellect, St. Bonaventure wrote: "Sed adhuc isti in tenebris fuerunt, quia non habuerunt lumen fidei." *In Hexaëmeron,* VII. 1-3, t.V, 366a. Cf. *ibid.,* I. 6-8, t.V, 330. "Intellectus est semper rectus . . . secundum respicit leges aeternas et ab ipsis recipit et in eis speculatur, non autem qualitercumque ex se movetur, immo frequenter est obliquus et erroneus." *III Sent.,* d.33, q.3, ad 5, t.III, 718b. "Ratio non solum infirmatur per ignorantiam, sed etiam per hebetudinem et praecipitationem." *Ibid.,* d.34, p.1, a.2, q.1, ad 2, t.III, 746b.

It seems needless to state that all references to the works of St. Bonaventure are to the Quaracchi edition of the *Opera Omnia.* As to Patristic quotations, we refer to the volume and column of the Greek or Latin Patrology of Migne by the abbreviation MPG or MPL respectively. All translations, unless otherwise indicated, are mine.

part of later scholars, intent upon searching into, and abiding by the exegetical tradition of former ages, but imbued with other philosophical doctrines, not to mention an increased knowledge of the secrets of nature. Thus, while the dogmatic definitions of the Church are infallibly true, while the living Catholic tradition is not subject to error, while theology is certain in its conclusions, subsequent explanations proposed by the Fathers, Doctors, Theologians, or particular schools or traditions can be deficient and imperfect. In fact, they risk being so in proportion as they include human, contingent, and uncertain elements.

As there was a human element, even by his own acknowledgment, in the life of the greatest of the Apostles, so is there a human element in the Church and it has left its infirmities behind it in the track of history. Darkened understanding is a part of the common heritage left us by our first parents and it is not surprising that men, always limited in some respects, sometimes fail to arrive at a full discovery of all the aspects of a difficult truth. Even less surprising is the fact that they sometimes unconsciously fall into error because, starting from incontrovertible, even revealed principles, they attach to these principles some inexact notions or false data. Thus, counterfeit exegetical traditions have been—innocently, to be sure,—and are still occasionally palmed off upon uncritical minds. These stray opinions merely serve to show that theology is a progressive science. The advanced thought of the age in nowise affects the contents of Sacred Scripture and the fallibility of human understanding in nowise alters the truth as revealed in the Word of God.

Moreover, one should not forget that from the Middle Ages to the beginning of the Renaissance the baneful tendency of the times to trust authority rather than to depend on one's own observations and experiments made itself felt even in the sciences, especially in medicine and biology. There were also not a few thinkers who merely speculated with regard to the processes of development and differentiation. These were the philosophers, more specifically the so-called nature philosophers, who preferred to reason out the order of nature rather than to determine it by observation and experimentation.

There is no reason, therefore, to be disconcerted or scandalized by defects in the human interpretations that Churchmen have given to the divine idea of woman. We are the heirs of the ages and the influence of Greco-Latin philosophy and literature, of Roman law, of the laws of uncivilized peoples, even of rabbinical exegesis, could unduly affect some theologians, bias their minds with prejudices or ideas that were altogether unfavorable to woman. Every man is of his own time and he cannot raise himself very far out of the mass of knowledge and opinion furnished by it. It is enough to recall how long it took to get rid of the vexatious Aristotelian phrase, *femina est mas occasionatus,* and to consider the efforts of several Doctors, indeed some of the greatest, to propose an explanation of it that would be acceptable to Christianity.

There is a synthesis common to the great doctors of the West, a harmony of philosophy with dogma and a remarkable agreement upon all fundamental questions. In every period of medieval philosophy, however, it is easy to detect manifold and contradictory types, currents moving in divergent directions—a divergence springing now from the philosophic content of the systems, now from the varying attitudes of medieval thinkers towards reason and authority and even from their different views upon the limits of the field of salutary knowledge. These differences, exemplified in their methods, or rather in the variations of their common method, insure individuality and originality of thought. The powerful movement at work within Christian thought in the Thirteenth Century, the Golden Age of Scholasticism, projected two high peaks. One of these is the doctrine of St. Thomas, who with St. Albert built Aristotelianism into a Christian system of thought; the other, that of St. Bonaventure in whom the Augustinian thought of the Middle Ages reached its highest development. These two saints, the Franciscan Bonaventure and the Dominican Thomas, were important personages in the construction of the scholastic synthesis of the Middle Ages. Though the spirit which animates the work of each is quite different, both Doctors represent a Christian philosophy; both are champions of the same faith. They are, in the words of Pope Sixtus V, twin stars rising by the special providence of God at the same time from two great Orders of the Church and merging their pure rays into one glorious light to shine forever before the infinite purity of the Triune God,—stars which by the intensity of their love and the light of their learning to this day illumine the Church of God.[2] They are "the two olive trees and the two candlesticks" that shine in the house of the Lord, and yet, like the majority of the Schoolmen, they assigned a certain inferiority to woman. Of the Angelic Doctor, Hans Meyer says: "Seldom has it occurred that a thinker who has had such a profound influence on the thought of centuries has erred so profoundly with regard to the nature of woman as the medieval, cloistered Saint Thomas."[3] In the Seraphic Doctor, the prejudice seems less marked, and a slight trend toward a higher appreciation of woman is noticeable.

Every age has offered an interpretation of the Gospel and an attempt at its fulfillment. On many matters neither the interpretation of the Church

(2) "Hi enim sunt *duae olivae et duo candelabra* (Apoc. 11,4) in domo Dei lucentia, qui et caritatis pinguedine et scientiae luce totam Ecclesiam collustrant; hi singulari Dei providentia eodem tempore tamquam duae stellae exorientes ex duabus clarissimis regularium Ordinum familiis prodierunt, quae sanctae Ecclesiae ad catholicam religionem propugnandam maxime utiles, et ad omnes labores et pericula pro orthodoxa fide subeunda paratae semper existunt, . . . " *Bulla Sixti V,* §13, *S. Bonaventurae Opera Omnia,* t.I, L.

(3) *The Philosophy of St. Thomas Aquinas;* translated by Rev. Frederic Eckhoff, p. 209. B. Herder Book Co., St. Louis, Mo., 1944.

Fathers, nor that of the Middle Ages satisfies us now, and by our further understanding of life and the Gospel of life, we criticize the judgment of medieval men. We have to sympathize with their best and understand their lives out of their lives and the conditions in which they were passed, but we must judge according to our own best wisdom, and out of ourselves offer comment.

PART ONE

WOMAN IN NATURE

To My Earthly Mother

Chapter I

WOMAN'S EQUALITY WITH MAN

THE LORD has wrought all His works by two and two, says Holy Writ, and contrast is one of the laws of creation: "So look upon all the works of the Most High two and two, and one against another" (Ecclus. 42:25). This contrast is particularly striking in the creation of man and woman, and in the distribution of their various qualities.

The biblical data concerning Adam and Eve are confined almost exclusively to the second, third, and fourth chapters of Genesis. For the pure version of the wonderful story stripped of all the cumbersome tinsel accumulated by ages of idolatry and superstition, let us refer to the first chapter of the Book of Genesis:

> "And God said: Let the earth bring forth the living creature in its kind, cattle and creeping things, and beasts of the earth, according to their kinds. And it was so done. And God made the beasts of the earth according to their kinds, and cattle, and every thing that creepeth on the earth after its kind. And God saw that it was good (1:24-25).
>
> "And he said: Let us make man to our image and likeness; and let him have dominion over the fishes of the sea, and the fowls of the air, and the beasts, and the whole earth, and every creeping creature that moveth upon the earth. And God created man to his own image; to the image of God he created him. Male and female he created them. And God blessed them saying: Increase and multiply, and fill the earth, and subdue it . . . (1:26-28). And God saw all the things that he had made, and they were very good. And the evening and morning were the sixth day" (1:31).

The second account is more explicit and detailed:

> "But a spring rose out of the earth, watering all the surface of the earth. And the Lord God formed man of the slime of the earth, and breathed into his face the breath of life; and man became a living soul. And the Lord God had planted a paradise of pleasure from the beginning, wherein he placed man whom he had formed. And the Lord God brought forth of the ground all manner of trees, fair to behold, and pleasant to eat of: the tree of life also in the midst of paradise, and the tree of knowledge of good and evil" (Gen. 2:6-9).
>
> "And the Lord God took man, and put him into the paradise of pleasure, to dress it, and to keep it. And he commanded him saying: Of every tree of paradise thou shalt eat. But of the tree of knowledge of good and evil, thou shalt not eat. For in what day soever thou shalt eat of it, thou shalt die the death. And the Lord God said: It is not good for man to be alone, let us make him a help like unto himself. And the Lord God having formed out of the ground all the beasts of the earth, and all the fowls of the air, brought them to Adam to see what he would call them,

> for whatsoever Adam called any living creature the same is its name. And Adam called all the beasts by their names, and all the fowls of the air, and all the cattle of the field, but for Adam there was not found a helper like himself. Then the Lord God cast a deep sleep upon Adam, and when he was fast asleep, he took one of his ribs, and filled up flesh for it. And the Lord God built the rib which he took from Adam into a woman, and brought her to Adam. And Adam said: This now is bone of my bones, and flesh of my flesh: she shall be called woman, because she was taken out of man. Wherefore a man shall leave father and mother, and shall cleave to his wife: and they shall be two in one flesh. And they were both naked, to wit, Adam and his wife: and were not ashamed" (Gen. 2:15-25).

"In the beginning God created heaven and earth" (Gen. 1:1). After this simple but majestic introduction to the history of the world, the Sacred Writer narrates in detail how God called forth the beasts of the field, the fishes of the sea, and the birds of the air from the dark depths of nothingness into the light of the visible kingdom which He had planned for His own honor and glory.

In relating the creation of man, Scripture seems to move more slowly, in reverent awe, as it were. The modeling of the shapeless clay, the vitalizing warmth of divine breath on the lifeless mass are most carefully described. "And the Lord God formed man of the slime of the earth, and breathed into his face the breath of life, and man became a living soul." Here we have a description of two actions: the first not a creative one by which man's body was prepared from matter already existing; the second a purely creative one, since it produced what in no way existed before.[1] The result, man, is a complete being. The Divine Artist moulds the body of man, not from some pre-existing animal, but from the finer particles of the earth.[2] His spirit is a separate creation, nearer to God as spirit is more like to God. This creative act is expressed by the word *breathing,* a term which connotes both the formation of the spirit and the communication to that spirit of spiritual light and life. Man rose up from the earth "a living soul." The rational soul is the principle of life of the human body; it makes the body a living thing.[3] In

(1) "Fecit itaque Deus hominem ex duplici substantia corpus de terra fingens, animam vero de nihilo faciens." *II Sent.,* d.1, p.II, 13b. Cf. pseudo-Augustine, *Libr. de Spiritu et anima,* c.14. MPL 40. 789, 790.

(2) For the composition and the movement of the human body, refer to St. Bonaventure, *II Sent.,* d.15, a.1, q.3, t.II, 380, and *ibid.,* d.17, a.2, q.2, t.II, 422.

(3) There are two ways of having and of giving life to another: *per modum efficientis,* with absolute perfection, a mode which belongs to God alone, and *per modum informantis,* without absolute perfection, a mode proper to the soul inasmuch as it gives life after the manner of an informant. In the words of St. Bonaventure: "Dicendum, quod aliquid communicare sive dare vitam alii potest dupliciter aut per modum efficientis, et hoc simpliciter perfectionis est, et sic competit soli Deo; aut per modum informantis, et sic non est simpliciter perfectionis, immo perfectionis cum imperfectione junctae." II Sent., d.8, a.1, q.1, ad 5, t.II, 211b. Vivifying is an act proper to the rational soul only when existing in the body. When not united to the body it does not vivify but lives by its own intrinsic nature. "Vivificare est actus animae rationalis, quem habet in corpus: aut ergo actus accidentalis aut essentialis. Si accidentalis, ergo vita accidit homini; quod manifeste falsum est, quia tunc accideret ei esse animal. Si est actus substantialis sive essentialis, ergo inest animae rationi sui quo est, sive formalis et completivi. Ergo si penes illud accipitur differentia formalis et completiva uniuscuiusque, quod est formale et completivum, penes illud, quo anima nata est vivficare corpus, sumitur illa differentia, sed eo ipso nata est anima uniri corpori, quo nata est corpus vivificare." *II Sent.,* d.1, p.2, a.3, q.2, t.II, 49a.

living things there is but one principle of life; in man there is but one soul, namely, the rational soul, which is *per se* the immediate substantial form of the body, giving not only being but also life, feeling, and intelligence. From the spiritual soul, then, as from their principle, proceed man's vegetative, sensitive, and intellectual powers.[4] Adam rose up from the earth "a living soul," a soul endowed with three natural faculties—memory, understanding, and will by which it became an image of the Most Holy Trinity,[5] a soul possessed of sanctifying grace, the likeness of God, for the Holy Ghost dwelt within him.[6] In addition to natural life, then, the first man received the life of original justice which brought him into living communion with God as his final end.

The biblical narrative concludes with an exclamation of breathless wonder: "Unto his own image and likeness did God make man." The end crowns the work; man's superior perfection required that he be created after all other creatures in a world fully prepared to receive him.[7]

The excellence of man, according to St. Bonaventure, consists simply and solely in the fact that God, by giving him a rational soul, made him to His own image and likeness. The three constituent powers of the soul—memory, understanding, and will—correspond in number to the three Divine Persons;[8] and this correspondence can be extended further, for it is not enough to say that there exist three spiritual powers in man as there exist three Divine Persons in God. We must also say that these three powers of the soul, emanating from the substance of the soul to which they belong, reproduce an internal arrangement upon the model of the Divine Essence. In God there is unity of essence and distinction of persons; in man there is unity of essence and distinction of acts.[9] Still further, there is an exact correspondence between the order and the reciprocal relations of the elements which constitute these two trinities. The three powers of the soul—memory, understanding, and will—act together in the one simple and indivisible substance of the soul. Just as the Father engenders the eternal knowledge of the Word Who expresses Him, and as the Word is in turn united with the Father by the Holy

(4) "Non tantum dat esse, verum etiam vivere et sentire et intelligere; ideo potentiam habet vegetativam, sensitivam, et intellectivam." *Breviloquium,* P.II, c.9, t.V, 227a. Cf. also *II Sent.,* d.15, a.1, q.3, t.II, 379-381.

(5) "Item, est creatura ad imaginem Dei facta; . . . illa est memoria, intelligentia et voluntas in quibus relucet Trinitas." *In Hexaem.,* II.27, t.V, 340b.

"Deiformis est creatura rationalis, quae potest redire super originem suam per memoriam, intelligentiam et voluntatem." *De sept. donis Spir. S.,* Col. III.5, t.V, 469a.

"Capax eius est et particeps esse potest, scil. per cognitionem et amorem." *Christus unus omnium Magister,* n.16, t.V, 571b.

(6) "Et ideo omnis creatura est vestigium, quae est a Deo; omnis est imago, quae cognoscit Deum; omnis et sola est similitudo, in qua habitat Deus." *De Scientia Christi,* q.4, concl., t.V, 24a.

(7) "Propter totius compositi *perfectionem* post cetera debuit homo produci. Quia enim homo sua dignitate et complemento finis est omnium corporalium; ideo post omnia erat producendus, ut sua productione finiret et compleret omnia praecedentia, tanquam finis complet quod ad ipsum ordinari habet." *II Sent.,* d.15, a.2, q.2, concl., t.II, 385a. Cf. Aristotle, II *de Anima,* text. 21. (c.2).

(8) Cf. *supra,* p.3, footnote 5.

(9) "Rursus, quia forma beatificabilis est capax Dei per memoriam, intelligentiam et voluntatem; et hoc est esse ad imaginem Trinitatis propter unitatem in essentia et trinitatem in potentiis: ideo animam necesse fuit esse *intelligentem* Deum et omnia, ac per hoc Dei imagine insignitam." *Breviloquium,* P. II, c.9, t.V, 227a.

Spirit, so memory or thought, teeming with the ideas enclosed within it, engenders the knowledge of the intellect or the word, and love is born from both as the bond which unites them.[10]

It is no accidental correspondence that is here described;[11] the structure of the creative Trinity conditions and therefore explains the structure of the human soul. It is, indeed, a definition of the soul in its very essence that is here in point, and to explain its nature is to discover in it the image of God[12] by means of which, with the assistance of divine grace, it may take possession of God.[13] It is hardly necessary to observe that the consciousness of this fact must transform the moral and religious life of man. That is why the idea of analogy is at the very root of St. Bonaventure's anthropology.

"And God created man to his own image." It was in this setting of matchless dignity and splendor that the masterpiece of God's creative power appeared upon the earth. "To the image of God he created him. Male and female he created them." It may be asked why in the case of the human race alone the distinction of sex was expressly mentioned in Genesis. Perhaps in order to make it clear that woman also was created to the image of God. Such a statement would by no means be a useless or unnecessary one in a country and at a time when woman was commonly held in low esteem. This text of Sacred Scripture, "Male and female he created them," makes it clear that the distinction of the sexes is immediately from God; that the sexes were equally created to the image of God and have consequently one and the same divine end. From these words of Sacred Scripture follows woman's claim to the possession of full and complete human nature, and therefore to complete equality in moral value and position as compared with man before the Creator.[14] The same essentially identical human nature appears in the male and female sex in twofold personal form. There are, consequently, male and female persons. Since man's likeness to God resides in his intellectual nature

(10) "Quia Filius missus est a Patre, et Spiritus Sanctus ab utroque, qui tamen semper est cum eis et nunquam recedit ab eis." *Itinerarium,* 6,6, t.V, 311b.

"Secundum autem harum potentiarum ordinem et originem et habitudinem, ducit in ipsam beatissimam Trinitatem. Nam ex memoria oritur intelligentia ut ipsius proles, quia tunc intelligimus, cum similitudo quae est in memoria resultat in acie intellectus, quae nihil aliud est quam verbum; ex memoria et intelligentia spiratur amor tanquam nexus amborum. Haec tria scilicit *mens generans, verbum* et *amor,* sunt in anima quoad memoriam, intelligentiam et voluntatem, quae sunt consubstantiales, coaequales et coaevae, se invicem circumincedentes." *Ibid.,* 3,5 t.V, 305a.

(11) "Esse imaginem Dei non est homini accidens, sed potius substantiale, sicut esse vestigium nulli accidit creaturae." *II Sent.,* d.16, a.1, q.2. fund.4, t.II, 397a.

(12) ". . . imago naturalis est, quae repraesentat per id quod habet a natura." *Ibid.,* concl., t.II, 397b.

(13) "Per hunc modum intellige quod a summo Opifice nulla creatura processit nisi per Verbum aeternum 'in quo omnia disposuit' e per quod produxit non solum creaturas habentes rationem vestigii, sed etiam imaginis, ut eidem assimilari possint per cognitionem et amorem." *De reduc. art. ad theol.,* 12, t.V, 323a.

"Et hoc est quod dicit Augustinus *de Trinitate* decimo quarto, quod 'eo est anima imago Dei, quo capax ejus est et particeps esse potest.' Quia enim ei immediate ordinatur, ideo capax ejus est, vel e converso; et quia capax est, nata est ei configurari; et propter hoc fert in se a sua origine lumen vultus divini (Ps., IV, 7). Et ideo quantum ad similitudinem quae attenditur ad convenientiam ordinis, perfecte dicitur imago Dei, quia in hoc ei assimilatur expresse." *II Sent.,* d.16, a.1, q.1, concl., t.II, 395a.

(14) "Ad praedictorum intelligentiam est notandum, quod, sicut ex praecedentibus patet, imago quantum ad suum *esse* principaliter consistit in anima et eius potentiis, et in his potissime, prout habent ad Deum converti; et quantum ad hoc non est distinctio masculi et feminae, servi et liberi. Ideo imago, quantum ad id quod est de complemento eius et se eius *esse,* non magis reperitur in viro quam in muliere." *II Sent.,* d.16, a.2, q.2, concl., t.II, 403b.

and, since woman is endowed with the same nature, she, too, is the image of God. Man and woman, then, distinct from each other by their sex, but equal to each other by their nature, share the same dignity. "If woman was created to the image of God and the equal of man," says St. Bonaventure, "it seems that the divine image is found equally in man and in woman."[15] St. Thomas, likewise, states this same opinion: "Therefore, we must understand," he says, "that when Sacred Scripture has said *to the image of God He created him,* it added, *male and female He created them,* not to imply that the image of God came through the distinction of sex, but that the image belonged to both sexes, since it is in the rational soul, in which there is no sexual distinction."[16] It is not permissible, therefore, to take one sex as the one absolutely perfect and as the standard of value for the other.

(15) "*Creavit Deus hominem ad imaginem et similitudinem suam, masculum et feminam creavit illos:* si igitur mulier creata est imaginem Dei et ad aequalitatem viri . . . videtur ergo, quod in viro et muliere aequaliter reperiatur ratio imaginis." *II Sent.*, d.16, a.2, q.2, f.1, t.II, 403a.

(16) *Summa Theologica, 1,* q.93, a.6.

Chapter II

HER PHYSICAL NATURE

"MALE AND FEMALE HE CREATED THEM. And God blessed them, saying: Increase and multiply." From the far-reaching physical differences in the two sexes there follows the combination of the sexes for the purpose of an organic social union of the human race, which we call humanity. In other words, humanity cannot be represented by any number, however large, of individuals of like sex but is to be found solely in the social and organic union of man and woman. Thus, one man and one woman constitute by nature a complete human being. On the other hand, the entire male sex in itself represents only the half of humanity and the female sex the other half, while one man and one woman together suffice to represent humanity. Man and woman, then, are mutually dependent and the one is the complement of the other. As St. Bonaventure says: "For the completion of their nature, God endowed the bodies of Adam and Eve with the nobility of sex."[1] Each of the two sexes, then, requires the other for its social complement; a complete social equality would nullify this purpose of the Creator. Nature intends the race to continue, and this continuance demands that children should be born and reared. Evidently, the intention at the basis of the differences mentioned is to force the complemental union of the two sexes as a necessity of nature.

When man was created male and female, difference was made, not in the soul, but in the body. The difference between the human sexes, then, which is largely a difference of body, was the result of God's special action. There is nothing in the biblical narrative to suggest the idea advanced by St. Athanasius and accepted by St. Gregory of Nyssa and by St. Ambrose, that the distinction of sex is intended and realized by God only in view of the Fall and sin. This distinction was God's plan from the very beginning, not a concession made to human weakness and human passion.[2] Adam and Eve were

(1) "Quaedam enim spectant ad complementum naturae, . . . Ad complementum naturae spectat, quod dedit Deus ex parte corporis: membrorum integritatem, complexionis sanitatem, sexus nobilitatem." *De Triplici Via,* §2, t.VIII, 6b.

(2) "Dicendum, quod in statu innocentiae absque dubio haberet generari ex homine; et hoc attestatur auctoritate *Scripturae* et iudicio *rationis rectae.* Dicitur enim hominibus in statu innocentiae, sicut scribitur Genesis primo: *Crescite et multiplicamini et replete terram.* Et alius textus dicit, mulierem *in adiutorium viri esse factam.—Rationi* etiam *rectae* hoc consonat, quae dicit, potentiam generandi spectare ad completionem naturae, usum vero generationis ad complementum et perfectionem civitatis supernae. Et quia in statu innocentiae natura perfectior erat quam in statu viae; et si homo stetisset, superna civitas suorum civium numerositate nequaquam fraudata esset; ponendum est, quod homo in statu innocentiae generare poterat et genuisset. Et quia nec vir per se, nec mulier per se suffecisset ad generandum; ideo per commixtionem fieret coniunctio unius ad alterum, et mutuum sibi praeberent auxilium in procreatione prolis ad multiplicandum genus humanum.—Et ideo concedendae sunt rationes ostendentes, quod si homo stetisset, et esset generatio et sexuum commixtio." *II Sent.,* d.20, a.1, q.1, t.II, p. 478ab.

still perfect and unspoiled as they had come from the Hand of God. Allowing them to be the instruments of God in peopling the world was rather a privilege accorded to their nobility in the eyes of their Creator. "And God blessed them and said: Increase and multiply" (Gen.1:27). As a proof of the nobility and sanctity of this power of their human nature, God gave them the command to perpetuate themselves in their children. At that moment the divine Hand of God was raised in blessing on the marital union of husband and wife, and marriage became a divine institution, the perfect natural state. With the words, "Increase and multiply," God enunciated the primary physical end of marriage—the procreation of children—and, by making them male and female, He showed that it was His divine will that mankind be perpetuated through generation.

As we examine the text, we can find no justification for the strange opinion of St. John Chrysostom that God had provided for the multiplication of the human race in the state of innocence otherwise than by sex relations and generative functions. Augustine taught steadfastly and with utmost precision that the distinction of the sexes in view of their generative relations in marriage was in conformity with the primitive purpose of the Creator.

Though God entrusted human generation to man and woman, He kept for Himself the direct infusion of divine life into the souls of those whom Adam and Eve and their children after them would beget. These priceless souls would be the direct work of His divine Hands, a circumstance in keeping with their dignity and immortality: with their dignity, because, created in the image of God, they would be bound by ties of love to Him from Whom they received their being; with their immortality, because only from God, Who in Himself possesses inexhaustible life, could they receive the principle of life which is never to be extinguished.[3] Thus, even in its natural condition, marriage oversteps the boundaries and limits of this world and its powers; it cannot accomplish its highest physical purpose, the procreation of children, without the co-operation of the Almighty. God Himself must supplement and complement the marriage union by the creation of the child's soul.

According to the second chapter of Genesis, the formation of the first woman took place after Adam had been placed in the terrestrial Paradise, that is to say, after his human nature had been supernaturalized. Adam had already received the divine command on the fulfillment of which was to depend the propagation of his descendants in the state of original justice in which he himself was constituted.[4] "And the Lord God said: It is not good

(3) "Animarum enim creationem Deus sibi soli debuit reservare, tum propter earum *dignitatem*, tum propter earum *immortalitatem*. Propter animarum *dignitatem*, quia, cum anima sit imago Dei et nata immediate ferri in Deum et beatificari in ipso diligendo eum ex toto corde, totum suum *esse* immediate debuit ab ipso habere, ut ipsum ex toto corde teneretur diligere. Decuit etiam hoc propter animarum *immortalitatem*. Cum enim solus Deus sit, qui habeat vitam in semetipso et vitam indeficientem; solus est, qui potest producere principium vitae perpetuum." *II Sent.*, d.18, a.2, q.3, t.II, 453ab.

(4) Cf. *supra*, p. 6, footnote 2.

for man to be alone; let us make him a help like unto himself." Since his helpmate was intended for the propagation of this holy race, she was to be altogether "like unto himself," a member of the same human species and possessed of the racial characteristics of justice and sanctity. The production of such a helpmate required a supernatural operation. "Then the Lord God cast a deep sleep upon Adam, and when he was fast asleep, he took one of his ribs, and filled up flesh for it. And the Lord God built the rib which he took from Adam into a woman." Eve, then, was produced not by the natural method of procreation but by the power of Almighty God and the efficient causality properly so-called of the seminal principle contained in the rib of Adam. She is the object of a special creative act, a circumstance which indicates her natural equality with man in her relationship to God. We may add that the Seraphic Doctor is convinced that God formed woman without the help of the ministrations of the angels, not only because the mode of production was above the power of nature but also in order that both sexes might immediately tend toward and love with their whole hearts Him by Whom they knew they had been immediately created.[5]

And the Lord God "brought her to Adam." It was for a very specific purpose that God brought man and woman together by giving Adam a helper and companion like in all things unto himself. He intended to allow these two noble creatures to be His instruments in peopling the world with sons of God. They were to play an essential part, limited though it be, in the propagation of their kind. And Adam himself, recognizing the secret designs of the Most High, exclaimed in awe at the wonders of the divine plan: "This now is bone of my bones, and flesh of my flesh. She shall be called woman, because she was taken out of man. Wherefore a man shall leave father and mother, and shall cleave to his wife; and they shall be two in one flesh" (Gen. 2:23-24),—the first human utterance recorded on the pages of Sacred Scripture.

The act that continues the human race, the act of reproduction, is the fulfillment of nature's urge as well as of God's command to increase and multiply. Stripped of its conscious aspects, it is a purely vegetative process since its goal—the merging of two cells into one and the producing of a new organism—is the fruit of a purely vegetative power. In man, the begetting of offspring is linked up with the highest as well as the lowest functions of his nature. Behind it we find two of the strongest forces in his life: the impulsion of his instincts, which makes him love the things of sense; and the impulsion

(5) "Si quis autem quaerat, utrum hoc opus *supra* naturam fecit, ministrante sibi virtute angelica; respondet Augustinus super Genesim ad litteram libro nono, ita inquiens: 'Quale ministerium exhibuere Angeli in illa mulieris formatione, quis audeat assignare? Certissime tamen dixerim, . . . non nisi illo opere Dei factum, quod Deus non per Angelos, sed per se ipsum operatus est'. Ratio autem potissima, quare Deus ita formavit, est, tum quia modus ille formandi erat supra potestatem naturae; tum etiam, ut homo in utroque sexu immediate in eum tenderet et ex se toto eum diligeret, a quo se nosset immediate esse factum." *II Sent.*, d.18, a.2, q.3, t.II, 454ab.

of his will, which makes him seek the things of spirit. The act of reproduction has been made holy by the sacred offices of wedlock. Proper to the state of marriage and to that state alone, it is connected in the most intimate way with the pattern of man's life on earth and with his eternal salvation.

After all, apart from the statements in Genesis, the problem of our origins resolves itself into a problem of metaphysics and of biology. While the metaphysics of the School had well-nigh reached its perfection and remained unaltered since the golden age of Scholasticism, biological sciences, particularly in the last one or two hundred years, have made giant strides. Formerly it was held that the male sex alone has of itself the germ and germinating power in human procreation; that the female sex merely supplies the matter and the application of germination. Hence the female sex has been likened to the earth which receives the seed of a plant. This principle of Aristotelian biology, namely, that the father alone is the active principle, and the mother the passive principle in the generation of the offspring, was accepted by St. Thomas Aquinas who says: "The seed of the male is the active principle in the generation of an animal, but the term *seed* can also be applied to that which belongs to the female, which is the passive principle."[6] And Hans Meyer expresses the Angelic Doctor's evaluation of man and woman in this respect in the following words: "The woman possessed an imperfect faculty of procreation, she merely contributed the material for the production of the living being, and in contrast to man she was the passive principle while man was the active and form-giving principle. The superiority of form over matter is sufficiently well known."[7]

In his *De generatione animalium,* Aristotle in a brilliant discussion develops his theory in which he states that, since the father contributes the formal element, the variations in degree of masculinity which the offspring can exhibit will reflect only the degree of the mother's reaction and resistance to the controlling form.[8] We may conclude that a daughter who takes after her mother is a walking criticism of her father's vital capacity. The female is, in fact, "a stunted male."[9] Her physical conformation is (a) a sign that her function is mainly nutritive—to provide within her womb its whole material embodiment for the male form, and to nourish the newborn infant at her breast; and (b)—as her smaller body, weaker veins, and comparatively anaemic pallor show—a symptom of her failure to be male.

St. Thomas holds the same opinion—that woman is an undeveloped man; therefore, he treats her as a child. "As regards the individual nature," he says, "woman is defective and misbegotten, for the active force in the male seed

(6) "Semen maris est principium activum in generatione animalis; sed potest etiam dici semen id quod est ex parte feminae, quod est principium passivum." *Summa Theol.,* I, q.115, a.2, ad 3.
(7) *Op. cit.,* p. 208.
(8) Cf. Book IV.3, 768ª 28ff. *The Works of Aristotle* translated into English under the editorship of J. A. Smith and W. D. Ross. Vol. V. Oxford at the Clarendon Press, 1912.
(9) *Ibid.,* Book II.3, 737ª 27.

tends to the production of a perfect likeness in the masculine sex; while the production of woman comes from defect in the active force or from some material indisposition, or even from some external influence; such as that of a south wind, which is moist, as the Philosopher observes."[10]

Regarding this teaching of St. Thomas, Hans Meyer says:

> "His observations about man and woman are based on the conviction that woman is inferior to man. He was greatly influenced in this respect by the Stagirite's lack of esteem for woman and also perhaps by the opinions of the age. In agreement with Aristotle, St. Thomas reiterates the opinion that man represents in himself perfection, while woman stands for the imperfect, and that nature is at all times bent on the production of the male and produces the female only when it is thwarted by inner or outer factors. The woman comes into existence only *per accidens,* because some process of nature has gone awry, and woman is therefore actually "the male gone awry," *mas occasionatus.* Christian thought, however, forestalled any cruder conclusions and obliged St. Thomas to make the following distinctions: with respect to human nature in general, woman is not a mere accidental result, she is rather something intended by nature and willed by the Creator because of the propagation of the race. With respect to her own particular nature, however, woman is something defective and accidental, *aliquid deficiens et occasionatum,* because the active power of generation in man seeks to produce something perfect like to man himself. If a woman is produced, this is owing to weakness in the man's power of generation, to some indisposition in the matter, or to some external factor, such as dampness which is often caused by the south wind."[11]

St. Bonaventure, likewise, uses the expression, "femina est vir occasionatus," but it is to explain away an objection to his theory that in the state of innocence before the Fall the number of men and women would have been equal.[12] According to Aristotle, the female is a male which, for some accidental reason, did not attain its full development; consequently, the objection states, she would not be included in nature's intention as directed to the work of generation and no women at all or at least very few of them would have been born.[13] St. Bonaventure then tries to reconcile the opinion of Aristotle with his own and states that the Philosopher did not mean to say that the female sex is "praeter naturae intentionem," but that in comparison with the production of man there is some "defectus" in the production of woman; that he is "fortior;" she, "minus fortior." That *occasionem,* says St. Bonaventure, is not "praeter naturam" nor "contra naturam" but "secundum

(10) *Summa Theol.,* I, q.92, a.1.

(11) *Op. cit.,* pp. 207, 208. Cf. St. Thomas, *Summa Theol.,* I. q.92,a.I; q.99,a.2 ad I; q.115, a.3 ad 4.

(12) "Et quoniam ratio dictaret, omnia facienda esse ordinata, et tot producere mulieres quot viros, ut quilibet vir haberet *adiutorium simile sibi* secundum exigentiam legis matrimonii; ideo tunc viros et mulieres produceret in numero aequali." *II Sent.,* d.20, a.1, q.6, concl., t.II, 486b.

(13) Sed contra: 1. "Sicut dicit Philosophus in libro de Animalibus, 'femina est vir occasionatus,' ergo videtur esse praeter naturae intentionem; sed tempore naturae institutae, cum natura esset recta, nihil produceretur praeter intentionem ipsius: ergo videtur, quod nulla mulier generatur, vel saltem paucae: ergo plures essent viri quam mulieres." *II Sent.,* d.20, a.1, q.6, t.II, 485a.

naturam."[14] In fact, nature requires it. In other words, woman is the salvation of nature which cannot get along without her.[15] It is true, says the Saint, that nature is at all times bent on the production of the perfect, but this is to be understood in the relative, not in the absolute, sense. The male sex in itself may excel the female, but the interests of nature would not be furthered by the production of the male sex alone but rather by the production of both male and female. Both sexes are intimately co-ordinated. Each requires the other as its social complement; therefore nature desires both sexes rather than the one or the other alone. The deficiency, then, is a deficiency of measure; hence no real deficiency and the authority of Aristotle disappears.[16]

St. Bonaventure rejected the teaching that the active power of generation belongs exclusively to the male sex, and the passive power to the female. If this were so, generation would create no bond of true parentage on the part of the mother. The mere fact that woman contributes the material for the production of the child, says the Saint, does not make her a mother, as is evident from the formation of woman from the rib of Adam. Though man furnished the material principle for woman when Eve was formed from his side, he cannot for that reason be called the father or the mother of that same woman, inasmuch as he took no active part in her formation.[17] The true mother takes an active part; she co-operates in the generation of the child.[18] The position of the Philosopher, then, is untenable; it is an understatement of the facts, for a mother has not only a *passive* power but an *active* power as well.[19]

The controversy regarding woman's part in human generation dates back, as we have seen, to classical antiquity. The two currents of the dispute, namely, the philosophers and the physicians, are represented respectively by Aristotle and Galen, or Hippocrates, whose two interpretations were followed by the two different schools of Scholastics. Albert the Great, Thomas

(14) "Ad illud autem quod primo obiicitur, quod femina dicitur vir occasionatus; dicendum, quod Philosophus non vult dicere, quod femina sit praeter naturae intentionem, sed quod virtus naturae aliquem defectum habet in productionem mulieris respectu productionis viri; ille autem defectus non repugnat ordini naturae, sed potius salvat. Secundum enim ordinem naturae, sicut producuntur in eodem corpore quaedam membra magis fortia, quaedam minus; sic producuntur in eadem specie quaedam individua unius sexus, quaedam alterius. Et ideo, licet ille defectus, qui ordinem naturae corrumpit, utputa est ille, qui est causa defectus membri vel bonae complexionis, sit *praeter* naturae intentionem; *generatio* tamen mulieris nec est *praeter* naturam nec *contra* naturam, sed *secundum* naturam." *Ibid.*, concl., t.II, 486b.

(15) "Hinc est, quod mulier generatur et dicitur vir occasionatus. Tamen quia istam occasionem necesse est evenire, nec sine ea potest natura salvari in esse; ideo natura, quae intendit salvari, utrumque sexum intendit." *IV Sent.*, d.44, p.1, dub.2, t.IV, 918a.

(16) "Ad illud quod obiicitur, quod natura semper desiderat illud quod melius est; dicendum, quod non intelligitur, quod semper desiderat melius *simpliciter,* sed melius *in ordine;* licet autem sexus masculinus melior sit in se quam femineus, non tamen esset ita sufficienter salus naturae in solo virili sexu, sicut est in virili et muliebri; et ideo natura magis desiderat utrumque quam alterum solum." *II Sent.*, d.20, a.1, q.6, concl., t.II, 487a.

"Item, generatio hominis non poterat continuari nisi per masculum et feminam, et ita necessaria est ad generationem mulier, sicut et masculus; ergo videtur, quod natura aequaliter intenderet utrumque sexum." *Ibid.*, f.2, t.II, 485a.

(17) "Item, vir praebuit mulieri materiale principium, quando de eius costa formata est Eva; sed propter hoc ipsius mulieris non dicitur esse pater, aut mater, quia cooperatus non fuit in eius formatione." *III Sent.*, d.4, a.3, q.1, t.III, 110ab.

(18) "Item, vera mater cooperatur in filii generatione." *Ibid.*, 110a.

(19) "Sed haec positio nimis parum dicit: primum, quia mater in generatione non solum habet potentiam *passivam,* sed *activam.*" *III Sent.*, d.4, a.3, q.1, concl., t.III, 111b.

Aquinas, Peter of Tarantasia, Egidius Colonna, and most Thomists follow Aristotle and deny any active contribution of woman in human generation. Alexander of Hales, St. Bonaventure and his disciples, Duns Scotus and his followers, according to the Greek physicians and Avicenna, hold that woman contributes actively in human generation.[20] This teaching, so emphatically stressed by the Seraphic Doctor, has always been defended by the Franciscan School and in our day has become the common doctrine of Catholic thinkers.[21] Duns Scotus, expressly following the opinion of St. Bonaventure, says that it does not matter that Aristotle taught the contrary; that the physicians Galen and Avicenna did not agree with him, and that on questions of this kind we must give more credit to authorities on the subject than to the Philosopher.[22] After all, in the field of medicine, Hippocrates and Galen reflected the same enlightenment of the great age in Greece as did Aristotle in the field of philosophy.

The science of eugenics has revealed the fallacy of the teaching that the physical, mental, and moral condition of the mother is inconsequential to the welfare of her offspring; that the vigor of the progeny is derived from the sire. It has been found that the maternal influence is as great, and along physical lines even greater than the paternal. For this reason, as St. Bonaventure says, the child often bears a closer physical resemblance to the mother than to the father. Hence when the physiologists call the father the active principle, it is only by way of "appropriation" that they do so.[23] As in theology, creation is appropriated to the Father, though it belongs to all three Persons of the Trinity, so in generation the active principle is by "appropriation" attributed to the father specifically, though in reality it belongs to the mother as well. Mothers generate their children by a causality which is active and not merely passive, as the disciples of Aristotle taught. Woman is not an instrument but an integrating part in the work of generation.

Thus, St. Bonaventure's view is more in keeping with that of modern physiologists who hold that human generation takes place by union of the male seed with the female germ cell or ovum with which it must grow into one body. The male seed perfects and completes the seed of the woman, determining it to unfold and bring forth the fruit. This doctrine establishes the perfect unity of nature between the male and the female sex inasmuch as from the very first formation of the fetus the woman meets the man not in a mere passive but in an active way, by truly generating. Moreover, it makes us

---

(20) Cf. the Scholion of the Editors of Quaracchi to the famous question of the Seraphic Doctor, *Sent. III,* d.4, a.3, q.1, t.III, 113ab.

(21) Cf. G. M. Roschini, *Mariologia* II, pars 1, Rome, 1947, p. 164, where the author, following the opinion of the Franciscan School based on Galen's theory, adds that it is confirmed by modern physiology: "moderna physiologia suffragatur."

(22) Cf. *Joannis Duns Scoti Theologiae Marianae elementa,* edited by C. Balich, Sibenik in Jugoslavia, 1933. *Ordinatio III,* d.4, q. un. in corp., p. 93. 111-112. Cf. also his reference to the same question in *Reportata Parisiensia* and in his *Lectura Completa,* also edited by Balich, p. 116-118.273.

(23) "Unde quod dicunt physici intelligendum est per appropriationem." *Ibid.*

understand more clearly the unity of flesh as a substantial unity of the same flesh in the fetus, or fruit, which is obtained materially and produced formally by both.[24] "And they shall be two in one flesh." Since the flesh of the generating parties grows together into one fetus as into a common fruit, that same flesh must be regarded as one flesh, so far as they are one by the act of carnal connection, the one using the flesh of the other as his own, or as a mere mingling of flesh.[25]

The equality as well as the inequality of the sexes is well expressed by the Seraphic Doctor in his discussion of the origin of Eve. He states that her formation from the rib of Adam was in perfect keeping with the nature of man, who excels woman in *dignity of origin, in power to act,* and *in authority to govern.*[26]

The formation of Eve from the rib of Adam was in harmony with the *dignity* of the first man who was the *principle* of all his species, men as well as women, just as God is the *principium* of the universe.[27] The source of Eve as well as of their joint descendants, Adam was in truth the source of the whole human race. The efficient causality properly so-called of the seminal cause contained in the rib of Adam makes him the principle of his species in a very definite way. To be sure, it was God who caused the woman to come forth from the man, just as it is God who makes the wheat come from the grain, but the grain, by its seminal power, is also the active, although subordinate cause. The seminal cause was in the rib; otherwise it would not be true to say that God created man in his causes, both male and female. But this active causality could develop in this particular way only under the influence of a divine volition. This conception of a causality properly called efficient, although acting in a way supernaturally determined under the influence of a divine *concursus* exceeding the natural *concursus,* provides us with an excellent explanation of the nature of, and the reason for, the origin of the first woman from the first man.[28] Eve was produced by the power of Almighty God and the efficient causality properly so-called of the seminal cause contained in the rib of Adam. The causality which is simply expressed

(24) ". . . nec poterant simul aliquem generare, nisi simul commiscerentur." *II Sent.,* d.20, a.1, q.1, f.1, t.II, 477a.

(25) "Dicendum, quod cum generatio prolis, quantum est de ordine et potestate naturae, habeat fieri per coniunctionem et commixtionem duorum sexuum in hominibus, qui respectu prolis habent se per modum materialis et efficientis, ita quod ratio materialis plus residet penes mulierem, et efficientis sive activi plus residet penes virum; necesse est ad generationem, aliquas particulas tam a muliere quam a viro decidi, in quibus esset virtus et ratio seminalis respectu corporis propagandi." *II Sent.,* d.20, a.1, q.2, t.II, 479b, 480a.

(26) "Excellit enim sexus virilis muliebrem et quantum ad *dignitatem in principiando,* et quantum ad *virtutem in agendo,* et quantum ad *auctoritatem in praesidendo.*" *III Sent.,* d.12, a.3, q.1, concl., t.III, 271a.

(27) "Quantum ad dignitatem in principiando, quia omnes tam viri quam mulieres ex uno viro fuerunt, in quo est expressa repraesentatio egressus rerum ab illo unico principio primo et summo." *Ibid.*

(28) "Et per hoc patet responsio ad sequens, quia formatio mulieris non fuit de consequentibus ad opera sex dierum; vel si fuit, *causaliter* dicitur fuisse facta, quia praecessit potentia obedientiae in costa, vel etiam aliqua *ratio seminalis longinqua,* licet secundum illam mulier non sit formata, sed secundum potentiam divinam." *II Sent.,* d.18, a.1, q.2, concl., t.II, 437ab. Cf. also *ibid.,* f.6, t.II, 435b.

by the fact that the matter taken from elsewhere became the matter of the woman *through the intermediary* of the rib, as taught by St. Thomas,[29] makes Adam the principle of his species only in a very attenuated way, by comparison with the *efficient causality properly so-called* of the seminal principle contained in the rib of Adam, as understood by St. Augustine and accepted by St. Bonaventure.

So much for the dignity of man as the principle of his species. Now as regards his *physical power or strength for action,* which St. Bonaventure considers his second title to excellence.[30] We know that women are commonly regarded as "the weaker sex." Physically, woman is no match for man. When we eliminate the effects of social habits, in so far as they tend to produce or increase differences in muscular strength and physical stamina, we still have a very large margin left which must be put down to the female physical balance. St. Bonaventure concedes this point, and all the evidence goes to support the assertion that, apart from the primary sexual differences, there are physical differences between the sexes and that women are by nature the weaker sex.[31]

If woman is physically weaker than man, her capacity for enduring severe suffering is undoubtedly greater. It is not only in her capacity of mother that she endures as a matter of course pain and suffering to an extent rarely demanded of man, but she likewise bears other illnesses more patiently, because "viri est *agere,* et mulieris est *pati.*" Whether woman's greater power of resistance to pain is biologically or morally determined is of no immediate importance; enough that it is a fact.

Thirdly, man excels woman in *authority to govern.* According to right order, woman is not appointed to govern man but man, as the head of the body, is appointed to govern woman, as the Apostle says. "The head of the woman is the man" (I Cor. 11:3).[32]

It should be emphasized here that man owes his authoritative pre-eminence in society not to personal achievements but to the appointment of the Creator, according to the words of the Apostle: "The man . . . is the image and glory of God; but the woman is the glory of the man" (I Cor. 11:7). The Apostle, in this reference to the creation of the first human pair, presupposes the image of God in the woman, though, as St. Bonaventure says, on account of corporeal differences in the sexes, it may be less distinct than

(29) *Summa Theol.,* I, q.92, a.3, ad. 1.

(30) "Quantum ad *virtutem in agendo* similiter praecellit, quoniam viri est *agere,* et mulieris est *pati.* Unde plus habet sexus virilis de virtute activa, propter quod et robustior est et re et nominatione." *III Sent.,* d.12, a.3, q.1, concl., t.III, 271a.

(31) "Si enim semen virile fuerit virtutis fortis ex concursu triplicis caloris et spiritus in ipso existentis, tunc fit fortior coagulatio et complexio, et generatur sexus vigorosus, id est masculinis. Si autem fuerit virtutis debilis, tunc fit coagulatio mollior et fragilior, et generatur ex eo infirmus, scilicet femineus." *II Sent.,* d.20, a.1, q.6, concl., t.II, 486a.

(32) "Quantum ad *auctoritatem in praesidendo* etiam praeexcellit. Nam secundum rectum ordinem non mulier viro, sed vir praeficitur mulieri tamquam caput corpori, sicut dicit Apostolus." *III Sent.,* d.12, a.3, q.1, concl., t.III, 271a.

in man.[33] As this likeness manifests itself exteriorly in man's supremacy over creation (Gen. 1:26), and as man as born leader of the family first exercised this supremacy, he is called directly God's image in this capacity. Woman takes part in this supremacy only indirectly under the guidance of man and as his help-meet. This was the subjection according to which man was from the beginning "the head of the woman."

Regarding St. Thomas' views on this question, Hans Meyer has this to say: "The duties of married life are distributed in the man's favor since man and woman in marriage have the relationship of master to servant."[34] St. Bonaventure's view is more tolerant. Although woman is in a certain sense inferior to man by reason of the weakness of her sex, she was created to be man's help-meet, not as a *slave,* but as a *companion,* and the Seraphic Doctor goes on to describe her position with classic clearness. "The head of the woman is the man," as the Apostle says. Although the man is said to be the *head* of the woman, he is not said to be her *master,* for she is not his handmaid. Therefore the Lombard says that woman was made the equal of man. She was formed not from his head, for in the social union between them, her part is not to rule; nor was she formed from his feet, for her part is not that of servile subjection. She was formed from man's side to show that she was to be esteemed as his *companion.*[35]

(33) "Et quoniam ex parte corporis est sexuum *distinctio,* et secundum sexuum distinctionem maior est *repraesentatio* sive quantum ad rationem praesidendi, sive quantum ad rationem *principiandi,* quia *vir est caput mulieris,* et vir est principium mulieris, et *non vir propter mulierem,* sed *mulier propter virum:* quantum ad hunc utique modum excellentiori modo reperitur imago in sexu masculino quam feminino, non ratione eius quod est de *esse* ipsius imaginis, sed ratione ipsius quod adiacet." *II Sent.,* d.16, a.2, q.2, concl., t.II, 403b.

(34) *Op. cit.,* p. 209.

(35) "Nam etsi mulier sit viro quodam modo inferior ratione infirmioris sexus, nihilominus, quia non est creata, ut esset ei in adiutorium ut *famula,* sed ut *socia;* hinc est, quod quamvis dicatur *caput* eius, non tamen dicitur *dominus,* quia ipsa non est ancilla eius. Et ideo supra dixit Magister distinctione decima octava, quod mulier ad aequalitatem fuit condita; ideo fuit formata de latere, non de pedibus vel de capite, ut viri videretur esse *socia,* non *domina,* vel *ancilla.*" *II Sent.,* d.44, a.2, q.2, concl., t.II, 1008b. Cf. also Augustine, XVIII. *de Civ. Dei,* c.2. MPL 41, 560-562.

Chapter III

HER PSYCHOLOGICAL NATURE

LOOKING BACK THUS FAR over St. Bonaventure's treatment of our subject, one fact seems to strike us particularly—his evident care, in spite of his use of Aristotelian terms, to safeguard the dignity of woman. In trying to come to a decision in any problem concerning man as a whole, we must consider the data of all relevant sciences. The data of anatomy and physiology, which treat of the functions and structure of man's bodily frame, must be supplemented by those of psychology, the study of man's mental processes. For us, biological facts are not so important. It is the psychological, not the physical nature of woman which St. Bonaventure stresses.

Modern psychology and anthropology make a far more extensive study of these two subjects than did the Middle Ages. What theologian approaching the problem of woman today would neglect to learn the facts of the sciences that concern her, including those of psychology, which deals with the basic natural urges and with the natural inclinations, all of which are concerned with the preservation of the individual and the species, the formation of the community, and also the development of the spiritual, mental, moral, and religious qualities of the personality? Although occasional references remind us that the great Doctors of the Middle Ages were not entirely ignorant of the implications of psychology and anthropology, an examination of their contributions shows that they are far removed from the ideal of a differential study of character and personality.

Our daily contact with different people makes us fully aware of the fact that all possess peculiar traits and characteristics. Here is the problem of individual differences in souls. As we note differences of race and sex, differences in mental ability and temperament, we are led to inquire into the cause of these differences. Are they the result of education, of social environment, of heredity, of the perfection of the bodily organs, or of a graded perfection of the souls themselves? In other words, are these differences accidental or substantial? In order to answer this question, we must first answer another, namely: Are souls substantially equal or unequal? Limiting the question merely to specific perfection, we must agree that all souls are equal, since they are substances of the same species, made up of the same essential qualifications, possessed of the same genus and difference. As regards individual perfection, however, there are two schools of thought, —one that holds that the inequality is substantial, the other that it is accidental. Again, of the two groups that hold the substantial inequality of souls, the first group, including such men as St. Bonaventure, Peter Lombard, and Duns Scotus, teaches that the soul itself gives rise to this inequality. The second group which claims St. Thomas Aquinas as an adherent maintains that the inequality arises from the relation of the soul to matter.

St. Bonaventure defends the substantial union of body and soul in the human composite. This substantial unity is an *unum per se,* not an *unum per accidens,* i.e., body and soul form a substantial union in the human composite without the aid of another form.[1] The being of the soul is united to that of the body intrinsically and the basis of this union is the life-giving principle of the body.[2] The organized body which is perfected by the vital principle owes its organization not to the soul but to its own form of organization, "which is from the formative power carried with the seed."[3] It is essential that the form of organization be unified and since it is essential, the perfecting by the vital principle is an essential or substantial perfection.

St. Bonaventure, then, insists that the substantial inequality of souls arises from the soul itself. Since the soul does not exist for the sake of the body, but the body for the sake of the soul, the excellence of the composite comes from the soul. One soul excels another not by reason of its origin, since it is from nothing, but rather by reason of the wisdom of the Creator Who brings all things into existence according to due order.[4] Although the substantial inequality is from the soul itself, the Seraphic Doctor does not deny that the body plays a large part in the exercise of the powers of the soul.[5]

Man's physical organization requires a differentiation in the person. The rational soul, as rational, is the form of man as man. Individuals must then necessarily differ from one another not only in their bodies, like the animals, but also in their souls and in the intellectual part of their rational souls. For that reason we say that human souls are diversified as are the human bodies that they inform, each of them exactly proportioned to the organized body that it brings to its perfection.

St. Thomas likewise insists that the difference in souls is substantial. He teaches, however, that a soul has greater perfection and nobility because of its proportion to a better disposed body, which perfection it receives not from the body or from its dependence on the body, but from God, Who

(1) "Unio animae et corporis . . . est unum per essentiam." *II Sent.,* d.25, p. 2, a.1, q.6, t.II, 623a.
"Licet autem anima rationalis compositionem habeat ex materia et forma, appetitum tamen habet ad perficiendam corporalem naturam; sicut corpus organicum ex materia et forma compositum est et tamen habet appetitum ad suscipiendam animam." *II Sent.,* d.17, a.1, q.2, ad 6, t.II, 416ab.
"Dicendum quod esse unibile adhaeret inseparabiliter, quia aptitudo, semper inest, quamvis non semper insit actus, sicut patet in rationabilitate et gressibilitate." *II Sent.,* d.1, p. 2, a.3, q.2, ad 4, t.II, 51a.

(2) *Ibid.*

(3) "Quae quidem est a virtute formativa cum seminibus delata." *II Sent.,* d.8, p.1, a.2, q.1, ad 2, t.II, 215b.

(4) "Cum anima non sit propter corpus, sed corpus propter animam, ista praecellentia ex parte animae venit. In hac autem praecellit una anima alteram, non ratione principii ex quo, cum sit ex nihilo, sed ratione sapientiae Conditoris, qui producit omnia secundum debitum ordinem." *II Sent.,* d.32, dub.6, t.II, 777b.

(5) "Non est tamen negandum quin multum faciat corpus ad exercitium illarum habilitatum, quae animae a sua creatione insunt. *Ibid.*

shapes the soul He creates according to the body into which it is to be infused.[6] Being convinced of the substantial difference between individuals, both Saints drew the conclusion that person is not above sex, and that the difference between man and woman reaches down into the very substance of human beings. Sex, therefore, is the basis for different physical characters.

As God made man male and female, so did He make the elements of reproduction male and female. In the human species these organs have a tremendous role to play, not only in the drama of begetting children, but also in the larger drama of living and loving and learning. From them, we derive the shape of our bodies, along with the differences of face, form, and organic features that distinguish the sexes; and the shape of our minds, which includes the differences of outlook with which men and women approach reality. From the male and female reproductive organs are poured into the blood stream certain chemicals that seem to impress themselves on every living muscle and fiber of the body. So far-reaching are the results that it is common to speak of a man's world and a woman's; of a man's way of looking at things and a woman's; of a man's sense of values and a woman's; of a man's psychology and a woman's; of a man's virtues and a woman's. Just as God gave man and woman complementary physical structures, so did He give them complementary dispositions, tastes, and consequently complementary roles to play in life. The indisputable results of anatomical, physiological, and psychological research show a difference so far-reaching between man and woman that the following is established as a scientific result: the feminine personality assumes the complete human nature in a different manner from the masculine. Each finds what is wanting to self supplied by the other. Only where there is the closest moral union and the fullest reciprocal service does human nature find its true realization.

It is this fundamental difference in temperament which accounts, in part at least, for the strong propensity of love between the sexes. St. Bonaventure likens this mutual attraction to the mutual attraction of matter and form, of soul and body, the union of which constitutes a new entity. The completion of nature, he says, requires that man be at once constituted of body and soul as of matter and form, which have a mutual appetite and a mutual inclination.[7] The soul can exist separated from the body, but it always has a longing for its counterpart, and thus, though the soul does not depend on the body for its being, we may consider body and soul as mutually depen-

(6) "Multitudo igitur animarum a corporibus separatarum consequitur quidem diversitatem formarum secundum substantiam, quia alia est substantia hujus animae et illius, non tamen ista diversitas procedit ex diversitate principiorum essentialium ipsius animae, sed est secundum diversam commensurationem animarum ad corpora; haec enim anima est commensurata huic corpori et non illi, illa autem alii, et sic de omnibus. . . . Sunt enim animae secundum substantias suas formae corporum." *Summa contra Gentiles,* II, c.81, ad 2. Cf. *Summa Theologica,* I, q.91, a.3; *ibid.,* q.96, a.3, and 4.

(7) "Completio vero naturae requirit, ut homo constet simul ex corpore et anima tamquam, ex materia et forma, quae mutuum habent appetitum et inclinationem mutuam." *Breviloquium,* p.7, c.5.2, t.V, 286b.

dent.[8] The soul does not depend on the body for its continuance in existence; its dependence is merely its inclination to the body as its own proper matter. Just as the natural form is dependent on the matter in which it is produced for its *mode* of being, so the human soul is dependent on the body in which it is produced for its *mode* of being.[9] The soul is dependent on the body because it has not complete being *(ens naturae)* without the body. The one depends on the other.[10] Since the human body is the highest and most noble complexity, it is destined for and inclines to the most noble form, the soul.[11] It is not an accidental and ignoble act for the soul to be united to the body to vivify it: not accidental, for the soul is the substantial form of the body; not ignoble, for the soul is the noblest of all forms and in it is the longing for its complete nature.[12]

Precisely because they are complementary to each other and correspond to each other by way of contrast, do man and woman appeal to each other as objects of attraction, tending to a union which will blend their lives into one complete and harmonious whole. The imperfect nature of woman seeks man as matter seeks its form.[13] But man also finds completion in woman. Before the advent of woman there was incompleteness; animate nature was inadequate to man's needs; his yearnings were unsatisfied. "And the Lord God said: It is not good for man to be alone; let us make him a help like unto himself" (Gen. 2:18).

Commenting on this passage, St. Bonaventure remarks that woman was needed as a helper to man in the work of generation which requires the union of both sexes.[14] At first sight, it would seem that the relation of the female sex to procreation impressed him too exclusively, for he says that man does not need the help of woman except in the act of procreation.[15] Here the Seraphic Doctor is speaking in the absolute sense. It is one thing to recognize the essential role which woman plays in the propagation of the race and another to say that this is her only function. Nowhere does St.

(8) "Et esto quod educerentur, adhuc non competerent sicut tactum est in objiciendo, tum propter appetitum, quem haberent ad animam rationalem, tum propter gravitatem." *II Sent.,* d.8, p.1, a.2, q.1, t.II, 215ab.

(9) "Naturalis appetitus animae ad corpus, qui est ad ipsam unionem et unionem antecedit natura, quamvis non antecedat tempore, se habeat in ratione efficientis eo modo, quo est dicere, peccatum habere causam efficientem." *II Sent.,* d.31, a.2, q.2, t.II, 752b.

(10) "Ad illud quod objicitur de corporibus miscibilibus, dicendum, quod non est simile, quia elementa, quae miscentur, non dependent ab invicem et unum potest habere esse completum sine altero; non sic autem est de anima et eius corpore, quorum utrumque ab altero dependet." *II Sent.,* d.17, a.1, q.3, ad 5, t.II, 418b.

(11) "Corpus enim humanum nobilissima complexione et organizatione, quae sit in natura, est organizatum et complexionatum; ideo non completur nec natum est compleri nisi nobilissima forma sive natura." *II Sent.,* d.1, p.2, a.3, q.2, t.II, 50b.

(12) "Hoc enim, quod est animam uniri corpori humano sive vivificare corpus humanum, non dicit actum *accidentalem* nec dicit actum *ignobilem; non accidentalem,* quia ratione illius est anima forma substantialis; non *ignobilem,* quia ratione illius est anima nobilissima formarum omnium, et in anima stat appetitus totius naturae." *Ibid.*

(13) ". . . natura imperfecta in muliere appetit virum, sicut materia formam." *IV Sent.,* d.36, a.2, q.1, concl., t.IV, 796b.

(14) Cf. *supra,* p. 13, footnote 25.

(15) "Primo per textum Genesis secundo: *Faciamus ei adiutorium simile sibi.* Sed vir non indiget adiutorio mulieris nisi quantum ad actum generationis, nec poterant simul aliquem generare, nisi simul commiscerentur." *II Sent.,* d.20, a.1, q.1, t.II, 477a.

Bonaventure disregard the richness and value of qualities that are peculiar to the feminine side of humanity, independently of generative and maternal functions; nowhere does he deny that apart from generation there are some things that woman does better than man according to the words of Ecclesiasticus: "Where there is no wife, he mourneth that is in want" (36:27). We may not, then, interpret St. Bonaventure's statement as even a mild reflection of the opinion of St. Augustine who sees no plausible reason for the creation of woman with her sexual difference than that of aiding man in the duty of procreation.[16] In his *De Genesi ad litteram* he says that if there had been a question of giving Adam a helper for the cultivation of the garden of Eden or the gladdening of its solitude, one who would afford him the consolation of friendship and the benefits of social life, then, in all these respects, a male companion would have been better than a female.[17]

As regards St. Thomas' view on this point, Hans Meyer says:

> "In the same way St. Thomas depreciates the functions of the woman. Woman depends on man in the act of procreation and for guidance throughout life, whereas man needs woman only in the act of procreation. His erroneous notion about the act of generation impelled St. Thomas to look on man as the master, and the woman as a mere helper. Man is able to accomplish all other tasks in life better than woman, even the care of the home and the education and training of the children."[18]

And again:

> "He thought that man would be able to perform household duties better than woman because he saw only brothers performing these tasks in the monastery. His lack of appreciation of woman as mother and wife is more amazing, as are his astounding views about women's souls and minds. The problem is partly explained by the fact that St. Thomas entered the monastery when he was only five years old, and thus saw no women about nor did he need the ministrations of women. Besides the influence of his monastic life, he came under the influence of the thought of his times, which accorded scant consideration to woman's civil rights and her position in the state."[19]

Speaking of the Saint's views about women's souls and minds, the same author states:

> "Not only does woman contribute the less important part to the production of the offspring, but she has the weaker body, the smaller growth, and a weaker intellect and less will power. Woman is to man as the senses are to the reason, or as the lower reason is to the higher reason. In woman the concupiscible appetite predominates, while man is the expression of the more stable element. Because both have reason, man and woman are said to be in the likeness of God, but man is the

(16) *De Genesi ad litt.* lib. IX, c. 3. MPL 34.395. "Quapropter non invenio, ad quod adjutorium facta sit mulier viro, si pariendi causa subtrahatur." *Ibid.*, lib. IX, c.5, MPL 34.396.
(17) *Ibid.*
(18) *Op. cit.*, p. 208.
(19) *Ibid.*, p. 209.

image of God in a special manner, because he is the principle and the end of woman, as God is the principle and ultimate end of the universe."[20]

St. Bonaventure explains that for accidental reasons connected with the corporeal difference between the sexes—virility and strength in the one, weakness and frailty in the other, the image is more distinct in man than in woman.[21] These accidental differences in the individual, however, in no way affect the essential character of the image of God which is the substantial form of the human species and belongs to man and woman alike.[22]

The Fathers and Doctors of the Church, and medieval theologians in general, interpreting in a strictly literal sense the production of woman from the rib of man, make use of every possible detail to stress the fitness and harmony of the arrangement which for them summarizes the natural relations of man and woman in general, or at least those of husband and wife. Flesh and bones are necessary to the human body, and flesh naturally is and must be softer than the bones. In the same way in the plans of the Creator, in the magnificent ideal of the union of man and woman, two different characters were necessary—one strong, the other weak; and though sin has somewhat disarranged this primitive order, the foundation stones still remain.

Interpreting the formation of woman from man in a metaphorical sense, man, the stronger of the two, symbolizes the higher faculty of the mind; woman, the weaker of the two, the lower. As woman is formed from man, so is the lower reason the result of directing the mind to things below. In the consideration of lower or material elements, it departs from the wakefulness of contemplation; it is in a sense weakened and gradually takes on the softness of woman. For this reason, the intellect is said *to be asleep,* and a *bone* is said to be taken from it from which woman is formed.[23] The difference in function, then, between the higher and the lower reason depends upon the influence exerted upon these two faculties of one and the same intellect by their objects. If the soul turns towards purely intelligible objects, it is informed by properties which are inseparable from their nature and assumes a definite unvarying character, that is, a true, perfect image, an ideal object, worthy of the noble faculty which conceived and produced it. If, on the

---

(20) *Ibid.*, p. 208.

(21) "Hoc autem est ratione virilitatis ex parte una, et infirmitatis sive fragilitatis ex altera, quae non respiciunt imaginem secundum se, sed ratione corporis annexi, et ita non essentialiter, sed accidentaliter." *II Sent.*, d.16, a.2, q.2, t.II, 404b.

(22) "Item, sexus non variat speciem, ergo vir et mulier sunt eiusdem speciei; imago consequitur hominem quantum ad formam speciei, non quantum ad formam individui: ergo aequaliter est in viro et muliere." *Ibid.*, f.3, 403a.

(23) "Concordat etiam haec formatio significationi, prout per virum et mulierem *superior portio rationis* et *inferior* habet significari. Sicut enim vir est fortior, et mulier est infirmior, sic superior portio et inferior; et sicut mulier ex viro, sic inferior portio est ex conversione spiritus ad haec inferiora. Dum autem ad haec inferiora convertitur, cessat a vigilantia contemplationis et quodam modo efficitur infirmior semetipso et tendit ad mollitiem mulieris; et ideo quodam modo *soporari* dicitur, et *os* ei auferri, et exinde mulier formari." *II Sent.*, d.18, a.1, q.1, concl., t.II, 433a.

other hand, it turns towards external and sensible objects, it receives from these objects a disposition which is to some extent sensual, which debilitates and enfeebles it, making it like to them,— changeable, contingent, and uncertain. The same reasoning power is always in operation, but when considering the intelligible, it is *superior;* when considering the sensible, *inferior.* In the first case, it is a virile reason; in the second, effeminate, as it were, and for this reason the names higher and lower are given to these two functions of the reason.[24]

In explaining the transition from sense knowledge to intellectual knowledge, St. Thomas draws attention to the Aristotelian distinction between the active and possible intellects. They are two faculties, not one and the same power viewed under two different aspects,[25] and they are really distinct from the essence of the soul, although inseparable from it.[26] In the process of knowledge, the intellect plays a double part. According to St. Thomas, it manifests itself, on the one hand, as an active agent inasmuch as it operates on the object presented by the sentient faculty and renders it intelligible; on the other, as a passive agent inasmuch as it manifests modifiability, passivity, and susceptibility to the reception of different forms. This interpretation St. Bonaventure refuses to accept, as does every true follower of St. Augustine, for the reason that he cannot concede the existence of a purely passive element in the human soul.

Thus, in the conception of St. Thomas and of St. Bonaventure, the terms active and passive intellects have entirely different significations. In the doctrine of St. Thomas, the passive intellect receives and preserves the forms which have been stripped of their individuating notes by the active intellect. In the doctrine of St. Bonaventure, the passive intellect turns toward the sensible and receives from the active intellect the power to strip it of all materiality and form a judgment concerning it. According to the latter interpretation, it is impossible for either intellect to exercise its activity without the aid of the other. The active intellect is not entirely active, nor is the possible intellect entirely passive. They are dependent upon each other, the activity of the one sharing in the passivity of the other and vice versa.[27]

(24) Cf. *Breviloquium,* p.2, c.9, t.V, 227; *II Sent.,* 24, 1, 2, 2, concl., t.II, 564. Regarding the two degrees of the single sensitive faculty and the four degrees of the single intellect, cf. *De triplici via,* I, 4, 19, t.VIII, 7.

(25) "Phantasmata et illuminantur ab intellectu agente et iterum ab eis per virtutem intellectus agentis, species intelligibilis abstrahuntur." *Summa Theol.,* I, q.85, 1.

(26) "Nec in angelo, nec in aliqua creatura, virtus vel potentia operative est idem quod sua essentia." *Summa Theol.,* I, q.54, a.3.

(27) "Appropriatur autem intellectus agens formae et possibilis materiae, quia intellectus possibilis ordinatur ad suscipiendum, intellectus agens ordinatur ad abstrahendum; nec intellectus possibilis est pure passivus; habet enim supra speciem existentem in phantasmate se convertere, et convertendo per auxilium intellectus agentis illam suscipere, et de ea judicare. Similiter nec intellectus agens est *omnino in actu;* non enim potest intelligere aliud a se, nisi adjuvetur a *specie,* quae abstracta a phantasmate intellectui habet uniri. Unde nec possibilis intelligit sine agente, nec agens sine possibili." *II Sent.,* 24, 1, 2, 4, concl., t.II, 569a.

There is no question here of two really distinct faculties.[28] The active and passive intellects are merely modes of mental activity, and the mind, like the will, is reduced to the substance of the soul. Scholastics solve the problem in terms of the general theory of double causality in which agents which are diverse and distinct in nature contribute each in its own way to a common result and produce one effect. As the active and passive intellects are mutually dependent and the complement one of the other, so, too, man and woman, for as St. Paul says: Neither is the man without the woman, nor the woman without the man, in the Lord. For as the woman is of the man, so also is man by the woman; but all things of God" (I Cor. 11:11,12).

If the two sexes are designed by nature for a homogeneous co-operation, then the leading position or social pre-eminence must necessarily fall to one of them. Man is called by the Creator to this position of leader, as is shown by his entire bodily and intellectual make-up. On the other hand, as a result of this supremacy, a certain social subordination in respect to man which in no way injures her personal independence is assigned to woman, as soon as she enters into union with him.

St. Paul, writing to the Corinthians, tells them that Christ is the head of the man, and that man is the head of the woman, and that God is the head of Christ; that man has not sprung from woman, but that woman has sprung from man; in other words, that man was not created for woman, but that woman was created for man, and that, whereas man is the image and glory of God, so, in a special way, is woman the glory of man.[29] These words of St. Paul reveal to us a profound knowledge of woman's nature, and of the end assigned her by the very essence of her nature. She is the glory of man, and she was created for him. Man is the image and glory of God, and he has for direct head Jesus Christ, His Divine Son. Does the Apostle infer that man is the end of woman, as God is the end of man? Evidently not, for he continues: "But yet neither is the man without the woman, nor the woman without the man, in the Lord. For as the woman is of the man, so also is the man by the woman; but all things of God" (I Cor. 11:11, 12). Man and woman have the same end. Both were created for God, and must tend to Him, although by different ways, because of the difference in their natures.

Following up the idea of *inferior portio rationis* and *superior,* what distinguishes man from woman is the fact that he can cling to an idea, conse-

(28) "Et ita cum cogitamus de intellectu agente et possibili, non debemus cogitari quasi de duabus substantiis, vel quasi de duabus potentiis ita separatis, quod una sine alia habeat operationem suam perficere, et aliquid intelligat intellectus agens sine possibili, et aliquid cognoscat intellectus agens, quod tamen homo, cuius est ille intellectus, ignoret." *Ibid.*, 571a.

(29) I Cor. 11:3, 7-9.

crate and devote his life to it, while woman cleaves principally to a person.[30] This difference arises from the fact that man was created to act while woman was destined especially to love, and by her love to render action easier to man whose companion she is, and whose glory she should be, according to the Apostle. Woman, therefore, needs some one on whom to lean, some one to guide her, to be her head, as Christ is the head of the man; some one whose glory she may be, as man is the glory of God. And this necessity, by corresponding to the need of acting and guiding by which man is distinguished from woman, renders the marriage union sweet and profitable. Woman depends on man, man supports woman, and both by mutual aid advance more surely toward their common end.

In nature, the most perfect scene is that which results from the combination of the sublime and the beautiful. So it is with the fellowship existing between ideal types of sexes in which man, the embodiment of strength, power, and greatness, stands for the sublime; woman, the embodiment of the smooth, the soft, and the gentle, for the beautiful. The feelings of the two sexes have been so arranged that each finds an instinctive pleasure in the qualities of the other. In the close union existing between them, one sex finds strength and support; the other, rest and comfort. And though he cannot speak from experience, as the Seraphic Doctor himself tells us, it is a wonderful thing that man finds in his wife a certain contentment and satisfaction which he could never find in another woman.[31]

This is the thought which St. Bonaventure brings out in his *Sentences.* In keeping with the qualities and nature of their sexes, man and woman were created for the most intimate relationship, the closest union, in which the one finds comfort and satisfaction; the other, strength and support. Because woman is united to man and man is united to woman by a strong and singular bond, for that reason the one sex was brought forth from the other. And because that union brings to man comfort and rest, the woman was formed from *man as he slept.* Since man, on the contrary, gives strength and support to woman, she is for that reason said to have been made *from bone.* And because the relations between them are in every respect mutual and equal, woman was formed not from any bone whatsoever but from a *rib* and *his side.* And so it is evident how the manner of the formation of man and

(30) In the consideration of the faculty of knowledge as turned toward superior objects, it is apparent that it is not so much the specific diversity of the objects towards which it turns that gives it its title of superior reason but rather the original internal disposition which directs its search always to the same superior object in the most varied beings. The inferior reason can consider the same objects as the superior reason; it is inferior only because it considers their lower elements. Thus, although the human soul is always the image of God, it does not always appear as such to one who does not make an effort to see it. Cf. *supra,* pp. 21-22.

(31) "Est enim ibi quoddam mirabile, quia homo invenit in muliere aliquam complacentiam, quam nunquam posset in alia invenire, ut dicunt experti." *IV Sent.,* d.36, a.2, q.2, concl., t.IV, 797b.

woman is in keeping with the characteristics of the mutual union which exists between them.[32]

Answering the objection that woman should not be formed from bone, St. Bonaventure explains that she was formed not from bone or the rib alone but from the bone clothed with Adam's flesh, as the following passage testifies: "This is now bone of my bones and flesh of my flesh." She is said to be formed *from bone,* he continues, either because that was the more important part of the formation, or because man gives strength to woman. The hardy vigor of the man will communicate to the gentler nature of the woman a certain backbone of strength, while man, on the other hand, becomes gentle and tender by companionship with woman.[33] Since man gives strength and receives tenderness, Sacred Scripture says that God "filled up flesh for the rib" (cf. Gen. 2:21), or it may be, continues the Seraphic Doctor, because that rib occupied the place of flesh, for it was fashioned in Adam not that it might remain there, but that woman might be formed from it.[34]

In the richness of His wisdom the perfect Artist formed from the region of the heart this perfect creature in all things like to man, able to help him in the crises and trials which mark his life. As Milton says:

> "Under his forming hands a creature grew
> Manlike, but diff'rent sex, so lovely fair,
> That what seem'd fair in all the world seem'd now
> Mean, or in her summ'd up."

In the tenderness, compassion, mercy, and loving sympathy of woman, we read a thought expressive of her glory—that her formation from such perfect material as a part taken from the body close to the heart of man, is an evidence of the delicacy and refinement of the feminine organism serving as an instrument of soul that is still more delicate and refined.[35] And when the Creator brought the last and best of His gifts to the man whom He had formed, that man spoke the first words of love which, as the greatest Authority tells us (Matt. 19:4-6), were the words of God Himself: "This

(32) "Vir enim et mulier secundum suorum sexuum proprietatem et naturam sic facti sunt, ut invicem coniungerentur, et ex hoc unus in altero quietaretur et unus ab altero sustentaretur. Quia igitur forti vinculo et singulari mulier coniungitur viro et e converso, ideo unus sexus productus est de altero. Quia vero illa coniunctio dat viro quietationem, ideo producta est *de viro dormiente.* Rursus, quia vir dat mulieri fortitudinem et sustentationem, hinc est, quod mulier dicitur esse facta *de osse.* Et quia in omnibus his est quaedam aequalitas mutuae societatis, ideo formata est mulier de osse non quocumque, sed *de costa* et *eius latere.* Et sic patet, quomodo modus formationis respondet proprietatibus illius mutuae coniunctionis, quae est inter virum et mulierem secundum rem." *II Sent.,* d.18, a.1, q.1, concl., t.II, 432b.

(33) "Ad illa quae obiiciuntur, quod non debuit fieri de osse; dicendum, quod non tantummodo mulier facta est de osse sive de costa, sed etiam aliqua particula fuit sumta de carne Adae, sicut sequens littera innuit: *Hoc nunc os de osse et caro de carne mea.* Magis autem fit denominatio ab osse, sive quia illa fuit pars principalior; sive quia vir mulieri confert robur, et mulier per viri consortium vigoratur, vir autem per mulieris consortium emollitur." *Ibid.,* 434b.

(34) " . . . et ideo dicitur esse caro repleta pro costa, quia vir dat fortitudinem et suscipit infirmitatem–sive etiam, quia costa illa locum carnis occupabat; non enim facta fuit in Adam, ut in eo maneret, sed ut de ea formaretur mulier." *Ibid.*

(35) "Corpus enim mulieris tenerius est quam corpus viri. Quanto quid tenerius, tanto patitur gravius." *De Perfectione Vitae ad Sorores,* Cap. VI, t.VIII, 121b.

now is bone of my bone and flesh of my flesh." And then with prophetic vision into the distant future, he proclaims the law for all his progeny: "Wherefore a man shall leave father and mother, and shall cleave to his wife, and they shall be two in one flesh." These words completed the union between man and woman by bestowing on it three qualities,—indissolubility, unity, and inviolable sacredness. The union thus made could be severed only by death; it was between one and one; and it was to be held sacred and inviolate by both.

Looking back over the foregoing pages we see how, in the creation of the sexes, the wisdom of God provided for a high moral union to perfect the corporal unity of mankind.[36] He took woman from man, and then reunited them in the divine institution of marriage. The production of woman from the side of man is in perfect keeping with the nature of the qualities which characterize the intimate union existing between them—a union in which man and woman enjoy companionship on equal terms.[37] All the qualities that have, with almost absurd precision and definiteness, been apportioned to the two individual sexes, can attain their highest point of beauty and excellence only when modified, aided, and illumined by the opposite characteristics. Man and woman are essentially peers. To man God gave the stronger mind and greater force, to be the guide, support, and protection of woman. To woman He gave the stronger heart and finer sensibility, tenderness, and patience, to be the consolation of man. The man protects the woman; the woman gives her loyal devotion to the man. Though tendentially different by nature, they ought by mutual intercourse and love converge rather than diverge—the woman acquiring something of the strength of man, man acquiring something of the sweetness of woman. The world will never know the possibilities of humanity until that eternal balance is recognized, and man and woman stand face to face, unequal in stature and physical strength, but on the level ground of moral and spiritual equality. Each is the complement of the other, and when their union is formed in God according to His divine institution, that union is the completion of humanity in all its attributes and qualities. Woman the helpmate, not the slave; man the protector, not the master; only thus shall we have a perfect union.

(36) "Hoc autem clarius apparet, si consideretur ordinis congruentia, quam servavit divina sapientia, dum produxit mulierem de latere viri. Congruum enim erat, mulierem sic de viro produci, tum propter ordinis habitudinem, quae attenditur inter *virum* et *mulierem* in humana specie; tum etiam propter ordinem et habitudinem, quae attenditur inter ea quae per virum et mulierem habent *significari*. *II Sent.*, d.18, a.1, q.1, concl., t.II, 432b.

(37) "Et quia in omnibus his est quaedam aequalitas mutuae societatis, ideo formata est mulier de osse non quocumque, sed de costa et eius latere." *Ibid.*

Chapter IV

HER PART IN THE FALL

THE UTTER HAPPINESS of Adam and Eve, fresh from the hand of God, is described in the Book of Genesis. Besides the essential gift of the state of grace, God's friendship, they enjoyed the plenitude of a threefold integrity—integrity of intellect, of will, and of the faculties which render possible the achievement of what is willed. In the book of nature spread out before them in the lovely garden of Paradise, they could read the handwriting of the Eternal Wisdom and know things in the threefold manner of their existence, namely, in sensible matter, in the mind, and in their eternal Exemplar.[1] Their wills, likewise, tended toward God alone as their last end and towards things only for the sake of God to Whom they were perfectly subject and faultlessly obedient.[2]

The precious freedoms of Paradise—freedom from ignorance, freedom from concupiscence, freedom from sickness and death, from pain and sorrow—were theirs to enjoy as long as they fulfilled the condition under which they were bestowed, namely, that they should not eat of the tree of the knowledge of good and evil. "For in what day soever thou shalt eat of it," God made plain to them, "thou shalt die the death." Such was the original condition which grace bestowed on human nature, wherein man not only had a supernatural end but likewise the power of attaining it.[3]

The innocence of the newly created couple is clearly indicated in Genesis 2:25: "And they were both naked, to wit, Adam and his wife: and they were not ashamed." This passage tells us that man was free from concupiscence until after the Fall. This special prerogative of our first parents is called the gift of integrity because it effected a harmonious relation between

(1) "Et ideo in statu innocentiae, cum imago non erat vitiata, sed deiformis affecta per gratiam, sufficiebat liber creaturae, in quo seipsum exerceret homo ad contuendum lumen divinae sapientiae; ut sic sapiens esset, cum universas res videret in se, videret in proprio genere, videret etiam in arte, secundum quod res tripliciter habent esse, scilicet in materia vel natura propria, in intelligentia creata et in arte aeterna." *Breviloquium,* II, 12, t.V, 230b.

(2) *II Sent.,* prooem., t.II, 4, 5.

(3) "Postremo, ut in homine manifestaretur Dei *bonitas* et benevolentia, ideo fecit hominem absque omni macula et culpa et absque omni poena sive miseria. Cum enim primum principium simul sit *optimum* et *iustissimum;* quia *optimum,* non debuit facere hominem nisi bonum, ac per hoc innocentem et rectum; quia *iustissimum,* poenam non debuit infligere ei qui nullum omnino habebat peccatum: ac per hoc tale corpus constituit illi animae rationali, quod ita sibi esset *obtemperans,* ut nulla esset in ea pugna rebellionis, nulla pronitas libidinis, nulla immunitio vigoris, nulla corruptio mortis; ita etiam esset *animae conforme,* ut, sicut anima erat innocens, et tamen poterat cadere in culpam, sic corpus esset impassible, et tamen cadere in poenam; et ideo 'poterat non mori, et poterat mori'; poterat habere sufficientiam, et poterat habere indigentiam; poterat animae obtemperare, et poterat etiam adversus eam rebellionem et pugnam habere." *Breviloquium,* II, 10, t.V, 228b.

flesh and spirit by completely subordinating man's animal passions to his reason.

Sacred Scripture immediately proceeds to relate how they soon acquired, through actual transgression, the knowledge of good and evil, and with it the sense of shame which had been previously unknown to them.

> "Now the serpent was more subtle than any of the beasts of the earth which the Lord had made. And he said to the woman: Why hath God commanded you, that you should not eat of every tree of paradise? And the woman answered him saying: Of the fruit of the trees that are in paradise we do eat. But of the fruit of the tree which is in the midst of paradise, God hath commanded us that we should not eat; and that we should not touch it, lest perhaps we die. And the serpent said to the woman: No, you shall not die the death. For God doth know that in what day soever you shall eat thereof, your eyes shall be opened, and you shall be as Gods, knowing good and evil. And the woman saw that the tree was good to eat, and fair to the eyes, and delightful to behold: and she took of the fruit thereof, and did eat, and gave to her husband who did eat. And the eyes of them both were opened and when they perceived themselves to be naked, they sewed together fig-leaves, and made themselves aprons. And when they heard the voice of the Lord God walking in paradise at the afternoon air, Adam and his wife hid themselves from the face of the Lord God, amidst the trees of paradise. And the Lord God called Adam, and said to him: Where art thou? And he said: I heard thy voice in paradise; and I was afraid, because I was naked, and I hid myself. And He said to him; And who hath told thee that thou wast naked, but that thou hast eaten of the tree whereof I commanded thee that thou shouldst not eat? And Adam said: The woman, whom thou gavest me to be my companion, gave me of the tree, and I did eat. And the Lord God said to the woman: Why hast thou done this? And she answered: The serpent deceived me, and I did eat. And the Lord God said to the serpent: Because thou hast done this thing, thou art cursed among all cattle, and beasts of the earth; upon thy breast shalt thou go, and earth shalt thou eat all the days of thy life. I will put enmities between thee and the woman, and thy seed and her seed. She shall crush thy head, and thou shalt lie in wait for her heel" (Gen. 3:1-15).

When Almighty Wisdom constituted the human race in one common humanity, He designed that all men should be of one mind in His Eternal Word of Truth, and of one spirit in His Holy Spirit, as they are of one body, through propagation from one common father of their race. Such was the divine plan. But how perversely has the unity of mankind been thrown into disorder through the weakness of human wills, and through that perverted love of self that puts pride in the place of charity, and revolt in the place of obedience! In the story of the Fall, the original cause of evil is the serpent, which in later Jewish tradition is identified with Satan: "But by the envy of the devil, death came into the world" (Wis. 2:24). When God had placed man in double sex, male and female, in the happiness of Paradise, the devil, envious of their lot, under the guise of a serpent attacked the woman, first with the *question:* "Why has God commanded you that you should not eat?" and secondly with the *assertion:* "You shall be as Gods, knowing good and evil." By this temptation the devil wished to overcome the weaker woman and through her later to encompass the ruin of the male sex. And the Lord permitting it, this is what he actually accomplished.[4] Evil approached the woman from without, feebly and insidiously, for it had no hold on the inner sanctuary of her mind. In view of the magnificent grace with which she was dowered, she could have repelled it with one effort, but she listened to it, she yielded to it, and persuaded man to yield also; and she carried his race and hers with her in the Fall.

There is something very solemn and arresting about the freedom of choice which God accords to His creatures. The success of their lives here on earth and their destiny for all eternity depend on their own decisions. Though God had created Adam and Eve with sufficient grace to enable them to emerge victorious from the struggle and though He knew that they would succumb to the temptation, nevertheless, He permitted them to be tried and to be tried well by one who had the required *knowledge,* the *power* and the *will* to do so. It was according to the dispensation of Divine Providence that the devil assumed the form of a serpent, that, from that effigy, the wiles and snares of the devil might be detected and made known to all the sons of Adam.[5]

Again it was by a dispensation of Divine Providence that our first parents were tempted against the fulfillment of a command, for whether they conquered the temptation or succumbed to it, the merit of obedience and the punishment of disobedience would be made known to all.[6] To tempt the woman first, however, was the idea of the devil himself and evidence of his cunning. Since it is easier to overthrow the less strong of two adversaries, the wily enemy attacks the city from the weaker side.[7]

The cunning of the devil is likewise evident in the manner in which he

(4) "Haec autem de tentatione tenenda sunt, quod cum Deus hominem condidisset in felicitate paradisi in duplici sexu, virili scilicet et muliebri; diabolus invidens homini, assumta specie serpentina, aggressus est mulierem, primo *quaerendo: Cur praecepit vobis Deus, ne comederetis?* (2), secundo *asserendo: Eritis sicut dii, scientes bonum et malum;* volens ista tentatione deiicere mulierem infirmiorem et per illam postea prosternere sexum virilem; quod et fecit, Domino permittente." *Breviloquium,* III, 2, t.V, 232a.

(5) "Ratio autem ad intelligentiam praedictorum haec est: quia, sicut primum principium est potentissimum in producendo, sic etiam est rectissimum gubernando; et ideo 'res, quas condidit, ita administrat, ut tamen eas agere proprios motus sinat'. Quoniam ergo homo sic factus erat, ut per victoriam pugnae perveniret ad praemium quietis aeternae; licet Deus sciret, hominem tentationi succumbere, debuit tamen permittere, hominem tentari ab eo qui *sciret, posset et vellet.*—Quoniam igitur diabolus qui prius erat sciens et rectus, per superbiam cadendo factus est versutus et invidus, et ideo per invidiam tentare *volebat* et per astutiam *sciebat;* ideo tentavit, iuxta quod *potuit* et Deus permisit. Quod ergo in tentando speciem serpentinam assumsit, hoc fuit dispensationis divinae, ut non solum posset deprehendi eius versutia, verum etiam ex illa effigie versutia diabolica in tentando innotescere posset cunctis filiis Adae." *Ibid.*

(6) "Rursus, quod tentavit de praecepto *disciplinae,* hoc similiter fuit dispensationis divinae, ut sive vinceretur, sive vinceret, cunctis innotesceret meritum obedientiae, sive demeritum inobedientiae." *Ibid.*

(7) "Quod autem incepit a *muliere,* hoc fuit versutiae suae, quia facilius est deiicere minus fortem; unde versutia hostis ex infirmiori parte aggreditur civitatem." *Ibid.*

proceeded with the temptation; it was an orderly procedure of *testing, motivating,* and *enticing.* He *tried her out* by a question: "And he said to the woman: Why hath God commanded you that you should not eat of every tree of paradise?" He *urged her on* by his assurance: "No, you shall not die the death." He *allured* her with his promise: "You shall be as Gods, knowing good and evil." First, he *questioned* her concerning the reason for the command, that he might introduce a doubt in her mind; secondly, after she had doubted, he *assured* her that they would not die, that he might lead her to despise the command; thirdly, *he held out a promise,* that he might make her desire the forbidden fruit. By this threefold device, he succeeded in making her consent of her own free choice; he was in possession of her intellect and will, wherein reside the rational, the irascible, and the concupiscible powers. Thus the wily serpent allured the woman and ensnared her by the desire of a threefold good: the desire of *knowledge* which resides in the rational appetite; the desire to possess *the perfect nature of God,* which resides in the irascible appetite; the desire for *the sweetness of the tree,* which resides in the concupiscible appetite. And so he tried every device; he appealed to every power of her soul by which she could be led into temptation, "for all that is in the world is concupiscence of the flesh, concupiscence of the eyes and the pride of life" (I John 2:16). And herein is found the source of every temptation—the world, the flesh, or the devil.[8]

Interpreters of Sacred Scripture have asked why the devil tempted the woman first, permitting her, in turn, to seduce the man. St. Bonaventure is very clear on this point, as shown by his a priori reasons in favor of the devil's plan of attacking the woman first: The order of destruction is the reverse of the order of construction. As Aristotle says, things last put together are the first to disintegrate. Since woman was the last of creation, it seems that the way of disintegration and corruption should have its origin in her and that the devil, therefore, should approach her first.[9] Then, too, exterior temptation should follow the same procedure as interior temptation. As sin first takes possession of the sensitive faculty of the soul and makes its way to the higher reason through the lower reason, so the exterior temptation, the work of the devil, should make its way to man, who in humanity represents the higher

(8) "Similiter modus, quo in tentatione processit, magnae fuit versutiae, quia *experiendo, impellendo* et *alliciendo* processit. *Experientiam* enim sumsit in interrogatione, *impulit* in assecuratione, *allexit* autem in promissione. Primo enim *interrogavit* de causa mandati, ut rationem duceret in dubium; secundo, dubitatione habita: *Ne forte moriamur* assecuravit, ut irascibilem duceret in contemptum; tertio *promisit,* ut concupiscibilem duceret ad consensum, quae facultas est *rationis et voluntatis,* complectens nihilominus tres praedictas vires, rationalem, irascibilem et concupiscibilem; respectu quarum diabolus allexit mulierem per triplex appetibile, scilicet per *scientiam,* quae est appetibilis rationali; per *excellentiam* ad modum Dei, quae est appetibilis irascibili; per *suavitatem ligni,* quae est appetibilis concupiscibili. Et sic tentavit omne, quod erat in muliere tentabile, per omne illud, per quod poterat in tentationem induci, quod est triplex appetibile mundi, scilicet *concupiscentia carnis, concupiscentia oculorum* et *superbia vitae;* secundum quae tria attenditur omnis tentationis origo, sive a mundo, sive a carne, sive a diabolo." *Ibid.,* 232ab.

(9) "Ordo enim destructionis contrarius est ordini constructionis, quae enim sunt ultima in componendo sunt priora in resolvendo; sed mulier fuit ultimo facta et formata: ergo videtur, quod via deformationis et corruptionis a muliere debuit habere exortum: ergo tentator debuit eam prius aggredi." *II Sent.,* d.21, a.1, q.3, t.II, 496a. Cf. also Aristotle, III. *Ethic.* c.3.

faculty of reason, through woman who represents the lower faculty.[10] Again, the more easily a foe can be overpowered, the more speedily does a cautious warrior make an advance against him. If woman can be overpowered more easily than man, it seems that the temptation should come to the man through her.[11] Lastly, an attack upon a strong enemy is often accomplished more easily through a member of his own household than through an outside foe. Man was strong and endowed with a spiritual mind. Since the devil dared not attack him directly, it seems fitting that he should start with the woman, in the hope of using her as a tool in the later conquest of a more powerful enemy.[12]

On the other hand, there were considerations which brought out the lack of motive for putting the woman to the test first; in fact, there were many good reasons why the devil should make a direct attack upon Adam. First of all, it is not the flesh which sins, but the soul, which knows no distinction of sex but bears the image of God equally in man and woman alike. There seems to be no reason, therefore, why the temptation should begin with the woman rather than with the man.[13] Secondly, woman had no inclination to sin. Like man, she was created in a state of original justice. Well balanced and self-controlled, she was free from the weight of inordinate passions, and therefore could be overcome with no less difficulty than the man.[14] Thirdly, it is more shameful to be vanquished by a woman than by a man, and more glorious to triumph over a man than over a woman. If the devil carefully flees from shame and disgrace and most eagerly seeks glory, it would seem that he should tempt the man first rather than the woman.[15] Again, it is the nature of the bold to rush eagerly against the strong. It would seem that the devil, who is very bold and daring and fully confident of his power, would have disdained to make an attack upon the woman, and that his boldness

(10) "Item, tentatio exterior debet conformari interiori; sed in tentatione interiori peccatum ascendit a sensualitate ad superiorem partem mediante inferiori portione rationis: si ergo superior portio est vir, et inferior est mulier; sicut tentatio interior procedit ad virum mediante muliere, sic et tentatio exterior." *II Sent.*, d.21, a.1, q.3, t.II, 496a. On this question cf. August., II *de Gen. contra Manich.* c.14. n.21. MPL. 34.207; XII. *de Trin.* c.11. n.16. seq. MPL 42. 1006, 1007; XIV. *de Civ. Dei*, c.11. n.2. MPL 41.419, 420; also St. Bonaventure *Opera Omnia, II Sent.*, d.24, p.1, a.2, q.2, t.II, 563, 564 and p. II in its entirety, t.II, 573-588.

(11) "Item, cautus pugnator citius aggreditur ad bellandum illum, quem potest expugnare facilius: si ergo mulier facilius poterat expugnari quam vir, videtur, quod progressus tentationis pervenire debuit ad virum mediante muliere." *II Sent.*, d.21, a.1, q.3, t.II, 496a.

(12) "Item, facilius est alicui expugnare fortem inimicum per domesticum quam etiam per se ipsum; sed vir erat fortis et spirituali mente praeditus: ergo non videtur, quod diabolus ausus fuerit eum tentare per se ipsum, sed per suum domesticum: ergo mediante muliere tentatio pervenit ad virum." *Ibid.*

(13) "Peccatum non est in carne, sed in Dei imagine; sed mulier et vir aequaliter sunt ad imaginem Dei, quia in anima non est distinctio sexus: ergo videtur, quod tentatio non magis debuit inchoari a sexu muliebri quam a virili." *Ibid.*

(14) "Item, mulier nullam habebat pronitatem ad peccatum, sicut nec vir, et ita erat recta; sicut vir, nec caro eius aliquo modo animam incurvabat; ergo videtur, quod ita difficile erat mulierem sicut virum deiicere: nulla ergo ratio videtur esse, ob quam tentatio diaboli magis inciperet a muliere." *Ibid.*

(15) "Item, vituperabilius est vinci a muliere quam a viro, et gloriosius est vincere virum quam mulierem: si ergo diabolus maxime refugit vituperium et avidissime quaerit gloriam, videtur, quod magis tentationem a viro quam a muliere inchoaverit." *Ibid.*

would have moved him to direct his strength against the stronger of his foes.[16]

Although these a priori reasons seem to neutralize one another, the indisputable testimony of Sacred Scripture makes it clear that the temptation did commence with the woman and reached Adam through Eve. This order of procedure is, moreover, says the Seraphic Doctor, in accordance with the *wisdom of God* Who permitted it, and with the *cunning of the devil* who chose it.[17]

First, as regards the *wisdom of God.* The Lord permitted the devil to follow this order of procedure for a threefold reason: to train man, to deprive the woman of an apparent excuse for her sin, and to teach us a lesson. It was intended to train and exercise man, for he was so strong and so endowed with moral and intellectual strength that he could resist not only the temptation of the serpent but also the suggestion of the woman. Therefore, God permitted him to be tried by the stronger temptation.[18] Secondly, that the woman might have no apparent excuse for her sin, God permitted the temptation to begin with her. If the man had sinned first, it would cause no surprise if the woman followed him in sin, for *man is the head of the woman* and has dominion over her. As it was, woman had not a shred of excuse for her sin.[19] Thirdly, it was for our instruction that the wisdom of God permitted the devil to proceed as he did. From that temptation arising from a sensible object, we learn the method and the progress of invisible temptation, for as the former came from the serpent to man through the woman, so the latter begins in the sensible appetite and reaches the higher reason by means of the lower.[20]

Now, as regards the *cunning of the devil.* He had noticed that the woman was *less wise, less constant, and more tenacious of purpose* than the man. Being *less wise,* she could more easily be seduced; therefore the demon seducer wished to make a passage way for himself through her. Being *less constant,* she could more easily be led astray. It is good strategy to attack an enemy at its weakest point. The devil, therefore, attacked the human

(16) "Item, natura audacium est libenter fortibus occurere: sed diabolus est audacissimus et procacissimus et maxime praesumens de suis viribus: ergo videtur, quod dedignatus fuerit primo aggredi muliebrem sexum: non ergo videtur probabile, quod prius tentaverit mulierem quam virum." *Ibid.*

(17) "Respondeo: Dicendum, quod, sicut dicit Scriptura et Magister dicit in littera, non est dubitandum, quin tentatio diaboli a muliere, inchoaverit et per eam pervenerit ad virum. Ratio autem huius sumitur ex parte *sapientiae Dei,* et ex parte *astutiae diaboli.*" *Ibid.*

(18) "Ex parte *sapientia Dei.* Dominus enim tali ordine permisit diabolum tentare, tum propter viri exercitationem, tum ne mulier haberet excusationem, tum etiam propter nostram eruditionem. Propter viri exercitationem, quia ipse adeo fortis erat et spirituali mente praeditus, quod non solum poterat resistere tentationi serpentis, sed etiam suggestioni mulieris; et ideo fortiori tentatione permissus est tentari." *Ibid., concl.,* 496b.

(19) "Proper mulieris vero removendam excusationem primo debuit ab ipsa tentatio incipere. Nam si vir primo peccasset, cum *vir sit caput mulieris* et dominetur ei, non esset multum mirandum, si mulier ei consentiret; immo magnum haberet excusationis colorem." *Ibid.*

(20) "Propter nostram eruditionem etiam hoc permissum est. In illo enim modo tentandi sensibili cognoscimus nos modum et progressum tentationis invisibilis; et sicut ille a serpente venit ad virum mediante muliere, sic iste a sensualitate pervenit ad superiorem portionem rationis mediante inferiori." *Ibid.*

citadel on that side on which the entrance was less fortified. Since the woman was *more tenacious of purpose* than the man, the devil figured that once vanquished herself, she would not rest until she had perverted her husband. Does not Ecclesiastes (7:27) say that a woman is "the hunter's snare, and her heart is a net and her hands are bands?" These are the reasons, says St. Bonaventure, why the devil, the cunning instigator, began his attack with woman.[21]

While these facts confirm the first a priori reasons, a series of other reasons reveals their weakness. One may object that the question of sex does not enter into the matter when it is a question of the image of God. If we consider only the essential nature of the soul itself, it is true that the image of God is equally distinct in man and in woman. However, since the soul accommodates itself to the nature of the body which it informs and on account of the natural weakness of the sex takes on a certain effeminacy, the feminine sex by its very nature, unless sustained by a greater grace, is more easily inclined to evil.[22] But, comes the objection, woman had no inclination to evil. This St. Bonaventure admits but refuses to conclude therefrom that woman is equal to man in stability of character. Though apparently free from evil tendencies and deceit, she could fall into sin more easily than man, who was naturally stronger and presumably more abundantly blessed with grace.[23] As to the objection that it is more humiliating to be conquered by a woman than by a man, this is true, but it is likewise more glorious to achieve success over a woman than to suffer defeat in battling against a man. Since the devil feared a truly virile resistance in an encounter with Adam, he applied his mind with greater precaution to the attainment of glory by a victory over the woman.[24] Finally, answering the objection that the daring are more willing to attack the strong than the weak, St. Bonaventure says this is true of those who are openly daring. But the devil is not only a bold adventurer; he is likewise a wily deceiver. He chooses not the most difficult but the surest way to success. Besides, he is

(21) "Ex parte similiter *astutiae diaboli* potest sumi ratio. Diabolus enim attendebat, mulierem esse *minoris sapientiae* et *debilioris constantiae* et *importunioris adhaerentiae*. Quia *minoris sapientiae* erat, facilior erat ad seducendum; et ideo diabolus seductor per eam voluit sibi facere transitum et viam. Quia *debilioris constantiae*, facilior erat ad pervertendum; et ideo diabolus expugnator aggressus est hominis civitatem ex ea parte, ex qua erat aditus minus munitus. Quia vero *importunioris* erat *adhaerentiae*, cogitavit diabolus, quod si ipsa primo vinceretur, non quiesceret, quousque perverteret virum. Unde dicitur Ecclesiastis septimo de muliere, quod *laqueus est venatorum, et sagena cor eius, vincula sunt manus illius*. Propterea diabolus, astutus impulsor, incepit a sexu femineo." *Ibid.*, 497a.

(22) "Ad illud autem quod primo obiicitur in contrarium, quod quantum ad imaginem non est sexuum differentia; dicendum, quod licet in viro et muliere reperiatur imago aeque expresse, quantum est de natura ipsius animae; quia tamen anima, quamdiu est in corpore, complexionem corporis imitatur, ex ratione debilitatis complexionis et sexus contrahit anima quandam effeminationem; et propterea, quantum est ex parte naturae, nisi adsit fortitudo maioris gratiae, facilius incurvatur ad malum sexus femineus." *Ibid.*, 497ab.

(23) "Ad illud quod obiicit, quod mulier nullam habuit ad hoc pronitatem; dicendum, quod verum est; non tamen ex hoc sequitur, quod haberet aequalem stabilitatem. Quamvis enim non haberet curvationem in affectu nec deceptionem in aspectu, facilius tamen poterat in hoc incidere quam vir, in quo et natura erat fortior, et gratia creditur fuisse abundantior." *Ibid.*, 497b.

(24) "Ad illud quod obiicitur, quod vituperabile est vinci a muliere etc: dicendum, quod verum est; verumtamen gloriosius est mulierem luctando superare, quam cum viro luctando succumbere. Et quia diabolus, si incepisset a viro, timebat, ne viriliter sibi resisteret, ideo maiori cautela studuit gloriam adipisci." *Ibid.*

not permitted to exercise his full power and, since he conquers only those who are willing to embrace defeat, he is fundamentally weak. For this reason he directed the temptation not against the stronger but against the weaker of the two.[25]

It was not in vain that the evil spirit, already fallen and therefore jealous, first attacked woman and promised her knowledge—not the innate, simple, direct knowledge that belonged to man in his origin but an inferior knowledge of things considered in themselves which is acquired by reason alone and bears upon the things of sense, the knowledge of which Aristotle was later to construct the theory, codify the method and define the content.[26] From the moment Adam and Eve set aside the thought of God as the measure of all things and depended upon their senses alone as the measure of all things as they subsisted in the material world, they found themselves incapable of attaining any stable object or immutable truth; hence in the midst of things good but incomplete, they could satisfy neither their thoughts nor their desires. Such was the Fall: like Lucifer, by an act of curiosity and pride, man turned from the intelligible to the sensible and, limiting himself to the domain of the accidental and of non-being, he lost his way in a maze of perplexity.[27] "Only this have I found, that God made man right, and he hath entangled himself with an infinity of questions" (Eccles. 7:30). Natural knowledge can satisfy neither his need to know nor his need to love. Instability of knowledge results in instability of desire which, in turn, results in instability of faculties and acts. The original continuity and rectitude of nature which once bound man to God are utterly destroyed and the soul, striving with all its might for an infinite good which it can no longer attain, drags on, a prey to the most cruel suffering.[28]

"Turning his back on the true light to pursue the mutable good," says St. Bonaventure, "Adam found himself deprived of his pristine rectitude and the whole human race through original sin inherited mental ignorance which marred the divine image and carnal concupiscence which destroyed the divine likeness. Blinded and bent down, man sits in darkness and sees not the light of heaven, unless he be strengthened against concupiscence by grace with justice and against ignorance by knowledge with wisdom."[29]

(25) "Ad illud quod obiicitur, quod audaces libentius aggrediuntur fortes; dicendum, quod illud verum est, ubi est audacia sine astutia; diabolus autem non tantum est audax et procax, immo etiam est astutus et fallax: et ideo in tentando non aggressus est viam difficiliorem, sed potius efficaciorem. Praeterea, non permittebatur sibi totam suam exercere potentiam; cum enim non vincat nisi volentem, est debilis pugnando; et ideo non a fortiori, sed a debiliori suam inchoavit tentationem." *Ibid.*

(26) *Breviloquium* III, 3, 2, t.V, 232; *Hexaem.*, XXII, 35, t.V, 442; in *II Sent.*, d.30, a.2, q.1, fund. 4, t.II, 721, St. Bonaventure points out the analogy between sensible knowledge as suggested by the serpent and that which is recommended by Aristotle.

(27) Cf. *II Sent.*, prooem., t.II, 5; In Hexaem., I, 17, t.V, 332 and XIX, 4, t.V, 420.

(28) *II Sent.*, prooem., t.II, 5.

(29) "Secundum enim primam naturae institutionem creatus fuit homo habilis ad contemplationis quietem, et ideo *posuit eum Deus in paradiso deliciarum.* Sed avertens se a vero lumine ad commutabile bonum, incurvatus est ipse per culpam propriam, et totum genus suum per originale peccatum, quod dupliciter infecit humanam naturam, scilicet *ignorantia* mentem et *concupiscentia* carnem; ita quod *excaecatus* homo et *incurvatus* in tenebris sedet et caeli lumen non videt nisi succurrat gratia cum iustitia contra *concupiscentiam,* et scientia cum sapientia contra *ignorantiam.*" *Itinerarium,* I, 7, t.V, 298.

In his discussion of the guilt of Eve, St. Bonaventure follows in the footsteps of Peter Lombard whose opinion he voices in his *Commentaries on the Sentences* and, like the *Magister,* he begins with an analysis of the woman's sin.

By consenting to the suggestion of the devil and wishing to be as God, woman committed the sin of pride. Though not aiming at an absolute equality with God, she aspired to a dignity far surpassing human measure. By desiring an unbecoming knowledge of good and evil, which was not included in God's intention for her, she committed a kind of spiritual avarice. Finally, in wishing to taste the sweetness of the fruit of the forbidden tree, she fell into gluttony and by this act became guilty of transgression and entangled in the sin of disobedience. And so it is evident that woman's sin had its origin in pride; it spread to avarice and ended in gluttony. It is evident, too, that she introduced disorder into all the powers of her soul: into the irascible power by too lofty aspirations; into the rational power by seeking knowledge of forbidden things; into the concupiscible power by tasting the sweetness of the forbidden fruit. And from that sin sprouted the root of all sin, pride.[30] "Pride is the beginning of all sin," says the author of Ecclesiasticus (10:15) and St. Bonaventure in his *Breviloquium* calls it a double root—a debasing fear and a passionate love; a triple incitement to three evils—the concupiscence of the flesh, the concupiscence of the eyes, and the pride of life.[31]

After discussing various opinions regarding the sin of Adam, the Seraphic Doctor finally concluded that the man's aspirations were less lofty than his wife's. However, in preferring his own will to the divine command, Adam showed his unwillingness to subject himself to God, which is, in a way, the equivalent of wishing to be as great as God. Or it has been said that Adam desired in the person of Eve, who was formed from him, what she so foolishly desired, for by synecdoche what is true of a part is true of the whole. Thirdly, Adam had the responsibility of leading his wife and,

(30) "Considerans igitur diabolus, hanc esse viam ad praecipitandam mulierem in culpam, primo promisit *dignitatis excellentiam: Eritis sicut dii.* Secundo, subiunxit *cognitionis abundantiam: scientes bonum et malum.* Postremo, praetendit *suavitatis experientiam,* cum ostendit *lignum pulcrum visu et ad vescendum suave.* Quoniam igitur mulier diabolicae suggestioni consensit, ideo primo, in appetendo *esse sicut Deus,* fuit *superba.* Deinde, in appetendo scire bonum et malum, quod non oportebat, et scire plus quam oportebat, fuit *avara.* Postremo, in experiendo *suavitatem ligni vetiti* fuit *gulosa;* et in hoc fuit transgressionis rea et culpa inobedientiae involuta. Et sic patet, quod peccatum mulieris inchoatum fuit in superbia, progressum habuit in avaritia, consummationem habuit in gula. Patet etiam, quod inordinata fuit ad triplicem potentiam, scilicet quantum ad *irascibilem,* dum appetiit alta; quantum ad *rationalem,* dum appetiit scire occulta; quantum ad *concupiscibilem,* dum voluit degustare suavia. Unde ex illo peccato pullulaverunt radices omnium peccatorum." *II Sent.,* d.22, a.1, q.1, concl., t.II, 517a.

(31) "Circa ortum capitalium peccatorum hoc in summa tenendum est, quod peccatorum actualium unum est *initium,* duplex *radix,* triplex *fomentum,* septiforme *caput* sive capitale peccatum. Unum est *initium,* scilicet superbia, iuxta quod scriptum est: *Initium omnis peccati est superbia; duplex radix,* scilicet *timor* male humilians et *amor* male accedens; triplex *fomentum,* secundum tria, quae sunt in mundo, scilicet *concupiscentia carnis, concupiscentia oculorum et superbia vitae.*" *Breviloquium,* III, 9, t.V, 238a.

since he did not discourage her in her high aspirations, the sin of Eve is imputed to him and it is said that he wished to be as God.[32]

After these preliminary discussions, the Seraphic Doctor proceeds to determine the comparative guilt of Adam and Eve. One sin can be graver than another by reason of the greater ingratitude which it supposes, by reason of the inordinate desire from which it proceeds, or by reason of the disastrous effects which follow from it. From the viewpoint of *ingratitude,* man sinned more grievously than woman because he had received more abundant gifts. Forgetful of his blessings, he defied and offended his benefactor, and in his greater ingratitude lies his greater guilt.[33] As regards *inordinate desire,* the woman sinned more gravely. Her will was more wicked, for she wished to be as God; her desire more ardent, for she firmly believed in the promise of the devil, and in the greater eagerness of her desire lies her greater guilt.[34] But considering the gravity of the sin in the light of its *consequent corruption,* we must make a distinction, for an instrument of corruption may operate as either *cause* or *occasion.* Considering the *cause* of the corruption, it was the sin of the man which caused the transmission of sin to his descendants, and since he corrupted himself and others, greater corruption resulted from the sin of the man and in this respect his guilt is said to have been greater than the guilt of the woman.[35] But considering the *occasion,* it was the sin of the woman which was the occasion of the man's sin and consequently of the sins of all his descendants, and thus it can be said that woman corrupted the rest of the human race, not only her descendants but also her husband. Therefore Eve sinned not only *in herself,* but also *in her neighbor,* and considered as an occasion of the corruption of the whole race, we may say that her guilt was the greater.[36]

The Seraphic Doctor then goes on to explain that if it is a question of

(32) "Concedendum est igitur, quod Adam non appetiit esse sicut Deus, quemadmodum mulier, sicut ostendunt rationes ad hoc inductae. Si autem dicatur alicubi appetiisse esse sicut Deus, hoc potest esse dictum triplici ratione: aut quia divinum contempsit imperium, et voluntatem suam divinae praetulit iussioni, et se sibi tanquam Deo subiicere et ex hoc Deo aequiparari voluit. Aut dictum est, quia mulier de illo sumta, appetiit sicut Deus esse, et per synecdochem quod est partis attribuitur toti. Unde Sancti, quod appetiit *alter,* frequenter loquuntur synecdochice et attribuunt utrique. Aut potest hoc tertio modo dictum intelligi, quia ipse, cum esset mulieri praepositus, ipsam non compescuit, unde sibi imputatur culpa mulieris. Mulier autem intelligenda est appetiisse esse sicut Deus, non per *omnimodam aequalitatem,* sed per quandam sublimationem in dignitate supra humanum modum; quam cum vir non compescuit, immo potius eius voluntati paruit, sibi peccatum mulieris imputatur, et voluisse esse sicut Deus refertur." *II Sent.,* d.22, a.1, q.2, t.II, 519b.

(33) "Si igitur loquamur de maiori gravitate quantum ad *ingratitudinem,* gravius peccavit vir quam mulier, pro eo quod abundantiora dona suscepit; et ideo, cum beneficiorum oblitus, benefactorem suum contempsit et offendit, magis ingratus fuit et in sui ingratitudine maiori culpabilior exstitit." *Ibid.,* d.22, a.1, q.3, t.II, 520b.

(34) "Si autem loquamur de maioritate quantum ad *libidinem,* sic amplius peccavit mulier quam vir, pro eo quod magis *improba* voluntate peccavit, dum concupivit Deo assimilari; et *ardentius* appetiit, dum credidit, hoc se obtinere posse quod diabolus ei suggessit; et ideo propter voluntatem magis improbam mulier peccavit ex maiori libidine, et quantum ad hoc culpabilior viro fuit." *Ibid.*

(35) "Si autem loquamur de maioritate culpae quantum ad *corruptionem consequentem,* distinguendum est quia aliquid potest dici corrumpere dupliciter: aut per modum *causae,* aut per modum *occasionis.* Si per modum *causae* sic, quia peccatum viri fuit causa transfusionis peccati in posteros, et ita corrupit se et alios, maior consecuta est ex peccato viri corruptio et quantum ad hoc culpa viri dicitur fuisse gravior." *Ibid.*

(36) "Si vero per modum *occasionis,* sic, quia peccatum mulieris fuit occasio peccati viri et ita per consequens omnium aliorum, hoc modo mulier potest dici ceteros corrupisse, non solum posteros, sed etiam virum suum. Unde non solum peccavit *in se,* sed etiam *in proximum.* Et quantum ad hoc dici potest, in muliere gravius fuisse peccatum." *Ibid.*

the nature or rank of the *sinner,* the man sinned more grievously than the woman, not only because of his surpassing gifts but also because of the supremacy of his position as head of the race. But if it is a question of the intrinsic nature of the *sin,* then Eve was more guilty because of her impiety toward God and her injustice toward her neighbor, for by her ambition she dishonored God and by her suggestion she caused the downfall of her neighbor.[37]

And if any one should ask which sin was greater, we must say that, since the sin of Eve was greater in matters which constitute the essence of sin, as in the greater wickedness of her inordinate desires, which in this instance was greater and more far-reaching than that of her spouse, so, speaking in an absolute sense, the sin of Eve was more serious and more far-reaching than the sin of Adam. We have an indication of this in the fact that her punishment was more severe, and if she had descended into hell, she would have had greater punishment.[38] St. Thomas is of the same opinion. Though admitting that both Adam and Eve committed the sin of pride, he finds some excuse for the man because he sinned out of benevolence and love for another.[39]

Milton, too, in "Paradise Lost" attributes Adam's lapse to conjugal love. Devotion to Eve impelled him to share her downfall. O poet's fancy! Adam's charge against his wife immediately after the transgression was far from chivalrous and by no means symptomatic of undue affection on his part: "The woman, whom thou gavest me to be my companion, gave me of the tree, and I did eat."

In no passage of Sacred Scripture can we find justification for St. Bonaventure's idea that man, stronger than woman, had received a proportionally greater amount of supernatural grace. If he was stronger in his capacity to resist evil, he gave no evidence of it in his immediate acquiescence to the suggestion of his wife. Love for his help-meet, readiness to do whatever would please her, made it easy for him to lay aside all thought of his tremendous responsibilities. It was sense-affection which led to his ruin, the love of a beautiful wife, and that wife was the tool of the serpent.

Much has been made of the fact that the tempter approached Eve rather than Adam. According to St. Bonaventure, Eve was addressed because it was doubtful whether man would have yielded. Eve, "the weaker vessel,"

(37) "Si igitur pensemus conditiones ex parte *peccantis,* gravius peccasse dicitur vir quam mulier, tum propter donorum praeexcellentiam, tum etiam propter status praesidentiam, quia mulieri quodam modo praelatus erat. Si autem pensantur conditiones ex parte *peccati,* gravius peccavit mulier quam vir, tum propter impietatem in Deum, tum propter iniquitatem in proximum. Deum enim sua ambitione exhonoravit et proximum sua suggestione deiecit." *Ibid.,* 521a.

(38) "Si autem aliquis quaerat, quod eorum magis excedebat aliud; ad hoc dicendum est, quod cum peccatum Evae excedat peccatum Adae in conditionibus, quae respiciunt peccatum essentialiter, utpote in maiori improbitate libidinis, in hoc quod et maius et magis ambivit, peccatum Evae magis excessit et gravius fuit, simpliciter loquendo. Et huius signum est, quia magis punita fuit, et si ad infernum descendisset, maiorem poenam habuisset." *Ibid.,* 521b.

(39) *Summa Theol.,* II, q.163, a.4.

accomplishes the downfall of the stronger. The serpent could not subvert Adam; Eve apparently had little difficulty in this regard, thereby proving herself stronger than the Arch-Tempter.

Never will it escape the memory of man what the first Eve was and what she accomplished. To Eve came the Evil One; to Eve he made his addresses; to Eve he suggested fair things, adventurous but sure to repay the adventure; to Eve he opened vistas as yet undreamed in her virgin mind; to Eve he proposed that she and her husband make themselves very like to God, "as Gods, knowing good and evil." And Eve assented; she rebelled against the ordinance of God and won her husband Adam to the same transgression. She was in fact an active agent in his fall; and with him fell the human race. Whereas Eve had been called, and was in God's great plan to be "the Mother of all the living," she now in dreadful phrase became "the Mother of all the dead."

It is a controversial question among theologians whether original sin derives solely from Adam or from both Adam and Eve as its efficient cause; or rather whether there would be an original sin if Eve alone had fallen. Sacred Scripture seems to answer the question in the negative, for whenever it refers to original sin, it refers to it as the "sin of Adam" or the "sin of one man." It is a certain dogma of the Catholic Faith that the human individual known as Adam was the common ancestor of the whole of the present human race; that he alone was qualified to act as its head and representative. The apparent dissentient text: "From the woman came the beginning of sin, and by her we all die" (Ecclus. 25:33), is merely a statement of the historic fact that Eve seduced her husband. As St. Thomas says: "Original sin is contracted not from the mother, but from the father. Accordingly, if Adam had not sinned, even though Eve had, their children would not have contracted original sin; the case would be different if Adam had sinned and Eve had not."[40] It is the common teaching of theologians that original sin consists essentially in the privation of grace, so far as this is voluntary in all men through the will of their progenitor.[41] To Adam God had given original justice and its concomitant preternatural prerogatives not only as a personal privilege but also as a heritage which he was to transmit to all his descendants. When Adam voluntarily renounced original justice, he acted not for himself alone, but as the representative of his race, the moral and juridical head of the whole human family. Consequently original sin is not a personal sin but a sin of nature conditioned upon our relation to Adam who, contrary to the will of God, despoiled

(40) *Summa Theol.*, II, q.81, a.5.

(41) "Quoniam igitur certissimum est, quod a nostra origine multiplicem contrahimus miseriam poenae; certum est, quod omnes nascimur *natura filli irae,* ac per hoc privati rectitudine originalis iustitiae, quam privationem vocamus culpam originalem." *Brevtloquium,* III, 5, t.V, 234b.

human nature of grace and thereby rendered it hostile to its Maker.[42] The sin of Adam, which dealt a mortal blow to his soul and to the souls of all his descendants, also caused the death of his body and the death of all his descendants: "By one man sin came into the world and by sin death, and death passed on to all men" (Rom. 5:12).[43]

Original sin can be transmitted only by the natural mode of sexual generation, that is, by the commingling of male with female, because this is the way in which all children of Adam come into being, hence the frequent occurrence of the phrase *"ex semine Adae"* in the various definitions of the dogma.[44] The parents engender the whole child, not merely its body. This does not imply that they create the spiritual soul; they produce a material substratum which is disposed by the laws of nature to receive a spiritual soul. This soul incurs original sin, not on account of its creation by God, but as a result of its generic relation to Adam. We cannot say that Almighty God is responsible for original sin; He merely creates the soul and refrains from endowing it with sanctifying grace for the reason that it is destined to be the form of a body derived by generation from Adam, who purely and solely is the efficient cause of original sin.[45]

A perusal of the foregoing passages convinces us that the Seraphic Doctor was inclined to be rather severe toward Eve. She was, it is true, the occasion, the instigator of the Fall; but if it was begun by woman, it was consummated by man.[46] The ruin of the human race was encompassed

(42) "Sicut igitur, si Adam stetisset, corpus suum obediens spiritui fuisset, et tale ad posteros transmitteret, et Deus illi animam infunderet, ita quod, unita corpori immortali et sibi obedienti, haberet ordinem iustitiae et immunitatem omnis poenae: sic, ex quo Adam peccavit, et caro facta est rebellis spiritui, oportet, quod talem ad posteros transmittat, et quod Deus animam infundat secundum institutionem primariam; anima vero, cum unitur carni rebelli, incurrit defectum ordinis naturalis iustitiae, quo debebat omnibus inferioribus imperare. Et quia carni unita est, oportet, quod ipsam trahat, vel trahatur ab ipsa; et quia ipsam non potest trahere tanquam rebellem, necesse est, ut ab ipsa trahatur et incurrat *morbum* concupiscentiae." *Ibid.*, III, 6, t.V, 235b.

(43) "Modus autem *traductionis* peccati originalis hic est, quod licet anima non sit ex traduce, originalis tamen culpa ab anima Adae transit ad animas posterorum, mediante carne per concupiscentiam generata, ita quod, sicut ab anima peccante infecta fuit caro Adae et prona effecta ad libidinem, sic per libidinem seminata et secum trahens infectionem vitiosam, inficit et vitiat animam; quae quidem infectio in anima non tantum est *poena,* verum etiam *culpa.* Et sic persona corrumpit naturam, et natura corrupta corrumpit personam, salva in omnibus divina iustitia, cui nullo modo potest imputari infectio animae, licet eam creando infundat et infundendo uniat cum carne infecta." *Ibid.*, 235a.

"Rursus, quia deserens bonum incommutabile propter bonum commutabile efficitur indignus utroque: hinc est, quod ratione carentiae originalis iustitiae perdit anima quietem temporalem in *corpore* et multiplicem *corruptionem et mortem,* et tandem separatur a visione lucis aeternae, amittendo felicitatem gloriae tam in anima quam in corpore." *Ibid.*, III, 5, 234b.

(44) "Ratio autem ad intelligentiam praedictorum haec est: quia, cum primum principium hominem fecerit ad suam imaginem propter sui ipsius expressionem; sic condidit eum ex parte *corporis,* ut omnes homines propagarentur a primo homine tanquam ab uno radicali principio; sic ex parte animae, ut propter expressam similitudinem, tam in essendo et durando quam intelligendo et amando, immedate emanarent omnes spiritus rationales ab ipso Deo tanquam a primo principio et immediato. Et quoniam *spiritus,* tanquam excellentior, magis accedit ad primum principium; sic condidit Deus hominem, ut spiritus corpori praeesset, et corpus econtra, si spiritus non obediret Deo, iusto Dei iudicio *corpus* suum inciperet sibi rebellare; quod et factum est, cum Adam peccavit." *Ibid.*, III, 6, t.V, 235ab.

(45) "Rursus quia *culpa* originalis in animam transfundi non posset, nisi *poena* rebellionis in carne praecederet; et *poena* non esset, nisi culpa praecessisset; nec *culpa* processit a voluntate ordinata, sed inordinata, ac per hoc non a voluntate divina, sed humana: patet ergo, quod originalis peccati transfusio est a *peccato* primi hominis, non a Deo, non a natura condita, sed a vitio perpetrato." *Ibid.*, 235b.

(46) "Ad illud ergo quod primo obiicitur in contrarium, quod ruina fuerit per mulierem; dicendum, quod quamvis in sexu muliebri ruina nostra fuit inchoata, in sexu tamen virili est consummata." *III Sent.*, d.12, a.3, q.1, t.III, 270a.

not by the fall of Eve but by the fall of Adam. Original sin is an inheritance from Adam, not from Eve, from the father, not from the mother. If Eve alone had fallen, we should have had the first sinful woman, but not a race of sinful women.

We have likewise seen that the Seraphic Doctor did not believe that Adam committed the same internal sins of pride and infidelity as his wife, and herein is manifested an indulgence toward Adam, too great an indulgence, it would seem, in the light of his severity toward Eve.

In the evaluation of her mental capacities, we see in St. Bonaventure, and likewise in St. Thomas, a lack of understanding of the special psychology of woman. Following the age-old habit of appraising her by comparison with man as a standard of everything human, they judge her mind from the viewpoint of her aptitude for abstract reasoning without taking into account the natural dispositions of a concrete mentality which makes her the natural educator of her children.

Chapter V

HER PUNISHMENT

As Adam and Eve cowered in their now shameful nakedness, covered with a garment of leaves, God sought them out, pronounced His august condemnation, and singled out the woman for special castigation.

> "To the woman also he said: I will multiply thy sorrows, and thy conceptions: in sorrow shalt thou bring forth children, and thou shalt be under thy husband's power, and he shall have dominion over thee.
>
> "And to Adam he said: Because thou hast hearkened to the voice of thy wife, and hast eaten of the tree, whereof I commanded thee that thou shouldst not eat, cursed is the earth in thy work; with labor and toil shalt thou eat thereof all the days of thy life. Thorns and thistles shall it bring forth to thee; and thou shalt eat the herbs of the earth. In the sweat of thy face shalt thou eat bread until thou return to the earth, out of which thou wast taken: for dust thou art, and into dust thou shalt return. And Adam called the name of his wife Eve, because she was the mother of all the living. And the Lord God made for Adam and his wife, garments of skins, and clothed them.
>
> "And he said: Behold Adam is become as one of us, knowing good and evil; now, therefore, lest perhaps he put forth his hand, and take also of the tree of life, and eat, and live forever. And the Lord God sent him out of the paradise of pleasure, to till the earth from which he was taken. And he cast out Adam; and placed before the paradise of pleasure Cherubims, and a flaming sword, turning every way, to keep the way of the tree of life" (Gen. 3:16-24).

Sacred Scripture tells us that the loss of sanctifying grace entailed the forfeit of the preternatural gifts enjoyed by our first parents in the Garden. After the Fall, concupiscence, until then properly subdued, suddenly became rebellious (Gen. 3:7). To weakness of the will, ignorance, and inclination to evil were added many bodily punishments,—sickness, toil, disease, sorrow and pain. Then came death and dissolution, deprivation of the vision of God and loss of heavenly glory.[1] God accepted the special responsibility of Eve and met it with a special chastisement, over and above the lot of the human race. Before considering the special sentence addressed to her alone, we must remember that Eve, as well as Adam, participates in the general chastisement of the sin, even in that laborious, tiresome toil announced to

(1) "Modus autem, quo genus humanum per originale peccatum *corrumpitur*, hic est. Nam quilibet per concubitum generatus nascitur natura *filius irae*, quia privatus rectitudine originalis iustitiae; propter cuius absentiam incurrimus quantum ad *animam* quadruplicem poenam, scilicet *infirmitatem, ignorantiam, malitiam* et *concupiscentiam;* quae quatuor inflicta sunt propter originale peccatum; quas sane poenas spirituales comitatur in corpore multiplex poenalitas, multiplex defectus, multiplex labor, multiplex morbus et multiplex dolor. Ad has poenas subsequitur poena mortis et incinerationis, poena carentiae visionis Dei, et amissionis gloriae caelestis, . . . " *Breviloquium,* III, 5, t.V, 234ab.

Adam alone.[2] In the sentence imposed is mapped out the lifework of the two sexes. Upon both was laid a burden of labor and of pain—on the man, the earning of his livelihood; on the woman, the bearing of children and the care of the family. Thenceforth sorrow upon sorrow, in what seemed a never-ending flood, fell upon man's life; but how much more upon woman's, for the first seduction had been hers.

For her share in the transgression, Eve, and womankind after her, is sentenced to a life of sorrow and travail: "I will multiply thy sorrows, and thy conceptions, and thou shalt be under thy husband's power, and he shall have dominion over thee."[3] The multiplying of her conceptions was appointed as a punishment to woman, not on account of the begetting of children, which would have been the natural manner of procreation even in the state of innocence, but on account of the numerous sufferings to which woman is subject in carrying her offspring after conception, in the pains of parturition, in the labor involved in the nurturing of the tender years of her children, and in the sorrows which she experiences through them.[4]

As regards family life, the woman was punished by being subjected to her husband's authority, as conveyed in the words: "Thou shalt be under thy husband's power." Hitherto there had been no idea of servile subordination. Adam was titular lord of creation, the physical and juridical head of the human race and of the family which is its absolute unit. Woman was the mother of all living, the creator of the family and its queen. Here marriage was a perfect partnership of dignity and equality—the husband exercising ultimate theoretical supremacy; the woman, practical executive supremacy; both working together in perfect harmony, each depending on the other as complementary parts of one social organism. But now, because woman had exercised her influence on the man for evil, she would henceforth be "under his power."[5] Doubtless this does not imply that woman's essential condition of equality was altered, but the sentence expresses what, in the nature of things, was bound to follow in a world dominated by sin and its consequences. The natural dependence and subjection of the weaker party was destined inevitably to become something little short of slavery.

---

(2) "Post autem divino iudicio *vir* incurrit poenam *laboris* et angustiae, poenam *famis* et indigentiae, poenam mortis et resolutionis in cinerem; sicut dicit Scriptura: *Maledicta terra in opera tuo* etc." *Ibid.*, III, 4, t.V, 233b.

(3) "*Mulieri* autem *duplicata* est poena, quia inflicta est ei poenalitas multiplicium *aerumnarum* in conceptu, poena *dolorum* in partu, poena quoque *subiectionis* ad virum in convictu; ac per hoc, secundum quod apparet, satis graviter punitum fuit illud peccatum, scilicet ligni vetiti esus, licet fuerit faciliter perpetratum." *Ibid.*

(4) "Magis autem bonum prolis per *matris* nomen datur intelligi, quia mulier propter procreationem liberorum facta est; unde facta est in adiutorium viri; et quia in procreatione prolis magis incumbit sibi labor." *IV Sent.*, d.17, a.1, q.2, t.IV, 678a.

"Quarto, matrimonium dicitur *matris munium,* id est matris officium, pro eo quod prolis enutritio et acquisitio maxime spectat ad mulierem in concipiendo, in portando, in pariendo, in nutriendo, in compatiendo." *Ibid.*, 678b.

(5) "Ad illud ergo quod obiicitur, quare non permittitur mulieri, (ut repudiaret virum) dicendum, quod tempore Legis non iudicibantur ad paria vir cum muliere, tum ratione conditionis, quia vir est principium mulieris, tum ratione *praevaricationis,* quia mulier est initium peccati; ideo dictum est ei Genesis tertio: *Sub viri potestate eris.*" *IV Sent.*, d.33, a.3, q.2, concl., t.IV, 760b.

As we look back over the interval of several thousands of years since God Himself, the Author of human society, established it upon the perfect law of marriage, we are not surprised that the state of woman called down the pity of the Most High. An awful degradation had fallen on the women of pagan nations and even among the chosen people of God, woman was held in low esteem. Even as far back as the Antediluvian period, polygamy was rife and where such custom prevails, we find woman downcast and downtrodden. During the Patriarchal Age, wife-capture was foremost among the contributing influences which lowered the status of woman and finally accomplished the degradation of her sex. Women were the spoils of war. The mother of Sisara, looking through the lattice, wondered: "Why is his chariot so long in coming back? Why are the feet of his horses so slow? One that was wiser than the rest of his wives returned this answer to her mother-in-law: Perhaps he is now dividing the spoils and the fairest of the women is chosen out for him" (Judges 5:28-30).

Sacred Scripture is silent regarding the vicissitudes that befell the Israelites during the four centuries that elapsed between the time of Malachi, the last prophet of the Old Testament, and the dawn of the Christian era. Profane history, however, tells us that they were subject in turn to Persian, Greek, Egyptian, Syrian, Maccabean, and Roman rule, and we know that the seventy years of captivity in Babylon and subsequent intercourse with heathen nations did not fail to leave its imprint on the laws and customs of the Israelites.

Retrogression goes hand in hand with false religions. Lacking the power to raise man out of the mire, sooner or later the gratification of lust with the resulting debasement of woman becomes the central feature of their pagan worship. In Babylon every member of the sex was required to enter the Temple and prostitute herself in the presence of its idol; parents deemed it an honor to devote their daughter to a life of sexual commerce for the enlargement of the sacerdotal coffers; and every year the great slave markets of Babylon opened for the sale of women.

Throughout all heathendom, religion and law worked together for the degradation of the sex. In Persia, even at her best, woman was but "the maid of man." And when Athens won the hegemony of Greece in 476 B.C., women, under the wise rule of Solon, were separated into five classes "for the convenience of all conditions of men." Wives, who constituted the first class and who existed for the sole purpose of propagating Greek citizens, were kept under strictest surveillance. Practically prisoners in their own homes, they possessed no rights or privileges beyond the will of their lords. Regarded as inferior beings neglected in heart and intellect, they were barred from all education and intellectual pleasures. The second class, the heterae, were the only free women in Athens. They were the intellectuals, accomplished women who delivered public addresses, taught rhetoric and elocution and founded schools of philosophy. They associated freely with men of their own rank and station—philosophers, statesmen and poets. They wielded wide influence in affairs of state, but disdained the marriage relation on account of its enforced ignorance, seclusion, and subjection. Then, there were the auletrides or flute-players, fashionable imported slaves, who were auctioned off to the highest bidder; the concubines, likewise purchased slaves, who with full knowledge of the lawful wife became members of their master's household; and the dicteriades, slaves of ill-repute procured at the expense of the state and the revenue from whose services was used to enrich the general treasury.

Greek literature abounds in mockery of woman. We have seen how even the great Aristotle rates her as man's inferior, not exactly as a slave or a child, but incapable of courage and justice. Legally, she was a minor. Not only could she not transact any business on her own account, but even the transactions of her husband, if undertaken by her counsel and at her request, were rendered null and void. Pericles, one of the lights of classic antiquity, thought that women should be in utter self-effacement, unworthy of mention whatsoever, good or bad. Demosthenes, the world's greatest orator, said: "We have *heterae* for our pleasure, wives to bear us children and to care for the household." Even the divine Plato, the most naturally Christian of the pagan philosophers, advocated a community of wives on the ground that the children would then be the property of the State. And granted that Xantippe may not have been the most amiable of creatures, Socrates the Wise made a rather broad statement when he said that the society of a wife is the last thing in the world to be sought after by a husband.

In Rome at this period, every right of woman was invaded. In the time of Augustus, the very mention of the ancient Roman virtues would seem a bitter satire upon the actual corruption. Conquest had inundated Rome with slaves, and the license engendered by slavery infected every relation of the family. There was no pure and noble religious belief to preserve the weaker sex from this contagion and all the evils which were debasing Grecian life were in full force here. Hymen, the god of marriage, was represented in Roman mythology as the son of Venus, the goddess of impurity, by Bacchus, the god of drunkenness.

Roman law prescribed the perpetual tutelage of woman. A female, though released from her father's authority by his decease, continued subject through life to her nearest male relative, or to her father's nominee as her guardian. The right of manus, which carried with it the privilege of wife-lending, was acquired by the husband with every form of marriage. And according to the

Roman law, the wife was included in the "patria potestas" of her husband, who had absolute control over her person and property. Rome and Grece talked much about their respect for good women, but they saw to it that the life of a good woman was almost that of a slave.

Thus, instead of the dignity, indissolubility, and unity which characterized the first relationship between man and woman, we find man heaping every kind of degradation upon his hapless mate, continually forcing upon her the sense of her own weakness and incapacity. Carrying mistrust to the utmost point of barbarity, different heathen legislations actually obliged her in the full bloom of her youth and beauty to follow the corpse of her husband and to immolate herself on his funeral pile.

A passing glance at the actual position of woman during the last years of Augustus will convince us of the truth of this statement. Already dishonored by so many outrages offered to her weakness, she was liable to repudiation by her husband. Among the most civilized nations,—the Greeks, the Romans and the Jews—the sanctity of marriage was entirely disregarded on the part of man who exercised with the greatest abuse the right of absolute divorce. Over a large portion of the world where polygamy had destroyed the unity of marriage, there was an open proclamation that woman was not the partner of man's life, but the instrument of his selfish pleasure; that if made from him at all, she was made not from the region of his heart, but from his feet. But when we consider woman in marriage, we consider her in her highest position. Tarnished as was her honor as wife and mother, all her honor lay in these two characters. Outside of them, that is as a human being, she had none.

The condition of woman over the earth, taken under its fairest aspect, might indeed be expressed with the utmost severity of philosophic truth in those prophetic words: "I will multiply thy sorrows and thy conceptions; in sorrow shalt thou bring forth children; and thou shalt be under thy husband's power, and he shall have dominion over thee." As Chaucer says:

> "Women are born to thralldom and to penance,
> And to be under man's goverance."

And Dryden:

> "He shall rule, and she in thralldom live."

So far, the gentle subordination under a lawful headship had as a penalty been altered to a severe rule. Human sin had converted it into a servile subjection, a pitiless tyranny. Not only did the shadow of Eve rest on all her daughters since the fatal day of the first deceit, but to the divine sentence the hand of man had added such severity of degradation that the penance seemed turned into a curse. Such was the world when in the stable of Bethlehem, the birthplace of civilization, took place the most momentous event in all history.

Chapter VI

ST. BONAVENTURE'S ATTITUDE

THE SEARCH FOR THE PRINCIPLE OF EVIL is one of the eternal problems of philosophy. Matter, as opposed to spirit, has often been alleged to be that principle. Hesiod, the peasant poet of Greece, who lived about the eighth century B.C., found it in the person of Pandora, the beautiful woman whose feminine curiosity made her open the box given to her by the gods, whence escaped all human ills, all woe, all evil. Hesiod's ingenious explanation, though no longer in vogue, seems strangely reminiscent of theories advanced by some philosophers of the Middle Ages who attribute every evil to Eve, a woman surprisingly fair in body, fairer yet in mind, to whom it was given to bear in her single hands the destiny of man. Since the day that Eve plucked the forbidden fruit, woman has been regarded as the source of all evil in the world. Not only her own sins, but the sins of the race are charged against her. She is the temptress, and guileless man her hapless victim.

We must admit that in the writings of the Fathers and Doctors of the Church in general are found many passages most uncomplimentary to woman, and the Seraphic Doctor is no exception. "The Second Philosopher has spoken truly," he says. "Woman is an embarrassment to man, a beast in his quarters, a continual worry, a never-ending trouble, a daily annoyance, the destruction of the household, a hindrance to solitude, the undoing of a virtuous man, an oppressive burden, an insatiable bee, man's property and possession."[1] And St. Chrysostom, commenting on St. Matthew, says: "What is woman except an enemy of friendship, an inescapable punishment, a necessary evil, a natural temptation, an attractive affliction, a domestic danger, a tool of Satan, an ill-smelling rose, a sweet poison, a continual contradiction to herself?" In the words of Adam, Sacred Scripture says: *She gave me of the tree and I did eat*. That was the tree of the knowledge of good and evil.[2]

The Seraphic Doctor entertained great mistrust of worldly, beautiful women and issued many precepts in the practical order against "the first

(1) "Verum dixit Secundus Philosophus: 'Mulier est hominis confusio, contubernalis bestia, continua sollicitudo, indesinens pugna, quotidianum damnum, domus tempestas, solitudinis impedimentum, viri continentis naufragium, pondus gravissimum, apis insatiabilis, humanum mancipium'." *Sermones de Tempore, Dominica XXIV. Post Pentecosten. Sermo VI*, t.IX, 459a.

(2) "Unde Chrysostomus super Matthaeum: 'Quid est mulier nisi amicitiae inimica, ineffugabilis poena, necessarium malum, naturalis tentatio, desiderabilis calamitas, domesticum periculum, falx satanae, rosa foetens, dulce venenum, semper prompta in sibi contrarium?' Sequitur: *dedit mihi de ligno, et comedi*. Illud erat lignum scientiae boni et mali." *Ibid*. Cf. St. Chrysostom, *In Matthaeum. Homil. 2*, xxxii. MPG 56.805.

cause of evil on earth," advocating the strategy found most effective in modern warfare—successful retreat. Here is a domain where he who hesitates is lost. Most carefully avoid the intimacies, the conversations, and the glances of women, who have been an occasion of ruin for many. *Turn away thy eyes that they may not behold vanity* (Ps. 118:37), he counsels. Otherwise the imagination will quickly enkindle a conflagration; there will be a soiling of the mind, a searing of the conscience.[3] As Jeremiah the prophet says: "Death is come up through our windows; it is entered into our houses, to destroy the children from without, the young men from the streets" (Jer. 9:21). "Can a man hide fire in his bosom, and his garments not burn? Or can he walk upon hot coals, and his feet not be burnt?" (Prov. 6:27,28). Flee the occasions of sin, as did Blessed Nicolas, who fled from women as from a plague. Would that young men of our day, continues the Saint, would do the same, not frequenting public games nor walking through the village streets to gaze upon beautiful but designing women. What folly to walk along a crowded highway carrying a precious ointment in a fragile vessel which could easily be broken in the jostling crowd! What folly for a young man to court danger by exposing himself to the gaze of beautiful women who may rudely shake or even shatter the vessel of his heart, allowing the precious ointment of grace to be lost! You have heard it said to them of old: "Whosoever shall look upon a woman to lust after her, hath already committed adultery with her in his heart."[4]

To resist the luring seductive pleasures of the flesh demands backbone and courage. It is the path of valor and heroism. "For thou hast done manfully," says Holy Writ, "and thy heart has been strengthened because thou hast loved chastity." Though the difficulty of the temptation increases one's merit when virtue finally emerges untarnished from the struggle, still the danger is great and therefore to be avoided.[5] To flee the seductive foe is a

---

(3) "Mulierum familiaritates, colloquia et aspectus, quae multis occasio sunt ruinae, sollicitius evitari iubebat, asserens, per huiusmodi debilem frangi et fortem saepe spiritum infirmari. Harum contagionem evadere conversantem cum eis, nisi probatissimum virum, tam facile dixit, quam iuxta Scripturam, *in igne ambulare et non comburere plantas*. Siquidem ipse adeo averterat oculos suos, ne huiusmodi vanitatem viderent, quod sicut aliquando socio dixit, quasi nullam recognoscebat in facie. Non enim securum esse putabat earum formarum introrsus haurire imagines, quae possunt aut edomitae carnis resuscitare igniculum, aut pudicae mentis maculare nitorem." *Legenda Sancti Francisci.* Cap.V, t.VIII, 517b.

(4) "Item, *exterius* occasionem peccati fugiendo, sicut fecit beatus Nicolaus, qui mulieres quasi pestem fugiebat. Utinam sic facerent iuvenes nostri moderni, non ita frequentarent spectacula nec per villam ambularent, ut viderent mulieres pulcras et paratas! Quantae insaniae esset vas balsamo puro plenum portare in platea et exponere illud, ut quilibet posset percutere illud cum lapide et frangere! Qui sic faceret insanus iudicaretur. Ita insanus debet iudicari qui corpus et sensus suos exponit ad videndum mulieres et spectacula, ut a qualibet pulcra muliere cor suum percutiatur, et si videat illam ad concupiscendum, frangatur, et balsamum gratiae, quod intus erat, effundatur. Semper, quoties vidisti mulierem aut mulieres ad concupiscendum eas, toties letale vulnus in corde tuo habuisti, et vide, si securum est ire ad spectacula et ibi mulieres respicere." *Sermones de Sanctis: De Sancto Nicalao,* t.IX, 476a.

(5) Est et tertia difficultas ex *circumstantiis extrinsecus annexis* trahens originem, sicut difficilius est abstinere, cum apponuntur delicata cibaria, difficilius temporalia bona contemnere, quando offeruntur magna et pulcra, difficilius continere in consortio feminarum. Et haec difficultas per accidens et indirecte auget aliquando meritum, cum virtus inter haec illaesa triumphat; sed directe et quantum est de se, magis est via ad ruinam et ideo fugienda." *Apologia Pauperum,* c.3, t.VIII, 249a.

manifestation of valor and intelligence, for her wiles are many,—wanton glances, plaited hair, delightful kisses, and sweet perfumes.[6]

Once held fast by the slippery chain of bodily lust, men can no longer order and regulate their lives aright. Well does Sacred Scripture say: "I have found woman more bitter than death, who is the hunter's snare, and her heart is a net, and her hands are bands" (Eccles. 5:27). "I have found woman more bitter than death," for death kills the body for a time, but a wicked woman destroys body and soul for all eternity. "She is the hunter's snare," that is, the snare of the devil, for it was by the snare of a woman that the demon got possession of the human race in the person of our first parent. "From the woman came the beginning of sin, and by her we all die" (Ecclus. 25:33). Her inconstant heart is an infernal net to catch inconstant man in the waters of sensuality, and her hands, that is her works, are bands to draw him to the lewdness of sin. Wherefore he who does not wish to be ensnared by the devil through the allurement of the seductive pleasures of the flesh but who wishes to keep his heart pure ought to turn his eyes from the vanity of public shows and avoid the society of women, for as the rose or the lily begins to fade with frequent handling and loses its beauty and fragrance, so is the heart of the chaste man who exposes himself to vain amusements frequented by women sometimes so touched and even bruised that it immediately begins to languish with impure thoughts and to lose the beauty and fragrance of its inner purity through consent to the thought.[7]

Again and again the Seraphic Doctor counsels the avoidance of women.[8] Shun the society of women, he says, as you would a serpent and never speak with one except in case of urgent necessity. Never look a woman in the face and, if she should address you, put an end to the conversation as soon as possible, for David the prophet says: "Her words are smoother than oil, and the same are darts" (Ps. 54:22). And St. Augustine counsels: "Harsh

(6) "Solent enim peccatrices mulieres in his quatuor maxime delinquere, scilicet in *nutibus oculorum;* Isaiae tertio: 'Nutibus oculorum ibant'; *superfluitatibus capillorum;* primae Petri tertio: 'Non sit exterius capillatura'; in *voluptatibus osculorum;* Proverbiorum septimo: 'Apprehensumque deosculatur iuvenem'; *suavitatibus unguentorum,* sicut dicitur Esther secundo, quod puellae regis 'ungebantur oleo myrrhino' etc." *Comment. in Evangelium Lucae* C.VII, t.VII, 183.

(7) "Tertio ligantur *lubrici vinculo corporalis lasciviae,* ne possint moveri ad ordinandum et dirigendum se ipsos; unde Ecclesiastae septimo: *Inveni amariorem mulierem, quae laqueus venatorum est, et sagena cor eius, vincula sunt manus illius.* Bene dicit: *Inveni amariorem morte mulierem,* nam mors temporaliter occidit corpus, sed nequam mulier corpus et animam aeternaliter, *quae laqueus est venatorum,* id est daemonum. Isto enim muliebri laqueo daemones venati sunt genus humanum in primo parente; nam *a muliere initium factum est peccati. Sagena* infernalis est lubricum *cor eius* ad capiendum lubricos in aquis carnalitatis; et *manus illius,* id est opera, *vincula sunt,* ad trahendum ad lubricitatem peccati. Unde qui non vult illaqueari a daemonibus laqueo carnalis lasciviae, sed vult se ipsum mundum conservare per puritatem pudicitiae, debet, quantum potest, declinare spectacula vanitatum, fugere consortia mulierum, quia, sicut rosa vel lilium, cum frequenter tangitur, incipit marcescere et amittere colorem et odorem; sic castus homo, quando se exponit huiusmodi spectaculis vanitatum et mulierum, ita aliquando tangitur et percutitur cor eius, ut statim incipiat marcescere per immundam cogitationem et amittere colorem et odorem interioris munditiae per consensum ad illam cogitationem." *Sermones de Tempore: Dominica XI. Post Pentecosten. Sermo II,* t.IX, 396a.

(8) "Quartum-decimum, ut ubique mulieres omnes iuvenesque imberbes praeter necessitatis vel manifestae utilitatis causam devites." *Epistola de XXV Memorialibus,* t.VIII, 494b.

"Dicit ergo pro primo: *Praecipio firmiter Fratribus universis, ne habeant suspecta consortia vel consilia mulierum. Suspectum consortium* est non solum mulieris *suspectae,* immo cum *omni* muliere, ubi locus et tempus, gestus et aspectus et alia laudabilia iudicia suspicionem probabiliter non excludunt." *Expositio super Regulam Fratrum Minorum,* c.XI, t.VIII, 435a.

conversation, brief and severe in tone must be held with women. Even though they be holy, avoid them none the less, for the holier they are, the more they attract, and ofttimes the poison of unholy desires is injected under the covering of soft-spoken and flattering words. Believe me, he says; I am a bishop, and I speak the truth in Christ. I do not deceive you. I have seen the cedars of Lebanus and the rams of the flock fall beneath the spell of their beauty—men whose ruin I did not anticipate more than I would that of a Jerome or an Ambrose." Flee, then, the wiles of women, "for you are not holier than David, stronger than Samson nor wiser than Solomon."[9]

By concupiscence, which has its source in woman and in her finds its gratification, man is drawn on by the appearance of sweetness to untold bitterness. That is why Solomon in remorse says: "I have found a woman more bitter than death" (Eccles. 7:27). "The lips of a harlot are like a honeycomb dropping and her throat is smoother than oil" (Prov. 5:3). By her beauty she ensnares those who fall in love with her. Wherefore the wise King says: *She is the hunter's snare,* that is, the snare of the demons who go about craftily seeking the souls of men destined from all eternity to feast their eyes on the Beauty "ever ancient, ever new." By her *words* and *glances* she ensnares man, as the Proverb says. "She entangled him with many words and drew him away with the flattery of her lips" (Prov. 7:21). She ensnares him by the *beauty* of her face, "for many have perished by the beauty of a woman" (Ecclus. 9:9). Her *speech,* too, is a snare, "for her conversation burneth as fire" (Ecclus. 9:11). She draws man not only into love but also into the paths of wickedness when he fulfills his promise to sin. "Her heart is a net" (Eccles. 7:27); she is the net of the devil, closely resembling the evil one of whom Habacuc says: "He lifted up all them with his hook, he drew them in his drag and gathered them into his net" (1:15). And afterwards she *holds them fast* by her love, for which reason Solomon says: "Her hands are bands," (Eccles. 7:27), and in the Book of Proverbs he continues in the same strain: "Immediately he followeth her as an ox led to be a victim, and as a lamb playing the wanton, and not knowing that he is drawn like a fool to bonds" (7:22). Only by the grace of God can man resist her. "He that pleaseth God shall escape from her" (Eccles. 7:27). In his First Epistle to the Corinthians, St. Paul says: "Fly fornication" (6:18), and Solomon in the Book of Wisdom: "And I knew I could not otherwise be continent, except God gave it" (8:21). "But he that is a sinner shall be

(9) "Mulieres vero fugias, quantum potes, et nunquam loquaris cum aliqua, nisi urgens necessitas te compellat, nec unquam respicias in faciem alicuius mulieris, et si mulier tecum loquatur, verba sua citissime circumcide, nam, teste Propheta, *molliti sunt sermones eius super oleum, et ipsi sunt iacula.* Ideo dicit Augustinus: 'Asper sermo, brevis et rigidus cum mulieribus habendus est. Nec tamen quia sanctae sunt, ideo minus cavendae; quo enim sanctiores fuerint, eo magis alliciunt, et sub praetextu blandi sermonis immiscet se viscus impiissimae libidinis. Crede, inquit, mihi; episcopus sum, veritatem loquor in Christo, non mentior. Cedros Libani et gregum arietes sub hac specie corruisse reperi, de quorum casu non magis praesumebam quam Hieronymi et Ambrosii.' Fuge ergo laqueos mulierum 'quia non es David sanctior nec Samsone fortior nec sapientior Salomone'." *Regula Novitiorum,* c.12, t.VIII, 487.

caught by her" (Eccles. 7:27), continues the Wise King. "His own iniquities catch the wicked, and he is fast bound with the ropes of his own sins" (Prov. 5:22).[10]

"Lo, this have I found, said Ecclesiastes, weighing one thing after another that I might find out the account, which yet my soul seeketh and I have not found it. One man among a thousand I have found; a woman among them all I have not found" (Eccles. 7:28,29). Commenting on the foregoing passage, St. Bonaventure says that Solomon is speaking hyperbolically and is simply remarking that he himself has found very few men and not one woman in whom concupiscence does not reign,—a fact which doesn't surprise the Seraphic Doctor at all, as he says, for in the Book of Ecclesiasticus we read: "All malice is short to the malice of a woman" (25:26). Church writers especially seem convinced of the truth of the old maxim, "corruptio optimi pessima," "the worst corruption is that of the best." St. Gregory Nazianzen tells us, "There is nothing better than a good woman, nothing worse than a bad one" and Sacred Scripture says: "A man will choose any wickedness, but the wickedness of a woman" (Ecclus. 25:18, 19).[11]

We might wonder at St. Bonavenure's attitude toward women were it not for the fact that for the most part he is speaking of sinful women, as is evident from the passages quoted. Moreover, the words of the Seraphic Doctor must be modified to suit his purpose, which was the instruction of the Novices of his Order. Prudence in dealing with the opposite sex is of necessity for all religious, since they carry about with them the tinder of fallen nature. Surely St. Bonaventure, who lived in the midst of a busy world, would have been the last person to express a false conception regarding the relations between the two sexes. When he told his Novices that they should everywhere and

(10) "Primo igitur tangitur ipsius concupiscentiae vehemens *pronitas,* quia perducit ad maximam amaritudinem sub specie dulcedinis. Ideo dicit: *Inveni amariorem morte mulierem,* et hoc post nefarii operis perpetrationem, ad quod concupiscentia pertrahit; unde Proverbiorum quinto: 'Favus distillans labia meretricis, et nitidius oleo gutter eius'. Ad hoc pertrahit concupiscentia illa, quae a muliere habuit ortum et in muliere habet fomentum, quae sua pulcritudine *illaqueat* per dilectionem; ideo dicit: *Laqueus est venatorum,* id est daemonum, qui venantur animas hominum. Illaqueat *verbis* et *aspectibus:* Proverbiorum septimo: 'Irretivit eum multis sermonibus et blanditiis labiorum protraxit illum'. Illaqueat *pulcritudine* faciei; Ecclesiastici nono: 'Propter speciem mulieris multi pereunt'. Illaqueat etiam *verbis* unde ibidem: 'Colloquium illius quasi ignis exardescit'. Non solum *illaqueat* in dilectione, sed etiam deglutit in nefario operi. Haec est sagena diaboli; Habacuc primo: 'Totum in hamo sublevavit: traxit illud in sagena sua'. Sed postmodum *ligat* per affectionem; et ideo dicit: *Et vincula manus illius;* Proverbiorum septimo: 'Sequitur et ignorat, quod ad vincula stultus trahatur'. Ab hac pronitate nullus eripitur, nisi qui a Domino iuvatur, tanta est; ideo dicit: *Qui placet Deo effugiet illam,* secundum illud primae ad Corinthios sexto: 'Fugite fornicationem', Sapientiae octavo: 'Scivi, quoniam aliter non possem esse continens, nisi Deus det'; 'Qui autem peccator est capietur ab illa'; Proverbiorum quinto: 'Iniquitates suae capiunt impium, et funibus peccatorum suorum constringitur'." *Comment. in Ecclesiasten.* C.VII, t.VI, 62b, 63a.

(11) "Hic notatur secundum, scilicet concupiscentiae generalitas, cuius rationem videre fuit difficultas; ideo dicit: *Ecce, hoc inveni, dixit Ecclesiastes, unum,* scilicet ipsius concupiscentiae *pronitatem,* et *alterum,* scilicet ipsius *generalitatem. Et laboravi, supple, ut invenirem rationem, quam adhuc quaerit anima mea;* haec est *ratio* generalitatis concupiscentiae, quare in omnibus est. *Et non inveni,* scilicet proprio ingenio, quia hoc philosophi scire non noverunt; sed tamen *fide* cognovit *rationem* et *experientia* cognovit *effectum,* scilicet generalitatem. Ideo dicit: *Virum unum de mille reperi, et mulierem ex omnibus non inveni;* hyperbole est, et vult dicere, quod paucissimos invenit viros, in quibus concupiscentia non regnaret; sed ipse nullas invenit mulieres; nec mirum, quia Ecclesiastici vigesimo quinto: 'Brevis omnis malitia super malitiam mulieris'." *Comment. in Ecclesiasten.* C.VII, t.VI, 63a.

without exception avoid women, he had in mind only that kind of communication which might lead to sin. The severity in the Seraphic Doctor, strangely out of place though it may seem, is excusable too, perhaps, on the ground that, like most theologians of his time, he was a religious and may have considered it a safeguard to virtue to have a low opinion of woman.

Chapter VII

THE ATTITUDE OF CHRIST

WE HAVE OFTEN HEARD it said that women had little place in the life of Our Divine Lord,—an unintelligible statement utterly without foundation. Women without number walk the pages of Christ's life, not infrequently playing dramatic roles therein. They are His loyal followers, His devoted friends, the constant recipients of His kindness and gracious favors. Not only did women "sit at Our Lord's feet and hear His words" (Luke 10:39), but they, as well as the Twelve, accompanied Christ on His preaching tours through Palestine. Back of the Apostles who naturally enough, as Christ's helpers and partners in His Father's business, occupy the foreground in the Gospel stories, we now and then catch a glimpse of the little band of faithful women, who patiently, almost thanklessly, followed in their footsteps, of their own substance ministering to the wants of Christ and His apostolic band. It is from His dealings with these women and others that He met along the way, from the infinite tenderness and the immeasurable pity which He manifested at all times toward "the weaker vessels of humanity," that we glean the beauty and tenderness of the character of Christ, the Ideal Man,—strong but kind; heroic but gentle; sinless yet infinitely forgiving.

In the eighth chapter of St. Luke's Gospel, we read: "And it came to pass afterwards, that He was traveling through the cities and towns, preaching and evangelizing the Kingdom of God; and the twelve with Him. And certain women who had been healed of evil spirits and infirmities" (8:1, 2) accompanied Him, their physician and their saviour, thus fulfilling the admonition of the Wise Man: "Honor the physician" (Ecclus. 38:1) "and let him not depart from thee, for his works are necessary"(*ibid.,* 38:12). "And they that were troubled with unclean spirits were cured" (Luke 6:18). "And all the multitude sought to touch him, for virtue went out of him, and healed all"(*ibid.,* 6:19).[1] Though Our Lord "healed all," men and women alike, special mention, says St. Bonaventure, is made of the miracles performed in favor of the female sex. Wherever women were in need, Christ

(1) "Secundo, quantum ad *curatos* comitantes ratione *accepti beneficii* subditur: *Et mulieres aliquae,* supple: cum eo iter faciebant, et hoc ratione accepti beneficii; unde adiungit: *Quae erant curatae a spiritibus malignis et infirmitatibus.* Ideo comitabantur eum tanquam suum salvatorem et medicum, secundum consilium Sapientis, Ecclesiastici trigesimo octavo: 'Da locum medico, et non discedat a te, quia opera eius sunt necessaria'; unde supra sexto: 'Et qui vexabantur a spiritibus immundis curabantur. Et omnis turba quaerebat eum tangere, quia virtus de illo exibat et sanabat omnes'." *Comment. in Evangelium Lucae* C.VIII, t.VII, 189a.

wrought His miracles freely, either because He wished to "give honor to the female as to the weaker vessel" (I Peter 3:7), or because woman is more compassionate than man in pitying and alleviating the sufferings of others, as it is written of the good woman in the Book of Proverbs: "She hath opened her hand to the needy, and stretched out her hands to the poor" (31:20). Or it may be, continues the Saint, that the women who were healed were persons of note and distinction and for that reason received special mention in the Gospel stories.[2]

Of the well-known women who had been cured by Christ and who out of gratitude accompanied Him in His travels, St. Luke makes special mention of three. There was "Mary who is called Magdalen," a woman of wealth according to tradition, and notorious for the *enormity of her sin,* "out of whom seven devils were gone forth" (8:2) when Christ absolved her of her sins at the house of the Pharisee. There was "Joanna, the wife of Chusa, Herod's steward" (8:3), a woman of some renown on account of the *high position of her husband* in the royal household. "And Susanna," whose surname is not given, a woman of *some rank and title in her own right.* Doubtless there were other women of means "among the many others who ministered unto Him of their substance" *(ibid.),* but St. Luke makes special mention of these three, says the Seraphic Doctor, according to the three paths along which they accompanied Christ, namely, as a *widow,* as a *wife,* and as a *virgin.* Mary Magdalen, formerly a sinner, was according to St. Jerome, a widow; Joanna, a married woman; and of Susanna, no mention is made of either state. Or it may be, continues the Saint, that the Evangelist makes special mention of Mary Magdalen, of Joanna, and of Susanna to show the nature of the disease of which they were cured, namely, disease of soul, disease of body, and disease of both body and soul.[3]

Woman's mission and object is to know Truth, not so much in order to teach it, as to recognize it, to feel it, and to make it attractive to others. To proclaim the truth in the midst of an unbelieving people requires courage, the courage of "the woman from the crowd" who, in the midst of blasphemers who deride Christ, uplifts her voice in His praise. "And it came to pass, as

(2) "Et nota, quod licet curaverit utrumque sexum, magis tamen specificat de muliebri, sive quia sexus infirmior, secundum illud primae Petri tertio: 'Infirmiori vasculo muliebri impartientes honorem'; sive quia clementior quam vir respectu infirmitatis alienae, secundum illud, Proverbiorum ultimo, de bona muliere: 'Manum suam aperuit inopi et palmas suas extendit ad pauperes'; sive quia inter personas curatas erant nobiliores." *Ibid.*, 189b.

(3) "Et ideo exprimit aliquas nominaliter, cum addit: *Maria, quae vocatur Magdalena,* a Magdalo oppido secundo milliario a Tiberiade; et haec erat notabilis ratione *enormitatis peccati;* unde et addit: De qua septem daemonia eiecerat, id est universa vitia; Gregorius: 'Septem daemonia Maria habuit, quae universis vitiis plena fuit'. Haec daemonia exierunt, quando peccata dismissa fuerunt . . . Erat etiam aliqua nobilis ratione *nobilitatis viri;* Unde addit: *Et Ioannam uxor Chusae, procuratoris Herodis,* qui erat persona nobilis. Erat etiam aliqua nobilis ex *se ipsa,* de qua sine cognomine adiungitur: *Et Susanna.* Has autem tres nominat, ut *commendet castitatem* secundum triplicem differentiam in comitatu Christi, scilicet *vidualem, coniugalem* et *virginalem.* Unde prima dicitur prius fuisse peccatrix, secunda coniugata, de tertia tacetur utrumque. Vel, ut in hoc *ostendatur curatio* a *triplici aegritudine,* scilicet animae et carnis et utriusque; ideo tres personas curatas exprimit, scilicet Mariam, Ioannam et Susannam." *Ibid.*

He spoke these things," says St. Luke, "a certain woman from the crowd lifting her voice said to Him: Blessed is the womb that bore thee, and the paps that gave thee suck. But He said: Yea rather blessed are they who hear the word of God and keep it" (11:27, 28). How fitting it was, says the Seraphic Doctor, that having revealed the truth, Divine Truth Himself appearing in their midst should be praised openly in the presence of the whole multitude! The woman was not cowardly or afraid but courageous; she lifted up her voice, as Isaias admonishes: "Lift up thy voice with strength. Lift it up; fear not" (40:9). She was not of noble rank but of humble origin,—a woman "from the crowd," as the Gospel says, unnamed, unrenowned, that the words of the Psalm might be fulfilled: "The poor and needy shall praise thy name" (Ps. 73:21). This woman was not silent with those of the crowd who were afraid to speak nor did she blaspheme Christ with the proud Pharisees, but, courageous and humble, she lifted up her voice in praise of Truth. As the Gloss says: "Great faith confesses the Son of God in the midst of blasphemers." To her may be addressed the words of St. Matthew: "O woman, great is thy faith" (15:28) which has so strengthened thee, and the words of Solomon in the Book of Proverbs: "Who shall find a valiant woman?" (31:10). In the woman "from the crowd" have been verified the words: "As everlasting foundations upon a solid rock, so the commandments of God in the heart of a holy woman" (Ecclus. 26:24).[4]

Faith and the rewards of faith run all through the Gospels but it was the faith of the women whom He met that especially moved the heart of Christ. On one occasion in the midst of the dense crowd, all striving to be near the Master, there was a poor suffering woman, probably a Gentile, who "having an issue of blood twelve years, had bestowed all her substance on physicians and could not be healed by any" (cf. Luke 8:43-48). "She came behind Him and touched the hem of His garment." *She came near* to Jesus because she believed, for, as St. Paul says: "He that cometh to God must believe" (Hebr. 11:6). She came *behind Him* because *she was afraid,* as was Mary Magdalen, who stood behind at the Lord's feet (Luke 7:38). She *touched* Our Lord, because she *hoped* to be cured, as St. Matthew relates: "For she said within herself: If I shall touch only his garment, I shall be healed"

(4) "Et hoc quidem conveniens erat, ut, manifestata veritate, Veritas ipsa se ipsam manifestans laudaretur manifeste coram tota multitudine. . . . Primo igitur quantum ad *conditionem laudantis personae* dicit: *Factum est autem, dum haec diceret,* scilicet ad confutationem falsitatis; *extollens vocem quaedam mulier de turba dixit illi,* ad veritatis commendationem et Pharisaeorum confutationem; in quo duplex notatur conditio in persona laudante, scilicet *virilitas* et *modicitas. Virilitas* notatur in hoc, quod *vocem extollebat,* secundum illud Isaiae quadragesimo: 'Exalta in fortitudine vocem tuam, exalta, noli timere'; *modicitas* in hoc, quod *quaedam mulier,* non nominata nec nobilis, sed de turba, ut impleretur illud Psalmi: 'Pauper et inops laudabunt nomen tuum'. Ex quo apparet, quod laudator divini nominis non debet esse timidus, ut laudare non audeat, nec timidus, ut laudare erubescat, sed virilis et humilis. Unde cum quidam *tacerent* ex *timore,* quidam *blasphemarent* ex *superbia* et *tumore;* haec mulier humilis et virilis nec *tacuit* cum timidis nec *vituperavit* cum blasphemis; unde in Glossa: 'Magna fiducia inter blasphemos confitetur Dei Filium'. Ideo poterant sibi dicere illud Matthaei decimo quinto: 'O mulier, magna est fides tua', quae scilicet tantum te fortificavit, cum dicatur Proverbiorum ultimo: 'Mulierem fortem quis inveniet'? In te verificatum est illud Ecclesiastici vigesimo sexto: 'Fundamenta aeterna supra petram solidam, et mandata Dei in corde mulieris sanctae'." *Comment. in Evangelium Lucae* C.XI, t.VII, 295b, 296a.

(11:21). Moreover, *she touched the hem,* that is, the lowest part *of the garment,* considering herself unworthy and honoring the power of Christ Who can give health through the lowliest of instruments. And because she believed and hoped, she easily obtained her cure, as the Gospel adds: "And immediately the issue of blood stopped." Herein is manifested the miraculous power of God Who at the touch of a little piece of His garment cured a serious disease of long standing. It is the wondrous power of Christ, then, which according to one's belief makes the impossible easy, as St. Mark says: "If thou canst believe, all things are possible to him that believeth" (9:22).[5] And Christ commended the woman, saying: "Daughter, thy faith hath made thee whole; go thy way in peace" (Luke 8:48), as if to say: "Justly have you obtained this favor, because you have believed."[6] Our Lord looked approvingly on the faith of this poor woman, who in her humility and modest reserve had not the courage even to voice her appeal to Christ.

"And behold a woman from Canaan who came out of those coasts, crying out, said to Him: Have mercy on me, O Lord, thou son of David. My daughter is grievously troubled by a devil, Who answered her not a word. And His disciples besought Him, saying: Send her away, for she crieth after us. And He answering said: I was not sent but to the sheep that are lost of the house of Israel. But she came and adored Him, saying: Lord, help me. Who answering, said: It is not good to take the bread of the children, and cast it to the dogs. But she said: Yea, Lord, for the whelps also eat of the crumbs that fall from the tables of their masters. Then Jesus answering, said to her: O woman, great is thy faith; be it done to thee as thou wilt, and her daughter was cured from that hour" (Matt. 15:22-28).

We cannot but admire this woman from Canaan for her perseverance in her petition, in spite of the rebuffs of Our Lord, and for her humble prayer, now re-echoed throughout the whole world: "Have mercy on me, O, Lord, thou Son of David"; for her acknowledgment of her daughter's misfortune: "My daughter is grievously troubled by a devil"; for the fervor which brought her from the far-off coasts of Canaan to find out for herself the power of

---

(5) "Tertio quantum ad *facilitatem perfectae curationis* a Salvatore subditur: *Accessit retro et tetigit fimbriam vestimenti eius. Accessit,* quia credebat; ad Hebraeos undecimo: 'Oportet accedentem credere'; *retro,* quia *timebat,* sicut soror eiusdem Maria, supra septimo: 'Stans retro secus pedes Domini'. *Tetigit,* quia *speravit curari;* Matthaei nono: 'Dicebat intra se: Si tetigero fimbriam vestimenti, salva ero'. *Tetigit* autem *fimbriam,* id est infimam partem *vestimenti* reputans se immundam et honorificans Christi potentiam, qui potest salutem dare per infima. Et quia credidit et speravit, ideo faciliter obtinuit. Propter hoc additur: *Et confestim stetit fluxio sanguinis eius;* ex quo apparet mira Dei virtus, quae morbum tam diuturnum et tam gravem curavit statim ad tactum unius particulae. Mira est ergo virtus Christi, quae credulitate sui impossibilia facit facilia secundum illud Marci nono: 'Si potes credere, omnia possibilia sunt credenti'." *Comment. in Evangelium Lucae* C. VIII, t.VII, 211a.

(6) "Tertio adiungitur approbatio veritatis detectae per definitivam commendationem cum subditur: At ipse dixit illi: *Filia, fides tua te salvam fecit,* quasi dicat: Iuste hoc assecuta es, quia credidisti." *Ibid.,* 212ab.

Our Divine Lord; and for the example of her penitence, well worthy of our imitation: Have mercy on me, O Lord."[7]

St. Bonaventure takes note of the fact that Christ commended the faith of three women whom He had heard and made whole. To Magdalen at the house of the Pharisee He said: "Thy faith hath made thee safe" (Luke 7:50); to the woman with the issue of blood: "Daughter, thy faith hath made thee whole" (Luke 8:48); and likewise to the woman from Canaan, He said: "O woman, great is thy faith" (Matt. 15:28).[8]

Religion always has the greatest emotional appeal to those who most feel the need of strength and help, and this is the psychological reason why so many women are faithful believers. They take God at His word and lay down no conditions for their belief. The strong, vain, more aggressive male likes to feel that he is sufficient unto himself. It was no woman who wrote, "I thank whatever gods there be for my unconquerable soul!" Wiser, more intuitive woman is conscious of her relative weakness in a competitive and predatory world. She finds in religion strength and promise and a code of conduct which protects her and her children. Women, too, are more inclined to accept the sacrifices which religion requires because it is part of woman's strange, complex make-up bravely to accept sacrifice and even suffering.

The tenderness of Christ's heart was always betrayed in His dealings with the poor and afflicted. To console a heart-broken widow, He raised her only son from the dead. "And it came to pass afterwards that He went into a city called Naim . . . And when He came nigh to the gate of the city, behold a dead man was carried out, the only son of his mother, and she was a widow" (Luke 7:11, 12). Sorrow always attends death, as Ecclesiasticus says: "Weep for the dead, for his light hath failed" (22:10), but this woman's grief was uncontrolled, because the dead man was her only son. Her lamentation was more bitter, as he was more dear, as Jeremias says: "Make thee mourning as for an only son, a bitter lamentation" (Jer. 6:26). And David, mourning his brother Jonathan, said: "As the mother loveth her only son, so did I love thee" (II Kings 1:26). The mother's grief was overwhelming, for "she was a widow," and therefore utterly desolate, deprived of the consolation of her son as well as that of her husband. Like the woman of Thecua who won the pity of the king when she said: "Alas,

---

(7) "*Ecce, mulier Chananaea, a finibus illis egressa, clamavit, dicens ei: Miserere mei, Domine, fili David; filia mea male a daemonio vexatur,* Matthaei decimo quinto. Proponit verba ista mulier Chananaea dupliciter, scilicet quantum ad clamorem universalem sive infatigabilem quantum ad *orationem* humilem, ibi: *Miserere mei, Domine* etc.; quantum ad *confessionem veracem,* ibi: *filia mea* etc. . . . In *mysterium* Ecclesiae *investigandum* cum dicitur: *Ecce, mulier Chananaea a finibus illis egressa;* in *exemplum poenitentiae* imitandae, cum additur: *clamavit: Miserere mei, Domine* etc.; quantum ad hoc commendandus est fervor." *Sermones de Tempore: Feria V. Post Dominicam Primam in Quadragesima,* t.IX, 213.

(8) "Et nota, quod trium mulierum Dominus fidem commendat, quas exaudit et salvat. Commendavit Magdalenam supra septimo, dicens consimile verbum: 'Fides tua te salvam fecit'; et hanc commendat hic; el mulierem Chananaeam, Matthaei decimo quinto, cui dixit: 'Mulier, magna est fides tua'. " *Comment. in Evangelium Lucae* C. VIII. t.VII, 212b.

I am a widow woman; for my husband is dead" (II Kings 14:5), the widow of Naim in her misfortune had the sympathy of the whole city. "And a great multitude of the city was with her" to comfort and console her, as was the custom of the Jews. To all these she could only say: "O all ye who pass by the way, attend and see if there be any sorrow like to my sorrow"; "he hath made me desolate, wasted with sorrow all the day long" (Lam. 1:12, 13). Indeed, the poor widow needed consolation.[9] "Whom when the Lord had seen, being moved with mercy towards her, he said to her: Weep not" (Luke 7:13). Our Lord was moved with mercy. With Job He could say: "I wept heretofore for him that was afflicted" (Job 30:25), "for from my infancy mercy grew up with me" (Job 31:18). And since mercy hidden in the heart is made manifest in speech, He said: "Weep not," consoling her with kind words, as is said in Job (29:13): "And I comforted the heart of the widow" and in Jeremias (31:16): "Let thy voice cease from weeping, and thy eyes from tears."[10] "And He came near and touched the bier. And they that carried it stood still. And He said: Young man, I say to thee, arise. And he that was dead sat up and began to speak, and He gave him to his mother" (Luke 7:14, 15). "He gave him to his mother." These words, says St. Bonaventure, show that it was to console the mother that Christ raised the young man from the dead.[11]

Upon the poor widow casting her two mites into the treasury Our Lord looked with the kindly eyes with which He always looks upon the poor, according to the words of Isaias: "To whom shall I have respect, but to him that is poor and little and of a contrite spirit, and that trembleth at my words" (Isai. 66:2). The Lord hears the prayers of such as these. "He hath had regard to the prayer of the humble, and he hath not despised their petition" (Ps. 101:18). "Do not the widow's tears run down the cheek, and from the cheek go up even to heaven?" (Ecclus. 35:18, 19). The smallest offerings of such persons Our Lord accepts, for he looks not at the amount

(9) "Secundum quantum *ad occursum multitudinis consolandae* subditur: *Cum autem appropinquaret portae civitatis, ecce, defunctus efferebatur, filius unicus matris suae;* de quo erat moeror luctus, quia *mortuus,* secundum illud Ecclesiastici vigesimo secundo: 'Super mortuum plora; defecit enim lux eius'. *Maior* etiam luctus, quia erat *unigenitus,* de quo fit planctus tanto amarior, quanto et carior; Ieremiae sexto: 'Luctum David lugens Ionathan mortuum: Sicut mater unicum amat filium, ita te diligebam'. *Maximus* autem luctus, quia mater omnino erat desolata; propter quod dicit: *Et haec vidua erat,* et ita iam omnino desolata, carens tam solatio filii quam mariti. Quod allegat illa mulier Thecuitis ad misericordiam impetrandam, secundi Regum decimo quarto: 'Heu! mulier vidua ego sum'. Et ideo plangebat Ieremias viduitatem Ierusalem Threnorum primo: 'Quomodo sedet sola civitas plena populo' etc. Et propterea multi ei compatiebantur; unde addit: *Et turba civitatis multa cum illa,* scilicet ad condolendum et consolandum, quia hic erat mos Iudaeorum, secundum illud Ioannis undecimo: 'Multi ex Iudaeis venerant ad Mariam et Martham, ut consolarentur eas de fratre suo'. Ad quos autem omnes poterat haec vidua dicere: 'O vos omnes, qui transitis per viam, attendite et videte, si est dolor sicut dolor meus'! post parum: 'Posuit me desolatam, tota die moerore confectam'. Et ideo egebat consolatione." *Ibid.,* C.VII, t.VII, 170b, 171a.

(10) "Quantum ad *affectum, pietatis in corde* dicitur: Quam cum vidisset Dominus, misericordia motus, scilicet quantum *ad cordis affectum,* ut posset dicere illud Iob trigesimo: 'Flebam quondam super eo qui afflictus erat'; et trigesimo primo: 'Ab infantia mea crevit mecum miseratio'. Et quia misericordia latens in *affectu* apparet in *affatu,* dixit: Noli flere, benigno sermone eam consolando, secundum illud Iob vigesimo nono: 'Cor viduae consolatus sum'; et Ieremiae trigesimo primo: 'Quiescat vox tua a ploratu, et oculi tui a lacrymis'." *Ibid.,* 171a.

(11) "Nec tantum erat nota plebi assistenti, sed *grata matri desideranti;* unde et subdit: *Et dedit illum matri suae;* in quo ostendit, se illum suscitasse ad matris consolationem." *Ibid.,* 171b, 172a.

of the offering, but at the amount one keeps for himself; not at the gift itself, but at the heart of the giver, as St. Gregory says. And again: "The kingdom of heaven is worth as much as you have. To Zacheus, it was worth the half of his goods (cf. Luke 19:8); to Andrew and Peter, it was worth their torn nets and their ship (Matt. 4:20); to the widow, it was worth two brass mites (cf. Luke 21:2); to another it was worth a cup of cold water (cf. Matt. 10:42). The kingdom of heaven, then, is worth as much as you have." For it the widow gave all she had; "she cast in all the living that she had," two brass mites,—evidence at once of her poverty and her generosity.[12]

Some considered the widow worthy of blame rather than of praise because she had not followed the golden mean but, going beyond the requirements of charity, had exposed herself to want. But because she had placed all her hope in Christ and had fulfilled His counsel, preferring the worship of God to her own personal advantage, she was praised by His divine lips. Though she appeared indiscreet in the eyes of men, she was truly prudent, for in giving her all, she became like to Him Who "being rich became poor for your sakes, that through His poverty you might be rich" (II Cor. 8:9).[13]

The widow offered two mites,—the one, her faith; the other, her charity, or rather a twofold faith,—faith in the Divinity and in the Humanity of Christ, and a twofold charity, namely, love of God and of her neighbor. The two mites which the poor widow cast into the treasury in the spirit of humility were, through the good intention with which they were given, more acceptable in the eyes of God than all the works of the proud Jews, for "God resisteth the proud and giveth His grace to the humble" (James 4:6).[14]

Perhaps the severest test of a man's attitude toward womankind is found

---

(12) "Secundo quantum ad *oblationem viduae pauperculae* subdit: *Vidit autem et quandam viduam pauperculam mittentem duo aera minuta. Vidit,* inquam, oculo benignitatis, quo ad pauperes respicit, secundum illud Isaiae sexagesimo sexto: 'Ad quem respiciam nisi ad pauperculum et contritum spiritu et trementem sermones meos'? Talium audit Dominus preces; Psalmus: 'Respexit in orationem humilium et non sprevit preces eorum'; et Ecclesiastici trigesimo quinto: 'Nonne lacrymae viduae ad maxillam descendunt et a maxilla ascendunt ad caelum'? Talium suscipit quantumcumque parvas oblationes, quia, sicut dicit Glossa, 'non perpendit Deus, quantum in sacrificio offertur, sed ex quanto detur'. Unde et Matthaei decimo: 'Qui dederit uni ex minimis his calicem aquae frigidae, non perdet mercedem suam'. Ideo dicit Gregorius: 'Exteriora nostra quamlibet parva Deo sufficiunt; cor namque et non substantiam pensat'; et post: 'Regnum caelorum tantum valet, quantum habes. Valuit namque Zachaeo dimidium bonorum, valuit Andreae et Petro dimissis retibus et navi, valuit viduae duobus minutis, valuit et alteri calicem aquae frigidae. Regnum itaque caelorum tantum valet quantum habes'. Et nota, quod in hoc quod dicit, quod misit duo aera minuta, simul paupertatem insinuat et liberalitatem: paupertatem, quia, cum posset alterum offerre, obtulit utrumque, ut impleret illud Tobiae quarto: 'Si exiguum tibi fuerit, etiam illud libenter impartiri stude'." *Ibid.*, C.XXI, t.VII, 521a.

(13) "Sed videtur haec vidua ex hac ratione non esse laudanda, sed potius vituperanda, quia medium non servavit, quia *periculo* se exposuit, quia *ordinem caritatis* praetermisit, contra illud Apostoli: 'Non ut aliis sit remissio, vobis autem tribulatio, sed ex aequalitate. In praesenti tempore vestra abundantia illorum inopiae sit supplementum,' secundae ad Corinthios octavo. Sed ideo divino ore laudatur, quia spem ponens in Christo et divinum implens consilium, quia Dei cultus praeferens suae privatae utilitati. Licet secundum hominem non videatur fuisse discreta eius eleemosyna, prudentissima tamen fuit, dum totum dando facta est imitatrix Christi, de quo secundae ad Corinthios octavo: 'Scitis gratiam Domini nostri Iesu Christi, quoniam propter vos egenus factus est, cum esset dives, ut illius inopia vos divites essetis'." *Ibid.*, 521b, 522a.

(14) "*Offert* autem *duo minuta,* id est *fidem* et *caritatem,* vel *geminam fidem,* scilicet de *Divinitate* et *humanitate,* seu *geminam caritatem,* scilicet *Dei et proximi,* secundum illud Canticorum quarto: 'Omnes gemellis foetibus, et sterilis non est in eis.' Et haec *minuta* sunt propter humilitatem, sed Deo maxime accepta sunt; unde Glossa: 'Consideratione suae fragilitatis *minuta,* sed merito piae intentionis magis sunt accepta quam cuncta superbientium Iudaeorum opera,' quia Iacobi quarto, 'Deus superbis resistit, humilibus autem dat gratiam'." *Ibid.*, 523a.

in his conduct toward a sinful woman, whom even good men are quick to condemn, slow to forgive, unwilling to forget. As a rule they are loathe to risk their own reputation by any show of consideration toward her. Not so Our Lord Who always received penitent sinners with paternal affection, showing to them the open bosom of His divine mercy. To learn the tenderness of the heart of Christ we need only to watch Him in the presence of two sinful women, the sinner prostrate at His feet and the woman taken in adultery.[15]

> "And behold a woman that was in the city, a sinner, when she knew that he sat at meat in the Pharisee's house, brought an alabaster box of ointment, and standing behind at his feet, she began to wash his feet with tears, and wiped them with the hairs of her head, and kissed his feet, and anointed them with the ointment. And the Pharisee, who had invited him, seeing it, spoke within himself, saying: This man, if he were a prophet, would know surely who and what manner of woman this is that toucheth him, that she is a sinner" (Luke 7:37-39) . . . "And turning to the woman, he said unto Simon: Dost thou see this woman? I entered into thy house. Thou gavest me no water for my feet, but she with tears hath washed my feet, and with her hairs hath wiped them. Thou gavest me no kiss, but she, since she came in, hath not ceased to kiss my feet. My head with oil thou didst not anoint, but she with ointment hath anointed my feet. Wherefore, I say to thee: Many sins are forgiven her, because she has loved much. And he said to her: Thy sins are forgiven thee" (Luke 7:44-48). Thy faith hath made thee safe. Go in peace" (*ibid.,* 50).

Jesus preferred the love of this repentant woman to the possible faith of the proud Pharisees and, beneath the gaze of His merciful eyes, Mary the sinner became Mary the Saint. Mary Magdalen is set before us as the model of penitence for all time and Our Lord's praise of her may serve for our instruction, for here we note two things: first, the intensity of her love, "because she hath loved much"; secondly, the effect of her love, "many sins are forgiven her," for thus did Christ reward her unspeakable love.[16]

As for the woman taken in adultery, Our Divine Lord did not extenuate her guilt. He said to her: "Go, and now sin no more," but He refused to condemn her so long as her guilty paramour, whose apprehension would have been as easy as hers, was allowed to go free, and while her accusers stood self-condemned (cf. John 8:1-11). With Christ there is no double standard of right and wrong and never by word or deed did He lend en-

---

(15) "Ad poenitentes quoque paternum praetendebat affectum, apertum ostendens eis divinae misericordiae sinum. Testes horum invoco et adduco . . . peccatricem illam ad pedes eius prostratam et mulierem in adulterio deprehensam." *Opusculum III Lignum Vitae de Mysterio Originis,* t.VIII, 74a.

(16) "Haec igitur Maria proposita est nobis in exemplum poenitentiae, et de ista dicitur in Evangelio hodierno: *Dismissa sunt ei* etc. In verbo autem proposito ad ipsius commendationem et nostram instructionem possumus duo notare: primo, *caritatis affectum,* cum dicit: quoniam dilexit multum; secundo, *caritatis effectum,* cum dicit: *Dimissa sunt ei peccata multa;* ista enim prae ceteris videtur Christum dilexisse." *De S. Maria Magdalena,* Sermo II, t.IX, 558ab.

couragement to the disparagement of woman. His daily deportment toward the sex was a standing reproof to the spirit of His age and to every man-imposed restriction on woman. No wonder that the women whose devotion is here recorded attended Jesus on His mission tours "through cities and villages" and in company with the Twelve journeyed with Him to Jerusalem. No wonder that when He walked the Dolorous Way to Calvary "there followed Him a great multitude of people, and of women who bewailed and lamented Him" (Luke 23:27). The crowd followed Christ out of feelings of mingled wonder and admiration; the women, out of pity. The wicked followed that they might rejoice at His death; the women, that they might assist thereat in loving grief.[17]

"There followed women who lamented Him." These lamentations for Christ were made by women, not by men, remarks St. Bonaventure, not because the women were more fervent or more steadfast in their love of Christ but because they are naturally more inclined to tears and are more compassionate by nature. Sacred Scripture says that women lamented Our Lord, continues the Saint, because they could do so with greater security. Then quoting the Gloss: "It was not because women alone lamented. Aye, men, too, grieved, but because the feminine sex, more contemptible, as it were, and beneath the notice of the leaders of the priests standing by, could more safely show their feelings than could the men."[18] But Christ, forgetting His own sufferings, His agony of physical pain and bitter injustice, turned His eyes upon the women, whose terrible fate was bound up with the siege and doom He foresaw threatening Jerusalem, and said: "Daughters of Jerusalem, weep not over me; but weep for yourselves and for your children" (Luke 23:28). Not that the women did wrong in having compassion on Christ, for Job, a good and holy man, says: "I wept heretofore for him that was afflicted, and my soul had compassion on the poor" (Job 30:25). Wherefore, it was fitting that the poor Christ, afflicted and amiable and most beautiful, should be compassionated with loving affection, as Zacharias had foretold: "And they shall look upon me, whom they have pierced. And they shall mourn for him as one mourneth for an only son, and they shall grieve over him, as the manner is to grieve for the death of the firstborn" (Zach. 12:10). Therefore, Christ did not disapprove of the women's weeping but of their dejection of soul, against which St. Paul warns the Thessalonians: "Be not sorrowful, even as others who have no hope. For if we be-

---

(17) "Secundo quantum ad *lamentationem mulierum concomitantium* subditur: *Sequebatur autem illum multa turba populi et mulierum, quae plangebant et lamentabantur eum. Turba* quidem sequebatur ex admiratione, sed *mulieres* ex miseratione; unde Glossa: 'Mali sequuntur, ut morientem laeti aspiciant, mulieres, ut quem vivere desiderabant moriturum, morientem et mortuum plorarent'." *Comment. in Evangelium Lucae.* C.XXIII, t.VII, 573a.

(18) "Haec autem lamentatio fiebat de Christo a mulieribus, non a viris, non quia mulieres essent in amore Christi ferventiores seu stabiliores, sed quia magis sunt naturaliter ad lacrymas pronae et magis compassivae naturae, . . . et quia poterant hoc facere magis secure. Unde Glossa: 'Non ideo inducitur solus mulierum ploratus, quin et viri dolerent, sed quia femineus sexus quasi contemptibilior liberius poterat, praesentibus principibus sacerdotum, quid contra eos sentiret, ostentare'." *Ibid.*

lieve that Jesus died and rose again, even so them who have slept through Jesus, will God bring with him" (I Thess. 4:13 ff.). Christ likewise disapproved of the lamentations of the women because they were occasioned by a kind of sensible love, namely, by the withdrawal of His beloved presence.[19]

Later we find three of these women at the foot of the Cross. With St. John as he himself tells us, "there stood by the cross of Jesus, His mother and His mother's sister, Mary of Cleophas, and Mary Magdalen" (John 19:25). How few the mourners of Christ! Out of all His dear ones, there stood at the cross three women, one of whom was His mother. The compassion of the women is gathered from the words: "They stood by the cross of Jesus." Drawn by loving compassion they came near to Christ. The others, unpitying, departed at a distance, thus fulfilling the words of the Psalm: "My friends and my neighbours have drawn near, and stood against me. And they that were near me stood afar off" (Ps. 37:12). But those who loved Him best stood near, namely, His Mother, who compassionated Him beyond all others, as the aged Simeon had prophesied: "And thy own soul a sword shall pierce" (Luke 2:35) and His mother's sister, Mary of Cleophas, and Mary Magdalen" (John 19:25). These three women, compassionating Him more than others, stood near the cross of Christ.[20] Where were the twelve Apostles? Why are they not mentioned here? The three Evangelists record the devotion of only these three women.

"And the women that were come with him from Galilee, following after, saw the sepulchre, and how his body was laid" (Luke 23:55). "They saw the sepulchre," assisting thereat in loving devotion. Note that the others departed after the body of Jesus had been taken down from the cross; the women alone who loved Him with a closer, more intimate love remained to assist at the rites of burial. And this they did that they might mourn in death Him Whom they had loved in life and Whom they had followed along the dolorous way to Calvary. Their presence at the tomb was an expression of

(19) "Tertio quantum ad *reprehensionem lamentantium* adiungit: *Conversus autem Iesus* ad illas dixit: *Filiae Ierusalem, nolite flere super me.* Prohibet autem huiusmodi mulieres a fletu, non quia male facerent Christo compatiendo, cum dicat vir pius et sanctus Iob trigesimo: 'Flebam quondam super eo qui afflictus erat, et compatiebatur anima mea pauperi'; ... Unde de Christo pauperi, afflicto et amabili Christo et pulcherrimo compatiendum est affectu piissimo, secundum illud Zachariae duodecimo: 'Aspicient ad me, quem confixerunt, et plangent eum planctu quasi super unigenitum et dolebant super eum, sicut doleri solet in morte primogeniti.' Non ergo hoc arguitur a Christo, sed quia contristabantur ex *mentis deiectione;* contra quod primae ad Thessalonicenses quarto: 'Non contristemini sicut et ceteri, qui spem non habent; si enim credimus' etc.; ... quia etiam contristabantur *carnali quadam affectione,* scilicet de subtractione faciei desideratae." *Ibid.,* 573b.

(20) *"Stabant autem iuxta crucem* etc. Hic notatur compatientium *paucitas;* quia ex omnibus caris eius tres aderant mulieres, inter quas et Mater Domini, cui etiam Dominus compatiebatur. Et notandum hic quatuor: *mulierum ad Dominum compassio,* ... Notatur ergo *mulierum compassio* in hoc quod dicit: *Stabant iuxta crucem Iesu;* ideo corpore appropinquabant, quia affectus compassionis trahebat. Alii vero longe recesserant per incompassionem; unde dicitur in Psalmo: 'Qui iuxta me erant de longe steterunt.' Sed istae steterunt iuxta, quae magis diligebant, scilicet *Mater eius,* quae super omnes compatiebatur; unde Lucae secundo; 'Tuam ipsius animam pertransibit gladius'; et *soror Matris eius, Maria Cleophae;* haec fuit mater Iacobi. Notandum est, quod Anna dicitur habuisse tres viros: Ioachim, Cleopham et Salome, et ex istis tribus viris habuit tres Marias scilicet Matrem Domini, quae fuit filia Ioachim; matrem Iacobi, quae fuit filia Cleophae; matrem Simonis et Iudae, quae fuit filia Salome.—*Et Maria Magdalena,* quae dicta est a Magdalo castro. Istae tres mulieres tanquam magis compatientes stabant iuxta crucem Domini." *Comment. in Ioannem* C.XIX, t.VI, 497b, 498a.

their loyalty and devotion and a fulfillment of the words of Ecclesiasticus: "My son, shed tears over the dead, and begin to lament as if thou hadst suffered some great harm, and according to judgment cover his body, and neglect not his burial" (38:16). "And make mourning for him according to his merit" (*ibid.,* 18). Not only did these devoted women see the sepulchre but they also saw the body laid therein. Therefore the Gospel adds: "They saw how his body was laid," and this, because they wished to bestow the gift of their kindness.[21]

These "certain" women were early at the sepulchre on Easter morn.

> "And on the first day of the week, very early in the morning, they came to the sepulchre, bringing the spices which they had prepared. And they found the stone rolled back from the sepulchre. And going in, they found not the body of the Lord Jesus. And it came to pass, as they were astonished in their mind at this, behold, two men stood by them in shining apparel" (Luke 24:1-4).

As Daniel, in fear and reverence "cast down his countenance to the ground and held his peace" (Dan. 10:15) when the angel addressed him, so the holy women "were afraid and bowed down their countenance toward the ground" (Luke 24.5). Women of such humility and reverential fear deserve to hear the truth, comments the Seraphic Doctor,[22] and the angels "said unto them: Why seek you the living with the dead? He is not here, but is risen. Remember how He spoke unto you, when He was yet in Galilee, saying: The Son of man must be delivered into the hands of sinful men and be crucified and the third day rise again. And they remembered His words" (*ibid.,* 5-8). Happy women, the first to hear of the resurrection from angels' lips! They had merited such happiness by following the Saviour, not only when He revealed His power by astounding miracles, but also when, laden with the cross, He walked the painful road to the Calvary, and again now, when they had come to bestow marks of faithful love on Christ in the tomb.

It is a notable fact that all the Evangelists mention Mary Magdalen first in the group of women who went to the tomb at dawn "on the first day of the week" to complete the anointing of the Lord's body, but St. John makes mention of her alone. We may well wonder why St. John in his Gospel

(21) "Quarto quantum ad *reverentiam mulierum in subsecutione* subiungit: *Subsecutae autem mulieres, quae cum ipso venerant de Galilaea, vicerunt monumentum.* Hoc autem faciebant ex pietatis affectu; unde Glossa: 'Aliis nota Iesu post depositum corpus recedentibus, solae mulieres, quae arctius amabant, officium funeris inspiciebant'; et haec faciebant, ut lugerent mortuum, quem prius dilexerant moriturum. Et hoc pietatis est et religionis, secundum illud Ecclesiastici trigesimo octavo: 'Fili in mortuum produc lacrymas, et quasi dira passus, incipe plorare et secundum iudicium contege corpus illius et non despicias sepulturam illius.' 'Et fac luctum secundum meritus eius.' Ideo hae mulieres piae non solum aspiciebant sepulturam, verum etiam corpus sepultum; et ideo addit: Et *quemadmodum positum erat corpus eius,* scilicet viderunt, et hoc ad impendendum humanitatis beneficium." *Comment. in Evangelium Lucae* C.XXIII, t.VII, 586a.

(22) "Et ideo Lucas subdit: *Cum timerent autem et declinarent vultum in terram,* prae timore scilicet et reverentia, sicut Daniel, Danielis decimo: 'Cum loqueretur mihi, deieci vultum meum ad terram et tacui'; et tales sunt idonei ad veritatem audiendam.—Unde addit: *Dixerunt ad illas: Quid quaeritis viventem cum mortuis? Non est hic sed surrexit;* in quo simul arguunt incredulitatem et asseverant veritatem." *Ibid.,* C.XXIV, t.VII, 589b.

mentions only the Magdalen, especially when we know that she went to the sepulchre in company of the other women. The Seraphic Doctor allows St. Augustine to give the answer: Mary Magdalen, he says, who had ministered to the Lord, loved Him far more ardently than the other woman, and since the other Evangelists had given the names of the women who had been with her, St. John mentions only Mary Magdalen who was most worthy of the tribute.[23]

For the same reason, St. Bonaventure considers Mary Magdalen worthy of special mention: "After the Lord was buried and soldiers had been assigned to guard the sepulchre, these devoted and holy women who had ministered to Christ during life, came with sweet spices to anoint the most sacred body of Jesus, that, in death, as in life, they might bestow upon Him a service of loving devotion. Of these women, Mary Magdalen was so carried away by the burning love of her heart, so affected by the sweetness of her deep devotion, so drawn by the strong bonds of love, that, forgetful of her woman's weakness, she braved the darkness of the shadows and the cruelty of the persecutors to visit the sepulchre. Nay more, she did not depart when the disciples left the sepulchre, but remained standing outside and moistened the tomb with her tears. Inflamed with the fire of divine love, consumed with ardent longing, and wounded by the darts of her overwhelming love, she could only weep and bewail her Lord. Truly could she utter the words of David (Ps. 41:4): 'My tears have been my bread day and night, whilst it is said to me daily: Where is thy God?' "[24]

In another passage St. Bonaventure commends the love and admirable courage of the Magdalen. "You seek Jesus of Nazareth, who was crucified" (Mark 16:6). The holy women to whom the angel addressed the foregoing words, were seeking Christ with such longing love that they did not rest even during the night. Did not Mary Magdalen seek Christ with the most fervent love? In spite of the faint-heartedness of the feminine sex, she braved every obstacle and came alone "before it was light" to the sepulchre; love made her bold. Neither the apparition of the angels nor the companionship of the Apostles satisfied her heart; nay, the sight of every creature wearied her. She would seek Jesus of Nazareth until she would find Him, and in possessing

(23) "Sed quaeritur hic primo: cum aliae mulieres Magdalena venissent ad monumentum, propter quid tantum de ea loquitur Ioannes? Respondet Augustinus in tertio libro de Concordia Evangelistarum: 'Maria, inquit, Magdalena ceteris mulieribus, quae Domino ministraverant, plurimum ferventior erat; propter quod solam non immerito Ioannes commemoravit, tactis aliis, quae cum ea fuerunt, sicut alii testantur'." *Comment. in Ioannem* C.XX, t.VI, 506ab.

(24) "Porro sepulto Domino, et ad custodiam sepulcri deputatis militibus, devotae illae mulieres et sanctae, quae fuerant obsecutae viventi, ut iam mortuo pietate officiosa famulatum impenderent, *emerunt aromata* ad corpus Iesu sacratissimum perungendum. Inter quas Maria Magdalena tanto cordis ferebatur incendio, tantae pietatis afficiebatur dulcedine, tam validis trahebatur vinculis caritatis, ut, femineae infirmitatis oblita, nec tenebrarum caligine nec persecutorum immanitate retraheretur a visitatione sepulcri, quin potius foris stans et rigans lacrymis monumentum, recedentibus discipulis, non recedebat, pro eo quos divinae dilectionis igne succensa, et tam invalescente urebatur desiderio et tam impatiente vulnerabatur amore, ut nihil ei saperet nisi flere possetque propheticum illud eructare veraciter: *Fuerunt mihi lacrymae meae panes die et nocte, dum dicitur mihi quotidie: Ubi est Deus tuus?" Lignum Vitae. De Mysterio Glorificationis,* t.VIII, 80b.

Him, she would possess every blessing. For Christ *crucified* confers the blessing of pardon in absolution of sin; Christ, the *Nazarene,* the living Christ, bestows the dew of grace for growth in holiness; *Jesus,* the Saviour, bestows perfect glory, the glorification of body and soul. Surely Mary Magdalen would find Jesus, for "You shall seek me, and shall find me when you shall seek me with all your heart, saith the Lord" (Jer. 29:13).[25]

No wonder when Easter dawned that Christ appeared to the holy women who had been with Him on Calvary and to Magdalen weeping near the tomb. Women had shared His ignominy; He made them the first to share His glory.

> "But Mary stood at the sepulchre without, weeping. Now as she was weeping, she stooped down and looked into the sepulchre. And she saw two angels in white, sitting, one at the head, and one at the feet, where the body of Jesus had been laid. They say to her: Woman, why weepest thou? She saith to them: Because they have taken away my Lord; and I know not where they have laid him. When she had thus said, she turned herself back and saw Jesus standing, and she knew not that it was Jesus. Jesus saith to her: Woman, why weepest thou? Whom seekest thou? She, thinking that it was the gardener, saith to him: Sir, if thou hast taken him hence, tell me where thou hast laid him, and I will take him away. Jesus saith to her: Mary. She turning, saith to him: Rabboni (which is to say, Master). Jesus saith to her: Do not touch me, for I am not yet ascended to my Father. But go to my brethren and say to them: I ascend to my Father and to your Father, to my God and to your God. Mary Magdalen cometh and telleth the disciples: I have seen the Lord; and these things he said to me" (John 20:11-18).

Jesus appeared first, not to James, who was to become head of the Church at Jerusalem; not to Peter, to whom Christ gave the keys of the kingdom; not to John, the disciple whom Jesus loved,—to none of these. St. Mark says: "He appeared first to Mary Magdalen" (16:9). She was the first to see the risen Christ.

"What fem'nine charm in woman so endeared
Her to the Lord as to be first to see
Him Risen, glowing with Divinity?
Her heart—which neither death nor failure feared."

It would seem, some may object, that if the disciples were more worthy, Our Lord should first appear to them and that they, in turn, should announce the resurrection to the women, rather than that the women should announce

(25) "Secundo quaesivit eum cum *latitudine benevolentiae* in diligendo; unde dicitur Marci decimo sexto: *Iesum quaeritis Nazarenum.* Istae sanctae mulieres, quas alloquitur Angelus, cum tanto desiderio amoris quaerebant Christum, ut etiam in nocte non quiescerent. Nonne cum magno fervore amoris quaerebat Christum Maria Magdalena, quae sola in sepulcro moras contrahere non timebat, cum sexus muliebris sit timidus ex natura? Non enim erat contenta visione Angelorum nec consortio Apostolorum; immo, taedium erat sibi videre omnem creaturam, quousque tamen quaereret, donec inveniret *Iesum Nazarenum crucifixum,* quia eo habito, habetur omne bonum. Nam Christus, in quantum *crucifixus,* confert beneficium veniae in absolutione culpae; in quantum *Nazarenus,* id est floridus, confert stillicidium gratiae in promotione iustitiae; sed in quantum *Iesus,* qui interpretatur salus, confert complementum gloriae in glorificatione corporis et animae. Et de hoc dicitur Ieremiae vigesimo nono: *Cum quaesieritis me in toto corde vestro, inveniar a vobis, dicit Dominus." Dominica infra Octavam Epiphaniae, Sermo I,* t.IX, 173ab.

it to the disciples. The order in which the resurrection was made known, says the Seraphic Doctor, was in keeping with the dispensation of Divine Providence and the merits or just reward of tender solicitude. It was the order of divine dispensation, as St. Gregory says: "Since in Paradise a woman delivered man to death, so from the tomb a woman brings to men tidings of life. A woman of *tender solicitude* conveys the message of the Restorer of Life, for, when the disciples had departed, she remained at the tomb, afflicted and disconsolate, and therefore deserved to be the first to be consoled and encouraged by the appearance of the Lord.[26]

Though St. John says: "Mary Magdalen cometh and telleth the disciples: I have seen the Lord" (20:18), St. Luke says: "It was Mary Magdalen and Joanna and Mary of James and the other women that were with them, who told these things to the Apostles" (24:10). St. Matthew, too (28:8-10), says that the holy women, following the injunction of the angel, announced the tidings of the resurrection to the disciples. Commenting upon this fact, St. Bonaventure says: "It was in the design of God that the tidings of the resurrection should come to men through women. As woman was the source from which issued sin and death, so now through women would come back to men the announcement and knowledge of life and immortality. This arrangement of our Lord provided the men with an opportunity of setting an example of humility. Wherefore St. Chrysostom, commenting on the Gospel of St. John, says: "The Evangelist does not deprive the women of praise, nor does he consider it disgraceful for the men to have learned from a woman." And St. Ambrose: "As in the beginning woman was the source of sin to man, and man was the consummator of the wrong, so now she, who had first tasted death, was the first to see Him Who is the Resurrection and the Life, and that she might not everlastingly bear the opprobrium of guilt in the eyes of men, woman, who had brought sin to man now brought him tidings of grace. The opprobrium of women, and especially of sinful women, concludes the Seraphic Doctor, has been taken away by the fact that from a woman came the announcement and knowledge of life and immortality.[27]

(26) "Sed quaeritur hic primo de ordine istius manifestationis.—Si enim discipuli digniores erant, videtur, quod primo eis Dominus apparere debebat, et iterum discipuli docere mulieres, quam mulieres discipulos. Respondeo: Dicendum, quod hoc factum est *ordine divinae dispensationis* et *merito humanae sollicitudinis;* ordo divinae dispensationis; propter quod dicit Gregorius: 'Quia in paradiso mulier viro propinavit mortem, a sepulcro mulier viris annuntiat vitam, et dicta vivificatoris narrat quae *magnae sollicitudinis,* quia, discipulis recedentibus, mulier remansit afflicta et desolata; et ideo citius meruit apparitione dominica consolari et refici'." *Comment. in Ioannen* C.XX, t.VI, 510ab.

(27) "Primo igitur quantum ad *testimonium mulierum* subdit: *Et egressae a monumento nuntiaverunt haec omnia illis undecim et ceteris omnibus.* Haec autem nuntiaverunt mulieres, quia sic est eis iniunctum ab Angelis; unde Matthaei ultimo: 'Cito euntes, dicite discipulis eius, quia surrexit, et ecce, praecedit vos in Galilaeam.' Hoc enim divina ordinatione gestum est, ut nuntiatio resurrectionis per mulieres veniret ad viros; sicut a muliere initium sumsit mors et peccatum, ita nunc per mulieres ad viros rediret annuntiatio et cognitio vitae et immortalitatis, ut etiam per hoc humilitatis daretur exemplum. Unde Chrysostomus: 'Evangelista non privat mulierem laude nec verecundum putat a muliere didicisse.' Aufertur etiam mulierum opprobrium, et maxime peccatricum." *Comment. in Evangelium Lucae* C.XXIV, t.VII, 590ab.

Ibid. footnote 1 reads: Glossa ordinaria (ex Ambros., X, in Luc. c.24. n.156. seq.) in Luc. 24, 9: "Sicut in principio mulier auctor culpae viro fuit, vir exsecutor fuit erroris, ita nunc quae mortem prior gustaverat resurrectionem vidit, et ne perpetuo reatus opprobrium apud viros sustineret, quae culpam viro transfuderat transfudit et gratiam."

PART TWO

WOMAN IN GRACE

Woman in Christian Marriage

Woman in the Virginal Life

To My Spiritual Mother

INTRODUCTION

If the magnificent portrayal of the beauty and splendor of the original creation as disclosed by the great Hebrew prophet and lawgiver in the Book of Genesis has a parallel in Sacred Scripture, it is to be found in the fourteen verses which stand at the opening of St. John's Gospel wherein are recorded the Godhead and Incarnation of the Divine Word.[1] Nowhere else in all literature, perhaps, do we find such an assemblage of important truths crowded into so few words, and, as we peruse the two passages, first the one, then the other, we are again reminded of the admonition of Ecclesiasticus to "look upon all the works of the Most High two and two, and one against another" (Ecclus. 42:25).

In the beginning man was great, the image of God and the recipient of His grace, but the Creator's glorious workmanship had been defiled. A real destruction, or as St. Bonaventure expresses it, an annihilation in the moral order and in the order of grace, had occurred;[2] fallen man stood in absolute need of a spiritual re-creation before he could attain his destined end.[3] A designer of finite capacities would have stood powerless before the task, but He Who had fashioned His masterpiece with infinite care could gather up the fragments and remake the thing of beauty that had originally proceeded from His creative hands,[4] and this He would do in a manner most worthy of the Redeemer and best suited to fallen man and to the restoration itself, namely, through the Incarnation of His Eternal Word.[5] It was most fitting, says St. Bonaventure, that the Restorer of the world should be the same Divine Artist Who had first fashioned it, and that He Who by His Eternal Word had brought all things into existence should by the same Divine Word made

(1) "In the beginning was the Word, and the Word was with God, and the Word was God. The same was in the beginning with God. All things were made by him, and without him was made nothing that was made. In him was life, and the life was the light of men. And the light shineth in darkness, and the darkness did not comprehend it. There was a man sent from God, whose name was John. This man came for a witness, to give testimony of the light, that all men might believe through him. He was not the light, but was to give testimony of the light. That was the true light, which enlighteneth every man that cometh into this world. He was in the world, and the world was made by him, and the world knew him not. He came unto his own, and his own received him not. But as many as received him, he gave them power to be made the sons of God, to them that believe in his name. Who are born, not of blood, nor of the will of the flesh, nor of the will of man, but of God. And the Word was made flesh and dwelt among us (and we saw his glory, the glory as it were of the only begotten of the Father), full of grace and truth" (John 1:1-14).

(2) "Cum igitur deformatio imaginis et peremptio gratiae sit quasi annihilatio in esse moris et vitae gratuitae;" *Breviloquium,* V, 3, t.V, 255a.

(3) ". . . cum offensa Dei sit tantum ponderanda, quantus est ipse; cum reatus poenae aeternae rationem teneat infiniti: impossibile est, quod homo resurgat a culpa, nisi *recreetur* in vita gratuita, nisi *remittatur* offensa, et poena relaxetur aeterna." *Ibid.*

(4) "Solus igitur, qui fuit principium creativum, est et principium recreativum." *Ibid.*

(5) "Restat nunc aliqua breviter dicere de incarnatione Verbi, per quod quidem Verbum incarnatum facta est salus et reparatio generis humani, non quia aliter Deus non potuerit humanum genus salvare et liberare, sed quia nullus alius modus erat ita congruus et conveniens ipsi reparatori et reparabili et reparationi." *Ibid.,* IV, 1, 241a.

Incarnate restore all things to the Father.[6] Since the first creation had been a manifestation of God's power, wisdom, and goodness, it was fitting that the restoration should likewise bear the stamp of this triple perfection. What greater manifestation of power than to unite in one person two extremes, natures separated by an unfathomable chasm? What greater evidence of wisdom and congruity than to perfect the universe by joining the Beginning and the end, namely, the Word of God, the Beginning of all things, and man, the last of creation? What greater mark of benevolence, nay, of inconceivable mercy, kindness, and love, than that a Master to save a servant should take the form of a servant?[7]

The stupendous plan of the Incarnation of the Son of God was a perfect one not only for manifesting the attributes of God but also for reaching fallen man who in abandoning his all-powerful, all-wise and all-loving Creator had become a victim of weakness, ignorance, and sin. To reclaim His creature from this degraded state and to make Himself known, loved, and imitated by him whom He had made "a little less than the angels," the Creator came down from heaven in visible, human form with human affections and sympathies, that through visible works done in the body He might draw man even "by the cords of Adam" and cure him of the disease of sin.[8] With the utmost benignity He came into this carnal and corruptible world, and from a pure Virgin, not through the intervention of man, but through the power of the Holy Ghost, He took a body like to ours. That body He made the instrument of His service, in which He might dwell, through which He might make Himself known, and by which He might claim kindred with us, with which He might offer an acceptable sacrifice to the Father for His brethren. "Sacrifice and oblation thou wouldst not; but a body thou hast fitted me. Holocausts for sin did not please thee. Then I said: Behold I come. In the head of the book it is written of me, that I should do thy will, O God" (Heb. 10:5-7). The Son of God stooped to the earth. To atone for the pride and disobedience of man, He "emptied Himself taking the form of a servant"

---

(6) "Ratio autem ad intelligentiam praedictorum haec est: quia, cum principium effectivum rerum non potuerit nec decuerit esse nisi Deum; et non minus sit res conditas reparare quam in *esse* producere, sicut non minus est *bene esse* quam *simpliciter esse:* decentissimum fuit, rerum principium reparativum esse Deum summum, ut, sicut omnia creaverat Deus per Verbum increatum, sic omnia curaret per Verbum incarnatum." *Ibid.*

(7) "Quoniam ergo Deus omnia fecit potenter, sapienter et optime seu benevolenter; decuit, ut sic repararet, quod suam *potentiam, sapientiam* et *benevolentiam* ostenderet. Quid autem *potentius,* quam coniungere extrema summe distantia in unam personam? Quid *sapientius* et congruentius, quam quod ad perfectionem totius universi fieret coniunctio primi ultimi, Verbi scilicet Dei, quod est omnium principium, et humanae naturae, quae fuit ultima omnium creaturarum? Quid *benevolentius,* quam quod Dominus propter servi salutem accipiat *formam servi? Ibid.*

(8) "Rursus, quia homo, cadens in culpam, averterat se et recesserat a principio potentissimo, sapientissimo et benevolentissimo; ideo corruerat in *infirmitatem,* ignorantiam et malignitatem, ac per hoc de spirituali effectus est carnalis, animalis et sensualis; et ideo ineptus erat ad divinam *virtutem imitandam,* ad *lucem cognoscendam,* ad *bonitatem diligendam.* Ad hoc igitur quod homo ab isto statu repararetur, congruentissimum fuit, ut ei condescenderet primum principium, reddendo se illi noscibile, amabile et imitabile. Et quia homo carnalis, animalis et sensualis non noverat nec amabat nec sequebatur nisi proportionalia et consimilia; ideo ad eripiendum hominem de hoc statu *Verbum caro factum est,* ut ab homine, qui caro erat, et *cognosci* posset et *amari* et *imitari,* ac per hoc et homo Deum cognoscens et amans et imitans remediaretur a morbo peccati." *Ibid.,* 241b.

(Phil. 2:7).[9] Of His own free will, He elected to suffer all the horrors of His Passion and Death. "He humbled Himself, becoming obedient unto death: even to the death of the cross" (Phil. 2:8).

What seemed to man an ending was but a beginning. In the living Church, the living Mystical Body which Christ formed to Himself as a result of His sacrifice, He continues on earth a real but mystical life. His Heart opened with the lance gave birth to the Church, His Bride, making "two in one Flesh" (Gen. 2:24). As Eve was derived from Adam, so was the Church derived from Christ. Just as Eve, the spouse of Adam, was the common mother of men generated in sin, so is the Church the Spouse of Christ and our Mother in the order of regeneration and sanctification. St. Bonaventure says: "As Eve was formed from Adam, so was the Church formed from Christ. The efficacy of the Blood and Water which flowed from the side of Christ as He slept on the Cross overflowed into the Sacraments of the Church, through which Sacraments the Church was founded; and so *man* corresponds to *Christ; sleep,* to *death; the taking of the rib, to the opening of the side.*"[10] Born on the Cross from the pierced side of the Saviour, the Church by her apostolic ministry perpetuates the beneficent and redeeming action of the Man-God. This ministry, willed by Jesus Christ, becomes the essential factor for propagating the Church throughout the nations, and the ordinary instruments of her conquests. The Blood and Water which flowed from the Heart of Christ on the Cross have never ceased to flow in a constant stream, giving and sustaining the life of the Church in every age and clime. From her fruitful womb are born "a chosen race, a royal priesthood, a holy nation, a purchased people." As her title of Bride suggests her fidelity and deep love for Christ, her Spouse; as her title of Body proclaims her union, submission and unfailing reception of life, so does her title of Mother express with great force the truth that all the saved are born to Christ by her. As St. Cyprian says: "He cannot have God for his father who has not the Church for his mother."[11]

As it would have profited us little to have been born of Adam if we had not been redeemed by Christ, so even the redemption of Christ would not have profited us unless that redemption were conveyed unto us through our regeneration into His body. This regeneration is our second birth of which Christ said to Nicodemus: "Amen, amen, I say to thee; unless a man be

(9) "Honor autem Deo subtractus per superbiam et inobedientiam respectu rei, ad quam homo astringitur, nullo modo melius restituitur quam per *humiliationem* et *obedientiam* ad eam rem, ad quam nullatenus tenebatur. Quoniam ergo Christus Iesus in quantum Deus aequalis erat Patri *in forma Dei;* in quantum homo innocens nullatenus erat debitor mortis; dum *semetipsum exinanivit et factus est obediens usque ad mortem,* exsolvit Deo quae non rapuit per obsequium satisfactionis perfectae, et obtulit sacrificium suavitatis summae pro perfecta Dei placatione." *Ibid.,* IV, 9, 250a.

(10) "Similiter correspondet, secundum quod per virum et mulierem significatur *Christus* et *Ecclesia.* Ecclesia enim ex Christo formatur, dum de latere Christi dormientis in cruce profluxit sanguis et aqua, ex quibus in Sacramentis Ecclesiae redundavit efficacia, per quae Sacramenta fundatur Ecclesia; et sic *vir* respondet *Christo, dormitio* respondet *morti, ablatio costae apertioni lateris.*" *II Sent.,* d.18, a.1, q.1, concl., t.II, 443a. Cf. also St. Thomas, *Summa Theologica,* I, q.92, a.1.

(11) *De Unitate Ecclesiae,* 5. MPL 4. 518.

born again, he cannot see the kingdom of God. Nicodemus saith to him: How can a man be born when he is old? How can he enter a second time into his mother's womb and be born again? Jesus answered: Amen, amen, I say to thee, unless a man be born again of water and the Holy Ghost, he cannot enter into the kingdom of God. That which is born of the flesh is flesh: and that which is born of the Spirit is spirit" (John 3:3-6). "We form one body," says St. Paul, "for we have been baptized in one Spirit" (I Cor. 12:12). So close the joining of Christ, the Head, with His members and the Body, that all make one. "For you are all one in Christ Jesus" (Gal. 3:28).

Because of our incorporation into Christ, our prerogative as members of Christ, the Holy Trinity dwells within us, sanctifies us, and makes us sharers in the divine nature.[12] By appropriation, all the marvels done in us in the order of our sanctification are attributed to the Holy Spirit. This is because these marvels are pre-eminently works of divine charity and gifts of divine love. They bespeak, therefore, especially Him Who within the Trinity Itself proceeds by way of love, is substantial Love Itself, and is called "the Gift."[13] But only within the Mystical Body are we beneficiaries of this divine indwelling. The mission of the gift of any of the Persons of the Blessed Trinity comes not to us except under the title of sanctifying grace, the divine life of the soul.[14] The Holy Spirit Himself, the Gift and Giver par excellence, proceeds from the Father and the Son, Who became Incarnate and Who is our Head.

Without the Incarnation there would be no Mystical Body. When God so loved the world as to give His only Son, did He not in giving Him give all else besides? What the natural sonship of Christ as Man wrought in the highest degree in our Lord's Incarnation, effecting the union of the divine and human natures in the Person of the Eternal Son, was wrought in a lower degree, but in the same order, in the redemption of each individual. By the infusion of the three theological virtues, the image of the Ever-blessed Trinity is restored to the soul. Corresponding to the natural image of God in the soul—the trinity of the faculties in the unity of its essence—is the supernatural image, the trinity of the infused virtues—faith, hope and charity—in the unity of grace.[15] This divine likeness which grace confers upon the soul, St. Bonaventure calls the "imago recreationis," thus distinguishing it from the divine reflection which every soul naturally bears, namely, the

(12) "Et quoniam ad ipsum accedere est per fidem, vel per fidei Sacramentum; et fides Christi eadem est in praeteritis, praesentibus et futuris: ideo ratio influendi in Christo ponitur respectu omnium, tam praeteritorum quam praesentium quam etiam futurorum, in Christum credentium et in Christo renatorum, qui per fidem copulantur Christo et per gratiam influentem fiunt *membra Christi* et *templa Spiritus sancti*, ac per hoc *filii Dei Patris*, connexi ad invicem per indivisible vinculum caritatis." *Breviloquium*, IV,5, t.V, 246a.

(13) "Ratione ejus quod subest aliqua dona approprientur Filio, ut sapientia et intelligentia, aliqua Spiritui Sancto, ut caritas. Ratione vero donationis, omnia approprientur Spiritui Sancto . . . quia per ipsum tanquam per primum donum donantur alia." *I Sent.*, d.18, q.1, ad 2, t.I, 324b.

(14) "Rursus, quoniam qui fruitur Deo Deum habet; ideo cum gratia, quae sua deiformitate disponit ad Dei fruitionem, datur donum increatum, quod est Spiritus sanctus, quod qui habet habet Deum." *Breviloquium*, V,1, t.V, 253a.

(15) "Consistit enim imago recreationis in tribus virtutibus theologicis et unitate gratiae, sicut imago creationis in tribus potentiis et unitate substantiae." *III Sent.*, 27, 1, t.III, 592.

"imago creationis."[16] The participation of the divine nature communicated to the soul by the gift of sanctifying grace constitutes the adopted sonship, on which rests the whole operation of the Christian, the whole merit of eternal life. In the individual, as we have seen, it is a "new creation"; in the mass it is entitled "the Body of Christ." By entrance into this state of adoption, all relative superiority or inferiority arising from nationality, color, race or sex disappears; for what are these to a creature renewed after the likeness of his Creator? "For you are all the children of God in Christ Jesus" (Gal. 3:26). So close the joining of Christ, the Head, with His members and the Body, that all make one. "For you are all one in Christ Jesus" (Gal. 3:28).

In the light of these facts, the truth of the admonition of Ecclesiasticus "to look upon all the works of the Most High two and two, and one against another," is self-evident. The first creation finds its counterpart in the second. The restoration of man by the personal action of God alone surpasses, or more truly may be said to complete, the idea of His original formation by the same personal action of the same Divine Word, Who, great as He is in creating, is greater still in redeeming, but is one in both, and in both carries out one original design. Through the continuing fathership of Adam, the Fathership of Christ appears as the completion of an original plan, devised before the foundation of the world, and actually carried out at the appointed time. Adam fashioned to the image and likeness of God on the sixth day of creation finds his counterpart in Christ born in the likness of man in the sixth period of time, the perfect number six symbolizing the fullness of time and the completion and perfection of the universe.[17] Just as the first man, the masterpiece of the material world, was fashioned on the sixth day, so it was fitting that the Second Man, Christ, the Restorer of the whole world Who united in His Person the First and the last, namely, "God and clay," should come toward the end of time, that is in the sixth age, which St. Bonaventure calls an age of grace or of the New Testament, an age suited for the exercise

(16) "Et quoniam qui hoc habet immediate ad Deum reducitur, sicut immediate ei conformatur; ideo donum illud immediate donatur a Deo tanquam a principio influxivo; ut, sicut immediate emanat a Deo Dei imago, sic immediate manet ab ipso Dei *similitudo* quae est divinae imaginis perfectio deiformis, et ideo dicitur *imago recreationis.*" *Breviloquium,* V.1, t.V, 252b, 253a.

(17) "Et hoc idem voluit per *senarium* dierum differre, ut in perfectione numeri simul ostenderetur perfectio universi." *II Sent.,* d.12, a.1, q.2, t.II, 297a.

Six is a perfect number, the first number which is the sum of its aliquot parts, i.e., of its sixth, third, and half. An aliquot part is a part which will exactly divide a number. *Four* is a part of *nine,* but not an aliquot part, but *one* is, for it is the ninth part; and *three* is, for it is the third part. Yet these two parts, the ninth and the third, or one and three, do not make the sum *nine*. Therefore *nine* is not a perfect number. In the words of St. Bonaventure: "Secundum enim arithmeticum *senarius* est numerus perfectus, quia constat ex omnibus suis partibus aliquotis, ita quod nec deficit nec excrescit. Partes autem *aliquotae* dicuntur, quae sumtae aliquoties reddunt totum." *Ibid.* Cf. St. Augustine, *De genesi ad litt.,* IV, 21, 38 ff. MPL 34, 311.

The three periods of time through which the world passes, namely, the time of the natural law, of the written law, and of the law of grace, are divided into seven ages. St. Bonaventure says: "Habet etiam haec Scriptura sacra *longitudinem,* quae consistit in descriptione tam *temporum* quam *aetatum,* a principio scilicet mundi usque ad diem iudicii. Describit autem per tria *tempora* mundum decurrere, scilicet per tempus legis *naturae,* legis *scriptae* et legis *gratiae,* et in his tribus temporibus septem distinguit *aetates*. Quarum prima est ab Adam usque ad Noe, secunda a Noe usque ad Abraham, tertia ab Abraham usque ad David, quarta a David usque ad transmigrationem Babylonis, quinta a transmigratione usque ad Christum, sexta a Christo usque ad finem mundi, septima decurrit cum sexta, quae incipit a quiete Christi in sepulchro, usque ad resurrectionem universalem, quando incipiet resurrectionis octava." *Breviloquium,* Prologus §2, t.V, 203b.

of wisdom and for a transition from a state of turmoil to peace.[18] And "when the fullness of time was come, God sent His Son, made of woman, and made under the law: that He might redeem them who were under the law; that we might receive the adoption of sons" (Gal. 4:4).

"The first man was of the earth, earthly; the second man from heaven, heavenly" (I Cor. 15:47). Over against the fathership which brought death and corruption and interminable ills of life, we see all the supernatural blessings of the new covenant, a triple dowry of adoption, betrothal, and consecration,[19]—man's inheritance as a spiritual race descending from the Second Adam. By the Incarnation, Christ became indissolubly united to the nature of man; by His sacramental union, He becomes united to our individual person, a union which occurs in the first instance through Baptism when we become "new creatures" and later through the Holy Eucharist by which "we live by Him." "O wonderful exchange! The Creator of the human race, assuming a human body, has deigned to be born of a virgin, and coming forth as man without a human father, has bestowed upon us His divinity" (Antiphon of the Feast of the Epiphany). Or as St. Augustine says in the second nocturn of the same feast: "God has become man, that man may become God; that man might eat the bread of angels, the Lord of the angels has today become man." In Jesus Christ, the second Adam, we behold human nature more wonderfully restored; and as He is our brother, the first-born among many brethren, we know that His glory is meant also for us, "that as sin hath reigned to death, so also grace might reign by justice unto life everlasting, through Jesus Christ our Lord" (Rom. 5:21).

Everything perfect travels in circles; the end of all things must in some way get back to its beginning. Our Saviour Himself set forth this fundamental principle: "I came forth from the Father, and I came into the world: again I leave the world and I go to the Father" (John 16:28). The soul that came from God must one day go back to God. Hence the Seraphic Doctor's recommendation to each of his students: "Sic dicat quilibet: 'Domine, exivi a te summo, venio ad te summum, et per te summum'."[20] The way is pointed out in an opening paragraph of the Saint's *Collationes in Hexaëmeron* which states that the "Verbum" is the "medium faciens scire, scilicet veritas."[21] As creatures went forth from God by the Word of God, so for a perfect return, it was necessary that the Mediator between God and man be not only

(18) "Hinc est, quod opus illud debuit fieri in *fine temporum*, ut sicut primus homo, qui erat totius mundi sensibilis ornamentum, ultimo fuerat conditus, scilicet sexto die ad totius mundi completionem: sic secundus homo, totius mundi reparati complementum, in quo primum principium coniungitur cum ultimo, scilicet 'Deus cum limo', fieret in fine temporum, hoc est in sexta aetate, quae est aetas apta ad exercitium sapientiae a statu turbinis ad quietem; quae omnia competunt sextae aetati decursus mundi propter incarnationem Filii Dei." *Ibid.*, IV,4, 244b, 245a.

(19) "Ipsa nihilominus est donum, per quod anima perficitur et efficitur sponsa Christi, filia Patris aeterni et templum Spiritus sancti;" *Ibid.*, V,1, 252a.

(20) Cf. *In Hexaëmeron,* I,17, t.V, 332.

(21) *Ibid.*

God but also man so that He might lead men back to God.[22] "For there is one God, and one mediator of God and men, the man Christ Jesus (I Tim. 2:5). In the Incarnation, the First Principle of all things was united to the last of creation; the human was joined with the divine; man, born in the fullness of time of a Virgin, was linked with the Eternal.[23] By taking flesh and dwelling among us, Christ has become the Center of the universe.[24] As the sun is the center of the macrocosm, the source of life and heat in the material world; as the heart is the center of the microcosm, the source from which the blood of life courses through the veins and arteries, so has the Son of God, in taking flesh and dwelling among us, become the very center of heaven and earth.[25] On His divinity rests the whole faith; on His Incarnation and death, the restoration of creation destroyed by the fall of man. He is the Light and Life of the soul.[26] He is the Mediator through whom the soul is united to God in this life[27] and the Source of its eternal happiness in heaven.[28] He is the Truth by which we arrive at Christian wisdom,[29] for in Him are contained all the treasures of wisdom and knowledge. As the Word and only-begotten Wisdom of the Father and as the God-Man, He is the source of all knowledge of God and of all salvation.[30] Whoever desires to return to the Father must return by and through Him, for through the Incarnate Word, the rational soul, in the manner of the circle is brought back to its Beginning in Whom it finds its perfection and its joy.[31] "Completus est circulus, completus est senarius, et propterea status."[32]

(22) "Sicut ergo res exierunt a Deo per Verbum Dei, sic ad completum reditum necesse est, Mediatorem *Dei et hominum* non tantum Deum esse, sed etiam hominem, ut homines reducat ad Deum." *De Reductione Artium ad Theologiam,* t.V, 325a.

(23) "Quod in ipso principium primum iunctum est cum postremo, Deus cum homine sexto die formato, aeternum iunctum est cum homine temporali, in plenitudine temporum de Virgine nato." *Itinerarium,* 6,5, t.V, 311b.

(24) "Incipiendum est a medio, quod est Christus." *In Hexaem.,* I, 10, t.V, 330.

(25) *In Hexaem.,* I, 19,20, t.V, 332.

(26) "Sicut ergo solus (Christus) eam (animam) proprie illuminat, sic eam solus proprie vivificat." *Dominica III Adventus,* Sermo XIV, t.IX, 73.

(27) "Postremo, quia est a primo principio, ut est reparativum reconciliando; et reconcilians est mediator, mediatio autem proprie convenit Dei Filio; ideo et incarnatio. Mediatoris namque est esse *medium* inter hominem et Deum ad reducendum hominem ad divinam *cognitionem,* ad divinam *conformitatem,* et ad divinam *filiationem.*" *Breviloquium,* IV,2, t.V, 242b, 243a.

(28) "Agnus Dei in media aquarum est Filius Dei, Filius dico, qui est media persona a qua omnis beatitudo." *In Hexaem.,* I, 38, t.V, 335.

(29) "Unde illud medium veritas est; . . . nec aliquo modo veritas sciri potest nisi per illam veritatem." *Ibid.,* I,13, t.V, 331b.

"Incipiendum est a medio, quod est Christus. . . . Unde ab illo incipiendum necessario, si quis vult venire ad sapientiam christianam." *Ibid.,* I,10, t.V, 330b.

(30) "Propositum igitur nostrum est ostendere, quod in Christo sunt omnes thesauri sapientiae et scientiae Dei absconditi, et ipse est medium omnium scientiarum." *Ibid.,* I,11, t.V, 331a.

(31) "Quasi ad modum circuli intelligibilis reducatur ad suum principium, in quo perficiatur et beatificetur." *Ibid.,* II,4, t.V, 221b.

(32) *De Reductione Artium ad Theologiam,* n.7, t.V, 321.

WOMAN IN CHRISTIAN MARRIAGE

Chapter I

CHRISTIAN MARRIAGE: ITS SYMBOLISM

CHRIST PROVED HIMSELF TO BE the central point in the history of mankind, and not least by the change His teaching effected in the position of woman. Society had altogether abandoned the high ideal which took concrete form in the Garden of Eden, and woman had fallen very low when the principles of the Church, primarily spiritual, were cast like a purifying element into the mass of corruption. It was the teaching of Christ that first brought freedom to the female sex, wherever this teaching was taken as the guide of life. In the society founded by Mary's Son woman takes equal rank with man, as a human being joint partaker with him of the promises made and the inheritance bequeathed. If man was to be a Christian, he was bound to regard woman in the light of Christ's teaching and example. She could no longer be a chattel, a slave, a beast of burden, an instrument of gratification, an inferior being. Possessed of an immortal soul made to the image and likeness of God, she could never be excluded from the dignity of having been created by the Eternal Father, redeemed by the Precious Blood of the Son, and made capable of a glorious sanctification in the Holy Spirit.

In his Epistle to the Galatians, St. Paul lays down the root principles of woman's freedom—a direct contradiction of the pagan teaching that woman is an inferior being. Aristotle, as we have seen, had described her as an incomplete version of man, and Plato wrote that "the souls of wicked men will be punished by passing, in the second generation, into the body of a woman, and in the third, into the body of an animal." But St. Paul says: "You are all the children of God . . . There is neither Jew nor Greek: there is neither bond nor free: there is neither male nor female. For you are all one in Christ Jesus" (3:26-28). This declaration of equal value puts us in touch with the special principle of Catholicity that woman's soul is of equal importance with man's.[1] Without Jesus Christ, the great lesson that before God there is no distinction of rich or poor, Jew or Gentile, bond or free, male or female, would be meaningless. He restored man to the sonship of God. "For you are all children of God by faith, in Christ Jesus. For as many of you as have been baptized in Christ, have put on Christ. And if you be Christ's then are you the seed of Abraham, heirs according to the promise" (*ibid.,* 26-29).

(1) Cf. *supra,* Part I, pp. 4-5.

Either through ignorance of the terminology of Sacred Scripture or through prejudice against woman, certain heretics point with confidence to passages of Sacred Scripture in which the use of the masculine noun or pronoun would seem to exclude woman from the heritage which is hers.[2] "He that believeth and is baptized shall be saved" (Mark 16:16). "Except a man be born again, he shall not see the kingdom of God (John 3:3). St. Bonaventure warns these men that: "The harlots shall go into the kingdom of God before you" (Matt. 21:31); that the Master received both sexes, healed both, and called both through His Apostles; that the Wise Solomon praised both sexes and of the valiant woman said: "And she shall laugh in the latter day."[3]

In his *De Civitate Dei,* St. Augustine took occasion to refute the heresy that women will not share in the resurrection.[4] And St. Bonaventure, quoting the passage on which the heresy is based, "Until we all meet into the unity of faith, and of the knowledge of the Son of God, unto a perfect man," shows that the words of St. Paul do not deny the resurrection of women but clearly proclaim it.[5] Since woman as well as man is according to nature's intention and, like man, was formed by God; since the two sexes form a composite and together constitute a complete human being, the male sex alone representing only half of humanity, and the female sex, the other half, it is clear that without the female sex, there can be no perfection of the species. The bodies of men and women alike shall rise from the dead, each sex preserving its own nature, all defilement removed. As men shall rise in the male sex, not for the propagation of the race, but for the perfection and glory of the elect; so women, in the female sex. As Christ rose, so shall all men rise with perfected growth in glory, their bodies freed from all dishonor and corruption, their members no longer inciting to lust but to the praise of God.[6]

These lofty ideas of Christianity, which apply without any difference to

---

(2) "Quod obiiciunt de Evangelio, quia in masculino; dicendum, quod confusum est illud masculinum et stat ibi pro natura, non pro sexu; et frequenter masculinum genus concipit femininum secundum morem Scripturae." *Comment. in Ecclesiasten,* C.VIII, t.VI, 64.

"Secundum hoc videtur confirmare haeresim illam, quod nulla mulier salvatur; et hoc nituntur probare haeretici.... Et hoc nituntur probare per illud quod dicitur Marci ultimo: *Qui crediderit et baptizatus fuerit;* non dicit: *quae baptizata fuerit.* Et id ipsum dicitur Ioannis tertio." *Ibid.*

(3) "Contrarium huius ostenditur: 1. Per illud quod dicitur Matthaei vigesimo primo: *Meretrices praecedent vos in regnum Dei.* 2. Item, hoc ostenditur, quia Dominus utrumque sexum recepit, utrumque sanavit corporaliter, utrumque vocavit per Apostolos. Ipse etiam Salomon utrumque laudavit, et de forti muliere Proverbiorum ultimo: *Ridebit in die novissimo." Ibid.*

(4) Lib. xiii C. 17, 18. MPL. 41. 389-391.

(5) "Respondeo: Dicendum, quod, sicut dicit Augustinus vigesimo secundo *de Civitate Dei,* aliqui voluerunt dicere, quod sexus femineus non resurget propter praedictam auctoritatem Apostoli: *Donec occurramus omnes in virum perfectum;* sed sicut ipse dicit ibi dicitur vir non a *sexu,* sed a *virtute,* non corporis, sed mentis, per quem modum mulier facta vir est, secundum quem modum dicitur in Psalmo: *Beatus vir, qui non abiit in consilio* etc.; quod intelligi etiam potest de muliere." *IV Sent.,* d.44, p.1, dub.2, t.IV, 917b, 918a.

(6) "Et ideo auctoritas ista non negat resurrectionem mulierum; sed manifesta ratio confirmat. Quoniam enim sexus femineus est naturalis et a Deo formatus, qui formavit virilem,—quod patet, quia sine ipso non esset perfectio speciei—et in corporibus nostris 'natura servabitur, et vitia detrahentur': sicut viri resurgent cum sexu virili, non propter generationem, sed propter perfectionem et decorem quantum ad electos, sic feminae in sexu femineo; quia tunc a membris illis dedecus et inhonestas per omnia auferetur, et quod excitat ad libidinem, excitabit ad Dei laudem." *Ibid.,* 918a. Here St. Bonaventure seems to be thinking of those properties named by St. Paul as belonging to a risen body. Cf. I Cor. 15:42-49.

woman as well as to man, were an energetic protest against the state of degradation in which one-half of the human race was placed and must have contributed, in an extraordinary manner, to the improvement of the lot of woman. Henceforth the philosophy which attempted to degrade her was silenced; that unblushing literature which treated woman with so much insolence found a check in the Christian precepts, and a reprimand no less eloquent than severe in the dignified manner in which all the ecclesiastical writers, in imitation of the Scriptures, express themselves on woman. The Christian doctrine, dissipating the repugnant fiction of her inferiority, made the existing prejudices against woman vanish forever; it made her equal to man by unity of origin and destiny, and in the participation of heavenly gifts; it enrolled her in the universal brotherhood of man, with his fellows and with Jesus Christ; it considered her as a child of God, the coheiress of Jesus Christ, as the companion of man, and no longer a slave and the vile instrument of pleasure. Once convinced of her high aim and mission, woman acquired a sense of appreciation of her own value, a sense of self-esteem and respect, which is at once the warrant and the measure of that which men would bear her. Thus ennobled in herself, how could she fail to be noble in her virginal purity, or in her special relations of wife and mother? In spite of the beneficent influence which the Christian doctrines of themselves exercised on man and woman, the desired end would not have been completely attained had not marriage, the primary relation of society, been restored.

Christians have ever been impressed with a deep-rooted conviction regarding the sacred character of marriage, and necessarily so, for it is a conviction based not only on reason but on the teaching of Christ Himself. We have seen that God Himself brought about the union of our first parents; that woman was formed to be the companion and helpmeet of man; that from the first, human marriage was not a civil contract, the work of man naturally yearning for society, not a mere pairing of sexes, but a partnership made under God's blessing, in which, according to His design, each should aid the other to serve Him and thereby attain eternal happiness.[7]

> "The Lord cast a deep sleep upon Adam: and when he was fast asleep, he took one of his ribs and made woman and brought her to Adam. And Adam said that she would be called woman, because she was taken out of man. *This now,* he said, *is bone of my bones and flesh of my flesh.* And the Lord said: *For this cause shall a man leave father and mother* and sons and daughters, *and shall cleave to his wife.* And the Apostle said: *This is a great sacrament, but I speak in Christ and in the Church.*[8]

(7) Cf. Gen. 2:23,24 and *supra,* Part I, pp. 25-26.

(8) "*Immisit Dominus soporem in Adam; cumque obdormisset tulit unam de costis eius* et fecit mulierem *et adduxit eam ad Adam.* Et dixit Adam, quod esset *virago, quia de viro sumta est. Hoc,* inquit, *os ex ossibus meis, et caro de carne mea.* Et dixit Dominus: *Propter hoc relinquet homo patrem et matrem* et filios et filias, et *adhaerebit uxori.* Et Apostolus dixit: Sacramentum hoc magnum est; ego autem dico, *in Christo et in Ecclesia.*" *De Donis Spiritus S.* Coll. VI, t.V, 487b. For the Scriptural text cf. Eph. 5:31,32.

In the sacred hour of creation on the hallowed spot of Eden was spoken the first human utterance recorded on the pages of Holy Writ. With prophetic vision into the unwritten future Adam proclaims the law for all his progeny. St. Matthew (19:5) ascribes the words of Adam to the Lord because, as St. Bonaventure explains, Adam had received a revelation from above during sleep and spoke under the inspiration of the Holy Ghost.[9] In these words prophetically spoken by God through Adam is contained the institution of the marriage union. God did not command Adam to take Eve as a wife but He enlightened his mind so that he would understand that she was to be given to him as a wife and that all his progeny might know that their wives are to be joined to them in the same way by free consent. Whereupon Adam thus enlightened by the Holy Ghost said: "This now is bone of my bones and flesh of my flesh," and, as Peter Lombard says, he spoke prophetically and the words which came from his lips were spoken not by him but by God Himself who on that occasion instituted the marriage union.[10] "And the Apostle said: *This is a great sacrament,* but I speak in Christ and in the Church" (Eph. 5:32). With these significant words, St. Paul writing under the inspiration of the Holy Spirit, proclaimed the God-given dignity of Christian marriage. "This is a great sacrament," comments St. Bonaventure; therefore, it was instituted not by man but by the Most High God.[11]

As a natural institution, then, marriage is as old as the human race, and as such the first to be blessed by Almighty God. For four thousand years it remained a mere contract between man and wife. In the present order of Providence, the marriage contract between baptized persons is a sacrament, under the superintendence of the Church, the fertile theme of canonists and theologians. Since marriage was in existence at the time of His coming, says St. Bonaventure, Christ did not institute it anew, but this marriage union already instituted in the Garden of Eden in which husband and wife should "cleave to each other" because they were "two in one flesh," Christ con-

(9) Cf. also Mark 10:7 and Gen. 2:24.
"Consonat nihilominus ratione *revelationis desuper datae.* Nam Adam prophetice dixit post soporationem: *Hoc nunc os ex ossibus meis et caro de carne mea. Quamobrem relinquet homo patrem suum et matrem et adhaerebit uxori suae, et erunt duo in carne una.* Hoc verbum dicitur *Deus* dixisse Matthaei decimo nono, quia Adam illud dixit divino Spiritu illustratus." *Quaestiones Disputatae.* Q.III. *De Continentia,* t.V, 168a.

(10) "Respondeo: Dicendum, quod institutio matrimonii est a Deo. Sed notandum, quod *quaedam* sunt Sacramenta, quae sunt pure fidei sicut baptismus et confirmatio et consimilia; *quaedam* autem non tantum sunt fidei, sed etiam naturalis dictaminis; et talia sunt poenitentia et matrimonium, sed tamen non *omnino* sunt de dictamine iuris naturalis. Quae primo modo sunt Deus instituit *mandando;* quae secundo modo instituit *interius illustrando;* et sic instituit matrimonium. Unde ipse non praecepit Adam, quod Evam duceret in uxorem, sed illustravit eum interius, ut intelligeret, eam sibi dandam in uxorem, et omnibus posteris per liberum consensum uxores illo modo coniungi. Unde Adam sic illustratus dixit: *Hoc nunc os* etc., et sicut dicit Magister in littera, prophetice est locutus; et ideo verbum illud non fuit a semetipso, sed a Deo: et ideo institutio huius Sacramenti fuit a Deo." *IV Sent.,* d.26, a.1, q.2, concl., t.IV, 664a.

(11) "Item, Sacramenta, quanto maiora sunt, tanto a maiore instituenda sunt; sed Sacramentum matrimonii est praecipue magnum, sicut dicitur ad Ephesios quinto: *Sacramentum hoc magnum est:* ergo a maximo Deo, non ab homine institutum fuit." *Ibid.,* 663.

summated and ratified in the New Law.[12] The exact occasion on which Our Lord elevated the purely natural marriage bond to the dignity of a sacrament, is not stated in Sacred Scripture. That He did so, however, is evident from the words of the Apostle in which the bond between husband and wife is compared to the sacred union existing between Christ and His Church. It is usually conceded, and the Seraphic Doctor intimates as much, that the sacrament was instituted at the marriage feast of Cana, which Christ honored by His Divine Presence and which He made memorable by the performance of His first miracle. In any event, His very presence at the nuptial rites was an indication of His approval of the marriage contract.[13]

Marriage, then, is a natural institution which Christ raised to the dignity of a sacrament, that it might typify and exemplify the union between Him, the Divine Bridegroom, and His Church, the Bride. Nor must we forget that in the special part from which woman was formed lay deeply veiled but fully intended the great sacrament which was to be unfolded only when the most astonishing and affecting of all events had taken place. To show her dependence and her dignity, and the love that should unite her to her spouse, woman was taken from the side of the sleeping man. She thus became an expressive figure of the Church.

Originally the marriage union was instituted as a duty binding upon the race; now, not only as a duty but also as a remedy against concupiscence.[14] The original marriage, and consequently marriage as it was conceived in the original plan of God before sin, was to be the means not merely of the natural propagation of the race, but also the means by which personal supernatural sanctity should be transmitted to the individual descendants of our first parents. It was, therefore, a great mystery, a sacrament, the Seraphic Doctor calls it, intended not only for the personal sanctification of those united by the marriage tie, but also for the sanctification of others, namely, their offspring. But this divinely ordered sanctity of marriage was destroyed by original sin and, instead of sanctity, the disease of concupiscence was transmitted to every child of Adam. And since the original state of man was one of close union with God by a pure and undivided love of Him alone, the remedy came through the union of the divine and the human natures joined

(12) "Postremo, quoniam, etsi Verbum incarnatum sit fons gratiae sacramentalis, *aliqua* tamen gratia sacramentalis fuit *ante incarnationem, aliqua* vero non nisi *post Spiritus sancti missionem, quaedam* autem *medio modo se habens;* hinc est, quod oportuit, Sacramenta institui *diversimode.* Nam *ante incarnationem* necessaria fuit et compunctio *poenitentialis* et generatio matrimonialis; ideo haec duo Sacramenta non de novo instituit, sed iam a se instituta et naturali dictamini quodam modo impressa consummavit et confirmavit in lege evangelica, dum poenitentiam praedicavit et nuptiis interfuit et legem coniugii approbavit, secundum quod colligitur ex diversis Evangelii locis." ***Breviloquium*** VI,4, t.V, 268b. Cf. John 2:1 ff. and Matt. 19:4 ff.

(13) "Item, Ioannis secundo: *Vocatus est Iesus et discipuli eius ad nuptias;* et consequenter ostendit, quod primum miraculum fecit ibi; sed si actus nuptialis non esset consonus legi Dei, Christus per sui ipsius praesentiam non approbasset." *Quaestiones Disputatae.* Q.III, a.1, t.V, 166.

"Instituit autem praedicta Sacramenta diversimode, quaedam scilicet ex eis *confirmando, approbando* et *consummando,* ut matrimonium et poenitentiam." *Breviloquium* VI,4, t.V, 268a.

(14) "Haec autem coniunctio non solum fuit post peccatum, verum etiam ante peccatum; sed prius fuit institutum Sacramentum coniugii in *officium,* nunc autem non solum in *officium,* verum etiam in *remedium* contra libidinis morbum; . . ." *Ibid.,* VI,13, t.V, 279a.

in one substance and person, a union realized by divine grace in every single individual soul. Hence it is that from the beginning God decreed that the propagation of the race should take place through the inseparable union of one man and one woman, which before the Fall symbolized the union of God and the individual soul, but after the Fall, the union of God and human nature as accomplished in the Incarnation of the Son of God, or the one and indissoluble union of Christ with His mystic spouse, the Church.[15]

The term marriage may be taken to denote the action, contract, or formality by which the conjugal union is formed or it may designate the union itself as an enduring condition. According to Catholic doctrine, the rite of marriage is a sacrament—an outward symbol to which Christ has attached a gift of inward grace. It is for this reason that the Church insists on the sacredness of marriage, bidding her children hold it in reverence, and view it not merely as a natural bond, but as a source of supernatural blessings. The matrimonial contract signifies the graces that flow from the union of Christ with His Church. This is true, however, only in the marriage of Christians. For them alone Matrimony has this signification, because for them alone Christ instituted the Sacrament of Matrimony. The marriage of those who are not Christians is a mere natural contract as it was before the coming of Christ; it is *res* not *sacramentum.*

It would be rash, of course, to infer from the Apostle's expression, "This is a great sacrament," that marriage was at that time a sacrament of the New Law in the strict sense, for not until a late period did the term *sacrament* acquire the exclusively technical meaning it has today; both in pre-Christian times and in the first centuries of the Christian era it had a much broader and more indefinite signification, as the Seraphic Doctor explicitly testifies.[16] Considering the expression in relation to the preceding words, however, we are justified in the conclusion that it is to be taken in the strict sense of a sacrament of the New Law. The love of Christian spouses for each other should be modeled on the love existing between Christ and the Church, because Christian marriage, as a copy and token of the union of Christ with the Church, is a great mystery or sacrament.

In order to be a solemn, mysterious symbol of the union of Christ with the Church, which takes concrete form in the individual members of the

(15) "Quoniam ergo Verbum Dei in sua sapientia hominem fecit, sicut et congruum fuit, potentem *stare, cadere* et *surgere;* hinc est, quod genus humanum eo modo propagandum ordinavit, quod ex ipso modo propagandi haberet quod manuduceret ipsum ad *standum;* haberet etiam quod manuduceret ad remedium, sicut etiam in propagatione illa est aliquid per peccatum scilicet libido, quod traducit morbum. Et quia *status* hominis erat ex coniunctione ipsius animae ad Deum per amorem unitivum modo castissimo, singulari et individuo; *remedium* veniebat ex coniunctione divinae naturae et humanae in unitatem hypostasis et personae, unitatem, inquam, divina gratia introductam ut *singularem* et *individuam;* hinc est, quod Deus ab initio instituit, ut propagatio fieret per coniunctionem maris et feminae *individuam* et *singularem,* quae significaret *ante* peccatum coniunctionem Dei et animae, seu Dei et subcaelestis hierarchiae, *post* peccatum vero coniunctionem Dei et humanae naturae, seu Christi et Ecclesiae; et ideo utrobique est *Sacramentum,* scilicet *ante* et *post,* licet alio et alio modo, quantum ad *significationem* et *usum.*" *Ibid.,* 279b.

(16) *Ibid.*

Church, Christian marriage must efficaciously represent this union, not merely by signifying the supernatural life-union of Christ with the Church, but also by causing that union to be realized in the individual members; or, in other words, by conferring the supernatural life of grace. The first marriage between Adam and Eve in Paradise was a symbol of this union; in fact, merely as a symbol, it surpassed individual Christian marriages, inasmuch as it was an antecedent type, whereas individual Christian marriages are subsequent representations. There would be no reason, therefore, why the Apostle should refer with such emphasis to Christian marriage as so *great* a sacrament, if the greatness of Christian marriage did not lie in the fact that it is not a mere sign, but an efficacious one, a sacrament in the true sense of the word.

St. Bonaventure defines a sacrament as a sensible sign, a remedy, as it were, instituted by Christ, in which under the covering of sensible things the divine power operates secretly, conferring some spiritual grace by which the soul is cured of the infirmity of sin.[17] St. Paul (Gal. 4:9) emphasizes the difference between the Old and the New Testament, when he calls the religious rites of the former "weak and needy elements" which could not of themselves confer true sanctity, the effect of true justice and sanctity being reserved for the New Testament and its religious rites. If, therefore, he terms Christian marriage, as a religious act, a great sacrament, he means not to reduce it to the low level of the Old Testament rites, but rather to show its importance as a sign of the life of grace and, like the other sacraments, an efficacious sign.[18] Though St. Paul does not speak of marriage as a true sacrament in clear and explicit terms, the doctrine is implied in his words and is easily deduced therefrom.

Many of the leading scholastics spoke of marriage as a remedy against sensuality, as is evidenced in the writings of Peter Lombard and his most distinguished commentators, St. Thomas Aquinas and St. Bonaventure. This aspect of the sacrament, however, does not exclude the conferring of sanctifying grace *ex opere operato,* but, on the contrary, recognizes it as the foundation of that actual grace, and as the root from which springs the right to

(17) "De origine igitur Sacramentorum hoc tenendum est, quod Sacramenta sunt signa sensibilia, divinitus instituta tanquam medicamenta, in quibus 'sub tegumento rerum sensibilium divina virtus secretius operatur'; ita quod ipsa 'ex *similitudine* repraesentant, ex *institutione* significant, ex *sanctificatione* conferunt aliquam spiritualem gratiam', per quam anima curatur ab infirmitatibus vitiorum, et ad hoc principaliter ordinantur tanquam ad finem ultimum." ***Breviloquium*** **VI,1, t.V, 265a.**

(18) "Quoniam ergo signa sensibilia, quantum est de se, non habent efficacem ordinationem ad gratiam licet habeant longinquam *repraesentationem* de sui natura; hinc est, quod oportuit, quod ab auctore gratiae *instituerentur* ad *significandum* et *benedicerentur ad sanctificandum:* ut sic essent ex naturali similitudine *repraesentantia,* ex adiuncta institutione *significantia,* ex superaddita benedictione *sanctificantia* et ad gratiam praeparantia, per quam sanetur et curetur anima nostra." *Ibid.,* 265b.

"Et quia 'denominatio fit a forma et a fine': hinc est, quod dicuntur Sacramenta, quasi medicamenta sanctificantia. Per haec enim anima a foeditate vitiorum reducitur ad sanctificationem perfectam. Et ideo, licet sint corporalia et sensibilia, sunt tamen veneranda tanquam sancta, quia sacra significant mysteria, ad sacra praeparant charismata, a sacratissimo Deo data, sacra institutione et benedictione divinitus consecrata, ad cultum sacratissimum Dei in sacra Ecclesia constituta, ita ut merito dici debeant *Sacramenta.*" *Ibid.,* 266a.

receive the divine assistance as occasion requires. This teaching of these great theologians is evident partly from their explicit declarations concerning the sacrament of marriage, and partly from what they defined as the essential element of the Sacraments of the New Law in general.[19] St. Augustine is of the same opinion. Though he fails to state explicitly that marriage carries with it a special gift of grace, the whole scope of his teaching calls for this interpretation as its logical conclusion.[20] Marriage, he assures us, is the divinely appointed remedy for human concupiscence, but, as the great theologians of later ages pointed out, this check on human passion is possible only through the succor which grace affords.

(19) For the doctrine of St. Bonaventure cf. *Breviloquium* VI,3, t.V, 267b; *ibid.*, VI,13, t.V, 279b; *IV Sent.* d.26, a.2, q.2 and d.31, a.2, q.1, in corp. For the views of St. Thomas cf. *Summa Theol.*, II,2, q.108, a.2.

(20) Cf. B. Alves Pereira, O.F.M., *La Doctrine du Mariage selon Saint Augustin,* (Paris, 1930), pp. 192-222.

Chapter II

ITS NATURE AND THREEFOLD PURPOSE

MARRIAGE, according to Peter Lombard, is *the marital union of a man and woman involving their living together in undivided partnership.*[1] Commenting on the Lombard's definition, the Seraphic Doctor says that it is a definition of marriage in its perfect or consummated state; that, though the definition covers the essential elements, he would like to make it clear that marriage is a *legitimate* contract to be entered into only by those who have a right to marry, for, even between persons who are free to marry each other, there are impediments which would render the contract illegitimate.[2] These impediments the Saint enumerates in hexameters.[3] Therefore, since the sacramentality of the marriage between baptized Christians always depends on its legitimacy and since the validity of the one is conditioned by the validity of the other, the Seraphic Doctor prefers to enlarge upon the Master's definition by the insertion of the word "legitima." His definition then reads: "Matrimony is the legitimate union of a man and woman involving their living together in undivided partnership."[4] The definition of the Lombard, however, continues the Saint, embraces the four causes, namely, the *formal* cause as expressed by the words "the marital union"; the *efficient* cause, by the words "of a man and woman," who give their consent; *the material* cause, by the implied words "inter legitimas personas," the addition of which St. Bonaventure suggests for the clarity of the definition; and the *final* cause as expressed by the words "involving their living together in undivided partnership," wherein is found the blessing of the Sacrament, which is the principal blessing or good of Matrimony.[5]

(1) "Matrimonium est coniunctio maritalis maris et feminae 'individuam vitae consuetudinem retinens'." *IV Sent.*, d.27, a.3, q.1, f.3, t.IV, 681.

(2) "Ista autem definitio: *Matrimonium est maris et feminae coniunctio maritalis,* sufficiens est quantum ad esse definiti, et tangitur ibi *genus* et *differentia.* Sed quoniam maritalis coniunctio duo implicat in se, scilicet legitimitatem personarum et indivisionem personarum; ideo ad maiorem eruditionem superadditur aliud, scilicet *inter legitimas personas* etc.; et non est de *esse* definitionis, sed explicatio primi membri." *Ibid.*, dub.I, 684a.

(3) "Huius autem Sacramenti sunt . . . duodecim *impedimenta,* quae impediunt contrahendum et dirimunt iam contractum, quae in his versibus continentur:

Error, conditio, votum, cognatio, crimen,
Cultus disparitas, vis, ordo, ligamen, honestas;
Si sis affinis, si forte coire nequibus;
Haec socianda vetant coniugia, iuncta retractant."

Breviloquium VI,13, t.V, 279a.

(4) "De Sacramento *matrimonii* hoc in summa tenenda est, quod 'matrimonium est coniunctio legitima maris et feminae, individuam vitae consuetudinem retinens'." *Ibid.*

(5) "Posset tamen dici, quod notetur ibi quadruplex genus causae, scilicet *formalis,* in hoc quod dicitur: coniunctio maritalis; *efficiens,* in hoc quod dicitur: viri et mulieris, quae, in quantum consentiunt, se habent in ratione causae efficientis, *materialis,* in hoc quod dicitur: inter legitimas personas; finalis, in hoc quod dicitur: individuam vitae etc., ubi tangitur bonum Sacramenti, quod est principale bonum matrimonium. Et per hoc patent obiecta, quia non est *superfluitas* nec *falsitas,* quia non est indivisio quantum ad coniunctum, sed quantum ad Sacramentum." *IV Sent.*, d.27, dub.1, t.IV, 684ab.

The definition, then, comprises three essential elements:

a) Marriage is a legitimate contract.

b) Every true marriage is essentially a *maritalis coniunctio,* that is, a union of a man and woman entered into for the physical purpose of begetting and rearing children,—an object which differentiates marriage from every other kind of legitimate union between human beings.

c) Marriage takes place between rational beings, and hence the conjugal union is crowned and ennobled by a spiritual companionship, "individua vitae consuetudo," the principal blessing and advantage of marriage,[6] which implies the two essential attributes of Matrimony, namely, unity and indissolubility.

The marital union, continues the Seraphic Doctor, is *effected* by the free and deliberate consent of the parties concerned; it is *consummated* by the union of the sexes.[7] Once the consent is given between a man and a woman whose union is not barred by any impediment,[8] the contract is made and, if the parties are baptized persons, the Sacrament of Matrimony is received. Save in so far as the Church may have seen fit to lay down certain conditions under which the consent must be given, nothing else is needed than that the two parties should thus plight their troth. The consummation of the marriage is, however, required to give to the union the highest degree of firmness. No earthly power, not even that of the Church herself, can dissolve a consummated marriage between two baptized Christians.[9] Only the one, holy, and perpetual Spouse of Christ can uphold the nuptial bond, of which she bears the mystery in herself.

The sacrament of marriage confers certain rights, the exercise of which, according to Hugh of St. Victor, contains a distinct symbolism. This twofold symbolism of marriage, St. Bonaventure accepts and makes his own.[10] Inasmuch as there are two elements in marriage, namely, consent of minds and union of bodies: the former of the two symbolizing the charity which unites God to the justified soul, of which the Apostle says, *He who is joined to the Lord is one spirit:* whereas the latter signifies the corporal union of

(6) *Ibid.*

(7) "*Introducitur* autem haec coniunctio in esse per liberum consensum animorum ex parte utriusque personae, exterius expressum in aliquo signo sensibili, *consummari* autem habet in copula carnali." *Breviloquium* VI,13, t.V, 279a.

(8) Cf. *supra,* p. 87, footnote 3.

(9) "Sed nunquam debet nec potest matrimonium, quod legitime introductum est, annullare, quia *quos Deus coniunxit* non potest *homo,* quantumcumque sit magnae potentiae, *separare,* cum ipsius Dei iudicio iudicandi remaneant universi." *Breviloquium* VI,13, t.V, 280b.

(10) "Conjugium, ut dignum est, sacramentum est illius societatis quae in spiritu est inter Deum et animam. Officium vero conjugii sacramentum est illius societatis quae in carne est inter Christum et Ecclesiam. Hoc est sacramentum, quod ait Apostolus, magnum in Christo et Ecclesia, ad quod sacramentum pertinere non potest mulier cum qua noscitur non fuisse carnale commercium. Potest tamen pertinere ad aliud sacramentum non magnum in Christo et Ecclesia, sed majus in Deo et anima . . . et forte, ut expressius dicatur, ipsa societas et quae exterius in conjugio pacto foederis servatur, sacramentum est, et ipsius sacramenti res et dilectio mutua animorum, quae ad invicem in societatis et foederis vinculo custoditur. Et haec ipsa rursus dilectio qua masculus et femina in sanctitate conjugii animis uniuntur sacramentum est, et signum illius dilectionis qua Deus rationali animae intus per infusionem gratiae suae et Spiritus sui participationem conjungitur." *De Sacramentis,* lib.ii, p.xi, c.3. MPL 176.482.

Christ and the Church, which consists in (His assumption of) flesh, regarding which the Evangelist testifies, saying, *The Word was made flesh, and dwelt among us;* it follows that the marriage which is not consummated by physical union, cannot claim to represent those espousals which Christ contracted with His Church by the mystery of the Incarnation, as St. Paul teaches, where, explaining the words of our first father Adam, *This is now bone of my bone and flesh of my flesh, and for this cause shall a man leave his father and mother, and shall cleave to his wife, and they shall be two in one flesh:* he forthwith adds: *but this I say is a great sacrament in Christ and the Church.*[11] Only of a properly consummated Christian marriage can it be said in the full sense of the phrase that husband and wife are "two in one flesh," (Gen. 2:24) and that their union is a perfect symbol of Christ's mystic union with His Church, consummated by the Incarnation. The striking point in the mystical signification of marriage is the fact that the union of man and wife which St. Paul views on such a lofty plane is not merely the moral union which arises from living the same life and sharing the self-same ideals and interests. The union which fully and perfectly reflects the oneness of Christ and His Church is that very union which is so little appreciated and so grossly misunderstood by those who have no faith.[12] Surely, as St. Paul concludes in wonderment, "This is a great sacrament."

In this great Sacrament of the New Law, husband and wife give each other the most perfect gift within the reach of their human powers, the complete gifts of self. So perfectly do they give themselves to each other, that, as St. Paul points out to the Corinthians, "The wife hath not power over her own body, but the husband. And in like manner the husband also hath not power over his own body, but the wife" (I Cor. 7:3). This physical union is only the consummation of the outward expression of that noble love which unites all the best moral and spiritual qualities of man and wife. Stripped of this significance, the physical union is nothing short of desecration. As God's love is the creative principle of the universe, so God willed that the love of man and woman should be the creative principle of the family. This power of human beings to beget one of their likeness is something like God's creative power by which He made us to His image and likeness.

In this exalted idea of marriage which had once been established by the Creator, then spoiled by unruly human passions, and lastly re-established

(11) Eph. 5:31,32.

(12) "Quia vero consensus ut de futuro non est proprie consensus, sed ipsius promissio; consensus vero ante commixtionem non facit plenariam unionem, quia nondum sunt *una caro:* hinc est, quod per verba de futuro dicitur matrimonium esse *initiatum,* de praesenti *confirmatum,* sed in carnalis *consummatum,* quia tunc sunt *una caro* et *unum corpus* fiunt; ac per hoc plene significat unionem illam, quae est inter nos et Christum. Tunc enim plene traducitur corpus unius in corpus alterius secundum sui comparis potestatem ad procreandam prolem." *Breviloquium* VI,13, t.V, 280a.

and ennobled by the Man-God, there is nothing sordid, shameful, or disgraceful. How can it be sordid for man and woman to exercise those rights which the Creator has conferred upon them? We dare not call it shameful for those joined in holy wedlock to realize the physical purpose for which God brought them together. It is certainly anything but disgraceful for human beings to avail themselves of the sacred privileges of that state of life in which Divine Wisdom has willed that by far the majority of the human race should find its way to heaven.

In bringing out this point, St. Bonaventure quotes from St. Paul's Epistle to Timothy (I Tim. 4:3-5), in which he warns him against the Gnostics, the Manichaeans, and other ancient heretics: "Forbidding to marry, to abstain from meats, which God hath created to be received with thanksgiving by the faithful, and by them that have known the truth. For every creature of God is good, and nothing to be rejected that is received with thanksgiving: for it is sanctified by the word of God and prayer."[13] St. Bonaventure then supplements the words of St. Paul to Titus: "All things are clean to the clean" (Tit. 1:15), with the words of St. Augustine: "Imperfectionem non facit Dei creatura, sed mens infirma et nesciens uti ea; ideo magis ei competit abstinentia quam perfectae menti."[14] This is a rather forceful argument, says the Seraphic Doctor, for temporal goods are creatures of God, and woman was formed by God and what is more, marriage is a Sacrament of the Lord, and freedom of one's will is a divine gift. These creatures of God are not a source of evil; they are, in fact, holy instruments in the hands of those who know how to use them.[15] The hunger of sex, then, not less than the hunger for food, is of divine origin; the former being designed to secure the conservation of the race; the latter, that of the individual. Both are natural, wholesome, and inescapable. Since they have been implanted by God, they are sacred as well.[16] It is only when the function is isolated from the personality and separated from its purpose that it assumes a position out of proportion to its proper place. When exercised in accordance with God's plan in the holy institution of marriage, it acquires a high nobility.[17] It is the unique glory of love that in giving, the donor loses nothing, but is

(13) "Sane, quia studium esse consuevit errantium testimoniis veritatis perverse intellectis adversus ipsam veritatem confligere; ideo consequenter munire se nititur auctoritate Scripturarum, primo allegans illud Apostoli: Omnis creatura Dei bona." *Opusculum XI. Apologia Pauperum,* c.5, t.VIII, 261a.

(14) *Ibid.*

(15) "Hoc si verum est, et huiusmodi ratio aliquid roboris habet; cum bona temporalia sint creaturae Dei, et mulier formata a Deo, et coniugium, quod plus est, sit Domini Sacramentum, et libertas propriae voluntatis sit donum divinum; nihil horum ad imperfectionem facit, magisque competunt haec perfectis quam imperfectis, tanquam melius scientibus uti." *Ibid.*

(16) "Item, quod est cibus ad conservationem individui, hoc est concubitus ad conservationem speciei; sed moderatus usus cibi est virtutis, ut sobrietatis: ergo et moderatus concubitus est virtutis, scilicet castitatis: ergo est consonus legi Dei." *Quaestiones Disputatae.* Quaestio III, *De Continentia,* art.1, t.V, 167a.

(17) "Omne illud, quod consonat evangelicis Sacramentis, est bonum et laudabile; sed continentia coniugalis est huiusmodi: ergo est bona et laudabilis. *Maior* patet; *minor* probatur; ad Ephesios quinto: *Sacramentum hoc magnum est etc.:* ergo continentia coniugalis est consona legi Dei." *Ibid.,* 166b.

himself enriched. Whatever the Christian does in the state of grace, provided it is not evil in itself and is done with a good intention, is an act of virtue and brings him closer to the realization of his heavenly ideal.[18] In married life, which is the path most people will follow to reach heaven, there is nothing better, nothing holier, nothing more sacred than the act whereby husband and wife become the instruments of God for the spread of His Kingdom through the multiplication of children.[19] Without doubt, says the Seraphic Doctor, conjugal chastity is commendable and in accordance with the law of God, not only today or tomorrow, but it has been so from the very beginning of the world and will so continue till the number of the elect will be complete.[20]

St. Bonaventure goes on to say that conjugal chastity itself as well as its act and its exercise is in accord with the law of *nature,* with the law of *Sacred Scripture,* and with the law of *grace.*[21] Its conformity to the *natural* law is evident from the *complementary nature of the sexes:* "God created man to His own image and likeness; male and female He made them" (Gen. 1:27); it is evident, secondly, from the *precept given to Adam,* and subsequently to Noah and his sons that the earth might be peopled: "And God blessed them saying: Increase and multiply and fill the earth," (Gen. 1:28),—a precept possible of lawful fulfillment only through the exercise of conjugal chastity. That conjugal chastity is in conformity with the natural law is evident, thirdly, from *the revelation given to Adam* during his sleep, as recorded by St. Matthew (19:4-6), whereupon, enlightened by the Holy Ghost, he exclaimed: "This is now bone of my bone, and flesh of my flesh. Wherefore a man shall leave father and mother, and shall cleave unto his wife: and they shall be two in one flesh" (Gen. 2:23, 24). According to the first proof, the union of man and woman is *natural;* according to the second, it is *moral;* according to the third, it is *sacramental,* and this whole teaching is in accordance with the precept of the natural law upon which the act and the exercise of conjugal chastity are based.[22]

(18) "Item, quod consonat *naturali dictamini* et ex ratione procedit est opus virtutis; 'virtus enim est habitus in modum naturae rationi consentaneus'; sed continentia coniugalis consonat naturali dictamini et ex ratione procedit: ergo etc." *Ibid.,* 166b, 167a.

(19) "Item quod consonat bono *naturali et communi* consonat legi Dei; sed actus coniugalis est huiusmodi, quia est ad hominum multiplicationem seu speciei conservationem: ergo etc." *Ibid.,* 167a.

(20) "Respondeo: Dicendum, quod absque dubio pudicitia coniugalis approbabilis est et consona legi Dei, non solum secundum statum praesentis temporis aut futuri, verum etiam a principio mundi usque ad finem praesentis saeculi, quousque electorum numerus compleatur." *Ibid.,* 167b, 168a.

(21) "Ad cuius intelligentiam notandum, quod ipsa pudicitia coniugalis et ipsius actus et usus consonat legi *naturae* et legi *Scripturae* et legi *gratiae.*" *Ibid.* 168a.

(22) "Legi *naturae* consonat ratione ipsius *naturae conditae,* ratione *praeceptionis superadditae,* ratione *revelationis desuper ostensae.* Consonat, inquam, ipsi legi naturae ratione *naturae conditae,* quae formata fuit in sexuum distinctione, secundum illud Genesis primo: *Creavit Deus hominem ad imaginem et similitudinem suam, masculum et feminam creavit eos.* Consonat etiam ratione *praeceptionis superadditae,* adhuc lege naturae manente, secundum illud Genesis primo: *Benedixit illis Deus et ait: Crescite et multiplicamini et replete terram;* quod quidem non fit legitime nisi per usum pudicitiae coniugalis. Consonat nihilominus ratione *revelationis desuper datae.* Nam Adam prophetice dixit post soporationem: *Hoc nunc os ex ossibus meis et caro de carne mea. Quamobrem relinquet homo patrem suum et matrem et adhaerebit uxori suae, et erunt duo in carne una.* Hoc verbum dicitur *Deus* dixisse Matthaei decimo nono, quia Adam illud dixit divino Spiritu illustratus. Ex primo horum coniunctio viri et mulieris est *naturalis,* ex secundo est *moralis,* ex tertio est *sacramentalis;* et hoc totum sibi competit secundum statum legis naturae: ex quo primo originem trahit actus et usus ipsius pudicitiae coniugalis." *Ibid.*

Conjugal chastity is likewise in accord with the *written* law or the law of Scripture as revealed in God's *promise,* in His *miracle,* and in His *statute.* First, in His *promise,* for the Lord promised Abraham: "Thou shalt be a father of many nations; and I will make thee increase exceedingly, and I will make nations of thee, and kings shall come out of thee" (Gen. 17:4-6); secondly, in His *miracle,* according to the words of Genesis: "And the Lord visited Sara, as He had promised, and fulfilled what He had spoken. And she conceived and bore a son in her old age, at the time that God had foretold her" (21:1, 2); thirdly, in the *statute* of God regarding the legitimacy of the contracting parties, for He said: "I am the Lord your God. Keep my laws and my judgments, which if a man do, he shall live in them. No man shall approach to her that is near of kin to him" (Lev. 18:2, 5, 6). Since God promised the blessing of children to Abraham through the marriage union, since by a miracle He made fruitful the sterile womb of Sara, since He gave laws governing the marriage contract, it is evident that conjugal chastity is in accord with the *written* law, or the law of Sacred Scripture.[23]

Conjugal chastity is no less in accord with the law of *grace,* as is evident from the *angel's announcement:* "Fear not, Zachary, for thy prayer is heard; and thy wife Elizabeth shall bear thee a son" (Luke 1:13). This favor Zachary had merited by devout prayer and a holy life according to the law of chaste wedlock, for "both were just before God, walking in all the commandments and justifications of the Lord without blame" (Luke 1:6). Chaste wedlock, secondly, has the *approval of Christ,* as is indicated not only by His presence at the wedding of Cana but also by the stern admonition addressed to the Pharisees: "What therefore God hath joined together, let no man put asunder" (Matt. 19:6). Thirdly, chaste wedlock is in accord with the *teaching of the Apostles,* for both Peter and Paul, the chief organizers of the Church, commend marriage and the law and fidelity of the marriage bond and the payment of the debt and the mutual love of husband and wife.[24]

---

(23) "Consonat etiam legi *scriptae* ratione divini *promissi,* divini *miraculi* et divini *statuti.* Ratione divini *promissi:* quia Dominus promisit Abrahae, Genesis decimo septimo: *Eris pater multarum gentium; faciamque te crescere vehementissime, et ponam te in gentibus, regesque ex te egredientur.* Ratione divini *miraculi,* secundum illud Genesis vigesimo primo: *Visitavit Dominus Saram, sicut promiserat, et implevit quae locutus est, concepitque et peperit filium in senectute sua eo tempore, quo praedixerat ei Deus.* Consonat etiam ratione divini *statuti,* Levitici decimo octavo. Nam leges statuit Dominus, secundum quas attenditur legitimitas in personis, quae contrahunt. Ait enim: *Ego Dominus Deus vester; custodite leges meas atque iudicia, quae faciens homo, vivet in eis. Omnis homo ad proximam sanguinis sui non accedat* etc. Ex quo igitur Dominus tanquam beneficium promisit, se daturum prolem Abrahae per viam coniugii, et emortuam vulvam Sarae mirabiliter fecundavit, leges etiam dedit, secundum quas matrimonium contrahendum est: patet, quod pudicitia coniugalis consonat legis *scriptae.*" *Ibid.,* 168ab.

(24) "Consonat etiam nihilominus legi *gratiae,* primo quidem ratione *denunciationis angelicae,* secundum illud Lucae primo: *Ne timeas, Zacharia, quoniam exaudita est oratio tua, et Elisabeth, uxor tua, pariet tibi filium;* hoc autem meruerat Zacharias per orationem devotam et per vitam sanctam in lege coniugii pudice servata; unde dicitur Lucae primo, quod *ambo erant iusti ante Dominum, incedentes in omnibus mandatis et iustificationibus Domini, sine querela.* Secundo ratione *definitionis dominicae,* non solum per *factum,* quo nuptiis interfuit, sed etiam per *verbum,* quo sententialiter definivit, Matthaei decimo nono; *Quos Deus coniunxit homo non separet.* Tertio etiam consonat ratione *eruditionis apostolicae.* Nam Petrus et Paulus, principales ordinatores Ecclesiae, utrique commendant et matrimonium et legem et fidem tori et solutionem debiti et amorem mutuum uxoris et viri." *Ibid.* 168b.

Since chaste wedlock is approved by the words of the Apostle, of the Evangelist, of the angel, and of Our Divine Lord Himself; since it is approved also by the natural law written on man's heart, by Sacred Scripture as stated in the law of Moses or the evangelical law, it is clear that it is in admirable harmony with the law of God and, accordingly, worthy of sanction. It is hard to understand, says the Seraphic Doctor, how the senseless perfidy of heretics can condemn chaste wedlock, especially when it has been approved by so many irrefragable arguments. The doctrine that marriage is evil is, as St. Augustine says, the teaching not of the Christians but of the Manichaeans.[25] It is only when the malice of men disrupts the established order, robs a divine institution of its divine significance and clothes it with an utterly false meaning, that the use of marriage becomes evil and degrading.[26] When the husband, who according to St. Paul is "head of the wife, as Christ is the head of the Church" (Eph. 5:23), and the wife, who according to the same Scripture should be subject to her husband "as the Church is subject to Christ," so abuse the marriage act and degrade the union established for their mutual sanctification, they become occasions of sin to each other, and holy Matrimony is to them a sacrilege rather than a sacrament. The wife is no longer a figure of the Church but of the concupiscence of carnal pleasure.[27]

We have seen that an all-wise God through the creation of man, male and female, has laid the groundwork of the family and has made the conservation of the race dependent upon the cooperation of husband and wife in the divinely appointed mission of procreation. "Increase and multiply" is a law which God not only sounded in the ears of our first parents but which He also wrote on the fleshy tablet of man's heart. Thus God Himself is the Author of human society which He has established on the perfect law of marriage.

When we think of the physical expression as part of the whole pattern, we shall see that God has appointed that natural human act and that it is a part of His whole scheme for married happiness. It gives honor and glory to

(25) "Quoniam igitur coniugalis pudicitia approbatur et *ore apostolico* et *verbo evangelico* et *ore angelico* et *ore divino;* approbatur etiam a *natura,* quae est lex indita, et a *Scriptura* seu lege Moysaica et a lege evangelica; manifestum est, quod ipsa legi divinae consonat et secundum eam est approbanda. Et mirum est, quomodo haereticorum perfidia ita insanit, ut, coniugalem pudicitiam reprobet tot irrefragabilibus testimoniis approbatam. Unde Augustinus, de Ecclesiasticis Dogmatibus: 'Malas dicere nuptias, aut fornicationi comparandas, aut stupris, et cibos credere malos, non hoc Christianorum, sed Manichaeorum est'." *Ibid.*

(26) "Si vero quis habeat oculum ad morbum, hoc est ad concupiscentiam satiandam; aut aliquo modo respicit remedium, vel officium, et tunc non est actus virtutis, sed vitium veniale, quia excusatur per matrimonii Sacramentum; aut nullo modo habet oculum nisi ad satiandam concupiscentiae appetitum, quo tanto impetu fertur, quod etiam si non esset uxor, cognosceret eam; et tunc, quia actus ille pervertit matrimonii legem, non est actus pudicitiae consonans, sed repugnans. *Ibid.,* 169a.

(27) "Et nota hic, quod licet uxor licite habeatur, tamen propter abusum et propter vitium coniunctum per *rem bonam* intelligitur *malum.* Propter quod et Apostolus dicit primae ad Corinthios septimo: 'Reliquum est, ut qui habent uxores sint tanquam non habentes'; sicut et Glossa dicit, quod 'multi non propter fecunditatem, sed propter desideria carnis uxores ducunt. Ideo per rem istam carnalis voluptas designatur'; unde non est inconveniens, quod uxor ratione vinculi sacramentalis designat Ecclesiam, sponsam Christi, et ratione libidinis designare possit concupiscentiam carnalis voluptatis." *Comment. in Evangelium Lucae* C.XIV, t.VII, 373.

Himself; it gives husband and wife a share in the work of creation; it increases the mutual love of husband and wife in its completing of their unity; and it should raise their hearts to God in thanksgiving for His goodness.

In ministering to the sacrificial labors of child-bearing and child-rearing, the conjugal relation brings into play the physical and spiritual elements which constitute the deepest and most satisfying qualities of human love. Since the act is in conformity with the moral law and thus pleasing to the conscience of the individual, it involves an intimate participation of the soul, effecting a tremendous deepening of human love, intensifying its unity and strengthening its permanence as can no other action. To regard wedded love as exclusively an objective means to the union of wedlock, and the latter in turn as a means of procreation, would be to subordinate entirely man as a human being to man as an animal, looking upon him as essentially a physical organism. The physical union of man and woman in this sacrament is but the shadow of the spiritual union—that union of mind, and heart and purpose—that should exist between husband and wife, as the late Holy Father Pius XI said in his encyclical on Christian Marriage: "By Matrimony, therefore, the souls of the contracting parties are joined and knit together more directly and more intimately than their bodies; and that not by any passing affection or sense of spirit, but by a deliberate and firm act of the will; and from this union of souls, by God's decree, a sacred and inviolable bond arises."

"The primary purpose of this outward expression of love," says His Holiness, "is that man and wife help each other day by day in forming and perfecting themselves in the interior life, so that through their partnership in life they may advance ever more and more in virtue, and above all that they may grow in true love toward God and their neighbors." The Encyclical then proceeds to make clear the sense in which the end just mentioned is termed "the primary purpose" of the marriage relation. It states that the mutual good which the spouses can achieve by bringing out the best in each other's nature "may truly be called even the primary cause and reason of marriage, provided that marriage is understood, not in the narrower sense as an institution for the due begetting and rearing of children, but in the wider sense as an intimate communion, association and companionship in all life." This interpretation is in harmony with the thought of St. Bonaventure who regards the *individua vitae consuetudo,* spiritual companionship, as the final cause or purpose of the Sacrament.[28] Like Hugh of St. Victor, the Seraphic Doctor teaches that there may be marriage without consummation and where

(28) Cf. *supra*, p. 87.

"Ad aliud dicendum, quod *matrimonium* plus dicit quam *obligationem*. Unde dico, quod non sequitur: iste est obligatus isti mulieri, ut eam accipiat in uxorem: ergo est eius vir; sicut non sequitur: obligavit se ad persolvendum: ergo solvit. Unde matrimonium non tantum est obligatio, immo ipsius vinculi indissolubilis unio." *IV Sent.,* d.28, a. unicus, q.3, concl., 3, t.IV, 692b.

this is the case, the symbolism of Christ's union with the Church is wanting.[29] But marriage is likewise a symbol of the grace by which God espouses the soul to Himself; and it is in virtue of this symbolism that every Christian marriage is a sacrament. Marriage, as Hugh of St. Victor says, is an external sign representing the *dilectio mutua animorum* of the wedded pair; and this mutual affection symbolizes the love by which God and the soul are bound together when the latter is adorned with supernatural grace.[30] St. Bonaventure likewise describes the relations existing between Christ and the individual soul as typical of the relations which should exist between the bridegroom and the bride,[31]—a union "begun here in grace and consummated in glory."[32] These ideas about marriage come to us from one source, the Sacred Heart of Our Divine Lord, Who made marriage in a mysterious way the sign of His own love for us, than which nothing is more enduring and holy. This mystical signification of marriage carries with it unity and indissolubility.

First of all, unity. Marital unity is the only natural form of marriage and the only type that corresponds to the primitive marriage divinely instituted between Adam and Eve, of which it was said: "Wherefore a man shall leave father and mother, and shall cleave to his wife: and they shall be two in one flesh" (Gen. 2:24). In this first Scriptural reference to marriage, the idea of unity is clearly evident, and no plurality of wives or husbands is contemplated. According to God's holy will, the union is to be monogamous, that is, the union of one man with one woman as long as both parties shall live. This dictate of the natural law was the original intention of God, says St. Bonaventure, and if man had not fallen, the equal distribution of the two sexes would have prevented polygamy from becoming general.[33]

To be sure, after the Flood, the Mosaic Law permitted, and it is commonly taught that it was by temporary divine dispensation, a plurality of wives in order that the human race might be multiplied. With the advent of the

---

(29) Cf. *supra* p. 89, footnote 12.

(30) Cf. *supra* p. 88, footnote 10.

(31) "Quia enim omnes spiritus rationales immediate producuntur a Deo tanquam a primo principio et immediato; et Deus in eis requiescit et quasi soporatur, dum *deliciae suae sunt esse cum filiis hominum* (Prov. 8,31); et rationalis spiritus a divino spiritu inhabitante confortatur et roboratur; optima consonantia conformatur signum signato, secundum quod per virum et mulierem significatur *Deus* et *anima.*" *II Sent.*, d.18, a.1, q.1, concl., t.II, 432b, 433a.

(32) "Quae unitas inchoatur in via, sed consummatur in aeterna gloria, iuxta quod Dominus orat, *ut sint unum, sicut et nos unum sumus; et ego in eis, et tu in me, ut sint consummati in unum;* qua unitate consummata per vinculum caritatis, erit *Deus omnia in omnibus* aeternitate certa et pace perfecta, eruntque omnia per amorem communia communione ordinata et ordinatione connexa et connexione indissolubiliter alligata." *Breviloquium,* V,8, t.V, 262a.

(33) "Et illa multiplicatio ad omnes spectaret, et hoc solum secundum legem matrimonii, in qua tantum una erat unius; necesse est, si natura stetisset, tot fuisse mulieres, quot viros, cum nulla mulier careret viro, et nullus vir caperet uxore, nec una esset plurium, nec plures unius." *II Sent.*, d.20, a.1, q.6, concl., t.II, 485b.

"Et quoniam ratio dictaret, omnia facienda esse ordinata, et tot producere mulieres quot viros, ut quilibet vir haberet *adiutorium simile sibi* secundum exigentiam legis matrimonii; ideo tunc viros et mulieres produceret in numero aequali. Nunc autem, quia generativa non omnino subest virtuti animali, id est imaginariae, nec etiam rationali, licet ei aliquo modo conformetur, sed magis variatur penes dispositionem membri et exterioris adiutorii; hinc est, quod non est certa determinatio numeri nec in viris nec in feminis generandis; immo modo, quando credit generare masculum, generat feminam, et quando credit generare feminam, generat masculum; et aliqui plures habent feminas; et aliqui plures masculos. Sic ergo patet, quod si homo stetisset, in aequali numero fieret multiplicatio virorum et mulierum." *Ibid.*, 486b.

Christian dispensation, however, this relaxation of the divine law came to an end, probably because it had served its purpose; marriage was restored to its primitive unity and elevated to the dignity of a sacrament. Not only does a plurality of wives contradict the natural law, but because of the separations, the jealousies that would arise, it would seriously impair the mutual help, love and fidelity which should exist between husband and wife. Physical union there may be; but the moral union never could be realized. The wife assuredly will not give her whole heart to a husband who offers her but a share in his divided affections.[34] It is in the intensely exclusive character of conjugal love that St. Bonaventure finds an argument for monogamy. Neither man nor woman is content to receive a divided affection. In any case, if one believes Christian marriage to be a sacrament, a symbol of the union between Christ and His Church, one sees at once that a plurality of wives would utterly destroy the symbolism, for if Christ is one, the Church also is one. The Seraphic Doctor stresses the point that God is a jealous God and will not tolerate that the soul should hold anything as dear as Him; neither could the soul endure to be forsaken by God for others.[35]

The second attribute of Matrimony is that of indissolubility, or that element of permanence which gives the marriage bond force during the subsequent lifetime of the contracting parties and interprets literally their words when mutually pledging themselves in marriage "until death do us part." Wherefore it is the constant teaching of the Church that among Christians the bond of consummated marriage cannot be dissolved except by death. This is not only the doctrine of the Church but the law of God Himself Whose Spirit moved Adam, in speaking of his own union, the prototype of all future marriages, to declare: "Wherefore a man shall leave father and mother, and shall cleave to his wife: and they shall be two in one flesh" (Gen. 2:24). This positive law of God which made human marriage, from the first, indissoluble and monogamous was commonly recognized among Christians. Later, however, by the Mosaic Law, under certain conditions, the bond could be dissolved. That Christ restored the union to its primitive permanence is evident from the words of Our Lord to the Pharisees: "What therefore God hath joined together, let no man put asunder" (Matt. 19:6).

(34) "Pluribus uti uxoribus est contra ius naturae communiter et proprie sumtum. Respondeo: Dicendum, quod, sicut dictum est supra, illa distinctione praesupposita, si 'ius naturale dicatur quod in Lege et Evangelio scribitur'; sic ius naturale est, quod sit una unius. *Erunt,* inquit, *duo in carne una,* tam in veteri quam in novo. Si autem *ius naturale* dicatur quod ratio recta dictat; adhuc verum est, quia adhuc dictat natura, secundum quod rationis rectae est, quod non faciat alii quod sibi non vult fieri; sed vir non vult, quod uxor habeat alium virum: nec ergo debet velle habere aliam uxorem; cum in tali actu ut supra visum est, ad paria iudicentur et tanquam pares conveniant. Si dicatur *ius naturale* quod natura impressit animalibus; sic dicendum, quod *non omnibus,* sed aliquibus animalibus brutis impressit; sed tamen in natura est *aliquorum animalium* irrationalium, et in *nostra* natura plantavit." *IV Sent.,* d.33, a.1, q.2, concl., t.IV, 750a.

(35) "In matrimonio est quidam amor singularis in quo non communicat alienus; unde naturaliter vir zelat uxorem quantum ad hoc ut nullum diligat ut diligit ipsum in actu illo; et omnis uxor similiter zelat virum quantum ad hoc . . . Similiter, caritate adveniente, quae facit ut omnia sint communia, nunquam facit uxorem esse communem, propter privatum amorem qui debet esset in matrimonio, qui etiam est sacramentum illius amoris quo Deus zelat animam ut nolit aliquem tantum diligi: sic et anima a Deo nullo modo vult propter aliam deseri." *Ibid.,* 750ab.

The bond of Matrimony is by its very nature, says St. Bonaventure, indissoluble. Therefore, "he that shall marry her that is put away, committeth adultery," for the very evident reason that, regardless of apparent separation, she is the wife of him who had her first, as the Apostle St. Paul says to the Romans: "For the woman that hath a husband, while her husband liveth, is bound to the law. Therefore, while her husband liveth, she shall be called an adulteress, if she be with another man" (7:2, 3). And Jeremias, the prophet: "If a man put away his wife, and she go from him, and marry another man, shall he return to her any more? Shall not that woman be polluted and defiled?" (Jer. 3:1),[36] a reference, no doubt, to the Mosaic Law on divorce which read: "If a man take a wife, and have her, and she find not favor in his eyes, for some uncleanness: he shall write a bill of divorce, and shall give it in her hand, and send her out of his house. And when she is departed, and marrieth another husband, and he also hateth her, and hath given her a bill of divorce, and hath sent her out of his house or is dead: the former husband cannot take her again to wife: because she is defiled, and is become abominable before the Lord" (Deut. 29:1-4). Technically, divorce was always the husband's act. The Mosaic Law allowed the man to dismiss his partner, but accorded no such power to the woman, which discrimination against the female sex St. Bonaventure attributes to the low opinion in which woman was held during the time of the Mosaic dispensation. Both on account of her subordinate position, for "the woman was created for the man" (I Cor. 11:8), and on account of her heavier share in the first sin and curse: "And thou shalt be under thy husband's power" (Gen. 3:16), woman was not considered on equal terms with man.[37]

According to the Roman law a husband not merely could, but was bound to divorce an adulterous wife; the wife had no redress against an offending husband. In the man, loose morals were regarded as a minor offence; in the woman, as a cause of condemnation. Where moral questions were at issue, the teaching of Christ provided no double standard,—a fact which He impressed upon the Jews by making clear to them the original status of the law and noting the changes they had effected by civil enactments.[38] Christ re-

(36) "Et haec est quae dictat, quod 'matrimonium est maris et feminae coniunctio, individuam vitae retinens consuetudinem'; quae etiam dictat, quod illud est vinculum insolubile. Et ideo subdit: *Et qui dimissam a viro duxerit moechatur.* Et ratio huius est, quia uxor est illius cuius primo fuit, quantumcumque videatur separari; unde Apostolus ad Romanos septimo: 'Quae sub viro est mulier, vivente viro, alligata est legi. Igitur vivente viro, vocabitur adultera, si fuerit cum altero viro'. Et ideo Ieremiae tertio: 'Si dimiserit vir uxorem, et recedens ab eo duxerit virum alterum; nunquid revertetur ad eam ultra? Nunquid non polluta et contaminata erit mulier illa'?" *Comment. in Evangelium Lucae* C.XVI, t.VII, 415a.

(37) "Ad illud ergo quod obiicitur, quare non permittitur mulieri, dicendum, quod tempore Legis non iudicabantur ad paria vir cum muliere, tum ratione *conditionis,* quia vir est principium mulieris, tum ratione *praevaricationis,* quia mulier est initium peccati; ideo dictum est ei Genesis tertio: Sub viri potestate eris." *IV Sent.*, d. 33, a.3, q.2, concl., t.IV, 760b.

"From the woman came the beginning of sin" (*Ecclus.* 25:33).

(38) "Notandum est autem, quod licet nulla mentio fieret de uxoribus, Dominus tamen, volens ostendere *statum* Legis quantum ad moralia et transitum quantum ad *caeremonialia,* et *iudicialia,* exemplificat de matrimonio, pro eo quod in ipso libellus repudii dabatur." *Comment. in Evangelium Lucae* C.XVI, t.VII, 415ab.

buked the Pharisees who, seeking to tempt Him, proposed this question: "Is it lawful for a man to put away his wife for any cause?" "Have you not read," replied Christ, "that He Who made man from the beginning made them male and female? For this cause shall a man leave father and mother, and shall cleave to his wife, and they shall be two in one flesh? Therefore, now they are no longer two, but one flesh." Jesus concluded His discourse to the Pharisees with these words: "What therefore God hath joined together, let no man put asunder." But the Pharisees persisted: "Why then did Moses command to give a bill of divorce, and to put away?" "Because Moses," answered Christ, "by reason of the hardness of your heart, permitted you to put away your wives; but from the beginning it was not so. And I say to you, that whosoever shall put away his wife, except it be for fornication, and shall marry another, committeth adultery: and he that shall marry her that is put away, committeth adultery" (Matt. 19:4-9). This declaration of Christ can be true only on the supposition that the previous marriage remained intact, even though the husband has separated from his wife because of her infidelity. Hence, the meaning of Christ's answer to the Pharisees is: In case of infidelity to her marriage vows, a husband may separate from his wife, but if he contracts a new marriage he himself becomes an adulterer. In the Gospel teaching of Our Lord the law of Matrimony is confirmed as a moral law, and divorce is forbidden.[39] Because the provision of the Mosaic Law was inadequate and temporal, because it fell below the original standard, Christ abrogated it: He disannulled "a foregoing commandment because of its weakness and unprofitableness, for the law made nothing perfect" (Heb. 7:18,19). This is Our Lord's teaching concerning the marriage contract, says the Seraphic Doctor. From it you may gather how the law *stands,* how *it is annulled,* and how *it is fulfilled.* Here, too, we see how Christ confounded the pride of the Pharisees as they came to Him boasting of their fulfillment of the letter of the law.[40]

The words of Our Lord proclaim the true nature of marriage in God's sight. They are of absolutely general import, holding good not only for Christians as such but binding the whole human race. Regardless of country or racial customs, no man may contract a second marriage during the lifetime of his first wife, for such union is not marriage but adultery. Dealing with the conjugal relations of husband and wife, St. Paul says: "The wife hath not the control of her own body in this matter, but the husband; the husband likewise hath not control of his own body, but the wife" (I Cor. 7:4). A husband, therefore, who takes another wife is usurping rights which are not

---

(39) "Et matrimonii lex in Evangelio confirmatur tanquam ius *morale,* et libellus repudii reprobatur; unde Matthaei decimo nono: 'Moyses mandavit dare libellum repudii et dimittere uxores vestras'." *Ibid.,* 415b.

(40) "Ex his igitur colligitur, qualiter Lex *manet,* qualiter *evacuatur,* qualiter *impletur,* et nihilominus Pharisaeorum supercilium de litera Legis gloriantium confutatur." *Ibid.*

his; he is disposing of what does not belong to him, for he is no longer his own and he cannot transfer to another woman what has already been surrendered to his wife. Such was the intention in the original union of Adam and Eve and such is the intention of marriage as restored by Christ. The rights of both partners in this respect are precisely the same[41] and neither can contract a second marriage, while the former marriage endures. Both polyandry and polygamy are illicit, invalid, no marriage at all, but sheer adultery. The practice of polyandry would convert the family into a monstrosity, for there would be as many heads as there are husbands. Is the polyandrous wife herself to be the head of such a family? If so, there is perversion of the natural order of predominance between the sexes. The practice of polygamy, likewise, is contrary to the natural law, running counter, as we have seen, to one of the great purposes of marriage, "individua vitae consuetudo," spiritual companionship, and certainly no aid to the primary physical purpose of marriage, the begetting and rearing of children. Not only does the natural law demand the indissolubility of the marriage bond but, for the faithful, this demand is reinforced by the bond of the sacrament, which represents the union of Christ with the Church, the one Bridegroom with the one Spouse: "Behold I am with you all days even till the consummation of the world" (Matt. 28:20).

Because the integrity of this sacred symbolism is being destroyed; because modern legislators, in formulating and promulgating laws of divorce, are like the Jews of old who sought by man-made laws to break the sacred bond of marriage, the world today is rapidly reverting to that condition which presaged the fall of ancient Rome, when moral censors, philosophers, and statesmen discarded their wives at will, and when it was said by Seneca: "There is not a woman left who is ashamed of being divorced, now that the most distinguished ladies count their years not by consuls, but by their husbands." But no matter how much the world may repudiate this law of God, no matter how our society may claim to dissolve marriage by the power of civil law, the permanence of the bond remains, for God made it so. "What therefore God hath joined together, let no man put asunder" (Matt. 19:6).[42]

---

(41) "Item quaeritur de hoc quod dicit: *Iudicatum est, uxorem minime debere dimitti;* utrum vir possit se vendere, uxore invita. Et quod non, videtur: quia *vir non habet potestatem sui corporis, sed mulieri:* ergo etc. Item, mulier non potest se vendere, viro invito: ergo cum paria iudicentur, patet etc." *IV Sent.*, d.36, dub.4, t.IV, 800.

(42) Cf. *supra* p. 88, footnote 9.

Chapter III

ITS THREEFOLD BLESSING

FROM THE NATURE OF THE SACRAMENT as set forth in the foregoing discussion may be deduced its threefold purpose:

First, the begetting and rearing of offspring in compliance with the divine command to "increase and multiply" (Gen. 1:28).

Secondly, mutual help and assistance, both bodily and spiritual, for in creating Eve, God said: "It is not good for man to be alone. Let us make him a help like unto himself" (Gen. 2:18).

To these objects has been added since the Fall of our first parents a third, namely, the regulation of the sexual instinct in accordance with the dictates of reason.[1] "For fear of fornication, let every man have his own wife, and let every woman have her own husband" (I Cor. 7:2).

Corresponding to these three objects of Christian marriage are three distinct blessings which make the conjugal union a source of good, thereby rendering it pleasing to God and useful to men. Three centuries after Tacitus had denounced Christians and despaired of Rome's moral life, the great St. Augustine wrote:

> "The good of marriage consists, among all nations and all men, in the generation of children as its cause, and in the fidelity of chastity. Now as respects the people of God it consists likewise in the sanctity of the sacrament, by virtue of which it is a crime even for a repudiated woman to marry another while her husband lives, though it were done only to have offspring. This is the only object of marriage, and yet if it should fail, the nuptial bond is dissolved only by the death of husband or wife."[2]

In his *De Nuptiis et Concupiscentia,* the Bishop of Hippo again lists the advantages of marriage in the following order: the blessing of children, the chastity of married fidelity, and in the case of God's people, the holiness of the sacrament.[3]

According to St. Augustine, then, the first good of marriage is the *offspring* born of the union. If self-preservation be nature's first law, then self-perpetuation, through normal propagation, is her second law, but there is this difference between self-preservation and self-perpetuation—the one is bind-

(1) "Nam . . . *matrimonium* disponit ad temperantiam conservandam, quam maxime persequitur infirmitas carnis, sed honestas remediat nuptiarum." *Breviloquium,* VI,3, t.V, 267b.

(2) *De Bono Conjugali,* C.XXIX, n.32. MPL 40.394.

(3) Lib. i, c.17. MPL 44.424. Cf. *infra,* p. 102, footnote 8.

ing upon the individual, the other upon the race. The continuance of the human race must be effected by man and woman standing in that abiding and exclusive relation to each other, which constitutes the state of marriage. On natural grounds alone, you may counsel, but you cannot compel, either by positive law or ethical precept, any man or woman to seek to have children. Surely, they are not to be breeded like cattle, as Plato proposed, but the union of the sexes, especially the marriage union, should be entirely free, spontaneous, uncommanded, and unrestrained, a union of intense mutual love.[4] The blessing of offspring means the loving reception of children, the nourishing and rearing of them in a religious manner, as St. Thomas Aquinas succinctly said when he spoke of the "procreation and rearing of children" as the primary purpose of marriage.

Since St. Augustine expressly states that *proles* is the only object of marriage,[5] he is consistent when he ranks the *offspring* born of the union as the primary good. To be sure, a world without children would be a winter without a spring, yet nowhere does St. Bonaventure state that the procreation of children is the primary purpose of Matrimony. On the contrary, he expressly states that the final cause of the marriage union is the life-communion, the spiritual companionship, "individua vitae consuetudo" wherein is realized the principal blessing of Matrimony, the blessing of the sacrament.[6] Consequently, we are not surprised at the order in which the Seraphic Doctor enumerates the blessings which Christian marriage confers upon those who enter this holy state, namely, *fides, proles, sacramentum.*[7] This spiritual companionship, called by theologians *fides,* or mutual faith, is indeed the more characteristically human good, offspring being related to the animal side of human nature. It is the realization of the "two-in-oneship" of marriage by which husband and wife will mutually perfect each other's personalities; in which they will find the deep joys, physical and spiritual, of that intimate life towards which their love is urging them. As the very dualism of man's nature constitutes a oneness, so do *offspring* and *mutual faith* constitute the adequate good of that human union of the sexes, which we call marriage,—a union which requires a lifetime for the fulfillment of the partners' essential duties towards each other and towards their children.

The blessing of mutual fidelity and the blessing of children are realized even outside the Church, but the third blessing, the indissolubility consequent

(4) "Rursus quia quaelibet praedictarum spiritualium unionum in Sacramento matrimonii significatarum est unio unius sicut *agentis* et influentis, alterius sicut *patientis* et suscipientis; et hoc, faciente amoris vinculo, qui ex mera *voluntate* procedit: hinc est quod matrimonium debet esse coniunctio duplicis personae, differentis secundum rationem *agentis* et *patientis,* sicut virilis sexus et muliebris, et hoc ex mero *consensu voluntatis.*" *Breviloquium,* VI,13, t.V, 279b, 280a.

(5) Cf. *supra,* p. 100, footnote 2.

(6) Cf. *supra,* p. 87, footnote 5.

(7) "Huius autem Sacramenti tria sunt bona, 'scilicet fides, proles et Sacramentum'." *Breviloquium* VI, 13, t.V, 279a.

"Et ideo ipsius matrimonii sunt tria *bona,* scilicet *Sacramentum* propter vinculum insolubile, *fides* propter debiti solutionem, *proles* vero sicut effectus consequens ad utrumque." *Ibid.,* 280a.

on its sacred symbolism is, at least in its full perfection, peculiar to Matrimony within the Catholic Church. Since marriage between Christians has its archetype in the hallowed union between Christ and His Mystical Bride, the Church, the union between husband and wife must be cemented and effected by means of grace, for thus is Christ joined to His Church. The *bonum sacramenti* imprints upon the matrimonial contract the supernatural stamp of Christ's mystic union with His Church, and thereby elevates the two properties of every ideal marriage, namely, unity and indissolubility, to the supernatural sphere. The blessings of marriage as a sacrament are peculiar to Christian Matrimony, which supernaturally ennobles and perfects both the procreation and rearing of children as also the mutual fidelity of husband and wife, and imparts all graces necessary for the prevention of incontinency.

This, likewise, is the teaching of St. Augustine who strongly insists that the consecration thus acquired by Christian marriage reacts on the other two blessings and invests them with a new excellence. The blessing of children is for the faithful a far different responsibility than it is for those outside the Church, for Christian children are born that they may be nurtured and reared as children of God. So, too, does the consecration of Christian marriage exercise a wholesome influence in the fostering of mutual love and in the perfecting of their spiritual life.[8]

In the Catholic home the birth of children is viewed not as the mere continuance of the human family, but as the increase of God's people. The natural propagation and education of the race becomes the nursery for the corporeal increase of the Church. As the natural life is perfected by the propagation of the human species, so the supernatural life of the Kingdom of God is perfected by rearing children of God, perhaps eminent saints whom Christ will raise even to the dignity of Angels, thus filling their depleted ranks and compensating for the losses caused by the fall of Lucifer and his followers. In the words of St. Augustine, "How, indeed, would it profit the offspring to be born unless it be reborn, since it is born unto punishment unless it be reborn unto life?"[9] By elevating marriage to the dignity of a sacrament and restoring it to the perpetual union of one man with one woman, Christ provided in a special manner for the decent and orderly propagation of the race and the proper care and training of Christian offspring, future citizens of the state, children of God and heirs of the kingdom of heaven.[10]

(8) "In nuptiis tamen bona nuptialia diligantur, proles, fides, sacramentum. Sed proles, non ut nascatur tantum, verum etiam ut renascatur: nascitur enim ad poenam, nisi renascatur ad vitam. Fides autem, non qualem habent inter se etiam infideles, zelantes carnem. Quis enim vir, quamlibet impius, vult adulteram uxorem? . . . Sed membrum Christi conjugis adulterium conjugi debet timere non sibi: et a Christo sperare fidei praemium, quam exhibet conjugi." *De Nuptiis et Concupiscentia,* lib.i, c.17, MPL 44.424.

(9) *Ibid.*

(10) Cf. *supra,* p. 6, footnote 2.

St. Bonaventure's high esteem for the Sacrament of Matrimony is seen from the fact that he places it side by side with the Sacrament of Holy Orders, of which he considers it the complement.[11] Unlike the other five Sacraments, these two Sacraments were instituted for the preservation of the race, in the supernatural and physical orders, rather than for the sanctification of the individual soul. Both are destined to rebuild the empire of God; the one in the spiritual realm, the other in the material realm, the family, whose fruitful soil provides Mother Church with an increase of members and bearers of sacred traditions.[12] The priest serves God in the house of God; parents serve Him in His living temples, the souls of their children,—creatures of time, yet made after the image and likeness of God, ornamented with sanctifying grace, destined for eternal friendship and closest union with the Godhead.

(11) "Ordo (est) novos milites introducentium, matrimonium novos milites praeparantium." *Breviloquium* VI, 3, t.V, 268.

(12) "Sacramentum autem renovans aut renovat *in esse spirituali,* et sic est *ordo,* cuius est administrare Sacramenta; aut in *esse naturali,* et sic est *matrimonium,* quod quia renovat multitudinem in *esse* naturae, quod est omnium fundamentum, ideo primo fuit ante omnia introductum." *Ibid.,* 267b, 268a.

Chapter IV

ITS RECIPROCAL OBLIGATIONS

LIKE OTHER GREAT THEOLOGIANS, St. Bonaventure finds in the Epistle of St. Paul to the Ephesians his doctrine of the sacramental value of marriage. Here after a general exhortation, the Apostle passed to the first and tenderest relations of the family, singling out first the wives and then the husbands for special instruction:

> "Let women be subject to their husbands, as to the Lord; because the husband is the head of the wife, as Christ is the head of the Church. He is the saviour of his body. Therefore as the Church is subject to Christ, so also let the wives be to their husbands in all things. Husbands, love your wives, as Christ also loved the Church, and delivered himself up for it: that he might sanctify it, cleansing it by the laver of water in the word of life: that he might present it to himself, a glorious church, not having spot or wrinkle or any such thing; but that it should be holy and without blemish. So also ought men to love their wives as their own bodies. He that loveth his wife loveth himself. For no man ever hated his own flesh, but nourisheth and cherisheth it, as also Christ doth the Church: because we are members of his body, of his flesh and of his bones. *For this cause shall a man leave his father and mother: and shall cleave to his wife. And they shall be two in one flesh.* This is a great sacrament; but I speak in Christ and in the Church" (Eph. V:22-32).

The scope of the passage is to sum up the reciprocal obligations of husband and wife in Christian Matrimony. With this end in view the Apostle proceeds to exalt marriage by representing it as a type of the most sacred and intimate of all conceivable unions, the union of the Incarnate God with His mystical Bride, the Church. Just as Christ and the Church are, by reason of that union, comparable to the head and the body in a single person, so the same comparison holds good also of husband and wife.[1] From the archetype the two partners may gather their respective duties in the Christian home. The man is bound to love and cherish his wife as Christ loves the Church; the woman owes obedience to her husband in all wifely duties.

The Christian family, founded on the divinely ordained concept of marriage is therefore the Mystical Body of Christ in miniature. The father of

(1) Et si tu obiicias, quod Apostolus loquitur de viro et muliere ad litteram; dicendum, quod loquitur de eis non secundum se, sed secundum significationem. Vir enim, quia fortis est et praesidet mulieri, superiorem portionem rationis significat, mulier vero inferiorem. Unde etiam est in matrimonio, quod vir significat *Deum*, et mulier significat *Ecclesiam* sive animam." *II Sent.*, d.16, a.2, q.2, concl., t.II, 404ab.

the family is head of the body and holds the place of Christ. The mother is the body itself or the Church. The children of the family are the members of that body as they are members of the Church. The father is Christ; the mother is the Church; the children are the faithful within the family circle. The members of the family—father, mother, and children—form a simple, but a true society. It is a society decreed by nature, since it arises from the fundamental needs of man's being.

As every society must have some one to govern it, so there must be a head of the household, and God intends the father to be that head, and as such to be respected and obeyed. "The husband is the head of the wife." Even Catholics have been known to find something illiberal or "medieval" in this statement, though no one really acquainted with the Christian family formed in the plenitude of Catholic tradition is likely to make exception to its practice. Husbands and fathers occupy positions of trust in their households. Fatherhood in the natural order is likened to the Fatherhood of God.[2] It is obligatory for the husband and father, therefore, to sustain the ideal, not that he is expected to prove as unfailing as the Omnipotent One, Who is divine, but that he shall so live that his wife's trust in him will not falter nor his children's confidence be betrayed.

Roman law made the husband the sole and absolute head of the wife. Such was the status of the wife throughout the Roman Empire when the Apostle penned his epistle. Her husband was her legal head, her substitute in the courts of the state. As to the Angelic Doctor's opinion on this point, Hans Meyer has this to say:

> "St. Thomas makes woman intimately dependent on man; she is *aliquid viri,* a part, as it were, of man's body. Therefore, man is her head and superior; he must guide her and may correct and discipline her. Woman is like a minor. Her lowly position extends also into public life. Obviously, according to St. Thomas, she cannot fill any position in the Church; she is not a full-fledged citizen because she cannot exercise any civil rights. Within the home woman finds her position more favorable; here she is an equal to her husband and here she possesses some rights to personal freedom. But even here the rights of man and woman are proportional. Their rights to marital intercourse are not equal, and the duties of married life are distributed in the man's favor since man and woman in marriage have the relationship of master to servant. St. Thomas tries to preserve the religious dignity of woman; woman has the same supernatural end and is capable of receiving the same graces. Only in the natural sphere does she hold an inferior position, only with respect to her natural rights is she at a disadvantage."[3]

(2) "*Ortus* namque non est per humanam investigationem, sed per divinam revelationem, quae fluit a *Patre luminum, ex quo omnis paternitas in caelo et in terra nominatur,* a quo per Filium eius, Iesum Christum, manat in nos Spiritus sanctus, et per Spiritum sanctum dividentem et distribuentem dona *singulis, sicut vult,* datur fides, et per fidem habitat Christus in cordibus nostris." *Breviloquium,* Prol., t.V, 201.

(3) *Op. cit.,* pp. 208, 209.

In what sense is woman really subject to man? Not in her spiritual life, for here is a realm wherein she stands erect—"never in bondage to any man." In Christ Jesus "there can be no male or female," for "all are one," as St. Paul says (Gal. 3:28). In religious matters, the common obligations and responsibilities of men and women are the same. In this matter, the canons of the Church, of course, follow the teachings of Christ. Women, however, are incapable of exercising certain functions pertaining to religion, as St. Bonaventure explains; a woman cannot receive sacred orders or minister at the altar, even in a subordinate capacity.[4] St. Paul declares: "Let women keep silence in the churches: for it is not permitted them to speak, but to be subject, as also the law saith. But if they would learn anything, let them ask their husbands at home, for it is a shame for a woman to speak in the church" (I Cor. 14:34). Ample proof against the ecclesiastical equality of women is likewise found in his first Epistle to Timothy (2:11-14) in which he enjoins submission and silence upon woman: "Let the women learn in silence, with all subjection. But I suffer not a woman to teach, nor to use authority over the man, but to be in silence, for Adam was first formed; then Eve. And Adam was not seduced; but the woman being seduced, was in the transgression."[5] He who rules in the spiritual realm, is a type of Christ the Head. Since woman cannot be the head of man, she cannot be admitted to Holy Orders.[6] "For I would have you know, that the head of every man is Christ: and the head of every woman is the man: and the head of Christ is God" (I. Cor. 11:3). "For the husband is the head of the wife, as Christ is the head of the Church" (Eph. 5:23). The restriction against woman, then, is based not so much on the decretals of the Church as on a sense of fitness. In this Sacrament, the person who is ordained is a representative of Christ the Mediator. Man alone, therefore, who by the very nature of his sex represents the God-Man is capable of receiving the imprint of the sacramental character and of bearing the type of the Head of the Church, the source of grace and authority.[7]

---

(4) "Respondeo: Dicendum, quod communis hoc tenet opinio, quod mulieres ad sacros ordines admitti non debent. Nam expresse dicitur distinctione vigesima tertia: 'Sacratas Deo feminas vel monachas sacra vasa vel sacratas pallas penes vos contingere et incensum circum altare deferre, perlatum est ad apostolicam Sedem, quae omnia vituperatione et reprehensione plena esse, nulli recte sapientium et dubium. Quapropter huius sanctae Sedis auctoritate, ne pestis haec latius divulgetur, per omnes provincias abstergi citissime mandamus' (Can. 25)." *IV Sent.*, d.25, a.2, q.1, concl., t.IV, 649b, 650a.

(5) "Item, in ordine spiritualis potestas datur ordinato; sed talis potestatis non est mulier susceptibilis, sicut dicitur primae ad Timotheum secundo: *Mulierem in Ecclesia docere non permitto neque dominari in virum:* ergo nec ordinis." *Ibid.*, f.3, 649a.

(6) "Ad illud ergo quod obiicitur de Debboa, dicendum, quod illa fuit potestas *temporalis,* non spiritualis. Mulieribus autem bene licet temporaliter dominari, sed non spirituali dominio, quod est signum, quod ille qui dominatur gerit typum capitis Christi; quoniam ergo mulier non potest esse caput viri, ideo ordinari non potest." *Ibid.*, 650b.

(7) "Et si quaeratur ratio huius, dicendum, quod hoc non venit tam ex institutione Ecclesiae quam ex hoc, quod eis non competit ordinis Sacramentum. In hoc enim Sacramento persona, quae ordinatur, significat Christum mediatorem; et quoniam mediator solum in virili sexu fuit et per virilem sexum potest significari: ideo possibilitas suscipiendi ordines solum viris competit, qui soli possunt *naturaliter repraesentare* et secundum *characteris susceptionem* actu signum huius ferre. Et ista positio probabilior est et multis auctoritatibus Sanctorum potest probari." *Ibid.*, 650ab.

If we differentiate between the spiritual and the moral, the husband is likewise not the head of the wife in the latter realm. He may not stay her from the right, nor command her to the wrong. Here is a realm sacred to the individual, a domain wherein one law pervades and that the law of God, where any intruder, be he potentate or husband, may be defied, and that with divine approval. Neither is the wife the subject party in the marriage bond, since the Church has always insisted on the reciprocity of matrimonial rights and duties between husband and wife.[8]

Where, then, is subjection actually found? In the economic and political field. It is not religious or ethical, but human and historical. As to woman's place in the family, it is that of a co-partner in rights and duties. The husband is the ruler of the family and the head of the wife; the woman as flesh of his flesh and bone of his bone to be subordinate and obedient to the husband, not, however, as a hand-maid but as a companion of such kind that the obedience given is as honorable as it is dignified. The husband's relation to the family, properly termed *headship,* is not to be confused with *mastery.* It is the expression of the mystical bond, likened in the great words of St. Paul, to the mystical espousal of Christ and the Church. And while it is true that the wife must render to her husband a true, enduring, and affectionate respect, this "reverence" is the corollary of the command laid upon the husband to "love his wife as himself."[9] Do we not read: "And Christ died for all; that they also who live, may not now live to themselves, but unto Him who died for them." In His Passion, the Saviour took the Church as His Spouse. It was from the open side of Christ as He slept on the cross the sleep of love and death, of death out of love, that the sacraments came, the streams of blood and water by which the Church was established and formed.[10] The Passion manifests the charity and love Jesus Christ had for His Church, suffering for her that He might espouse her. In so doing He gives to Christian marriage its sublime grandeur. St. Paul himself, as we have seen, draws the parallel: "Husbands, love your wives, as Christ also loved the Church and delivered Himself up for it that He might sanctify it, cleansing

(8) ". . . tamen debet esse inter virum et mulierem obligatio, quia aliter non interveniret inseparabilis unio; et quoniam conformis est unio, ideo conformis est obligatio, et ideo quantum ad hoc *pares* iudicantur, quia conformiter sibi invicem obligantur." *IV Sent.,* d.32, t.IV, 742a.

(9) "In parte ista sunt dubitationes circa litteram, et primo de hoc quod dicit: *In hoc enim pares sunt* etc. Videtur enim falsum, quia in hoc Sacramento significatur coniunctio Christi et Ecclesiae, Dei et animae, inter quos nulla omnino est paritas: ergo nec viri ad uxorem.–Item, ad Ephesios quinto: *Mulieres subiectae sint viris suis;* post dicit de viris, quod *diligant eas sicut corpora sua:* ergo cum corpus sit pars inferior, patet etc. Respondeo: Dicendum, quod in matrimonio est considerare sexus *distinctionem* et *conformem coniunctionem* et postremo *mutuam obligationem.* Ratione duorum primorum significat Deum et Ecclesiam, quia, sicut mulier eget viro, sic Ecclesia Christo; ratione coniunctionis inseparabilis et conformitatis significat illa coniunctionem; sed ratione *obligationis* non est significatio, quia Deus omnino liber est et nulli omnino obligatur." *Ibid.*

(10) "Similiter correspondet, secundum quod per virum et mulierem significatur *Christus* et *Ecclesia.* Ecclesia enim ex Christo formatur, dum de latere Christi dormientis in cruce profluxit sanguis et aqua, ex quibus in Sacramentis Ecclesiae redundavit efficacia, per quae Sacramenta fundatur Ecclesia; et sic *vir* respondet *Christo, dormitio* respondet *morti, ablatio costae apertioni lateris.*" *II Sent.,* d.18, a.1, q.1, concl., t.II, 433a.

it by the laver of water in the word of life that He might present it to Himself a glorious Church" (Eph. 5:25-27, 32).

St. Paul goes on to delineate Christ as the Bridegroom, whose love after redeeming sanctifies one who shall be His Bride forever, one who obeys Him with the fidelity of conjugal love, one whose preservation of His faith unstained is not the dry fulfillment of a command, but the prompting of wedded affection. The image seems chosen to convey intensity of love, first on the part of the Bridegroom as bestowing it, and then on the part of the Bride as responding to it. As the Bride is subject to Christ with never-failing subjection, so does He cherish and foster her forever in an indefectible union of unbroken charity.

How would it be possible for St. Paul, the most practical of men, to exhort husbands to cherish their wives with love similar to that which Christ bears His Church, if marriage did not carry with it the endowment needed for this most holy fashion of love, a love, assuredly, beyond the reach of man's natural faculties? If Christian Matrimony were not cemented by grace, it would bear only a faint and far-off resemblance to the relation which exists between Christ and His Church.[11] It takes divine grace for husband and wife to cleave to each other in spite of every difficulty, in good times and bad, in riches or in poverty, in sickness or in health, until death do them part. The very intimacy of their relationship brings man and woman so close that tensions are bound to arise. As far back as 131 B.C., Q. Caecilius Metellus, censor, in a famous speech before the Senate summed up the matter by saying that nature had so ordained that it was impossible for a man to live without a wife and equally impossible to live in comfort with one.[12]

Here, then, the whole emphasis is on love, the most compelling force in the world, conscience alone excepted. A man is ruled by the woman he loves, and he would not have it otherwise; it is only when he loves himself the more, that he seeks to dominate her. "If you love Me, said our Lord to His disciples, "you will keep my commandments." Love is likewise an impelling force; it prompts to service and to sacrifice. Conformity of the will is acquired by love, says the Seraphic Doctor,[13] and to love is to be transformed into the likeness of the person loved.[14] When the Apostle enjoined husbands to love their wives as themselves, he insured their self-submission, for the major charge seemed to include the minor.

(11) "Item, ad Ephesios quinto: *Viri diligite uxores vestras, sicut et Christus Ecclesiam;* sed coniunctio Christi ad Ecclesiam est secundum amorem castissimum: ergo et coniunctio viri ad mulierem est secundum amorem castum. Sed amor castus est consonus legi Dei: ergo et eius actus." *Quaestiones Disputatae.* Q.III *De Continentia,* a.1, t.V, 166b.

(12) "Ita natura tradidit ut neque cum illis commode nec sine illis ullo modo vivi possit." Au. Gellius, *Noctes Atticae,* lib.i, c.6.

(13) "Tunc autem (voluntas) conformatur, cum ad ipsam convertitur diligendo." *II Sent.,* prooem., t.II, 4b.

(14) "Unde Hugo: 'Scio, anima mea, quod, dum aliquid diligis, in eius similitudinem transformaris'." *Ibid.*

Chapter V

ITS SPHERES OF ACTIVITY

THE GERM OF HUMAN SOCIETY which a sound sociology must take as its starting point is not the abstract human individual but the living union of man and woman primarily in the home. As the manifestation of human nature in woman necessarily differs from its manifestation in man, according to the intention of the Creator, so, too, must the social spheres of interest and the callings of the sexes differ. Just as it is not permitted to take one sex as the standard of the other, so from the social point of view, it is not allowed to confuse the vocational activities of the two sexes. The different characteristics in the equipment of the sexes indicate the role each is to fill in his lifework. Just as two colors, when properly mixed, can produce a white luminosity which has the perfection of all color, so man and woman can work together toward a common goal of virtue and excellence which may be out of the range of each, working individually. Only on the condition that they complement each other will they be able to supply for each other's weaknesses, to profit by each other's strength, to temper each other's excesses and defects. Nature has not given them the same training. Neither should we. Nature has not assigned them the same tasks to accomplish or the same burdens to bear. Then neither should we.

Plato never made a greater mistake than when he wrote that "the female sex differs from the male in mankind only in this, that the one bears children, while the other begets them"; and consequently that "no occupation of social life belongs to a woman because she is a woman or to a man because he is a man, but the natural capacities are distributed equally in both sexes, and woman naturally bears her share in all occupations, and man his share, only that in all woman is weaker than man."[1]

Over against this opinion of Plato, we must set Aristotle's correction: "Cohabitation among human kind is not for the mere raising of children, but also for the purpose of partnership in life: for from the first the offices of man and woman are distinct and different: thus they eventually supply for one another, putting their several advantages into the common stock."[2] Elsewhere he sets forth these several offices in detail: "The nature of both partners, man and woman, has been prearranged by a divine dispensation

(1) *The Republic,* Book V, c.5. 454 D; 455 D.
(2) *Nicomachean Ethics,* VIII, xii.7.

in view of their partnership: for they differ by not having their faculties available all to the same effect, but some even to opposite effects, though combining to a common end: for God made the one sex stronger and the other weaker, that the one for fear may be the more careful, and the other for courage the more capable of self-defense; and that the one may forage abroad, while the other keeps house: and for work the one is made competent for sedentary employments, but too delicate for an out-door life, while the other makes a poor figure at keeping still, but is vigorous and robust in movement; and touching children, the generation is special, but the improvement of the children is the joint labor of both parents, for it belongs to the one to nurture, to the other to chastise."[3]

The two spheres of human action corresponding to the two orders of human capacities, masculine and feminine, are comparable to two concentric circles of unlike circumference, the external, the larger circle representing the vocational labors of the man; the inner, those of the woman. The man becomes a father with paternal rights and duties which include the support of the family and, when necessary, their protection. His sphere is the outer, the industrial world. But there is also an industrial world for the woman,—one suited to her capacities, as is the external to man's, a world wherein her presence and efficiency are no less needed. It is the inner world, the home. From this divinely constituted sphere of maternal activity, she, in the role of Christian mother, exerts a powerful influence for good, second only to the Church of God, of which she is the symbol. She is its life-giving principle, its very heart.

What we have come to consider the most commonplace term for this union, the word "matrimony" is really one of its most beautiful names. If its roots be *matris munium,* it emphasizes the offices and duties of a mother. To woman, God has given the character of domesticity. By her physical nature He has made her the bearer of children and the nurturer of their tender years,—the most momentous, responsible and divine office which has been delegated to any mortal being, an office which brings with it the weary period of gestation, when all the vital forces of the mother are drawn upon to nourish the growing fetus; the pangs of parturition; months of lactation when she pours her life substance into the child; sleepless nights and watchful days and ceaseless ministries of love.[4] Maternity is designed to employ and absorb the Feminine, while Paternity is at most an important incident in the life of man. The obligations of the Feminine are *in* the office; those of the Masculine rather *to* it. The former center woman in their actual performance; the latter send man wherever he may best serve her who is engaged in them.

(3) *Econ.,* i.3.

(4) "Quarto, matrimonium dicitur *matris munium,* id est matris officium, pro eo quod prolis enutritio et acquisitio maxime spectat ad mulierem in concipiendo, in portando, in pariendo, in nutriendo, in compatiendo." *IV Sent.,* d.17, a.1, q.2, concl., t.IV, 678b.

If every child born into this world is not merely a human body, but a human *being* "created only a little less than the angels," and destined to live forever in a celestial Paradise, then is it not an honor to be an instrument in God's hands for the production of such immortal children of God? Christian mothers the world over do not refuse their sacred duty but cherish the privilege of giving to God those generations which on the last day will rise up, a mighty throng, with palms in their hands, a song of joy on their lips, to call them blessed. Herein is reversed the former punishment of woman that she should bear children in sorrow. "She shall be saved through child bearing, if she continue in faith, and love and sanctification" (I Tim. 2:15).[5] For the woman who accepts the pain along with the blessing, pain itself is the preparation for the purest kind of joy. In his last discourse to His disciples, Christ rendered a delicate homage to the office of woman when He drew from the pains of travail one of the most profound and human-sorrowful of His illustrations. "A woman when she is in labor hath sorrow because her hour is come; but when she hath brought forth the child, she remembereth no more the anguish, for joy that a man is born into the world" (John 16:21). Fecundity is woman's glory; motherhood, a joy; it is there that God applied His punishment: "I will multiply thy sorrows and thy conceptions; in sorrow shalt thou bring forth children" (Gen. 3:16). But by the grace of the Redeemer the pain of child-bearing will have a supernatural fertility, for through it will the woman be saved; her sorrow will be changed into joy.

The two reciprocal spheres of activity, taken in the narrowest sense, exclude each other. The actual task assigned by nature to woman cannot be performed by man, while the reverse is also true. There is, however, the mixed domain of the earning of a livelihood in which both sexes work, although in so doing neither can deny his or her characteristic qualities. Woman has physical necessities which only labor can supply. If not done for her, it must be done by her. It is a right, however, which her higher nature will lead her to forego as soon as the grasp of necessity permits. Nature forbids competition in the same field and, according to physical law, woman should be spared all industrial burdens which impair her most important duty in life. If man by his greater physical strength is fitted to be lord of the external, woman cannot share that sovereignty with him except as a pretender, an inferior, or a slave. Possession of the gifts in which he excels proves him to be the worker of and for his race. The newborn child, therefore, is doubly blessed since it shares in the heritage of both its father and its mother. Though each plays a vital part in the movements by which it is produced, the father may be called the more *honorable* source of its being;

(5) "Item primae ad Timotheum secundo dicitur de muliere: *Salvabitur per filiorum generationem, si permanserit in fide et dilectione cum sanctificatione;* sed in actu coniugali est generatio filiorum, et illud est consonum legi Dei." *Quaestiones Disputatae,* Q. III, *De Continentia,* a.1, t.V, 166a.

the mother, the more essential. To the father it is indebted for what it *has;* to the mother, for what it *is*. Therefore, civil laws have with good reason decreed that the child should be closely attached to its mother.[6]

In the important work of developing the spiritual and intellectual life of the child by a training which is rightly called the second birth, both parents play a part. The mother leaves her impress most strongly on the child's earliest years. During the years of adolescence the father's part becomes more important. Being the head of the woman, the man is representative of paternal authority,[7] a power held in reserve and sometimes needed to complement the mother's sweetness. As Goethe says: "The father is the head of the family; the mother, the heart." Woman prevails by affection where man rules by authority. Neither parent can supply the place of the other, for they are copartners in rights and duties, their diverse functions being suited in each particular instance to the individual temperaments concerned. Without woman, even from a moral point of view, the family would be incomplete, for there are almost necessary influences which would be impossible of exertion, if the home contained only the manly character of the husband. From the mother the child receives not only his life and nutriment but also a priceless moral and spiritual heritage. There is no substitute for a mother's tenderness, patience, compassion and love; no measurement of her influence. First impressions sink deepest and remain longest in the human heart. Though the early writing of the mother's hand may for a time be covered over by the hands of others, the acid of human suffering and the sobering experience of life will in the end bring out in all its clearness and beauty the manuscript once traced there by a mother's hand. As William Ross Wallace says:

"They say that man is mighty,
He governs land and sea,
He wields a mighty scepter
O'er lesser powers that be;
But a mightier power and stronger
Man from his throne has hurled
For the hand that rocks the cradle
Is the hand that rules the world."

The rule, *ceteris paribus,* is always necessary for a just comparison. Man, because of his superior brawn, is, in the order of nature, woman's defender,

(6) "Dicendum, quod secundum leges civiles sive ius imperiale "partus sequitur ventrem." Et ratio huius est valde conveniens, quoniam prolis duplex est principium, pater scilicet et mater. Pater est principium *honorabilius,* sed mater est principium *substantialius;* et ideo in honoribus et municipiis filius sequitur patrem, quoniam illa acquiruntur paterna sollicitudine et in *hereditate* patrimoniali. Sed quoniam mater est principium substantialius, quantum ad id quod est, sequitur matrem; et quoniam libertas et servitus respiciunt hominem secundum id quod *est,* non secundum id quod *habet:* hinc est, ut partus sequatur ventrem." *IV Sent.,* d.36, a.1, q.3, concl., t.IV, 794b.

(7) "Ad illud ergo obiicitur, quod vir est superior; dicendum, quod illud intelligitur quantum ad illos actus, qui respiciunt sexem virilem specialiter, scilicet quantum ad regimen domus et consimilium." *IV Sent.,* d.32, dub.1, t.IV, 742a.

her protector against physical harm.[8] But the law of compensation is still in operation. In the realm of morals, woman takes the precedence; she stands erect where man succumbs. Man has strength to act; woman, strength to endure. Strength is needed not only for action but more especially to bear up against and withstand shocks from without and misfortunes from within. Man's is a physical strength; woman's a moral strength, an energy of soul which enables her to bear calmly the trials and evils of life, a strength which gives her courage to carry out her designs with unshaken firmness, for "viri est *agere,* et mulieris est *pati.*"[9] Courage is generally considered a manly virtue; fortitude, a feminine virtue. The former is, at least, more adapted to the male sex, who are called upon to act; the latter, to the females, who are obliged to endure. A man without *courage* would be as ill-prepared to discharge his duty in his intercourse with the world, as a woman without *fortitude* would be to support herself under the complicated trials of body and mind with which she is liable to be assailed.

Shakespeare says that apparel oft proclaims the man and we see from his epistle that the Apostle St. Peter was not altogether unconscious of the matter of woman's attire. He is not condemning personal adornment but merely reminding Christian wives that these externals should not constitute the main feature of their attractiveness; it is beauty of heart and soul that really matters; it is the hidden man of the heart, the incorruptibility of a quiet and meek spirit, which is rich in the sight of God" (I Pet. 3:3, 4). In the Book of Proverbs it is written of the good wife that "Strength and beauty are her clothing, and she shall laugh in the latter day" (31:25) and again: "Favour is deceitful and beauty is vain: the woman that feareth the Lord, she shall be praised" (31:30). I think it was Keats who said, "A thing of beauty is a joy forever." Was he thinking of an effeminate beauty which addresses itself to the senses only, a beauty which fades, or was he referring to a spiritual beauty whose exterior loveliness is but as the outer husk or covering of noble, steadfast virtue? A good man will seek a wife of spiritual beauty, a woman who will be a complement to his own noble aspirations and high ideals, a "valiant woman" such as Solomon describes in the Book of Proverbs:

> "Who shall find a valiant woman? Far and from the uttermost coasts is the price of her. The heart of her husband trusteth in her, and he shall have no need of spoils. She will render him good, and not evil, all the days of her life. She hath sought wool and flax, and hath wrought by the counsel of her hands. She is like the merchant's ship; she bringeth her bread from afar. And she hath risen in the night, and given a prey to her household, and victuals to her maidens. She hath considered a field and bought it; with the fruit of her hands she hath planted a vine-

(8) "... quia matrem munit ac defendit per virum, tum per prolem, quia mulier indiget defensore, Isaiae primo: *Defendite viduam* (Isai. 1:17)." *IV Sent.,* d.27, a.1, q.2, concl., t.IV, 678b.
(9) Cf. *supra,* p. 14.

> yard. She hath girded her loins with strength, and hath strengthened her arm. She hath tasted and seen that her traffic is good; her lamp shall not be put out in the night. She hath put out her hand to strong things, and her fingers have taken hold of the spindle. She hath opened her hands to the needy, and stretched out her hands to the poor. She shall not fear for her house in the cold of snow, for all her domestics are clothed with double garments. She hath made for herself clothing of tapestry; fine linen and purple is her covering. Her husband is honorable in the gates, when he sitteth among the senators of the land. She made fine linen, and sold it, and delivered a girdle to the Chanaanite. Strength and beauty are her clothing, and she shall laugh in the latter day. She hath opened her mouth to wisdom, and the law of clemency is on her tongue. She hath looked well to the paths of her house, and hath not eaten her bread idle. Her children rose up and called her blessed; her husband, and he praised her. Many daughters have gathered together riches; thou hast surpassed them all. Favour is deceitful, and beauty is vain. The woman that feareth the Lord, she shall be praised. Give her of the fruit of her hands; and let her works praise her in the gates" (31:10-31).

What a noble institution is Christian wedlock rightly understood,—an institution in which two beings are joined together that their separate moral and intellectual qualities may make a perfect whole; the husband infusing strength, courage, and perseverance into the wife whom he covers with the shield of his manly protection; the wife softening all that is too rough and forceful in her husband's character, polishing his manners, correcting his tendency to sternness, toning down the harshness of his too hasty decisions. Thus, by the gentle contact of her finer nature, "the valiant woman" endeavors to refine the character of her husband, communicating to him some of that delicate perception of detail, of fine points, which is of so much importance in social relations and thus acquiring for him a certain distinction which will make her husband "honorable in the gates, when he sitteth among the senators of the land." "The valiant woman" need be neither a clinging vine nor a stalwart Amazon. She is not man's competitor, but his helpmate. She is the "soul of society," whose task it is to make men aware of the truth, beauty, and goodness of God. Her beauty is meant to soothe; her understanding sympathy, to soften; her love, to penetrate and reflect in the soul of man.

In the brightness of the North Star which, astronomers tell us, reflects the brilliance of two stars so close together that their light merges and appears as that from a single star, Robert Montgomery sees a beautiful analogy to the unity and constancy which should characterize man and wife.

"The cynosure of northern skies
Appears but one to seamen's eyes,
Yet twain there are,
And each a star—
Perhaps a sun.

"May you, my friends, reverse the view,
And while on earth you look like two,
From Heaven to be seen as one;
Yea, like that polar symbol be
A double star of constancy."

WOMAN IN THE VIRGINAL LIFE

Chapter I

VIRGINITY: ITS THREE ASPECTS

IN CHRISTIAN MARRIAGE we see the work of God as both Creator and Redeemer. He Who had established the union of man with woman in innocence in the Garden of Eden was the selfsame God Who, becoming Incarnate, restored it after the long night of the Fall as part of His organism for the renewal of things. As an institution, then, marriage dates back to the dawn of creation. It was not till four thousand years later, when Daniel's prophetic seventy weeks of years had rolled by from the day of Nehemias' labors in rebuilding Jerusalem and the fullness of time had dawned upon the world, that a thing so new, so strange as the Virginal Life was created upon the earth. The course of all preceding ages had advanced upon the divine command, "Increase and multiply." To have children, to have many children, was an honor hitherto coveted by man. To be unmarried, not to carry on the house of Israel, to exclude oneself from the possible parentage of "Him that was to come," was a reproach. But now that the blessing of "their children's children" had been realized and long lines of descendants filled the earth, there appeared the True Head of the race, the Virgin Son of a Virgin Mother, bearing aloft a new standard, ushering in a new order of things,—a life directly opposed to the practice and habits of the time and proclaimed by all ancient Christian writers as the *condition* of the perfect following of our Lord.

The personal character of the God-Man had attracted the undeviating gaze of the early Christians who strove to reproduce in themselves in varying degrees some likeness of the Master, but there was in the character of Our Lord one feature especially which called forth the tenderest love of His disciples, the imitation of which has brought about a moral revolution whose mighty current rushing on unceasingly during nineteen centuries will continue to roll forward till the end of time, bringing refreshment and restoration as it flows.

The example of the Virgin Christ, conceived and born of a Virgin and throughout His life, like His Virgin Mother, a Virgin still, the Author, Guardian and Lover of Virginity and its Reward exceeding great,[1] inspired many young souls to follow Him in virginity of heart and flesh. St. Bona-

(1) "Virgo enim in Virgine conceptus est, et natus Virgo de Virgine, et post nativitatem cum Virgine Matre Virgo permansit, auctor et custos et amator virginitatis et remunerator largissimus, Christus Iesus." Opusculum X. *Vitis Mystica,* Additamentum IV, t.VIII, 211b.

venture, voicing the opinion of all the ancient writers of the Church from the Ascension to St. Augustine, saw in virginity a special imitation of Christ. It is a life of self-denial and suffering; in other words, the crucified life, for Christ suffered for us, leaving us an example, as the Apostle Peter says. "Christ also suffered for us, leaving you an example that you should follow His steps" (I Pet. 2:21), but "to follow is to imitate." Each one follows Christ in the way in which he imitates Him. Christ has proposed many things for our imitation, but not to all did He propose virginity of the flesh.[2] The precepts of the Gospel are binding upon all. Yet Christ laid down further rules, intended only for those who seek Christian perfection and binding upon those alone who freely choose to follow them.[3] But this perfection consists in charity, a love of God so intense that it brooks no impediment which stands in the way of total surrender to Him. No sooner had Our Lord preceded and drawn in His own life the perfect lineaments of virginity than a crowd of privileged souls betrothed and espoused to Him arose all over the earth. In the sex that had known no other duties than those of the mother, had possessed no other hold on man than the charm belonging to the union of the sexes, there appeared suddenly young maidens who disregarded the joys of marriage and the condition which till then had seemed the only hope of woman's life. Whereas heretofore men had looked upon the unmarried state of adults as a mark of presumed profligacy, there were now seen those who freely renounced the bond of marriage and the ambition and success of the world in order to give themselves to a life either of contemplative piety or of active charity, the one and the other previously unknown. A great number of both sexes renounced that which no Christian precept called upon them to renounce, the state of marriage, and with it all the merely human and natural interests of life, in order to follow their Redeemer and His Mother in that virginal purity which they had introduced.[4] Thus, as time went on, this profession of virginity or continence, which was unknown before the coming of Christ, which was abhorrent to Jewish nature, which to an unbelieving Gentile world seemed a renunciation of man's task to multiply his race, became a reality, an institution, a power all over the earth.

This virginal life it is our purpose to study according to the views of St. Bonaventure. Quoting St. Augustine, the Seraphic Doctor defines virginity

(2) "Merito igitur eum sequimini etiam in hac vita virginitate cordis et carnis, quocumque ierit. Quid est enim sequi nisi imitari? quia *Christus passus est pro nobis, relinquens vobis exemplum,* sicut ait Apostolus Petrus. Hunc in eo quisque sequitur, in quo imitatur, in quo multa ad imitandum omnibus proponuntur, virginitas autem carnis non omnibus." *Ibid.*

(3) "Sed hoc potest esse non solum absque peccato mortali, quia nullus ad hoc tenetur, verum etiam absque veniali, in his potissimum, quae sunt consilii et in nostrae ponuntur liberae voluntatis arbitrio, ac per hoc omitti possunt absque ullo peccato, sicut expresse patet in voto paupertatis et continentiae virginalis." Opusculum XI. *Apologia Pauperum,* c.II, t.VIII, 240.
Our Lord looked upon the young man in the Gospel who had kept all the commandments from his youth and He loved him. "If thou wilt be perfect, go," He said, "sell all that thou hast, and give it to the poor, and thou shalt have treasure in heaven, and come, follow Me." And the young man went away sad, for he had great possessions. Cf. Matt.19: 16 ff.

(4) Cf. *supra* p. 119, footnote 1.

as "a firm resolution to preserve perpetual incorruption in corruptible flesh."[5] In virginity, then, there are two elements to be considered: the material element, that is to say, the absence in the past and in the present, of all complete and voluntary delectation, whether from lust or from the lawful use of marriage; and the formal element, that is the firm resolution to abstain forever from sexual pleasure. This definition of St. Augustine expresses directly the formal element in virginity, for "meditatio" denotes the mind's purpose, while the epithet "perpetuae" implies that a virgin should bear in mind the purpose of always persevering therein. The material element is expressed indirectly by the words "in carne corruptibili incorruptionem," "incorruption in corruptible flesh." Virginity in either sex, then, implies (a) physically, bodily integrity, visible evidence of which exists only in woman, (b) morally, reverence for bodily integrity which is suggested by a virtuous motive. The essence of virginity, then, like that of purity, resides in the soul, but its material element is in the body.[6] Wherefore St. Augustine says that *although virginity resides in the flesh* and is, therefore, a physical quality, *nevertheless it is a spiritual thing, which a holy continency fosters and preserves.*[7]

Inasmuch as perfection is not a fleeting and changeable thing but a permanent state ennobled by the creature's complete surrender to the Creator, this virtue must be consecrated and ratified by vow. Wherefore virginity as a virtue denotes the purpose, confirmed by vow, of preserving perpetual integrity. St. Augustine says *by virginity, integrity of the flesh is vowed, consecrated and observed in honor of the Creator of both soul and body.*[8] A vow can be solemnized in three ways, namely, *by the reception of Holy Orders, by receiving the habit of a religious community,* wherein there is a distinction between professed and non-professed, and *by one's own promise* provided it take place in the hands of an authorized person. Even though such women have not received the veil, nevertheless if they have taken a solemn vow of continence in the presence of an authorized person, they can in no way contract marriage, "neither by right nor in fact." Those who have bound themselves by simple vows cannot contract marriage *without sin,* although they can do so in fact.[9]

---

(5) "Item, hoc ostenditur per definitionem virginitatis, quam ponit Augustinus dicens: 'Virginitas est in carne corruptibili incorruptionis perpetuae meditatio'." *IV Sent.,* d.33, a.2, q.1, t.IV, 753.
Cf. St. Augustine, *De Sancta Virginitate,* c.13, n.12. MPL 40.401.
"Christus virgo, virgo Maria utrique sexui virginitatis dedicavere principia." St. Jerome, *Ep. 48 ad Pammach.,* n.21. MPL 22. 510.

(6) "Cum enim ad perfectam virginitatem duo concurrant, scilicet incorruptio mentis et incorruptio carnis: incorruptio mentis est sicut *formale* et complementum; incorruptio carnis est sicut materiale." *IV Sent.,* d.33, a.2, q.3, t.IV, 758ab.

(7) *De Virgin.* C.viii, n.8. MPL 40. 400.

(8) *Ibid.*

(9) "Respondeo: Dicendum, quod contingit votum solemnizari tribus modis, scilicet *ordinis susceptione, habitus assumtione,* ubi est distinctio professorum a non professis, et *propria testificatione,* dum tamen fiat in manu publicae personae. Quamvis ergo tales non susceperint velum; si tamen se astrinxerunt in manu publicae personae ad continentiam, nullo modo possunt contrahere, nec de iure nec de facto. Si autem se voto simplici astrinxerunt, non possunt, scilicet sine peccato; possunt de facto." *IV Sent.,* d.38, dub. VI, t.IV, 826.

Ordinarily the consecration of young girls is permitted to bishops alone, for it is fitting that souls be consecrated to Christ by those who are themselves espoused, according to the words of St. Paul: "For I have espoused you to one husband that I may present you as a chaste virgin to Christ" (II Cor. 11:2). And they ought to bring forth perfect sons; and for that reason they have the power of the keys in most important and worthy matters, with which they alone have been entrusted. The vows of widows, however, may be made in the hands of a priest delegated by the Bishop according to the approved form.[10]

Virginal continence or virginity, according to the Seraphic Doctor, postulates three conditions: first, *abstinence from all unlawful intercourse;* secondly, *abstinence from all lawful intercourse;* and thirdly, *integrity of mind and body.*[11] As regards the first, it is a "habitus," an habitual course or *rule of conduct;* as regards the second, it is a *state of virtue;* as regards the third, *it is a glory.*[12] In virginity, therefore, there are three aspects to be considered, namely, the *virtuous habit,* the *state,* and the *glory of virginal integrity.*[13]

First, the *virtuous habit* or practice of virginity. Moral or ethical virtue, as Aristotle says, is the product of habit, a habit of right action formed by acting rightly.[14] The virtues are not engendered in us by nature but, like the arts, they must be acquired by actual practice of them.[15] That virginity is a virtue is evident from the fact that it is a "habitus," not a spasmodic art, but a permanent disposition of soul, a habit of doing that which is the proper act of the power wherein the virtue resides.[16] The susceptibility of pleasure has grown up with us from the cradle; hence the difficulty of eradicating this feeling which is engrained in the very fabric of our lives. It is harder to fight against pleasure than against anger, says Aristotle, but virtue, like art, is constantly dealing with the more difficult, since the harder the task, the better the success.[17] The difficulty of virginity is shown by the words "in carne corruptibili incorruptionem," for if the flesh were incorruptible, it would not be difficult to maintain it in perpetual chastity.[18] If it is difficult

(10) "Respondeo: Dicendum, quod quantum est de iure communi, hoc licitum est solis episcopis, quia ipsi sunt sponsi, qui debent Christo animas consecrare, secundum quod dicit Apostolus secundae ad Corinthios undecimo: *Despondi vos uni viro virginem castam,* et debent filios perfectos generare; et ideo habent clavium potestatem in *excellentia,* et eis solis ista quae sunt excellentiae, sunt commissa. Unde hoc quod dicit Magister, locale solum fuit et nunc non habet locum nisi de viduis velandis, quibus potest sacerdos de consilio episcopi dare velum." *IV Sent.,* d.20, dub. VI, t.IV, 543.

(11) "Respondeo: Dicendum, quod continentia virginalis sive virginitas tria dicit: primum est *abstinentia* ab omni *coitu illicito;* secundum est abstinentia ab omni *coitu licito;* tertium est integritas mentis et carnis." *IV Sent.,* d.33, a.2, q.1, concl., t.IV, 753b.

(12) "Quantum ad primum dicit *habitum,* quantum ad secundum dicit *virtutis statum,* quantum ad tertium dicit *decorem.*" *Ibid.*

(13) "Respondeo: Dicendum, quod, sicut tactum est, in virginitate tria considerare, scilicet habitum, statum et decorem integritatis." *Ibid.,* q.2, concl., 755a.

(14) *Ethic.* Bk.II, c.1, 1103 a14-b25, Aristotle, *The Nicomachean Ethics,* a commentary by H. H. Joachim, Oxford at the Clarendon Press, 1951, p. 72.

(15) Cf. Aristotle, *ibid.,* c.4-6, 1103a 26 sqq. p. 74.

(16) "Concedendae igitur sunt rationes probantes, virginitatem *virtutem* esse, secundum id quod nominat habitum." *IV Sent.,* d.33, a.2, q.1, t.IV, 753b.

(17) "Nam, ut ait Aristot., II. *Ethic.* c.3, 'circa id quod difficilius est, semper et ars et virtus versatur'." *IV Sent.,* t.IV, 318; editors' footnote 5.

(18) "Sed meditari incorruptionem perpetuam hoc est maxime arduum et difficile, et tale est virtutis genus." *IV Sent.,* d.33, a.2, q.1, t.IV, 753.

to abstain from unlawful intercourse, how much more so from all intercourse and if the former is a virtue, how much more so the latter.[19] Conjugal chastity is deserving of praise merely because it abstains from unlawful pleasures; hence no excellence attaches to it above that of chastity in general. Virginity attains to perfection in this matter, namely, to entire freedom from sexual pleasure, and that not for a time only but for all time.[20]

But Aristotle defines virtue as the "medium duarum extremitatum, secundum quod sapiens determinabit";[21] and St. Augustine says that "virtus non aliud est quam modus."[22] Now the mean of virtue is fixed with reference not to quantity but to right reason, as Aristotle says.[23] Wherefore it is said of the magnanimous that in point of quantity, he goes to extremes, but in the matter of becomingness, he follows the mean.[24] The same may be said of virginity which postulates not only abstinence from lawful intercourse but the complete renunciation of all carnal pleasure, which renunciation constitutes the most perfect act of the concupiscible appetite.[25] All the unmarried who have preserved themselves from grave sin against purity are virgins. They possess the virtue of self-mastery; endurance in the war against the passions; the firm stand of fearless souls against the unholy demands of the flesh; the perfect and lovely virtue of continence.[26]

Though virginal chastity in itself excels conjugal chastity, we cannot conclude therefrom that a virgin is more chaste than a married woman. A thing may excel other things in two ways: first, in some particular genus, and in this sense virginity excels in the genus of chastity, since it surpasses the chastity of both widowhood and of marriage;[27] secondly, a thing may excel absolutely and in this sense virginity is not the most excellent of the virtues. Though the virtue of virginity excels in the genus of chastity, it does not follow that virginity is the greatest of the virtues. It is a question of one virtue excelling another and it depends upon the individual. Provided that she be possessed of greater virtue, a married woman can be continent as well as a virgin, and conversely.[28] Hence, St. Bonaventure's statements concerning

(19) "Item, hoc iterum videtur ratione: quia abstinere a coitu illicito est illud est virtutis; sed difficilius est ab omni coitu abstinere quam ab illicito: ergo si illud est virtutis, multo fortius istud." *Ibid.*

(20) "Secundo quaeritur de comparatione continentiae virginalis ad matrimonium sive coniugium; et quod virvinitas sit melior et perfectior, videtur: Quia "virtus consistit circa difficile et arduum": ergo circa magis arduum maior virtus; sed magis arduum est omnino abstinere a coitu quam aliquando tantum: ergo maioris virtutis." *Ibid.*, d.33, a.2, q.2, t.IV, 754a.

(21) *Ethica Nicomachea,* II.6.

(22) Cf. St. Bonaventure, *In Hexaem.*, VI, 12, t.V, 362.

(23) *Ethica Nicomachea,* II.6.

(24) "Et propterea dicendum, quod quando dicitur, quod virtus consistit in medietate, hoc non est intelligendum respectu obiecti—quia sic nullus esset castus, nisi cognosceret medietatem omnium mulierum de mundo, quia illud est medium inter aliquam et nullam—sed istud intelligitur, ut sic medium teneatur, et virtus sit medium circa delectationes et tristias." *IV Sent.*, d.33, a.2, q.1, t.IV, 754. Cf. Aristotle, II *Ethic.* c.3 and c.6.

(25) Cf. *supra* p. 121.

(26) "Unde virginitas est habitus continentiae perfectus et decorus." *IV Sent.*, d.33, a.2, q.1, t.IV, 753b.

(27) "Esto enim, quod tres in tribus statibus contineant, secundum quod melius possunt, adhuc excedit continentia vidualis coniugalem, et virginalis vidualem." *IV Sent.*, d.33, a.2, q.3, t.IV, 757a.

(28) "Si loquamur quantum ad *habitum;* sic se habent ut excedentia et excessam quia ex maiori virtute potest continere etiam coniugata quam virgo, et e converso." *Ibid.*, d.33, a.2, q.2, 755a.

the special virtue of virginity are not to be taken literally. Formally, virginity is but the purpose of perpetually preserving perfect chastity in one who abstains from sexual pleasure. Ordinarily this purpose is inspired by a virtue superior to that of chastity; the motive may be religious or apostolic. Then the higher virtues of charity or religion will ennoble this purpose and communicate to it their own beauty; but we shall not find in it any splendor or merit which are not the splendor or merit of another virtue.

The loss of virginity can be understood from a consideration of the two elements which constitute it, namely, integrity of purpose as the formal element and integrity of the flesh as the material element. If both elements are lost, that is, if there is a failure in the resolution and a loss of bodily integrity, then virginity is totally destroyed and never can be regained.[29] As the gift of original justice, which consisted in integrity of purpose and of the flesh, could not be restored by human reparation, so, too, virginity once lost never can be regained by penance.[30] In other words, virginity is irreparably lost by sexual pleasure, voluntarily and completely experienced. "I will tell you without hesitation," writes St. Jerome in his twenty-second Epistle to St. Eustochium "that though God is almighty, He cannot restore a virginity that has been lost."[31]

Though the integrity of the flesh would seem to consist in the seal of virginal purity, yet sometimes the seal is broken without the loss of virginity. Physical virginity may be lost by violation against one's will without the loss of moral virginity.[32] If integrity of the flesh be lost in spite of the mind's fixed purpose to preserve chastity, says the Seraphic Doctor, the formal and essential element, and accordingly the merit and reward, of virginity remains intact even though the material element has been destroyed. Virginity has been lost in the sight of men, but not in the sight of God, as St. Ambrose says.[33] Something has been lost, but the essence remains. We may say, then, that the integrity of the bodily organ is accidental to virginity.

If, however, integrity of purpose be lost, the integrity of the flesh remain-

(29) "Ex his potest patere, quando virginitas amittatur. Cur enim ad perfectam virginitatem duo concurrant, scilicet incorruptio mentis et incorruptio carnis: incorruptio mentis est sicut *formale* et complementum; incorruptio carnis est sicut *materiale*. Si ergo *utrumque* pereat, totum perditum est et nunquam recuperari potest." *Ibid.*, d.33, a.2, q.3, 758b.

(30) "Item, iustitia originalis consistit in quadam mentis et carnis integritate; sed quia virginitas dicit incorruptionem mentis et carnis, ex quo semel perditur, nunquam per satisfactionem potest recuperari: ergo pari ratione neque originalis iustitiae donum per satisfactionem recuperatur. Si ergo ex illius iustitiae privatione est in nobis originalis culpa, impossibile fuit, quod Adam satisfaceret pro posteritate sua." *II Sent.*, d.33, a.1, q.2, t.II, 785a.

(31) N.5. MPL 22. 397.

(32) "Item quaeritur de hoc quod dicit Isidorus: *Non potest corpus corrumpi, nisi prius corrumpatur animus.* Videtur enim illud manifeste falsum, quia multis virginibus a viris pessimis facta est iniuria, et corruptae sunt violenter. *Si tu intelligas* de corruptione peccati, sicut dicit Magister; *contra* omne peccatum est in libero arbitrio: ergo non est in carne vel in corpore. Respondeo: Dicendum, quod istud intelligitur de corruptione, quae redundat in amissionem decoris virginitatis; cum enim sit de magnis bonis, nullo modo potest perimi vel auferri omnino nolenti. Sed ipse opponit de qualicumque corruptione." *IV Sent.*, d.33, dub.7, t.IV, 764ab.

(33) "Si autem amittatur *incorruptio carnis,* salva *incorruptione mentis;* manet quod *formale* et completivum est virginitatis, ideo meritum et praemium, quamvis etiam illud quod materiale erat, sit perditum; unde perdita est *secundum quid,* manet tamen *simpliciter;* perdita est in conspectu hominum, non in conspectu Dei. Et hoc est quod dicit Ambrosius et habetur in littera." *IV Sent.*, a.2, q.3, t.IV, 758b.

ing intact, then the formal element is lost and the material element remains. When integrity of purpose is restored by the sincere resolve to preserve chastity, virginity likewise is restored and the person is considered a virgin, although her glory is not so great as it would have been had she never consented. This interpretation seems the more kind one.[34]

It is to be marked, on the one hand, that material virginity is not destroyed by every sin against the sixth and ninth commandment, and on the other hand, that the resolution of virginity extends to more than mere preservation of bodily integrity, for if it were restricted to material virginity, the resolution, at least outside the marriage state, might coexist with vicious desires, and could not then be virtuous. A failure in the resolution, or even incomplete faults, leave room for efficacious repentance, which restores virtue and the right to the reward.

Virtue can be recovered by penance as regards that which is formal in virtue, but not as to that which is material therein. As a man who has squandered his wealth does not recover his riches by repenting of his sin, in like manner a person who has lost virginity by sin, recovers by repenting, not the matter of virginity but the purpose of virginity. As regards the matter of virginity there is that which can be restored miraculously by God, namely, the integrity of the organ, but there is something else which cannot be restored even by a miracle; God cannot undo that which is done. St. Jerome says in his letter to Eustochium (*Epistle* xxii): *Other things God can do, but He cannot restore the virgin after her downfall.*

So much for the "habitus" or *virtue* of virginity. Now, as regards the "decor." The *glory* of virginity lies in its holy incorruption or bodily integrity, and for this reason it is always to be preferred to conjugal chastity which is characterized by base corruption.[35]

As regards the *state* of virginity, however, we must make a distinction as to time. Comparing the two states as they existed in the *Old Law,* the state of conjugal chastity is by all means preferable and the state of virginity is forbidden; being an unproductive state of life, it was considered a reproach and held in ignominy.[36] Comparing the two states in the time of *grace,* when fruitfulness of the womb is no longer required but when there is a need of holiness and incorruption and purity of mind, virginity is preferred to conjugal chastity.[37] If, however, we are speaking of different times and com-

(34) "Si autem perdatur incorruptio mentis, salva incorruptione carnis, tunc perditur quod *formale* est, et manet quod est materiale; et quia illa redit ad suum propositum et habet materiale substratum; reduente virginitate, virgo iudicanda est, licet non in tanta gloria, in quanta esset, si nunquam consensisset. Et hoc sentire videtur esse magis pium." *Ibid.*

(35) "Si autem loquamur quantum ad decorem; sic semper virginitas praefertur continentiae coniugali, quia ibi est corruptio foeda, hic autem est incorruptio sancta." *Ibid.*

(36) "Si autem quantum ad statum, tunc est loqui dupliciter; aut secundum *idem tempus,* aut secundum *diversa.* Si secundum *idem,* dupliciter: aut secundum tempus *Legis,* aut tempus *gratiae.* Si secundum tempus *Legis;* status continentiae coniugalis omnino praefertur, et status virginitatis prohibetur, et sterilis maledicitur et in contumelia habetur." *Ibid.*, 755b.

(37) "Si secundum statum *gratiae,* ubi non requiritur fecunditas ventris, sed sanctitas et incorruptio et puritas mentis; virginitas praefertur continentiae coniugali." *Ibid.*

paring the state of conjugal chastity in the time of the Law with virginity in the time of grace, each best suited to its own time, then the one *state* is not to be preferred to the other state, nor the *merit* of the one state to the merit of the other, provided, of course, that there be equal charity. This is what St. Augustine means when he says that the celibacy of John is not to be preferred to the marriage of Abraham.[38] Therefore, reasons proving that the state of virginal continence is more noble than that of marriage are based on a comparison of the two states in the time of grace, or on the consideration of the glory of virginity.[39] If any one should advance St. Augustine's view as being opposed to this, we must remind him that St. Augustine was speaking of the two states of life as they existed under different conditions,—conjugal chastity in the time of the Law and virginity in the time of grace.[40] The married person may be more prepared in mind to observe virginity, if it should be expedient, than the one who is actually a virgin. Hence St. Augustine charges the virgin to say: "I am no better than Abraham, although the chastity of celibacy is better than the chastity of marriage." Further on he gives the reason for this: "For what I do now, he would have done better, if it were fitting for him to do it then: and what they did I would even now do, if it behooved me now to do it."[41]

Objection has been made to the lawfulness of virginity inasmuch as it is contrary to a precept of the natural law. Just as the words of Genesis 2:16, *Of every tree that is in paradise, thou shalt eat,* indicate a precept of the natural law, in reference to the preservation of the individual, so also the words of Gen. 1:28, *Increase and multiply and fill the earth,* express a precept of the natural law, in reference to the preservation of the species. A precept implies a duty. But there are two kinds of duties: one which has to be fulfilled by the individual and which cannot be set aside without sin; the other which is binding on the multitude and not on the individual. The precept of the natural law which binds man to eat must be fulfilled by the individual, if life is to be sustained. The precept of procreation, on the other hand, regards the whole multitude of men, which needs not only to multiply in body, but also to advance spiritually.[42] Wherefore sufficient provision is made for the

(38) "Si autem secundum *diversa* tempora loquamur, utpote si continentiae statum consideremus in tempore Legis et virginitatis in tempore gratiae, sicut unusquisque in suo optimo; sic *status* statui non praefertur nec *meritum* merito, dum tamen sit caritas aequalis. Et hoc est quod dicit Augustinus, quod caelibatus Ioannis non praefertur coniugio Abrahae." *Ibid.*

(39) "Rationes igitur probantes, quod continentia virginalis est dignior, procedunt ratione statuum relatorum ad tempus gratiae, vel ratione decoris virginitatis." *Ibid.*

(40) "Ad illud quod obiicitur in contrarium de auctoritate Augustini, dicendum, quod loquitur secundum status diversos, scilicet Legis et gratiae." *Ibid.*

(41) *De Bono Conj.* c.xxii, n.27 and c.xxiii, n.28, MPL 40. 392.

(42) "Item quaeritur de hoc quod dicit: *Deus nondum iuserrat, ut coirent*. Hoc enim videtur esse falsum, quia dicitur Genesis primo: *Crescite et multiplicamini et replete terram;* constat, quod hoc dictum est quantum ad actum generativae: ergo etc. Iuxta hoc quaeritur, si mandatum illud omnes obligabat. Quodsi *sic:* ergo videtur, quod transgressi sunt, quia non coierunt in statu innocentiae: si *non:* ergo videtur, quod poterant continue servare virginitatem. *II Sent.*, d.20, dub. 3, t.II, 487b, 488a.

"Item quaero, utrum illud mandatum maneat adhuc. Quodsi manet: ergo non licet alicui servare virginitatem, quod est contra Apostolum, qui dicit ad Corinthios septimo: *Volo, omnes vos esse, sicut ego sum;* loquitur de castitate. Si non obligo modo, quaero: quando revocatum est. Videtur etiam, quod modo sint melioris conditionis homines quam tunc, quia modo possunt servare virginitatem, tunc autem non poterant." *Ibid.*, 488a.

human race, if some fulfill the precept of procreation, while others abstaining from the exercise of the duty betake themselves to the contemplation of the things of God, for the beauty and welfare of the whole human race, and follow the counsel of virginity.[43]

As to the objection that the sterile earth must be cursed, we answer it is true if it is devoid of the power to produce the fruit which it should yield at that time; but in the time of grace there is needed not the fruit of the womb but of the mind, not a corporal but a spiritual offspring.[44]

The counsel of virginity is expressly given in the New Testament; first in St. Matthew (19:11,12), where Christ, after reminding His disciples that besides those who are unfit for marriage by nature, or by reason of a mutilation inflicted by others, there are those who have made the same sacrifice for the kingdom of heaven, recommends them to imitate these. "He that can take it, let him take it." Tradition has always understood this text in the sense of a profession of perpetual continence. This counsel is suited to man's fallen nature and not to the state of original justice in which God created him, because then when there was no inclination to evil, to be continent would not be more virtuous than to marry and all would beget offspring for the worship of God. Now, however, on account of the difficulty and hardships undergone in its attainment, it is considered a work of great virtue and dignity.[45]

But, it has been objected, in the state of original justice man was endowed with perfect virtue and at that time the state of virginity was not in existence but only that of conjugal chastity. Virginity, therefore, does not excel conjugal chastity but is excelled by it.[46]

In the state of original justice, explains St. Augustine, marital intercourse would have taken place without any corruption of integrity,—a statement which might require some explanation, since woman's bodily integrity seems inconsistent with sexual intercourse.[47] Now the corruption of virginity implies three things, namely, the breaking of the virginal seal, the endurance

(43) "Respondeo: Dicendum, quod illud mandatum datum fuit viro et mulieri in statu innocentiae; sed cum esset mandatum *affirmativum,* non obligabat ad semper, sed pro loco et tempore. Determinatio autem temporis dependebat ex revelatione divinae voluntatis; quam quia Deus nondum eis revelaverat, ideo dicit Magister quod nondum iusserat. Ad illud quod quaeritur, utrum illud mandatum fuerit revocatum; dicendum, quod aliter obligabat tempore naturae institutae, aliter nunc. Tunc enim omnes obligabat, quia omnibus erat in officium; nunc autem non obligat omnes, pro eo quod multi sunt, qui sufficiunt illud implere, aliis consilium virginitatis servantibus." *Ibid.*

(44) "Ad illud quod obiicitur, quod terra sterilis est maledicenda; dicendum, quod verum est, si sterilis est a fructu, quem tempore illo debet producere; sed tempore gratiae non quaeritur fructus ventris, sed mentis, non corporalis, sed spiritualis." *IV Sent.,* d.33, a.2, q.2, t.IV, 755.

(45) "Hoc autem consilium competit statui naturae *lapsae,* non autem naturae *institutae,* quia tunc, cum nulla esset pronitas, non esset maior virtus continere quam nubere, et omnes prolem ad cultum Dei generarent; nunc autem propter difficultatem et arduitatem omnino continere magnae est virtutis et dignitatis." *II Sent.,* d.20, dub.3, t.IV, 488a.

(46) "Item, si homo stetisset, non minus perfectas habuisset virtutes; sed tunc non esset virginitas, sed tantum continentia coniugalis; ergo continentia coniugalis est continentia perfectissima: ergo virginitas non superexcellit, immo exceditur." *IV Sent.,* d.33, a.2, q.2, t.IV, 755a.

(47) "Respondeo: Dicendum, quod proposita quaestio habet plus curiositatis quam utilitatis; quam tamen habet ortum ex verbis Augustini, ideo introducta est, maxime propter explanationem illius verbi, quod dicit, quod maritus commisceretur uxori sine ulla corruptione integritatis; quod quidem non videtur esse intelligibile. Si enim mulier permaneret integra, nunquam esset viri ad mulierem carnis commixtio." *II Sent.,* d.20, a.1, q.4, t.II, 482b.

of suffering or remorse, and base delectation. The first is natural, the second is penal, but the third, which stands midway between sin and its punishment, is basely defiling.[48] If, therefore, a man had known his wife in the time of original justice, there would have been a breaking of the seal but it would have been unaccompanied by suffering or remorse or by base delectation, because the reproductive power would have been undefiled and untainted by sin. Indeed, those organs, like the mouth, the hand, and the tongue, would be subject to reason, as St. Augustine says. And as the hand or the mouth is opened or closed without resultant suffering or remorse and without base delectation, so in the state of nature it would have been with all the organs and it would not have been more shameful to speak of the reproductive organs than of the other members of the body as is now the case, when nature recoils in shame from mentioning the marital act on account of the defilement which it supposes.[49] In our fallen nature, carnal intercourse has its source in corruption and proceeds accordingly. This corruption makes itself felt in violence and remorse, in delectation and defilement, for which reason carnal intercourse is degrading to the dignity of a virgin.[50]

We have seen that the glory of virginity lies in its holy incorruption or bodily integrity.[51] For this reason the Seraphic Doctor compares it to the state of the blessed in heaven, thereby elevating it above the marriage state. The state of virginity is the more perfect, says the Saint, resembling as it does the state of the glorified body which knows no corruption. "For in the resurrection they shall neither marry nor be married; but shall be as the angels of God in heaven" (Matt. 22:30). Wherefore St. Jerome says that "virginity is known to the angels."[52] The Fathers of the Church in general develop this teaching. St. Augustine calls the virginal life "the portion of angels."[53] And St. Chrysostom says: "The state of virginity is good, I agree; indeed, it is better than the married state, I confess. And if you ask how much better, I answer: 'As much as heaven is better than earth, or angels are better than men'."[54]

(48) "Propter quod intelligendum est, quod integritatis corruptio tria dicit, scilicet claustrorum apertionem, poenalem passionem et foedam delectationem. Primum est naturae, secundum est poenae, tertium vere est corruptionis vitiosae, quae tenet medium inter culpam et poenam." *Ibid.*

(49) "Si igitur vir uxorem cognovisset in tempore naturae institutate, fuisset ibi claustrorum apertio, sicut ostendunt rationes secundo inductae; non tamen fuisset ibi poenalis passio ac foeda delectatio, quia vis generativa nec esset corrupta nec esset infecta; immo obedirent rationi illa membra, sicut dicit Augustinus, sicut obediunt os, manus et lingua. Unde sicut manus aperitur et clauditur, et os aperitur et clauditur, nec est ibi passio vel poena nec delectatio foeda, sic fuisset in natura; nec turpius fuisset tunc loqui de istis membris quam sit loqui de aliis. Nunc enim turpe est loqui propter hoc, quod natura horret et erubescit actum illum ratione foeditatis, quae in ipso consistit." *Ibid.*, 482b, 483ab.

(50) "Et sic patet responsio ad rationes ad partem oppositam. Omnes enim procedunt de corruptione, secundum quod corruptio sonat in violentiam et poenalitatem, et in delectationem et foeditatem; et sic minuit dignitatem virginalem." *Ibid.*, 483b.

(51) Cf. *supra*, p. 125, footnote 35.

(52) "Secundo quaeritur de comparatione continentiae virginalis ad matrimonium sive coniugium; et quod virginitas sit melior et perfectior videtur. Item, quod similius est statui gloriae est perfectius; sed continentia virginalis est similior statui gloriae, quia ibi est incorruptio, ibi non nubunt, unde Hieronymus dicit, quod 'Angelis est cognata virginitas'." *IV Sent.*, d.33, a.2, q.2, t.IV, 754.

(53) "Virginalis integritas et per piam continentiam ab omni concubitu immunitas angelica portio est." *De Sancta Virginitate*, c.13. MPL 40. 401.

(54) Cf. *De Virginitate*, c.10. MPG 64.37-44.

Chapter II

ITS EXCELLENCE

IN THE NEW LAW, then, the state of virginity excels the state of widowhood and of marriage.[1] Other things being equal, says St. Bonaventure, it is better because it is purer.[2] Marriage is good; virginity is better. Our Divine Lord Himself extolled virginity as a precious gift: "Who said to them: All men take not this word, but they to whom it is given" (Matt. 19:11). And St. Paul describes it as a higher call: "Therefore, both he that giveth his virgin in marriage, doth well; and he that giveth her not, doth better. A woman is bound by the law as long as her husband liveth; but if her husband die, she is at liberty. Let her marry to whom she will, only in the Lord. But more blessed shall she be, if she so remain, according to my counsel: and I think that I also have the spirit of God." The state of virginity is more befitting those who are set apart for the sacred ministry. The Council of Trent has defined as a matter of faith that it is "better and more blessed to remain in virginity or celibacy than to be married."[3] It is conditions, not persons, that are contrasted here, and hence it would be wrong to say that the preference given to virginity implies disrespect for the married state. No doubt a good mother who rears her children in the fear of God leads a more meritorious life than an indifferent nun.[4] The error of Jovinian, as St. Jerome says, consisted in holding that virginity and marriage were of equal merit in the sight of God.[5]

St. Paul, speaking as a faithful preacher of the doctrine of the Lord, formally declares that marriage is permissible, but that it would be better to follow his counsel and remain single, and he gives the reasons. Besides the considerations arising from the circumstances of his time, he gives this general reason, that the married man "is solicitous for the things of the

---

(1) "Esto enim, quod tres in tribus statibus contineant, secundum quod melius possunt, adhuc excedit continentia vidualis coniugalem, et virginalis vidualem." *IV Sent.*, d.33, a.2, q.3, t.IV, 757.

(2) "Ad illud quod obiicitur, quod laboriosius est etc.; dicendum, quod verum est, ceteris paribus; sed licet activa sit laboriosior, non tamen melior, quia alia purior." *IV Sent.*, d.33, a.2, q.2, t.IV, 755b.

(3) "Si quis dixerit, statum coniugalem anteponendum esse statui virginitatis vel coelibatus et non esse melium ac beatius manere in virginitate aut coelibatu quam iungi matrimonio, anathema sit." Sess. XXIV, can.10. (Denzinger-Bannwart, n.981.)

(4) "Insuper, et alia est comparatio *statuum*, et alia *personarum*. Unde sicut non sequitur, si perfectior est virginitas quam coniugium, quod ideo virgo sit semper perfectior coniugata, quia potest esse, quod virgo sit impia, et coniugata sit sancta." Opusculum XI. *Apologia Pauperum*, Cap.VI, t.VIII, 268.

(5) "Haec verba ipsius, quibus, ut excuset errorem proprium, exaggerat alienum. Nunquam enim Iovinianus, quamquam sit omnino detestandus, in hanc quam hic fiagit dementiam incidit, ut gulositatem aequaret abstinentiae, sicut nec luxuriam continentiae coaequavit, sed pudicitiam coniugalem et virginitatem, usum ciborum et abstinentiam aequalis apud Deum meriti censuit." *Ibid.*, Cap.V, t.VIII, 263.

world, how he may please his wife, and he is divided" (I Cor. 7:33); whereas he that is without a wife directs all his care to his own bodily and spiritual sanctification, and is at liberty to devote himself to prayer. Here we find the real reason why marriage is inferior to virginity. It is not because there is anything even remotely degrading about the married life.[6] It is simply for the psychological reason that marriage monopolizes the mind and heart and ordinarily leaves less freedom to serve God. "And the unmarried woman and the virgin thinketh on the things of the Lord, that she may be holy both in body and in spirit. But she that is married thinketh on the things of the world, how she may please her husband" (I Cor. 7:34).

Of the excellence of virginity we have proof from the lips of Our Divine Lord.

> "Now it came to pass as they went, that He entered into a certain town, and a certain woman named Martha received Him into her house. And she had a sister called Mary, who sitting also at the Lord's feet, heard His word. But Martha was busy about much serving, who stood and said: Lord, hast Thou no care that my sister hath left me alone to serve? Speak to her therefore that she help me. And the Lord answering, said to her: Martha, Martha, thou art careful, and art troubled about many things. But one thing is necessary. Mary hath chosen the better part, which shall not be taken away from her" (Luke 1:39-42).

A divine good, then, takes precedence over a human good; the good of the soul is preferable to the good of the body; and the good of the contemplative life is better than that of the active life.[7] Now virginity is directed to the good of the soul in respect to the contemplative life, which consists in thinking on the things of God, whereas marriage which is directed to the good of the body, namely, the corporeal increase of the human race, is an active way of life; the man and woman who embrace the married state have to think on the things of the world, as the Apostle says, while the virgin is free to devote herself entirely to the attainment of the one thing necessary.[8] The state of virginity means a signal victory over the lower appetites,[9] and an emancipation from earthly and worldly cares, which gives a man liberty to devote himself to the service of God. Although a person who is a virgin may fail to correspond to the sublime grace of his or her state, and may be inferior in merit to a married person, yet experience bears witness to the

(6) "Nunquam enim qui commendat virginitatem adversarius censendus est esse coniugii, aut qui laudat solitudinem adversarius dicendus est coenobiticae vitae." *Ibid.*, Cap.I, t.VIII, 236.

(7) Cf. *infra*, p. 133, footnote 23.

(8) "Ad illud quod obiicitur, quod valet ad plura est melius; dicendum, quod hoc est verum, si aeque intense valeat; sed aliquid intense valet ad unum, quod praevalet remisse valenti ad plura." *IV Sent.*, d.33, a.2, q.2, t.IV, 755b.

(9) "Nam qui omnino sentit de passionibus carnis, hic *insensibilis* iudicatur, sed hoc habet per naturam; qui vero omnino consentit, hic *luxuriosus est;* qui vero excitatur, sed tamen non consentit, talis *virtuosus* est; et hoc omnino bene est in virginibus, quia aliquo modo caro excitat, quamvis non ita, sicut in corruptis. Hoc autem intelligitur, loquendo secundum virtutes *politicas* et naturam *lapsam;* nam per superabundantem gratiam potest esse, quod non sentiat, et tamen virtutem habeat." *IV Sent.*, d.33, a.2, q.1, t.IV, 754b.

marvelous spiritual fruit produced by the examples of those men and women who emulate the purity of the angels.

By virginity, Man, who was created "a little less than the angels," rises above those celestial spirits in honor, for his state of life surpasses theirs in four respects: Man's virginity is *more inclusive* than that of the angels; his is a virginity of spirit and flesh; theirs, of spirit alone. Man's virginity is *more noble,* for it has its origin in grace; that of the angels, in nature. The former is voluntary; the latter, necessary and inevitable. Man's virginity is *more glorious,* for it is preserved through a struggle and victory; that of the angels, without a struggle, therefore without a victory. Man's virginity, likewise, is *more expedient,* for it is full of merit. Not so that of the angels, for their virginity is in accordance with their nature. And so, concludes St. Bonaventure, the virginity of man is *more inclusive, more noble, more glorious* and *more expedient* than that of the angels.[10]

In twelve proofs based on *authority,* on *example* and on *reason,* St. Bonaventure stresses the surpassing excellence of virginal chastity.
Proof from *authority:*

1. In the first Epistle to the Corinthians, already quoted, St. Paul says: "Therefore, both he that giveth his virgin in marriage doth well, and he that giveth her not doth better" (7:38). Therefore, virginal chastity excels other forms of chastity, according to the authority of the Apostle.[11]
Proofs from *example:*

2. This truth is likewise shown from the *example of Christ* Who in His human nature was a model of virtue and of all Christian perfection; but it is an established fact that Christ was a virgin. Therefore, virginal chastity is to be preferred to other forms of chastity.[12]

3. Likewise, this truth is evident from the *example of the most blessed Mary,* the Mother of God, whose fruitfulness did not destroy her virginity. Therefore, virginity is more commendable than other forms of chastity.[13]

4. Likewise, from the *example of John the Evangelist,* whom the Lord loved more than the other disciples. The reason for Christ's love of John is

---

(10) "Honore transcendit dominium et merito ipsum statum Angelorum quatuor gradibus: virginitas enim hominis *multiplicior* est Angelorum; haec est enim in corpore et in spiritu, illa in spiritu tantum. Item, *nobilior* est: haec enim est a gratia, illa a natura; item, haec voluntaria, illa necessaria. Item, *gloriosior;* haec enim est cum pugna et victoria; illa sine pugna, et ideo sine victoria. Item, *utilior;* haec enim est meritoria, illa non, quia natura. Et sic illa *universalior, nobilior, gloriosior, utilior." De Nativitate B. Virginis Mariae*, Sermo I, t.IX, 706.

(11) "Tertio quaeritur de sanctimonia virginali; et est quaestio utrum virginalis continentia sit omnibus praeferenda. Et videtur, quod sic, *auctoritate, exemplo* et *ratione; auctoritate* sic. 1. Primae ad Corinthios septimo: *Qui matrimonio iungit virginem suam bene facit, et qui non iungit melius facit:* ergo continentia virginalis est praeferenda aliis continentiae differentiis, secundum auctoritate Apostoli." *De Perfectione Evangelica,* Quaest. III, Art. III, t.V, 175.

(12) "Item, hoc ipsum ostenditur *exemplo Christi.* Christus enim secundum humanam naturam fuit exemplum virtutis et totius christianae perfectionis; sed constat, quod Christus fuit virgo: ergo virginalis continentia est omnibus praeponenda." *Ibid.*

(13) "Item, hoc idem ostenditur *exemplo beatissimae Mariae,* matris Domini, cuius fecunditas virginitatem non abstulit: ergo virginitas est prae omnibus commendanda." *Ibid.*

given by St. Jerome in the words: "A virgin chosen by the Lord, he remained a virgin forever."[14]

5. Likewise, from the *example of John the Precursor of Christ,* who is known to have been a virgin.[15]

6. Likewise, from the *example of Abel,* who was a virgin. Of him St. Augustine says: "This is perfect justice: virginity, priesthood, and martyrdom, which threefold justice was in Abel."[16]

From all these excellent examples it is shown that virginity or virginal chastity is to be preferred to all other forms of chastity.[17]
Proofs from *reason:*

7. That especially which makes us follow Christ is greatly to be preferred, but virginity especially makes us follow Christ, as St. John says: "For they are virgins. These follow the Lamb whithersoever he goeth" (Apoc. 14:4).[18]

8. Likewise, that especially which makes man like the angels is especially to be praised, but virginity more than other virtues makes man like the angels, because, as St. Jerome says, "to live in the flesh opposed to the flesh is a life, not of men, but of angels."[19]

9. Likewise, *to be continent* is good, *to be more continent* is a greater good, *to be most continent* is the greatest good; but the greatest continency is virginity. Therefore, etc.[20]

10. Likewise, the pure is good, the more pure is a greater good, and the highest purity is the highest good; but in virginity is the highest integrity and purity. Therefore, etc.[21]

11. Likewise, "that is whiter which is not mixed with black." By like reasoning, then, that is better which has no admixture of evil; but concupiscence is the source of all evil and virginity especially has no admixture of concupiscence. Therefore, etc.[22]

12. Likewise, that is more praiseworthy which better disposes for the most

(14) "Item, exemplo Ioannis evangelistae, quem Dominus maxime dilexit; et huius reddit Hieronymus dicens: "Qui virgo electus a Domino, virgo in aeternum permansit." *Ibid.*

(15) "Item, *exemplo Ioannis praecursoris Christi,* quem constat virginem fuisse." *Ibid.*

(16) "Item, exemplo Abel, qui virgo fuit; unde Augustinus, in libro de Mirabilibus sacrae Scripturae: Tota iustitia haec est: virginitas, sacerdotium et martyrium, quae triplex iustitia in Abel fuit." *Ibid.*

(17) "His omnibus exemplis praecipuis ostenditur, quod virginitas seu virginalis continentia sit omnibus aliis continentiae partibus praeferenda. Item, hoc ipsum ostenditur *ratione* sic. *Ibid.*

(18) "Quod maxime facit nos sequi Christum est maxime praeferendum; sed virginitas maxime facit sequi Christum, Apocalypsis decimo quarto: *Virgines enim sunt et sequuntur Agnum, quocumque ierit:* ergo etc." *Ibid.*

(19) "Item, quod maxime facit conformem Angelis est maxime commendandum; sed virginitas facit maxime conformem Angelis, quia, secundum Hieronymus, 'in carne praeter carnem vivere angelica vita est, non humana'; ergo etc." *Ibid.*

(20) "Item, *continere* bonum est, ergo *magis continere* magis bonum, et *maxime continere* est maxime bonum; sed maxima continentia est virginitas: ergo etc." *Ibid.*

(21) "Item, honestum est bonum, ergo magis honestum magis bonum et summe honestum summe bonum; sed in virginitate est summa honestas et puritas: ergo etc." *Ibid.*

(22) "Item, 'albius est quod nigro est impermixtius': ergo pari ratione melius est quod est malo impermixtius; sed libido est fons omnis mali, virginitas autem maxime impermixta libidini: ergo etc." *Ibid.* Cf. Aristotle, III *Topic.* c.4. for "albius est" etc.

noble act, but virginity better disposes for the act of contemplation, in which is required the greatest purity.[23]

Thus does St. Bonaventure extol the beautiful virtue of chastity which sheds such unmistakable radiance on its possessor that even those who lack it recognize its presence and pay it tribute. It preserves unsullied the noblest part of man,—his heart, his mind and soul.[24] It is a strong, manly, noble virtue, demanding fortitude, strength of character, and genuine virility. For man, it is a breastplate and a shield; for woman, the brightest jewel in her crown of loveliness. "What stronger breastplate," says Shakespeare, "than heart unstained!" "There is no jewel in the world," declared Cervantes, "so valuable as a chaste and virtuous woman." Milton sang the praises of chastity in immortal verse:

> "So dear to heaven is saintly chastity
> That when a soul is found sincerely so
> A thousand liveried angels lackey her."

"Ah, me! how weak a thing the heart of woman is!" says the English tragedian Shakespeare.[25] Woman is weak by nature, by constitution, and often in consequence of the education she receives, but let the mind of woman be ennobled by a generous devotion; above all, let the love of God be enkindled in her soul, and she becomes capable of all that is most elevated in thought, most noble in heart, most heroic in courage, and most persevering in combat. "There are some women," says Saint Chrysostom, "who have not only shown themselves more courageous than men, but have almost attained to the impassibility of angels. There are some who, like a steadfast rock, are not only undisturbed by the fury of the waves, but who even force the foaming waters to break harmlessly around them; theirs is the strength of iron and the transparent hardness of the diamond."[26]

Before the Son of God had given us life by His death, and restored our strength through the divine weakness of His passion, the world was under the dominion of violence, which was mistaken for power, the only attribute then known of the Deity. Women, children, and slaves counted as naught. Stripped of all rights, they laid claim to and received no esteem. But when men saw God working the greatest marvels with almost insignificant means, overcoming the strongest obstacles with the weakest instruments, they realized that God needs not man to manifest the power of His arm; that there

(23) "Item, quod magis disponit ad actum nobilissimum est laudabilius; sed ad actum contemplationis, in quo requiritur maxima puritas, magis disponit virginitas: ergo etc." *Ibid.*

(24) "Nam castitas non est in carne, sed in mente, et ex corde redundat in corpus; unde melior est castitas mentis quam corporis. Nam si cor fuerit castum, et corpus; non autem si corpus, et cor; quamvis Iudaei tempore Legis crederent, illud esse *dictum antiquis: Non moechaberis,* tantum de castitate carnis, sed Dominus ad Legis impletionem addidit, non solum castitatem esse servandam in carne et corpore, sed etiam in cogitatione, affectione et visione." *Sermones de Tempore. Dominica XI Post Pentecosten,* Sermo II, t.IX, 397a.

(25) *Julius Caesar,* Act ii, scene 4.

(26) *De stud. praesent.* Hom.v. n.3. MPG 63. 488-489.

is something greater than physical strength,—the complete surrender of self into the hands of God as docile instruments of His will. It is for this reason that God has sometimes chosen "the weaker sex" in preference to men to execute through her the designs of His mercy and love, for who better than she can rise to the occasion which demands great adaptation, entire submission, unalterable patience, or perfect resignation?

The grace of Christ imparts to the feminine character that firm resolution, forceful energy, and steady perseverance which are the crown of her noblest faculties. The union of Christ with the tender Agnes was the union of Spouse with spouse. Agnes the Virgin was likewise a Martyr. As perseverance in good is the gate of Paradise, so perseverance in evil is the gate of hell. If you persevere in good, as did the gentle Agnes, you will, like her, in death knock at the door of Paradise.[27] Without supernatural aid, woman's human nature is too weak to produce, far less ripen, those fruits of virtue, which the Holy Spirit is everywhere seeking under the title of a "valiant woman." This same Holy Spirit in words written of the "valiant woman" commends and extols the blessed Agatha. "Strength and beauty are her clothing," for she is garbed in the shining robe of virtue; "and she shall laugh in the latter day," for she is certain of salvation and eternal happiness.[28] "Who shall find the valiant woman?" She is formed and found in the school of Christ,—not only such Christian heroines as Agnes, Cecelia, Agatha, and Lucy, but countless numbers of Christ's martyrs who carry glorious valor into the obscure paths of daily life. Not warriors on the field of battle but valiant heroines in the spiritual combat, women, little women, the youngest, weakest, and frailest of their sex, whose tender minds and bodies are naturally opposed to endurance of suffering and steadfast perseverance, are for the strength of their weakness a source of wonderment to man, for "the weak things of the world hath God chosen, that He may confound the strong" (I. Cor. 1:27).[29]

(27) "Coniunctio Christi et Agnetis est coniunctio Sponsi et sponsae. Agnes Virgo fuit et Martyr. Sicut perseverantia in bono porta est paradisi, ita perseverantia in malo est porta inferni; si perseveras in bono, in morte pulsas ad portam paradisi." *De Sancta Agnete Virgine et Martyre.* Sermo II, t.IX, 505.

(28) "Spiritus sanctus in verbis istis de muliere forti scriptis commendat et extollit beatam Agatham: ab informatione *virtutis gratificantis,* ibi: *Fortitudo et decor indumentum eius;* et a certitudine sive tentione *salutis beatificantis,* ibi: *et ridebit in die novissimo." De Sancta Agatha Virgine et Martyre,* t.IX, 513. Cf. Prov. 31:10,25.

(29) "Ad illud ergo quod obiicitur de *mulieribus,* patet: quia, licet non competat bellum *materiale,* competit tamen *spirituale.* Multae enim in hoc bello strenues fuerunt, ut patet de sacris Virginibus, quae martyrizatae sunt pro confessione et nomine Christi." *IV Sent.,* d.7, a.3, q.1, concl., t.IV, 173a.

Chapter III

ITS REWARD

THIS PERFECT VIRGINITY OF BODY, enhanced by a purpose of perpetual chastity, produces a special likeness to Christ and creates a title to one of three "aureolae," which theologians mention.[1] According to the Seraphic Doctor, as we shall see, these "aureolae" are particular rewards added to the essential happiness of eternity, and are like so many laurel wreaths, crowning three conspicuous victories and three special points of resemblance to Christ: the victory over the flesh in virginity, the victory over the world in martyrdom, and the victory over the devil in the preaching of the truth.[2]

In Sacred Scripture we read of three rewards to be given to faithful souls, namely, the reward of the *"aurea"* or golden crown, the reward of the *fruit,* and the reward of the "aureola" or little golden crown. Different theologians interpret these rewards in different ways.[3] St. Bonaventure makes them correspond to the three aspects of virginity. To the *virtuous habit or practice of virginity,* he assigns the reward of the golden crown; to the *state* of virginity, the reward of the fruit; to the *glory of virginal integrity,* the reward of the "aureola," the aureole or halo, the little golden crown.[4]

There is no doubt, he says, that the "aurea" or golden crown is the reward of the *virtue.*[5] That the fruit is the reward of the *state of life* is evident from the parable of the sower as related by St. Matthew (13:8, 23). As more or less fruit is produced according to the fertility or excellence of the soil, so the *fruit* is greater or less according to one's *state of life.* And although married women, widows, and virgins practice chastity according to their state of life, nevertheless, the chastity of widowhood surpasses that of marriage and virginal chastity excels that of widowhood.[6] The greater the virtue, the greater the reward. Therefore, to virginal chastity is awarded the hundredfold fruit;[7] to chaste widowhood, the sixtyfold; to chaste marriage, the

(1) "Et ideo tertio modo dicendum, quod *aureola* debetur actui interiori per comparationem ad decorem exteriorem, et exteriori relato ad interius." *IV Sent.,* d.33, a.2, q.3, t.IV, 757b, 758a.

(2) "Multum etiam facit *genus et nobilitas operis,* quia, sicut clarum est, aureolae praemium non debetur habitui virtutis intrinseco, sed operi privilegiato utpote praedicationi, martyrio et virginitati." *Apologia Pauperum,* c.3, 19, t.VIII, 250.

(3) "Respondeo: Dicendum, quod triplex praemium legimus in Scriptura, scilicet praemium *aureae,* praemium, quod est *fructus,* et praemium *aureolae.* Distinguitur autem a diversis hoc diversimodo." *IV Sent.,* d.33, a.2, q.3, t.IV, 756b.

(4) "Aliter igitur in virginitate tria considerantur, scilicet *habitus, status* et *decor; habitui* respondet aurea, *statui* fructus, sed *decori integritatis* aureola." *Ibid.,* 757a.

(5) "Et quod *habitui* aurea, hoc non est dubium." *Ibid.*

(6) "Quod vero *statui* fructus, hoc patet sic: quia, sicut fructus maior et minor, quem ponit Dominus in Evangelio, attenditur secundum nobilitatem terrae, sic *fructus* maior et minor secundum statum. Esto enim, quod tres in tribus statibus contineant, secundum quod melius possunt, adhuc excedit continentia *vidualis coniugalem,* et *virginalis vidualem.*" *Ibid.*

(7) St. Matthew says: "And every one that hath left house, or brethren, or sisters, or father, or mother, or wife or children, or lands for My Name's sake shall receive an hundredfold and shall possess life everlasting" (19:29).

thirtyfold.[8] Moreover, it is evident that the reward of the "aureola" is due not to the practice of virtue in itself but to the kind and nobility of the work which it accomplishes.[9] It is the reward of certain acts which have to do with something extrinsic, as for instance something *inferior,* as the body, or with something *close at hand,* as the neighbor, whom he converts and leads to heaven by his good teaching. Wherefore *Doctors* and *Preachers* will experience a certain glory on account of the conversions they have made; the *Martyrs,* too, who have exposed themselves to sufferings for Christ, will possess a certain glory and joy in their bodies; *Virgins,* likewise, who have kept their bodies pure for Christ will be rewarded by a certain glory in their bodies. And that glory or joy resulting from that glory is rightly called the aureole, or golden halo. "However," continued the Seraphic Doctor, "I believe that the 'aureola' should be called *glory* rather than *joy,* because all will rejoice on account of the glory, but not all will have the 'aureola.' That the whole idea may be expressed by one phrase, it is better to say *glory with joy* and *joy with glory.*"[10]

That the aureole is the reward of the *glory* of virginity is proved from the description in the Book of Exodus (25:25) of a large crown surmounted by a small crown: "A polished crown, four inches high, and over the same another little golden crown," symbolizing the twofold reward which theologians mention,—the *essential* reward, the "aurea" in the likeness of a large crown, and the *accidental* reward, the "aureola" in the likeness of a small crown. This is the crown with which the lovely soul, and especially the virgin spouse of Christ, is to be crowned.[11] It is likewise proved from St. John's vision of "the woman clothed with the sun, and on her head a crown of twelve stars" (Apoc. 12:1). Just as Christ shares His throne with the victors, says St. Bonaventure, so does the Blessed Virgin share her crown with souls

(8) "Item, cui debetur fructus maior, illud est maioris virtutis, sed continentiae virginali debetur fructus centesimus, sicut dicitur Matthaei decimo tertio in Glossa, coniugali trigesimus: ergo etc." *IV Sent.,* d.33, a.2, q.2, t.IV, 754a. The editors have added the following footnote: "Glossa est ordinaria apud Strabum et Lyranum estque secundum Hieron. in hinc loc.: Centesimum fructum virginibus, sexagesimum viduis et continentibus, tricesimum casto matrimonia deputantes."

(9) Cf. *supra* p. 135, footnote 2.

(10) "Quod autem *aureola* respondeat alicui decori exteriori, patet: quia aureolae assignantur his actibus, qui considerant aliquid extrinsecum, ut puta quod est *infra,* ut corpus; vel quod est *iuxta,* ut proximus, quem convertit et ad patriam per bonam doctrinam ducit. Unde decor quidam erit *Doctoribus* de conversis per ipsos; et quidam etiam decor et gaudium erit *Martyribus* in corpore, qui se pro Christi passionibus exposuerunt; quidam decor *Virginibus* in corpore, quod pro Christo incorruptum servaverunt; et ille decor vel gaudium de illo decore *aureola* recte dicitur. Credo tamen, quod melius *decor* aureola dicatur quam *gaudium,* quia omnes gaudebunt de decore, non tamen omnes habebunt aureolam; sed ut totum ad unum dicatur, melius est dicere, quod utrumque, scilicet decor cum gaudio et gaudium cum decore." *IV Sent.,* d.33, a.2, q.3, t.IV, 757ab.

(11) "Tertio quaeritur de virginitate per comparationem ad praemium; et dicitur communiter, quod praemium virginitatis est aureola, et hoc probatur:

"1. Per figuram, Exodi vigesimo quinto praeceptum est, fieri supra magnam coronam aliam coronulam; et secundum hanc figuram duplex est praemium, ut dicunt magistri: *substantiale,* et hoc dicitur *aurea* ad similitudinem magnae coronae; et *accidentale,* et hoc dicitur *aureola* ad similitudinem parvae. Si ergo coronari debet illa corona anima decora, et maxime Christi sponsa; et talis est virgo: ergo etc." *Ibid.,* 755, 756a.

that are perfectly chaste.[12] Then, too, a crown is due one who has struggled manfully. The most bitter battle of life is with the flesh. Therefore, those who have distinguished themselves by a perfect and signal victory over the flesh, deserve to be crowned with a special crown. This perfect victory virgins achieve. They will, then, be crowned with a crown of distinction, one which the married will not possess.[13] They will receive not only the large crown, but the small golden crown as well.[14]

(12) "2. Item, hoc ostenditur per Scripturam, Apocalypsis duodecimo: *Mulier amicta sole, et in capite eius corona stellarum duodecim.* Si hoc de *beata Virgine* continentibus coronam; et sic etc." *Ibid.*, 756a.

(13) "3. Item, corona debetur certanti; sed maxima pugna est in carne: ergo qui ipsam perfecte vincit et notabiliter, debet notabiliter coronari. Sed perfecte vincunt virgines: ergo sunt notabiliter coronandi, ergo aliquam coronam habebunt, quam non coniugati." *Ibid.*

(14) "Item, in virginitate meremur non tantum *auream,* sed etiam *aureolam.*" *IV Sent.*, d.33, a.2, q.1, t.IV, 753.

Chapter IV

THE LILY OF CHRIST

On account of its rare grace and beauty, its ravishing whiteness and its infinite delicacy, the lily, the loveliest of flowers, is universally regarded as the emblem of virginal innocence and purity.[1] In the present treatise, the term is used to designate not those who observe the chastity of widowhood or of married life but pure virgins who have never lost the bloom of their virginal innocence.[2] "How to extol thee, O Virginal Purity," exclaims St. Bonaventure, "I know not. May that peerless Lily, the Uncreated Wisdom of God, the Lord Jesus, the Only-begotten Son of the Father and the only Son of the matchless Lily, the most chaste Virgin Mother Mary, who, standing on the border-line of the Old Covenant and the New, first pronounced the sacred vow of perpetual and perfect virginity, instruct my ignorance."[3] May the consideration of the snow-white lily, its beauty and surpassing loveliness, so highly praised by the virgin's Spouse, lead us to an appreciation of the lily of perfect virginity.[4] *"Consider the lilies of the field, how they grow. Amen, I say to you that not even Solomon in all his glory was arrayed as one of these"* (Matt. 6:28, 29). "King Solomon exceeded all the kings of the earth in riches and wisdom" (III Kings 10:23), and yet his glory could not compare with the glory of the lily, the symbol of the spiritual lily, the chaste virgin of Christ.[5] The Lord and Master of His creation could have

(1) "De hac igitur gratia lilii, in quo vitis nostra floruit, locuturi, videamus, vera luce nos illuminante, quare tanta virtus per *lilium* figuretur. Et manifeste quidem occurrit, quia propter candoris munditiam, qua ille flos ceteris floribus est praelatus, munditia virginalis merito figuratur. Nullus praeterae alius flos vel ipso prospectu tantum prae se fert gratiae, quantum hic unus; quare merito mundissima et omnibus piis gratiosa virginitas per hunc figuratur florem." *Vitis Mystica,* Additamentum IV, t.VIII, 196.

(2) "Sed hae iam minime *flores* appellantur, quia virginitatis florem lilii amiserunt. Eos igitur, qui deflorati non sunt, id est virgines, flore lilii in praesenti volumus nuncupari." *Ibid.*

(3) "Quibus itaque laudibus te efferam, o virginalis candor, prorsus nescio. Atqui nescientem me doceat singulare illud lilium, increata Dei sapientia, Dominus Iesus, unigenitus Patris Filius et unicus Filius lilii singularis id est castissimae Virginis Matris, quae in confinio utriusque legis votum consecravit perpetuae et integerrimae virginitatis." *Ibid.*

(4) "Doceat, inquam, me, quomodo per considerationem lilii materialis lilii virginalis circumstantias agnoscere valeam." *Ibid.*

(5) "Iam nunc ad contemplandum florem ipsum lilii veniamus. Vide, o virgo Christi, quanta pulcritudine praeemineat flos tuus, flos tuum florem designans, ceteris floribus. Vide, quantam prae omnibus floribus, qui sunt in terra, gratiam obtineat specialem. Vide, quantam ab ipso Sponso tuo laudem prae cunctis floribus mereatur. *Considerate,* inquit, *lilia agri, quomodo crescunt. Amen, dico vobis, quoniam nec Salomon in omni gloria sua coopertus est sicut unum ex istis.* Lege, o virgo, et perlege et saepe relege hoc verbum Sponsi tui et lege et intellige, quantum in huius floris commendatione tuam gloriam commendavit. Omnem mundi gloriam sapientissimus ille omnium Creator et cognitor unico tuo flosculo cooperuit nec gloriam flosculo, sed flosculum omni gloriae praetulit. In Salomone enim, de quo legitur, quod *magnificatus est super omnes reges universae terrae in divitiis* et honore, omnes mundi glorias debes intelligere; in flore vero lilii tui, qui tuam et omnium virginum Christi figuram gerit, virginitatis gloriam contemplare. Si ergo tantum commendatur ab ipsa Veritate decor lilii tui, ut ei iuste subiiciatur omnis gloria Salomonis, quem non dubium est secundum magnitudinem gloriae suae fuisse coopertum; quantum putas commendandum esse ipsum tuae virginitatis lilium incorruptum et nulla in perpetuum macula corrumpendum, cuius vel umbra et figura tantum meruit commendari? Si omne operimentum omnis gloriae Salomonis non potest decori unius materialis lilii comparari; quis decor comparabitur tuae florenti virginitati, quae est tuum lilium verum et spirituale? Nullus, inquam; quia ad claritatem altitudinis tui decoris decores terreni nequaquam possunt ascendere, quia *nec Salomon in omni gloria sua coopertus fuit sicut unum ex istis.*" *Ibid.,* 206ab.

raised her to the pinnacle of worldly glory. He could have placed her upon a throne and clothed her in queenly glory, but this was too little for His love. He reserved for her the very best that even He, the Almighty, could give. He made her His Bride.

We cannot help noticing that the flower of the lily, so tall, so white, so pleasing to the eye, is always bent towards the earth. The virgin of Christ, like the lily, in humility bends her head earthward, not presuming on herself but mindful of the dust and ashes whence she came and of her human frailty.[6] For no one is the virtue of humility more necessary than it is for virgins who, considering the excellence of their merits, are apt to fall into the abyss of pride. Virgins of Christ, even in this world, lead the life of angels; they are as the Lord said men would be in the resurrection. "For in the resurrection they shall neither marry nor be married; but shall be as the angels of God in heaven" (Matt. 22:30). They need not await the incorruption of the resurrection, for even now they lead an incorrupt life emulating that of the angels.[7] Lest, therefore, through pride they disgracefully fall from so high a step to which they have courageously mounted of their own free will, let them, like the flower of the lily, bend toward the earth. Let them remember that they are dust and that their "days are as grass." Let them consider that they have not yet risen to the happiness of immortality but are still hemmed in by a wall of flesh which separates them from their beloved Jesus. Let them beware of the wily serpent who endeavors to make them believe that their virginity is the result of their own virtue rather than the free gift of God, or that it was given them as a deserved recompense, or that on account of this singular gift they are better than others, or that the kingdom of heaven is already theirs. These are the four snares of Satan, according to St. Gregory, into which even good virgins not infrequently fall.[8]

Again and again the Seraphic Doctor recommends the virtue of humility to the virgins of Christ, whom Satan unceasingly labors to bring down from the lofty heights of chastity to which they have mounted. "Bow down," he

(6) "Nec praetereundum est, quod ipse flos lilii tam altus, tam candidus, tam iucundus semper reclinatur ad terram. Quid nobis per hoc aliud quam humilitas commendatur? Caput enim inclinare ad terram est mentem nostram ad generationem terrenam et fragilitatem de terra contractam inflectere, ne de nobis aliquid praesumere omnino audeamus, dum nos lutum et cinerem esse consideramus." *Ibid.*, 207b.

(7) "Nulli autem haec virtus tam necessaria est, ut virginibus, ne in profundum superbiae decidant, dum suorum considerant excellentiam meritorum. Virgines enim Christi etiam adhuc in terra viventes angelicam ducunt vitam, cum tales sint, quales dixit Dominus homines futuros esse post resurrectionem; quia tunc *neque nubent neque nubentur, sed erunt similes Angelis Dei in caelo.* Non exspectant autem virgines Christi incorruptionem resurrectionis solummodo, sed in praesenti, etiam vivunt incorruptae, vitam sine dubio angelicam aemulantes." *Ibid.*

(8) Ne igitur a tam altissimo gradu, quem non ex praecepto cuiusquam, sed propria voluntate viriliter ascenderunt, viliter per superbiam decidant; inclinentur ad terram, sicut flos lilii; recordentur, quoniam pulvis sunt, et quod dies eorum sicut foenum, et nondum aestiment, se ad immortalitatis beatitudinem resurrexisse, sed adhuc illo carneo pariete circumdatos, qui inter ipsos dividit et dilectum Iesum. Caveant illum astutum serpentem ipsis multipliciter insidiantem, ut vel ducat eas ad praesumendum aliquid de se, quatenus existiment, bonum, quod habent, non habere se a Deo, sed a propria virtute; vel credant, sibi pro meritis suis datum; vel propter hoc quod a Domino singulariter acceperunt, credant se meliores aliis; vel ut putent, se habere quod non habent. Haec sunt quatuor species iactantiae, quibus ille nequissimus serpens etiam bonos non raro decipit." *Ibid.*, 207b, 208a.

says, "that we may go over" (Isai. 51:23). "Bow down," that is, "direct earthward your intention which you have raised aloft to heavenly things that through you a passage may be open to crush you beneath our feet."[9] "O chaste soul, virgin of Christ, beloved of your Spouse and spouse of your Beloved," admonishes the Saint, "do not conspire with the enemy; do not bow down to seek the things of earth,—the praise of men, earthly honors and riches, for if you 'bow down' to these things, the Deceiver will 'go over.' He will trample upon you; he will overcome and crush you and upon you, who have cast aside the light and sweet yoke of Christ, he will place the insupportable yoke of his iniquity."[10]

Virgins who are delighted by the beauty of the lily should consider this point especially, that the flower of the lily is *white* within and without. For what does the white exterior of the flower symbolize if not purity of body? And what does the white interior signify if not the purity of the virgin's mind? It would be a sorry flower; indeed, 'twould be no lily at all, if either the interior or the exterior of the flower were deprived of its gleaming whiteness; so, too, that virgin would be a sorry virgin, indeed, no virgin at all, were she deprived of chastity both of mind and body.[11] I have no doubt that there are many virgins of both sexes who have finished their earthly course and attained salvation but who, nevertheless, are wholly undeserving of the virgin's crown. Many of these were pure in body but contaminated in mind, not unto eternal death, however, for they were awaiting lawful nuptials. "If," says the Apostle, "a virgin marry, she hath not sinned" (I Cor. 7:28). Far less has she sinned who has married in will only, although in her mind she has already desecrated the flower of her virginity. St. Augustine agrees with this opinion, saying: "A maiden aspiring to marriage is by no means better than a woman who has already entered the married state, for the latter is content with one man; the former, looking everywhere for a mate, necessarily commits fornication with many in her mind." One man pleases her today;

---

(9) "Vobis autem, o virgines Christi, humilitatis virtutem, quam iam saepius vestrae caritati commendavimus, ad propositi nostri rectitudinem pro maxima parte putamus sufficere. Quia enim in tantam altitudinem castitatis ascendistis, laborat adversarius vester, satanas, ut vos ab illa deflectat. Clamat enim nobis saepe, immo semper suggestionis internae voce dicens: *Incurvare, ut transeamus*. Quid est incurvare? Deflecte intentionem tuam ad terrena, quam ad caelestia erexisti, ut pateat nobis transitus per te, ut conculcemus te." *Ibid.*, 198b.

(10) "Ne consentias inimico tuo, o anima casta, virgo Christi, amica Sponsi tui, amici tui sponsa, ne consentias; ne incurveris; hoc est, nihil terrenum quaeras non laudes humanas, non honores, non divitias terrenas; quia si ad haec declinaveris, transibit per te mendax ille teque conculcabit et premet ac elidet te et iugum iniquitatis suae importabile ponet super te, si abieceris *iugum* Christi leve et suave. O quam insensati, qui recitudinem intentionis suae sic incurvant, ut accipiant illum deterrimum et iniquissimum satanam sessorem suum, abiecto illo pulcherrimo et optimo primo rectore Domino Iesu, cuius, ut ipse asserit, iugum suavissimum est et onus levissimum." *Ibid*. "For my yoke is sweet and my burden light" (Matt. 11:30).

(11) "Hoc autem virginibus est summopere considerandum, qui lilii pulcritudine delectantur, quod flos lilii tam interius quam exterius *albus* est. Quid enim per exteriorem partem floris albam nisi munditia corporis; quid per interiorem nisi mentis virginalis puritas figuratur? Turpe esset, immo non esset lilium, quod vel interius vel exterius candoris sui puritate careret; ita quoque turpis est virgo, immo non est virgo, quae non habet utramque, scilicet mentis et corporis castitatem." *Ibid.*, 206b, 207a.

another one, tomorrow; then the third and fourth, and perhaps more. How shall such a one, if she die, obtain the reward of incorrupt virginity?[12]

What of those virgins who after their vow have lost their physical virginity by violation against their will; or of those who sometime before their vow aspired to the wedded state but later, in the spirit of penitence, bound themselves by a vow of chastity; or of those who after their vow failed in their resolution to observe virginal chastity but later returned to the faithful observance of the vow and persevered in it even to the end? Shall virgins such as these be crowned with the reward? The Seraphic Doctor hesitates to say, but he gives it out as a matter of opinion rather than of definition that those who have been violated against their will without sensual gratification should not be deprived of the virgin's reward, according to the words of St. Lucy: "Si invitam iusseris violari, castitas mihi duplicabitur ad coronam" (cf. *Roman Breviary,* Feast of St. Lucy, December 13th, II Noct. lect. 6).[13] "If, however, their virginal chastity be lost," continues the Saint, "I hope that such loss will redound to their good, for perchance God permitted those virgins to be deprived of so great a privilege which He foresaw they would not use well. If a virgin uses her virginity to lord it over others, it would be to her advantage to lose her virginity and thereby acquire the virtue of humility."[14]

Wherefore, O virgins of Christ, do not sing in mournful tones: "The kingdom of the world and all the adornments of this present life I have despised for the love of the Lord Jesus Christ." By preserving for Himself the lily of your virginal purity, by specially consecrating it to Himself in preference to other beautiful virtues and holding it fast by a personal love, He has given you even in this life a glory greater than all the glory of the world. You will see this clearly in the Canticle of love, where, passing over

(12) "Unde non dubito, multos utriusque sexus virgines in corpore defunctos esse et salvandos, qui nequaquam virginale praemium merebuntur. Multi sunt mortui sunt, qui corpore quidem adhuc incorrupti, sed mente corrupti erant, ipsa tamen mentis corruptione non existente eis ad mortem aeternam, quia legitimas nuptias exspectabant, sine quibus nulla voluerunt illicita connubia perpetrare. *Si* enim, inquit Apostolus, *nupserit virgo, non peccavit;* multo minus peccavit quae sola tantum voluntate nupsit, quamvis iam in mente florem virginitatis corrupit. Consentit huic sententiae beatus Augustinus, dicens, "quod nequaquam melior est virgo aspirans ad nuptias muliere nuptias iam adepta, cum ea quae iam nupsit, uno sit viro contenta; nuptura vero, quaerens per omnem populum, cui adhaereat, cum pluribus necesse est fornicetur animo." Placet enim illi hodie unus, cras alius, deinde tertius et quartus et fortassis plures; et quomodo talis, si moritur, meritum obtinebit virginitatis incorruptae?" *Ibid.,* 207a.

(13) "Utrum autem illae virgines, quae vi opprimuntur post votum virginitatis nec aliquando consentiunt corruptioni; vel etiam illae quae ante votum aliquando ad nuptias aspiraverunt firma mente, sed postea, poenitentia ductae, voto castitatis se constrinxerunt; sive etiam illae quae post votum aliquando sola voluntate a voto continentiae resilierunt, sed rursus ad voti constantiam redierunt et usque in finem perseveraverunt: utrum, inquam, tales virgines sint praemio coronandae, fateor, me ex auctoritate nescire, et hoc magis peritiorum hominum, vel certe divino potius censeo arbitrio definiendum. Dico autem magis opinando quam definiendo de primis, quae vim patiuntur, si nunquam suae corruptioni nec voluntate nec delectatione consentiunt, virgineo non esse praemio spoliandas, quod ex verbis Luciae—si tamen authentica iudicantur—videtur posse comprobari." *Ibid.,* 207a.

(14) "Si autem per violentiam a non consentientibus castitas virginalis amittitur, spero, quod talis amissio castitatis ipsis amittentibus cedat in bonum, quia forte permisit eas benignus Iesus tali bono spoliari, quo praescivit, ipsas non bene usuras. Utile enim esset, aliquam, quae propter virginitatis meritum deberet superbire, perdere virginitatem et per hoc consequi humilitatis virtutem." *Ibid.* On this point, cf. St. Augustine, I. *de Civ. Dei,* c.28. n.1. MPL 41. 41, 42.

in silence nearly all the other flowers, Christ makes frequent mention of the flower of His spouse, repeating again and again the name of the *lily*. *As the lily among the thorns, so is my love among the daughters* (Cant. 2, 2). *My beloved has gone down into his garden, to the bed of aromatical spices, to feed in the gardens and to gather lilies* (Cant. 6:1). And again: *My beloved to me, and I to him who feedeth among the lilies* (Cant. 2:16).[15] O lily worthy of praise, beloved of thy Spouse! O lovable lily gathered by thy Spouse, gathered, as I think, not to droop and die but to be placed on the golden altar *which is before the throne of God* (Apoc. 8:3), that is, in the sanctuary of heaven, there to be the ornament of the other Saints in whom the Lord rests as if on a golden altar. O delicate, lovely lily, on which the Spouse feeds, not that He finds His delight in this flower alone but that He finds a special delight in it and bestows upon it His dearest love. And rightly so, for virgins possess a twofold endowment; other Saints not virgins, a single one. Now if the whole Church is virgin in mind, *not having spot or wrinkle,* as St. Paul says (Ephes. 5:27), incorrupt in faith, hope, and charity, and therefore worthy of the name of virgin and the praise of her Spouse, what great praise should be bestowed upon our lilies who have in body as well as in mind what the whole Church has only in mind! Indeed, the virgins of Christ are, as it were, the richness and the marrow, the most desirable part of the whole Church. These spiritual lilies, held fast in the close embrace of their Spouse, are the loveliest flowers in her garden.[16]

The six petals which form the perfect blossom of the dazzling white lily are symbolic of the six advantages which ought to inspire the maiden's heart with love of virginal purity. Three of these advantages pertain to the present life; three, to the life to come. Here the Seraphic Doctor notes the worries which usually accompany the state of marriage and praises in the most enthusiastic terms the incomparable sacrifice consummated by the virgin. By her espousal to her heavenly Bridegroom, the virgin escapes three dis-

---

(15) "Noli ergo subtristis cantare: 'Regnum mundi et omnem ornatum saeculi contempsi propter amorem Domini mei Iesu Christi', qui tibi etiam in praesenti vita decorem dedit omni decore mundano maiorem, lilium integritatis tuae sibi conservando et sibi prae ceteris pulcritudinibus virtutum specialiter dedicando et speciali dilectione adstringendo. Videbis luculenter hoc in Cantico amoris, ubi, ceteris floribus pene omissis, florem tuum saepius nominat nomen lilii saepius inculcando. *Sicut lilium inter spinas, sic amica mea inter filias;* et item: *Dilectus meus descendit ad areolam aromatum, ut lilia colligat;* et rursus: *Dilectus meus mihi, et ego illi qui pascitur inter lilia.*" *Vitis Mystica,* Additamentum IV, t.VIII, 206b.

(16) "Laudabile lilium, amica Sponsi; amabile lilium, quod colligitur a Sponso. Non enim, ut aestimo, colligitur, ut ultra marcescat; sed ut in altari aureo collocetur, *quod est ante thronum Domini,* id est, ut collocetur in caelesti sanctuario, ut sit ipsum lilium ad ornamentum aliorum Sanctorum, in quibus Dominus tanquam in altari aureo requiescit. Delicatum perfecto lilium, in quo pascitur Sponsus; non quod in hoc solo delectetur, sed in hoc quadam speciali praerogativa dilectionis plus aliis delectatur. Nec immerito. Duplex enim bonum in virginibus, quod in aliis Sanctis non virginibus simplex est. Cum enim tota Ecclesia virgo sin in anima, *non habens maculam neque rugam,* in fide et spe et caritate incorrupta, propter quod et *virgo* appellari meretur et a Sponso laudari; quanta laude putas digna esse lilia nostra, quae hoc habent tam in corpore quam in anima, quod tota Ecclesia habet tantum in anima? Quasi quidem adeps et medulla, medulla totius Ecclesiae sunt virgines Christi et quaedam singularis excellentia aliorum florum, Sponsi amplexibus familiarius inhaerentes." *Ibid.*

advantages of the present life and secures for herself three advantages of future glory.[17]

Two disadvantages of the present life are the result of the sentence pronounced on our first mother Eve after the transgression of the command, for against the serpent God pronounced three maledictions; against Eve, two; against Adam, one. To the serpent the Lord said: *Upon thy breast shalt thou go, and earth shalt thou eat and the woman shall crush thy head* (Gen. 3:14, 15). To Eve He said: *In sorrow shalt thou bring forth children and thou shalt be under thy husband's power* (Gen. 3:16). And to Adam God said: *In the sweat of thy face shalt thou eat bread* (Gen. 3:19).[18]

The maledictions pronounced against Eve and through her against all married women down to the present time are two, namely, that *in sorrow they bring forth children* and that *they are under the power of their husbands.*[19] How can we express the anguish of a woman in labor—sorrow so intense that it can be conceived only by those who have experienced it? Sacred Scripture makes frequent mention of this sorrow, and when we wish to express intensity of any pain we are accustomed to compare it to the pangs of childbirth. Our Lord Himself, Who understands all sorrow, did likewise. He willed to compare the sadness which His disciples felt at His approaching death to the sadness of a woman in labor, saying: *A woman, when she is in labor, hath sorrow, because her hour is come; so also you now indeed have sorrow* (John 16:21 ff.).[20] St. Paul, likewise, wishing to show the sorrow of those who come unprepared on the day of final judgment, says: *For when they shall say, peace and security; then shall sudden destruction come upon them, as the pains upon her that is with child, and they shall not escape* (I Thess. 5:3).[21] In the Prophets, too, and in many other passages of Sacred Scripture we find frequent reference to the intensity of this suffering. But since we have the more frequent testimony of the living

---

(17) "Tria sunt incommoda in praesenti vita in coniugatis, propter quae vitanda virginalis castitas est appetenda. Tria sunt quoque commoda futurae gloriae, propter quae acquirenda virginitas est vovenda Domino et conservanda." *Ibid.*, 209b.

(18) "Praesentis vitae incommoda duo habemus ex maledictione, quae inflicta fuit primae parenti nostrae Evae post transgressionem praecepti. Serpens enim tribus maledictionibus percussus fuit, Eva duobus, Adam una. Serpenti enim dictum est a Domino: *Supra pectus tuum gradieris, terram comedes, et mulier conculcabit caput tuum.* Evae autem dixit Deus: *In dolore paries filios et sub protestate viri eris.* Adae vero ait: *In sudore vultus tui comedes panem tuum.*" *Ibid.*

(19) "Maledictiones itaque Evae et per ipsam omnium mulierum nuptarum duae sunt in praesenti expressae, scilicet, quod *in dolore pariunt filios et sub potestate virorum sunt.*" *Ibid.*

(20) "Quis et quantus sit dolor mulierum parientium, nullus hominum cognovit, nisi quae expertae sunt. In Scripturis autem huius doloris testimonium frequenter invenimus, quia, cum magnitudinem alicuius doloris volumus exprimere, ipsum mulieri parturienti comparare solemus. Fecit hoc ipse Dominus, omnium dolorem cognitor; cum videret discipulos de morte sua nimium constristandos, ipsorum tristitiam mulieris parturientis tristitiae voluit comparare, dicens: *Mulier cum parit, tristiam habet, quia venit hora eius; ita et vos nunc quidem tristitiam habetis.*" *Ibid.* Cf. also Deut. 2:25; Ps. 47:7; Ecclus. 48:21; Isai. 13.8 and 21:3; Jer. 6:24 etc.

(21) "Similiter et beatus Paulus, volens ostendere dolorem eorum qui in èxtremi iudicii die imparati invenientur, ait: *Cum autem dixerint: Pax et securitas, tunc repentinus superveniet eis interitus, sicut dolor in utero habenti, et non effugient.*" *Ibid.*, 209b, 210a.

who have known it by experience, it seems useless to dwell longer on this point.[22]

But happy the virgins and truly wise, who beyond all worldly advantages have chosen to be united closely to the spirit of the Lord, procreating for their Eternal Spouse, the good Lord Jesus, not each year but every single day, offspring far better, far richer, and more secure—the spiritual offspring of good works; loving Him into Whose most chaste marriage chamber they have entered with sweet modesty, or Whom, rather, they have received into the marriage chamber of their own hearts, Whose living voice they have heard in His precepts and promises of heavenly rewards, and when their Spouse spoke, they were obediently responsive to Him Whose love brings with it a lasting chastity; Whose touch brings and preserves purity; Whose nuptials make and preserve virgins. O truly happy those who have consecrated the purity of their minds as well as of their bodies to such a Spouse! By intercourse with Him they are made so fruitful in soul that they become mothers of all the virtues; their children will dwell forever in their heavenly home, and face to face in His Presence shall the seed of their good works be directed to their Spouse forever. "The children of thy servants shall continue, and their seed shall be directed forever," says the Psalm (101:29).[23]

The virgin spouses of Christ likewise escape the second curse pronounced on the first mother Eve, and through her on all married women, for *they are not under the power of mortal man;* and in this regard consider diligently what a great evil they escape. St. Paul says: "The unmarried woman and the virgin thinketh on the things of the Lord, that she may be holy both in body and in spirit. But she that is married thinketh on the things of the world, how she may please her husband" (I Cor. 7:34). What does the virgin gain? Freedom from no small evil, worldly anxiety, "how she may please her husband." What an increase of devotion do you think takes place in virginal souls, who in accordance with their desires and duties, without hindering cares, can be free for prayer and other spiritual works? What great annoyance do you think devout married women experience who wish to have time for God but are prevented by their husbands to whom they must be subject? And indeed this is a heavy burden for women who are married to men whose characters and dispositions clash with their own good qualities and holy lives.

---

(22) "Saepius quoque in Prophetis et in aliis Scripturis de huius doloris magnitudine multa inveniuntur exempla. Sed quia vivorum plura suppetunt testimonia, quae id ad experientiam cognoverunt, videtur in his non diutius immorandum." *Ibid.*, 210a. Cf. also Gen. 35:18; I Kings 4:19; I Par. 4:9.

(23) "Sed felices virgines et vere prudentes, quae etiam praeter commoda carnalia spiritui Domini iungi vicinius elegerunt, spirituales fetus, id est bona opera, multo melius uberius et securius immortali Sponso suo, Domino bono Iesus non singulis annorum spatiis, sed diebus singulis procreantes, amantes eum, in cuius thalamum castissimum duce pudicitia intraverunt, vel quem potius in sui cordis thalamum receperunt, cuius vocem organicam in praeceptis suis et promissis praemiorum caelestium audierunt, et loquente Sponso suo, sibi per obedientiam responderunt; cuius amor castimoniam, cuius tactus munditiam, cuius nuptiae virgines faciunt et conservant. O vere felices, quae tali viro non solum animi, sed etiam corporis munditiam consecrarunt! Cuius commercio sic in anima fecundantur, ut omnium virtutum matres efficiantur, quorum *filii* in domo caelesti aeternaliter *habitabunt,* et *semen* operum suorum coram Sponso suo in saeculum dirigetur." *Ibid.*, t.VIII, 210a.

How many married women there are who would gladly purchase their independence at the price of death itself, that, freed from the power of wicked husbands, they might give unrestricted service to the Lord![24] And virgins who have tasted the sweetness of His attractions will never subject themselves to the power of an earthly spouse. Would one truly wise wish to free himself from the servitude of Him "to serve Whom is to reign?" Of the Saints we read that *they shall reign* with Christ *forever and ever* (Apoc. 22:5). If they will reign, they will be kings, "heirs indeed of God and joint heirs with Christ" (Rom. 8:17). Truly, then, will they be kings, heirs of God the King, joint heirs of Christ, the King. O happy virgins who are subject to the yoke of Him alone Who changes His servants into kings, of Whose kingdom there shall be no end![25]

The third advantage of virginity is *freedom from the countless cares* which are inevitably bound up with the rearing of children. The extent of this anxiety and worry only parents can know, for the greater the love, the greater the anxiety and who can fathom a parent's love for his child? It sometimes happens that this solicitude goes to such lengths that it takes full possession of all the powers of the soul and, excluding all else, makes the children the sole topic of conversation. Poor parents! their thoughts run hither and thither; they wander and traverse the course of land and sea; their bodies are worn with toil, that their children might enjoy money and possessions.[26] Nor are they at rest even when they have acquired more than they need, for, under the cover of paternal love, avarice steals into their hearts, as Juvenal says: "Crescit amor nummi, quantum ipsa pecunia crescit" (*Satyr.* 14, v.139). So great is their love of wealth that when deprived of it by reverses, their works of mercy are discontinued and those unhappy parents who cannot show compassion or mercy toward the unfortunate make themselves un-

(24) "Evadunt etiam virgines Christi maledictionem secundam Evae, matris primae, et per ipsam omnium mulierum maritatarum, scilicet quod *sub viri mortalis potestate non sunt;* et in hoc quantum malum effugias, diligentius intuere. Super quo Pauli Apostoli sententiam audiamus: *Virgo, quae innupta est, cogitat quae sunt Domini, ut sit sancta corpore et spiritu; quae autem nupta est cogitat quae sunt mundi, quomodo placeat viro.* Quid acquiritur? Evaditur malum non modicum, sollicitudo mundana, quomodo viro placeat. Quantum putas animis virginalibus devotionis augeri, quod libere, quando volunt et quando debent, nulla impediente cura, possunt orationibus ceterisque spiritualibus exercitiis vacare? Quantas, putas, habent coniugatae religiosae et Deo vacare volentes molestias, cum a viris propriis, quibus eas subiectas esse oportet, prohibentur? Est enim hoc magnum onus coniugii, cum mulieres viris talibus copulantur, qui a bonis earum moribus et bona conversatione discordant. Quantas putas esse coniugatas, quae supplicio mortis hoc emere vellent, quod a malorum virorum potestate liberatae, liberum possent Domino servitium exhibere?" *Ibid.*

(25) "Quem si recte gustaveris, ipso te trahente, iam nequaquam ulterius sub alterius potestate redigeris. Quis enim sapiens ab illius se vellet absolvere servitio, 'cui servire regnare est'. Quis autem regnare nolit? . . . Sic enim de Sanctis legitur, quia *cum Christo regnabunt* in aeternum. Quid est *regnabunt?* Reges erunt. Hoc enim et Apostolus ait: *Heredes quidem Dei, coheredes autem Christi.* Reges ergo vere erunt, heredes Dei regis, coheredes Christi regis. Felicissimae ergo virgines huius solius iugo subiectae, qui servos suos commutat in regis, quorum regnum non mutabitur in aeternum!" *Ibid.*, 210b.

(26) "Tertia causa appetendae virginitatis est *carentia multiplicium anxietatum,* quae inevitabiliter habentur circa pueros nutriendos. Quanta sit haec anxietas et sollicitudo, soli novere parentes. Secundum amorem enim, quo afficiuntur circa filios, extenditur sollicitudinis magnitudo, quem amorem, exceptis parentibus, nulli sciunt. Verum enim dixit qui ait: 'Quis sit amor prolis, soli novere parentes'. Unde nonnunquam sollicitudinem ipsam in tantum contingit extendi, ut omnes animi vires occupet, et omnibus postpositis, solummodo filiorum mentio habeatur. Discurrit animus et vagatur et circuit mare et aridam, nihil inexpertum relinquit, plurimumque et corpus miserorum parentum diverso labore atteritur, ut filiis pecunia et possessio comparetur." *Ibid.*, 210b, 211a.

worthy of obtaining mercy. Now you see the great evil caused by undue solicitude for one's children and where it leads. What untold anxiety do even good parents, and especially mothers, who generally have greater love for their children, suffer when they see these children leave the path of virtue and wander through the bypaths of vice, when they see them afflicted with divers diseases of body, when, finally, they see them overtaken by death! In such great trials, what place is left for divine contemplation? How will a heart weighed down by such heavy sorrows raise itself aloft?[27]

O happy virgins whose Spouse can die no more, whose sons, the virtues, always live and lead the virgins themselves to life, whose thoughts are directed not towards earthly goods, but, forgetful of children, tend to the only good! Even in this world, happy virgins bear in their own souls heaven with its joys, which later shall be made manifest to them. Already they wander through celestial joys, they pass through choirs of blessed spirits, and with the clear vision of the spiritual soul, they understand the particular duties of each of the choirs and, detained by no solicitude for earthly children, these peerless virgins taste the joys prepared for them by their King and their Spouse.[28]

Happy, therefore, are the virgins who in taking a Spouse have subjected themselves to Him alone "Whose yoke is sweet, Whose burden light" (Matt. 11:30). With every fiber of their hearts they desire to please Him alone Who is *beautiful above the sons of men.* With the purest affection unshared by any creature, they give themselves wholly and entirely to Him from Whom they have received all—their very existence in the order of nature and in the order of grace,—and Who out of pure love has given Himself as their Spouse. What worthy return, O Virgin of Christ, can you make for such great generosity? He gave you to yourself when He created you that you might exist; He gave you to yourself a second time when He re-created you that you might live a holy life, and, lest you faint on the way, He gave you as provision for your journey His own Body and Blood, His very Self, true God and true Man. And, you, what return will you make? If you know not how to repay

(27) "Nec adhuc quiescitur, etiam pluribus, quam necessitas exigat, conquisitis, quia occasione dilectionis filiorum subintrat avaritia etc. Crescit amor nummi, quantum ipsa pecunia crescit. Et nimis hanc optat, cum non habet, consequenterque moriuntur in miseriis opera misericordiae, dum miseris nec possunt compati nec volunt misereri et se ipsos miserrimi parentes faciunt indignos ad misericordiam consequendam. Iam, ut puto, vides, quantum malum faciat sollicitudo circa filios habita et ad quem finem tendat. Quantum autem putas anxietatis addioi etiam bonis parentibus, et maxime matribus, quae maiore solent circa filios affectu moveri, cum vident, vitam filiorum, virtutum tramite relicto, vagari per devia vitiorum, cum diversis illos affici vident corporum infirmitatibus, cum denique tandem ad mortis vident interitum devenire? Quis in tantis miseriis locus divinae contemplationi relinquitur? Quomodo cor sursum habebit tantis gravitatibus oppressum?" *Ibid.,* 211a.

(28) "O quam beatae virgines, quorum Sponsus non ultra mori potest, quarum filii, id est virtutes, semper vivunt, immo et ipsas ad vitam perducunt, quarum animus ad diversa terrena non distenditur, sed ad solum bonum extenditur, posteriorum oblitus! Portant iam virgines beatae in mente sua caelum cum gaudiis, quantum homini fas est, quod ipsis postea est laturum. Iam vagantur per gaudia caelestia, transeunt choros beatissimorum spirituum, singulorum chororum officia singula spirituali mentis vivacitate perspiciunt, et singularium virginum gaudia sibi a Rege et a Sponso suo praeparata libera mentis aviditate degustant, nulla filiorum terrenorum sollicitudine remoratae." *Ibid.*

Him for His gift of your creation, how can you repay Him for the gift of Himself? If you could give yourself a thousand times, what a poor offering you would be, compared to God! But for all that, give as much as you can; give yourself entirely to Him Who has given you entirely to yourself and Who has restored you entirely to yourself and, not satisfied with this, has in addition given Himself entirely to you. Love Him Who has loved you so much; love Him "with thy whole heart, and with thy whole soul, and with all thy strength" (Luke 10:27). Love your matchless Lover, for He has given you a heart of good will and a rational mind and strength to accomplish the things that are good. Let thy soul bless the Lord and never forget all that He hath done for thee (cf. Ps. 102:2); bind yourself to Him with bonds of love that without restraint you may "be still" (Ps. 45:11) and "taste and see that the Lord is sweet" (Ps. 33:9).[29]

Let us now consider the three advantages which virgins alone will enjoy in the life to come. St. John the Evangelist in his Apocalypse saw twelve times twelve thousand harpers, their virginal bodies undefiled, "follow the Lamb whithersoever He goeth" (cf. 14:1-4). Behold the singular reward of virgins, which is symbolized by the fourth petal of the lily, "they follow the Lamb whithersoever He goeth." Quoting St. Augustine, the Seraphic Doctor continues: "Where does this Lamb go where only virgins have the courage and strength to follow Him? Into what glades, into what meadows does He go? He goes there, I think, where true joys are found, not the empty joys of this world, deceiving transports, nor the joys which are experienced in the kingdom of God by those who are not virgins, but joys unlike all other joys,—the joys of the virgins of Christ, joys which they receive from Christ, in Christ, with Christ, after Christ, through Christ. The particular joys of the virgins of Christ are not the same as the joys of those who are not virgins, although the latter, too, are Christ's; for others there are other joys, but none such as these. Enter into these joys, *follow the Lamb, whithersoever He goeth.* Indeed, the flesh of the Lamb is likewise virginal, for when He had grown to man's estate, He preserved that virginity which His conception in

(29) "Felices igitur virgines, quae Sponsum accipientes, illi se soli subiecerunt, cuius *iugum suave est et onus leve,* eique soli tota et integra mente placere desiderant, qui sane est *speciosus forma prae filiis hominum,* non dividentes mentem suam, ut ex parte cupiant et sollicitae sint placere Deo et ex parte placere viro, sed se totas integras reddunt illi a quo semetipsas receperunt, ut essent, et receperunt, ut bene essent, ipsumque praeterea Sponsum gratuito acceperunt. Quid poterit tanto largitori digne rependi? Dedit te tibi, cum te creavit, ut esses; reddidit te tibi, cum te recreavit, ut bene esses; dedit in viaticum tibi, ne in via deficias, corpus et sanguinem suum, se verum Deum et verum hominem; et tu quid rependes? Si pro eo, quod te tibi dedit, cum te creavit, vicem nequis rependere; quid denique pro eo, quod se tibi dedit? Certe, si te millies posses rependere, quid esses tu in comparatione Dei? Repende tamen quantum potes, repende te totam illi qui te totam tibi et dedit et reddidit, et his non contentus, se quoque totum tibi dedit. Dilige hunc tantum te diligentem et singularem dilectum *ex toto corde et ex tota anima tua et ex omnibus viribus tuis;* quia et cor bonae voluntatis et animam rationabilem et vires ad implenda quae bona sunt, ipse dedit tibi. *Benedicat anima tua Domino et noli oblivisci* has et omnes retributiones eius; et te dilectionis illius vinculis adstringe, ut liberius *vacare possis et videre, quam suavis est Dominus.*" *Ibid.,* 210b.

the womb of His Mother did not destroy."[30] He was a Virgin conceived of a Virgin, a Virgin born of a Virgin and after His birth He remained with His Virgin Mother a Virgin, the Author, the Guardian and lover of virginity and its exceedingly great Reward, Christ Jesus.[31]

In this passage from the Apocalypse, St. Bonaventure finds proof of the high rank and excellence of the virginal life, and of its being a new thing upon the earth. The whole assembly of the redeemed, says the Evangelist, was a multitude which no man could number. But amongst them was a certain determinate number of the highest dignity and without spot, the first-fruits of the earth, those twelve times twelve thousand, the number which denotes perfection.[32] And *they follow the Lamb, whithersoever He goeth.* The rest, as St. Augustine says, may follow the Lord, at least follow His footprints, walking along the same path, but they do not set their feet perfectly in His very steps. The rest of the multitude may follow Him everywhere except where He walks in the glory of virginity; but these follow Him even there. "Continue to follow Him," exhorts St. Augustine, "O virgins of Christ, by persevering in your holy vows. Do everything in your power that the blessing of virginity may not be lost to you, for you can in no way regain it." O, with what great admiration, with what great joy will the rest of the multitude of the Saints who cannot follow the Lamb along this path, behold you and rejoice with you because they have in you what they do not have in themselves![33] Indeed, that Omnipotent Lamb Whom you follow whither-

(30) "Sequamur, et nos prosequamur in tractatu materiae propositae commoda futurae vitae, Christi virginibus singulariter accessura. Beatissimus evangelista Ioannes in Apocalypsi sua vidit duodecies duodena millia sanctorum citharoedorum illibatae virginitatis in corpore, inviolatae veritatis in corde, quod sequerentur *Agnum,* sponsum virginum *quocumque ierit." Ibid.* Quoting St. Augustine, *de Sancta Virginitate,* c.27, n.27, St. Bonaventure continues: "Ecce, virginum praemium singulare, quod per quartum folium floris lilii designatur, quia *sequuntur Agnum, quocumque ierit.* 'Quo ire putamus hunc Agnum, quo nemo eum sequi vel audeat vel valeat nisi vos? Quo, inquam putamus eum ire? In quos saltus, in quae prata? Illuc, aestimo, ubi sunt vera gaudia, non gaudia huius saeculi vana, insaniae mendaces, nec gaudia, qualia in ipso regno Dei ceteris non virginibus praestantur, sed a ceterorum omnium gaudiorum sorte distincta. Gaudia virginum Christi, de Christo, in Christo, cum Christo, post Christum, per Christum. Gaudia propria virginum Christi non sunt eadem non virginum, id est eorum qui non sunt virgines, quamvis tamen sint Christi. Nam sunt aliis alia gaudia, sed nullis talia. Ite in haec, sequimini *Agnum quocumque ierit;* quia et Agni caro utique virgo est. Hoc enim in se retinuit, cum esset in corpore auctus, quod non abstulit Matri conceptus'." *Ibid.,* 211ab.

(31) *Ibid.,* cf. *supra,* p. 119, footnote 1.

(32) The number *twelve* is twice perfect. *Six* is the perfect number. Cf. *supra,* p. 73, footnote 17.

(33) For references to St. Augustine in these passages, cf. *De Sancta Virginitate,* c.27, n.27 and *ibid.,* c.28, n.28 and c.29, n.29. MPL 40, 410, 411.

" 'Non enim habent, quid faciant, ut virgines sunt, in quibus iam factum est, ut virgines non sint'. . . . 'Sequantur itaque Agnum ceteri fideles, qui virginitatem corporis amiserunt, non quocumque ierit, sed quocumque ipsi poterunt. Possunt autem in omnibus virtutibus, nisi cum in decore virginitatis incedit. Quomodo enim post eum ibunt itinere virginali, qui hoc amiserunt, quod nullo modo recipiunt? Vos ergo, o virgines eius, vos ite post eum, quae propter hoc unum, quocumque ierit, sequimini eum. Sequimini eum tenendo perseverantur quod vovistis ardenter; facite quod potestis, ne virginitatis bonum vobis pereat, cui facere nihil potestis, ut redeat'. O quanta cum admiratione, o quanto cum gaudio videbit vos cetera multitudo Sanctorum, quae Agnum ad hoc sequi non potest. Videbit nec invidebit, et collaetando vobis, quod in se non habet habebit in vobis." Opusc. *X. Vitis Mystica, Additamentum IV,* t.VIII, 211b.

soever He goeth will not desert those who cannot follow Him as you do; He will go before them and He will not depart from them, for *God will be all in all* (I Cor. 15:28), and those who are less favored will not stand in awe and fear of you, for where there is no envy, difference is concord. Wherefore be courageous, confident, strong, and steadfast. *Vow ye, and pay to the Lord your God* (Ps. 75:12) your vows of perpetual chastity, not only that you may avoid the troubles of this present life but far more that you may enjoy the singular delights of the world to come, which Christ, your Lamb *passing will minister* especially *unto you* (Luke 12:37).[34]

Let not the virgins of Christ foolishly imagine that virginity alone suffices for them to follow the Lamb of God whithersoever He goeth, for the Lamb Himself treads the path not only of virginity but of all the virtues. The virgin of Christ, then, even in this life, must follow the example of the most gentle Lamb along the path of all the virtues if she wishes to reach the place where she will for all eternity follow Him wherever He shall go. How can a proud virgin follow the Lamb walking in the path of humility, if she in no way resembles Him? How can the passionate follow Him who is most mild? How can the envious follow One burning with love? How can the avaricious follow the most bountiful Jesus? How can the discouraged follow Him Who is courageous and strong? How can a virgin who is disposed to indulge herself follow Him Who is habitually temperate? The Lamb walks the path of all the virtues; so, too, let the virgin walk who wishes to imitate the Lamb. Let her be humble, mild, burning with love; let her be generous, courageous, and temperate and she is imitating and will imitate the Lamb whithersoever He goeth, and she will deserve to hear from her Spouse, the Lamb Himself, the words of the Canticle: "How beautiful are thy steps in sandals, O prince's daughter!" (7:1). Indeed, the virginal soul, whose steps in sandals are praised, will be the favored daughter of God, the Prince, and the favored Lady of the kings of earth. *Beautiful* are the virgins' *steps in sandals* when, directed along the path of all the virtues, they follow Christ the Lamb Who died for them, they themselves being prepared to follow the Lamb for the Lamb's sake even to death and through death, if necessary; in every deed by the example of the Good Lamb, Christ Jesus, strengthening the feet of their affections against the serpent laying snares for their virginal sandals, whose

(34) "Agnus quippe ille, quem vos quocumque ierit, sequimini, nec eos deseret, qui eum non valent sequi quo vos; omnipotentem Agnum loquimur, et vobis praeibit et ab eis non abibit, cum erit Deus *omnia in omnibus;* et qui minus habebunt a vobis non horrebunt; ubi enim nulla invidentia est, concors est differentia. Praesumite itaque, confidite, roboramini, permanete qui vovetis et *reddite Domino Deo vestro* vota perpetuae continentiae, non tantum propter aerumnas praesentis saeculi vitandas, sed multo magis propter futuri saeculi delicias singulares, quae vobis specialiter Agnus vester, Christus transiens ministrabit." *Ibid.*, 211b, 212a.

head, nevertheless, by the help of the Lamb Himself, is crushed by a Virgin's foot.[35]

The fifth petal of the flower of the lily symbolizes the fifth reason why virginity is desirable: *They will sing before the throne of God and of the Lamb a new canticle which virgins alone can sing* (cf. Apoc. 14:3). Happier than the rest of the multitude, o virgins, are you who bring to the eternal nuptials of the Lamb a new song which you will sing, harping on your harps, not a song such as all the earth sings, as the Psalm says: "Sing ye to the Lord a new canticle. Sing to the Lord, all the earth" (Ps. 95:1), but a song which you alone can sing.[36] The rest of the multitude will listen and will be delighted by the excellent gift which is yours alone, but you, who both sing and hear the song, will exult more happily, will reign more joyously than they. What mind can conceive the happiness, the delight, the exultant joy, for if all the virgins will sing that song, will not the Virgin of Virgins herself sing? Surely, she will sing and will sing more beautifully and more joyously than the other virgins, for she is the purest of them all, and in her singing she will be an example to the whole choir of virgins whom by her example she has inspired with a love of virginity. The virgins then with festive joy will sing their song to the heart of the Virgin Lamb, their Spouse, Who has bestowed upon them the privilege of being able to sing such a song.[37] Will not the Lamb Himself, Who surpasses not only the assembly of the other virgins but also the Virgin of Virgins, His Mother—the Lamb from Whom they have received not only their virginity but their very existence, the Spouse Himself, the most desirable Virgin of Virgins, will He not also sing? Yes, indeed, He will sing, and that most joyful voice of the Eternal Word of the

(35) "Caveant autem virgines Christi, ne pueriliter ista intelligant, ita ut solam virginitatem credant sibi sufficere ad sequendum Agnum Dei, quocumque ierit; cum ipse Agnus non solum virginitatis semitam, immo etiam omnium virtutum viam incedat. Oportet ergo, virginem Christi omnium virtutum itinere, etiam in hac vita, Agnum mansuetissimum imitari, si vult illuc pervenire, ubi sine fine eum, quocumque ierit, sequetur. Quomodo enim sequi potest virgo superba Agnum in humilitatis via gradientem, ad quem nullo modo accedit? Quomodo mitissimum iracunda, quomodo ferventem in caritate invida, quomodo largissimum avara, quomodo alacrem accidiosa, quomodo sobrium ebriosa? Ambulat in omni via omnium virtutum Agnus, ambulet sic et virgo cupiens Agnum imitari. Sit humilis, mitis sit, sit caritate fervens, sit larga, sit alacris, sit sobria, et imitatur et imitabitur Agnum, quocumque ierit, et meretur ab ipso Agno, Sponso suo audire: *Quam pulcri sunt gressus tui in calceamentis, filia principis!* Specialis quippe filia Dei principis, et domina regum universae terrae erit anima virginalis, cuius gressus commendantur in calceamentis. . . . Pulcri igitur sunt gressus virginum in calceamentis, cum directae per viam virtutum omnium Agnum Christum pro ipsis mortuum prosequuntur, paratae pro Agno etiam ipsae usque ad mortem et per mortem, si necesse fuerit, sequi Agnum; in omni facto munientes pedes affectuum suorum exemplis optimi Agni, Christi Iesu adversus serpentem insidiantem calcaneo virginali, cuius tamen caput virginali pede, ipsius Agni adiutorio, conculcatur." *Ibid.*, 212a.

(36) "Quintum folium floris lilii quintam causam designat, propter quam virginitas est appetenda, illam scilicet, quia *cantabunt canticum novum ante thronum Dei et Agni quod* praeter virgines, *nemo dicere potest.* O felices et ceteris feliciores virgines, quae "affertis ad illas Agni nuptias aeternales canticum novum, quod cantabitis in citharis vestris, non utique tale, quale cantat uinversa terra, ut dicitur: *Cantate Domino canticum novum, cantate Dominum omnis terra;* sed tale, quale nemo potest dicere nisi vos'." *Ibid.* Here St. Bonaventure is still quoting St. Augustine.

(37) "Audiet tamen et delectabitur omnis multitudo fidelium vestro proprio et tam excellenti dono. Vos autem, quae et dicetis et audietis, quia id quod dicetis a vobis audietur, felicius exsultabitis iucundiusque regnabitis. Quis istam felicitatem, quis istam iucunditatem poterit explicare, immo quis humana mente concipiet tantae exsultantis iubilum? Nam si omnes virgines canticum istud cantabunt, nunquid illa virginum Virgo no cantabit? Cantabit utique et tanto melius et iucundius, quanto castior ceteris, praebebitque toti virginum choro in cantando exemplum, quas ad virginitatis amorem suo incitavit exemplo. Cantabunt ergo virgines illa iucunditate festiva canticum suum in cor Agni virginis, Sponsi sui, a quo, ut tale canticum cantare possent, acceperunt." *Ibid.*, 212ab.

Father, accompanied by all the virgins in His midst, will be heard above all. O happy song! O joyous festivity without compare or end! Who would not sigh for it? Who would not labor to reach the place where he may hear the new song of so many virgins, the wondrous voice of the Lamb's Mother ringing out above the rest; where he may hear the All-sweet Lamb Himself singing the purest and sweetest melody? If, even in this body of living death, the words of the Lord are sweet to the palate (cf. Ps. 118, 103), "sweeter than honey and the honeycomb" (Ps. 18, 11), what will be the sweetness of His words in the home which knows no death, nor fear, nor grief, where there is no place for bitterness but where all, inebriated with the abundance of His house, will drink of the torrent of divine pleasure? Great will be the joy of all the multitude on hearing the sweet virginal canticle of the Lamb; unbounded the joy of the virgins, who alone sing the song with the Lamb.[38]

The sixth and last reason why virginity is desirable is symbolized by the sixth petal of the flower of the lily. This reason the prophet Isaias long foretold: "I will give to them in my house and within my walls, a place and a name better than sons and daughters. I will give them an everlasting name which shall never perish" (Isai. 56:5). O sublime honor, O surpassing glory, O singular reward of virgins! Let all virgins ponder these words, and let all those who are delighted by the sublimity of the reward but who have not yet vowed chastity to the most chaste Jesus, set out on the high and narrow path of virginity that they, too, may receive the reward of an everlasting name and a place far better than that given to those who have begotten sons and daughters.[39]

What is that *name* which the Lord has promised to give to His virgins? It is a certain characteristic and surpassing glory which virgins alone will possess. As men are distinguished by their names, so is this glory of virgins termed a *name* which will distinguish them from the multitude assembled in the same kingdom and in the same house. All the blessed who are destined

(38) "Quid autem? Nunquid et ipse Agnus non solum aliarum virginum coetum, sed etiam ipsam Virginem virginum, Matrem suam superexcellens, a quo, habent non solum, ut sint virgines, sed etiam ut sint; nunquid ipse Sponsus, virginum virgo optimus non etiam cantabit? Immo vero et ipse cantabit, et iucundissima illa vox Verbi Patris aeterni prae omnibus, cum omnibus, in omnibus audietur. O felix, felicius, felicissimum canticum! O festivitatem iucundissimam, comparatione et fine carentem! Quis istud non anhelet? Quis laborare contemnet, ut illuc perveniat, ubi tantarum virginum canticum novum audiat, ubi mirabiliter prae ceteris virginibus redundantem vocem Matris Agni percipiat; ubi et ipsum Agnum purissimum et dulcissimum melos, totem melleum audiat concinentem? Si enim *eloquia Domini*, teste Psalmista, et in isto corpore mortis existentis alicui tam *dulcia sunt, ut mel et favum superent;* quanta putas ea dulcedine superabundare deber, ubi omnis mortalitas, omnis timor, omnis dolor procul transierunt; ubi nulli amaritudini nullus locus relinquitur, sed omnes *torrente voluptatis* divinae potabuntur, inebriatae ab *ubertate domus* eius? Maxima omnibus felicitas canticum virgineum Agni dulcissimum audientibus, multo tamen abundantior virginibus ipsi et cum ipso Agno cantantibus." *Ibid.*, 212b.

(39) "Sexta et ultima causa, propter quam virginitas est appetenda, sexto floris lilii folio designatur. Ostenditur, quae sit haec causa, testimonio Isaiae ita dicentis: *Eunuchis,* id est virginibus meis, *dabo in domo mea et in muro meo locum nominatum multo meliorum quam filiorum atque filiarum; nomen aeternum dabo eis, quod nunquam deficiet.* O sublime meritum virginum, o gloriam excellentem, o praemium speciale! Legant et intelligant memoriaeque commendent verbum hoc, verbum bonum et suave, virgines omnes; pueri pariter et puellae gaudeant et perseveranter currant, qui iam continentiam voverunt, donec comprehendant. Audiant qui nondum voverunt et delectentur in altitudine praemiorum, ut voveant etiam ipsi votum castitatis castissimo Iesu et semitam virginitatis altissimam et arctissimam apprehendant, ut ipsi bravium accipiant nominis sempiterni et locum multo meliorem, quam qui filios et filias ex se genuerunt, incolere mereantur. *Ibid.*, 213a.

for eternal life will remain in one kingdom and will enjoy one God; nevertheless, as the Apostle says: "Star differeth from star in glory. So also is the resurrection of the dead" (I Cor. 15:41, 42), that is, the different merits of the Saints. Though all the stars are in the heavens, still, "one is the glory of the sun, another the glory of the moon, and another the glory of the stars" *(ibid.)*. So, too, though all the Saints will shine in glory, their lights will be more or less brilliant according to their merits. "In my Father's house there are many mansions" (John 14:2) says St. John. What will be the glory of the virgins who have followed Christ in purity of body and of mind? As the moon surpasses the other heavenly bodies in its resemblance to the sun, so do virgins surpass the other Saints in their resemblance to Christ. They alone follow Him whithersoever He goeth. Therefore, like the moon which shines high above the stars in glory, will the virgins of Christ possess in the house of the Lord a far better place than other sons and daughters who are not thus sealed with the honor of virginity.[40]

To these brides of Christ the Seraphic Doctor thus addresses himself:

> "If then you have despised the nuptials of the sons of men whereby you might bring forth sons of men, so much the more, O virgins, love with your whole heart the Son of Man *beautiful above the sons of men* (Ps. 44.3). Consider the beauty of your Lover, a beauty derided by the proud but discernible to you by the inner eyes of your soul. Consider His wounds as He hangs on the cross, His scars in the Resurrection, His blood shed in death, the price of your faith, the work of your redemption. Consider the great value of all these things; weigh them on the balance of charity, and whatever love you have to bestow upon a bridegroom, bestow it upon Him Who seeks not physical beauty but the inner beauty of your soul when *He gave you the power to be made the daughters of God* (John 1:12). Consider the great security of your love for Him Whom you do not fear to displease by ill-grounded suspicions. Earthly spouses love each other because they discern unmistakable signs of mutual love. Ofttimes, however, they suspect each other of some wrong because they cannot see the hidden secrets of their hearts. Not so with your Lover, the most sweet, the all-desirable Jesus, in Whom you will find nothing to reproach. Nor do you have to fear that

(40) "Quid per hoc *nomen* designatur, quod Dominus promittit se suis virginibus daturum? 'Quaedam utique gloria propria excellensque significatur, quae erit virginibus non communis cum multis, quamvis in eodem regno et eadem domo constitutis. Nam ideo fortassis *nomen* dictum est quod eos quibus datur, distinguit a ceteris,' sicut homines propriis nominibus distinguuntur. Licet enim omnes ad vitam aeternam praedestinati in uno regno sint mansuri et uno Deo fruituri; tamen, sicut ait Apostolus, *stella differt a stella in claritate; sic et resurrectio mortuorum;* 'haec sunt merita diversa Sanctorum'. Nam sicut commune est omnibus sideribus esse in caelo, et tamen est *alia gloria solis, alia lunae, alia stellarum;* sic in ipsa vita aeterna esse commune erit omnibus Sanctis, in ipsa autem vita aeterna distincte fulgebunt lumina meritorum. *In domo autem Patris aeterni mansiones multae sunt,* 'ubi non vivet alter altero prolixius, quia omnes habebunt vitam aeternam. 'In multis autem mansionibus honoratur alius alio clarius'. Quanta, putas, ibi gloria fulgebunt virgines Christi, corporis simul et mentis puritate Christum sequentes? Qui Sanctorum chorus melius lunae comparabitur quam virgines? Quod sidus soli similius quam luna? Quis chorus Sanctorum quo Sponso similior quam virgines? Solae sequentur eum, *quocumque ierit;* unde et solae illi similes sunt atque simillissimae. Honorabuntur ergo prae ceteris in eodem regno existentibus splendore quidem excellentiori, sicut lunam videmus prae ceteris sideribus praeeminere; possidebuntque in domo Domini locum meliorem multo quam ceterorum filiorum et filiarum ipsius, qui virginitatis merito non sunt insignes." *Ibid.,* 213ab.

He who looks into your hearts and *reins* may falsely suspect you of some evil. 'The searcher of hearts and reins is God' (Ps. 7:10). 'Man seeth those things that appear, but the Lord beholdeth the heart' (I Kings 16:7). If, then, you would owe great love to an earthly spouse, how dearly ought you to love Him for Whose sake you were willing to have no earthly spouse! Hold fast in your heart Him Who for you was fastened to the cross; be ever mindful of the great love He has shown for you who for Him have kept yourselves inviolate in body as well as in soul; be ever mindful, too, of the singular glory He has prepared for you whom He has honored by so singular a grace.[41]

"In heaven He will give to you, O virgins of Christ, a special glory, a special crown which the Fathers call the *aureole* or *little golden crown,* a word derived from *aurum, gold,* that the very name of the crown which will be given you as the reward of virginity may suggest the excellence of the virgin's glory. 'Why,' I ask, 'will it be given to the consecrated virgins of Christ?' 'That they might shine forth among the saints as gold among the metals,' for Isaias says: 'In that day the Lord of hosts shall be a crown of glory and a garland of joy to the residue of His people' (Isai. 28:5). Notice that the *crown* is made of gold and precious stones; the *garland,* of flowers,—roses, violets, and such blossoms. How glorious to have God Himself for a crown! Not only will virgins have God for a crown, a reward possessed by all the Glorified, but for the flowery garland of joy in their hair, they will have the special privilege of spiritual glory, which will shine forth in the virgins in their heavenly home. 'I will give to them in my house and within my walls, a place, and a name better than sons and daughters. I will give them an everlasting name which shall never perish' (Isai. 56:5). But what is that *place better than the sons of God;* that *everlasting name;* what is the *aureole?* Ineffable glory, exceedingly great and incomprehensible to those who have not experienced it. Wherefore, O virgins, who alone will be able to enjoy this experience, press on with great eagerness; persevere with great courage."[42]

(41) "Si ergo nuptias contempsistis filiorum hominum, ex quibus gigneretis filios hominis; tanto magis corde amate Filium hominis *speciosum forma prae filiis hominum.* Inspicite pulcritudinem amatoris vestri; etiam hoc ipsum, quod in eo derident superbi, inspicite, quam pulcrum sit interioribus luminibus. Inspicite vulnera pendentis, cicatrices resurgentis, sanguinem morientis, pretium credentis, commercium redimentis. Haec quanti valeant, cogitate; haec in statera caritatis appendite, et quidquid amoris in nuptias vestras impendendum habetis, illi rependite, qui non pulcram carnem, sed interiorem pulcritudinem vestram quaerit, ubi vobis *dedit potestatem filias Dei fieri.* Videte, cum quanta securitate amatis eum cui displicere falsis suspicionibus non timetis. Vir et uxor invicem se amant, quia in se vident in manifesto signa caritatis; saepe tamen de se aliquid mali invicem suspicantur, quia sua occulta invicem non contuentur. Non ita est de amatore vestro, dulcissimo Iesu, toto desiderabili, in quo nihil invenietis, quod reprehendere possitis; nec vobis timendum est de ipso, quod falso aliquid mali de vobis suspicetur qui *renes* intuetur et corda. Si ergo magnum amorem coniugibus deberetis, quantum amare debetis eum, propter quem coniuges habere noluistis? Totus vobis figatur in corde qui pro vobis fixus est in cruce; semper habentes in mente, quantam caritatem vobis exhibuit qui vos sibi inviolatas tam in corpore quam in anima conservavit, quantam vobis et quam specialem gloriam praeparavit, quas tam speciali gratia sublimavit?" *Ibid.,* 214a.

(42) "Specialem, inquam, gloriam, specialem coronam donabit vobis in caelis, quam nostri majores *aureolam* appellant, quam idcirco ab auro aestimo nominatam, ut ipsum coronae nomen, quae dabitur vobis in praemium virginitatis, insinuet excellentiam gloriae virginalis. Quid, inquam, dabitur sacris virginibus Christi? Ceteris sanctis ut praeemineant, sicut aurum cetera metalla praecellit. Dicit enim Isaias: *In die illa erit Dominus corona gloriae et sertum exsultationis residuo populi sui.* Attende, quod *corona* fit de auro et de lapidibus pretiosis, *sertum* de floribus, puta rosis, violis et huiusmodi. Attende, quam magnum est ipsum Deum habere pro corona! Et virgines non tantum habebunt Deum pro corona, id quod est commune omnibus glorificatis; sed habebunt pro capillo florido exsultationis praerogativam spiritualis excellentiae, quae in virginibus in patria caelesti apparebit. Quid autem est ille *locus multo melior quam filiorum Dei;* quid illud nomen aeternum; quid aureola? Magnum est valde et inexplicable inexpertis. Sed propterea cum magna aviditate currendum, magna fortitudine perseverandum est eis qui soli fruendo poterunt hoc experiri." *Ibid.,* 214.

Glancing backward over St. Bonaventure's treatment of woman thus far, we see that motherhood is the object of her life,—the cause of her liveliest joys, the source of her deepest sorrows. If to follow a higher vocation, she renounces the joys of the motherhood of flesh and blood, it is to consecrate herself to the functions of a holier and loftier motherhood,—a motherhood all spiritual in its nature and in its end. To live as a virgin either in the world or in religious life requires not only the renunciation of the pleasures of the flesh, but a life of sacrifice for the love of Christ, her Spouse. As the love which prompted the initial sacrifice, grows and expands in her heart, it reaches the point where it merges into love of souls, for whom Christ died. Just as a true mother longs to bring children into the world, so does the true virgin long to be an instrument in the transmission of divine life to souls. She becomes the spouse of Christ in order to become the mother of little children whom she nourishes with the doctrine of life; or of the poor, the sick, and the infirm, whom she relieves by her ministrations and purifies by her prayers. She becomes the mother of poor sinful women, who have grown weary in the paths of iniquity, or, consecrating herself to a more sublime vocation, she spends her life in prayer. These spouses of Christ do not renounce the glorious privilege of motherhood, for in their hearts are formed the germs of life which are carried to languishing souls and are there fructified by divine grace. At this point virginity is complemented by spiritual motherhood; virginity and motherhood are reconciled and for the physical fecundity sacrificed by the virgin there is substituted a spiritual fecundity limited only by love.

Though the state of virginity is in itself more perfect than that of motherhood, a devoted mother may, through greater love, be closer to God than the virgin. In fulfilling the duties of her state, she relinquishes virginal integrity, but the growth of charity in a truly holy marriage leads always to virginity of heart,—spiritual virginity. To both virgins and mothers, the liturgy of the Church applies the beautiful words: "Come, spouse of Christ." The mother who has consecrated to Christ her functions as mother, who strives to be utterly pure of heart and free from sin, becomes more and more like Christ and His Mother. Her espousal to man is a stepping-stone to a higher espousal to Christ, and her motherhood is a means to virginity of spirit. Thus though no aureole of virginity surround her in heaven, in terms of love and love's reward, she may be closer to the Source of virginity than many a virgin.

PART THREE

WOMAN IN GLORY

To My Heavenly Mother

Chapter I

THE IDEAL WOMAN: VIRGIN AND MOTHER

AT THE VERY ZENITH OF HUMAN HISTORY, at the crossroads of two worlds where the Old Law meets the New, stands the masterpiece of God's creation, the world's loveliest lady, the incomparable Woman, Mary. Behind her lies the Old Covenant, whose God of armies was a mighty Prince, whose Will was law, whose Justice, inexorable. Before her lies the New Covenant of grace, whose Prince of Peace is a little Child, whose Law is love, whose Mercy, boundless. There she stands, the miracle of exception, all the loveliness of womanhood surrounding her, for though a stainless Virgin, her curving arms enshrine a Child, the Desired of the Ages.

From out the mists of antiquity she comes, shrouded in mystery, veiled under a glorious list of types and symbols which foreshadow and prophesy her dignity.[1] From the remotest years, eons before her name was on the lips of men, she was the noble theme of prophets, who, searching in vain through all creation,—the vast expanse of earth and sea and sky—for one sole emblem worthy to portray her splendor, ended in heaping countless metaphors in despairing tribute of her praise. She is the flowering rod of Aaron, rod of Jesse, blossom-crowned; she is the fleece of Gedeon heaven-dewed 'mid arid ground; the virgin earth, a hallowed land, whence sprang the Fairest Flower; she is a fountain ever clear, the protecting mantle of a cloud, a rainbow of perpetual peace; she is all the glory of the heavens,—the sun, the moon, the bright and shining morning star.[2] She is the mirror of the prophets and the fulfillment of their predictions, the Woman whom St. John in vision saw, when finally through the broken gleams and partial light of the Old Testament she emerged into the bright noonday of Revelation as Nature's Queen with the moon as her footstool, the stars as her wreath, the sun as her gown.[3] Not daring to raise our eyes to her starry heights lest, as Gray says of Milton, we should be "blasted with excess of light," let us contemplate her as the simple little Hebrew maid, clad in gown of homespun, her feet bare, on her head no crown of stars but a veil of Nazareth weaving.

---

(1) "Hoc ergo signum magnum, id est beatissima Virgo, quae diu sub umbra Legis latuit in Scripturis involuta, sub figuris abscondita, praedicta Prophetarum clamore et praeconio, educta Sanctorum desiderio." *De Assumtione B. Virginis Mariae. Sermo VI,* t.IX, 701b.

(2) "Unde et Spiritus sanctus per ora Prophetarum commendat eam non solum verbis, verum etiam figuris et similitudinibus parabolicis; et quia nulla similitudo parabolica perfecte sufficit ad eius excellentiam exprimendam, ideo ad ipsius laudem multiformes introducuntur similitudines et metaphorae. Aliquando enim ad ipsius laudem introducuntur similitudines metaphoricae a natura inferiori, utpote similitudo *radicis, terrae* et *virgae;* modo, a natura media, utpote *fontis, nebulae* et *nubeculae;* aliquando, a natura supercaelesti, ut est metaphora *solis* et *lunae* et *stellae.* Inter omnes autem metaphoricas similitudines excellentissima videtur metaphorica similitudo sumta a *sole." De Nativitate B. Virginis Mariae. Sermo II,* t.IX, 708b.

(3) "And a great sign appeared in heaven, a woman clothed with the sun, and the moon under her feet and on her head a crown of stars" (Apoc. 12:1).

The Perfect Virgin

A sinless child, fair as the morning, radiant and fragrant with God's grace, we meet her, the pure Virgin of Juda,

> "Standing with reluctant feet,
> Where the brook and river meet,
> Womanhood and childhood fleet."

Though born under the law of fear, there burned in her pure heart a flame of love far brighter than that which enkindled the fiery Isaias, the pure Jeremias, the rapt Ezechiel, the wise and holy Daniel. A more valiant lover of her Lord than David, she breathed into the love songs of the Prophet King a fervor and tenderness which his own great heart had not comprehended. Mary's God was a hidden God, revealed only in dim prophecies and types and figures but, unlike the pagan world about her which worshipped the sun and everything under the sun, "gods many and lords many" (I Cor. 8:5), she had learned to discern the lineaments of the Creator in the work of His Hands and, rising above the beauty and glory of His creatures, she had caught an unforgettable glimpse of the Beauty ever ancient, ever new. While her virginal mind dwelt perpetually on the Infinite Loveliness, her pure affections yearned for the God of Israel with unimaginable tenderness and power. Not yet had the Saviour uttered the sublime words: "Blessed are the clean of heart, for they shall see God" (Matt. 5:8). Not yet had the Evangelist revealed that virgin souls will in heaven "follow the Lamb whithersoever He goeth" (Apoc. 14:4), but chastity was already the vowed resolve of her heart. A few more years would Anna the Prophetess watch and pray and the eyes of the aged Simeon grow more dim watching for the Consolation of Israel before the glory foretold by Aggeus should come to pass and the Desired of Nations Himself should be presented in the Temple, but Mary had already consecrated herself to the Most High. "While she was yet a little one, she pleased the Lord of grace," and as a handmaid solemnly dedicated herself to His service. "Thou art the God of my heart, and the God that is my portion forever" (Ps. 72:26). Multitudes of holy Nazarites had chosen the Lord for their inheritance in the holy Temple. There many generations of the children of Israel had offered their victims and the even more acceptable homage of their hearts, but not since the days when the blood of Abel mingled with his holocaust and Isaac laid himself upon the wood of sacrifice, did the eyes of the Almighty rest upon anything more pleasing than the little maiden who now offered herself a "living" sacrifice to the Lord. The Spouse Himself in the Canticle proclaims the white splendor of her virginal purity: "I am the flower of the field and the lily of the valleys" (Cant. 2:1). "As the lily among thorns, so is my love among the daughters" (Cant. 2:2). The other daughters and virgins in whom the pricks and stings of concupiscence are not altogether extinct are the *thorns.* Mary is the pure-white fragrant lily, unspotted by carnal defilement,—pure in thought, pure in affection, pure in word and stainless flesh. Like the Nazarites of old, she was, as the prophet Jeremias foretold (Lam. 4.7), a dazzling mirror of purity. *Whiter than snow,* the cool purity of her flesh untarnished by the fire of concupiscence; *purer than milk,* the holy words that fell from her lips; *more ruddy than old ivory,* the pure affections of her heart; *fairer than the sapphire,* the purity of her thoughts, for the sapphire is a heavenly blue and, being a virgin, Mary's thoughts were thoughts of God and things divine, for, as St. Paul says: "The unmarried woman and the virgin thinketh on the things of the Lord, that she may be holy both in body and in spirit" (I Cor. 7:34).[4]

There must have been many holy virgins in Israel, chaste maidens who kept their bodies and souls pure for God, but Mary's virginity was unique. It was perfect and complete, spiritual as well as physical, for, as theologians from the days of St. Augustine and St. Gregory of Nyssa have maintained, she had given it the stability and perfection of a vow. Mary, says St. Bonaventure, was "a virgin in flesh, a virgin in mind, a virgin who had sealed her virginity by vow, a virgin holy in spirit and body."[5] Not merely her act but her very power to act, not merely the use of her body but its whole substance she had consecrated to God, thus accomplishing in a unique and supernatural manner that self-surrender which is the characteristic act and function of womankind.

The higher appreciation of virginity does not generally find expression in the morals of the Israelites. A vow, to be sure, was no new thing among the Jews, as a perusal of the Old Testament will testify, but a vow never to marry, and that from spiritual motives, was an entirely new and unprecedented honor. In view of the divine decree that the Messiah should arise out of Israel, the striving for the propagation of the people of God held a relative precedence over the observance of virginity. Marriage and motherhood were the cherished ideals of every Jewish maiden. Hebrew women, even the most renowned among them, such as Sara, Rebecca, Lia, Rachel, Ruth rejoiced in the married state. Even the daughters of the tribe of Levi, dedicated to the

(4) "Candor *continentiae* Virginis designatur in candore floris; unde de ipsa merito dicit Sponsus Canticorum secundo: *Ego flos campi et lilium convallium. Sicut lilium inter spinas, sic amica mea inter filias.* Aliae enim filiae et virgines *spinae* sunt propter aculeos et punctiones concupiscentiae non omnino in eis exstinctae; haec autem fuit *lilium* candens et redolens, quia nihil impuritatis nec foeditatis carnalis sensit, sed omnimodum nitorem habuit in cogitatione, affectione, locutione et carnis incorruptione. Et hoc designatur Threnorum quarto: *Candidiores Nazaraei eius nive,* ratione incorruptionis in carne, ubi nihil erat de calore concupiscentiae; *Nazaraeus enim interpretatur floridus: nitidiores lacte,* ratione incorruptionis in sermone; *rubicundiores ebore antiquo,* in affectione; *sapphiro pulcriores,* in cogitatione; *sapphirus* est caelestis coloris, et Virgo semper supercaelestia cogitabat, secundum illud primae ad Corinthios septimo: *Mulier innupta et virgo cogitat quae Domini sunt, ut sit sancta corpore et spiritu." De Assumptione B. Virginis Mariae. Sermo V,* t.IX, 699a.

(5) ". . . virgo erat carne, virgo mente, virgo professione, virgo sancta spiritu et corpore." *De Annuntiatione B. Virginis Mariae. Sermo II,* t.IX, 660b.

service of the high priest, all without exception married. Sacred Scripture tells us that the daughter of Jephte, who was to be offered as a holocaust to the Lord by her own father, mourned only her misfortune in dying a virgin and her one desire, before the consummation of the sacrifice, was to retire to the solitude of the mountains, and there, with her companions, to bewail her virginity (Judges 11:34-40). Still the Lord accepted the sacrifice of Jephte; He did not give him back his child,—a circumstance which should give the Israelites pause, it would seem, in the thought that perpetual virginity might be pleasing to the Lord.

The resolution of Mary to remain in the state of virginity in no way indicated an abandonment of the vocation of a true Israelite who longingly expected the Messiah. Furthermore, if the vocation of the people of the Covenant—to have the Messiah to proceed from amongst them—brought with it a universality of marriage for the sake of posterity, could it possibly be opposed to the spirit of the Old Testament if, toward its end, souls to whom a deeper knowledge of the Law and the Prophets, to whom prayer and meditation, and even a special revelation had made known the fullness of time, should resolve not to marry again,[6] or even not to choose that state of life at all?

The virginity of Mary, so diametrically opposed to the ingrained prepossessions of her people, was in the mind of God at the very dawn of creation when He separated the land from the waters, as recorded in the Book of Genesis: "Let the waters that are under the heavens be gathered together in one place, and let the dry land appear. And it was so done, and God called the dry land Earth" (Gen. 1:9,10). The *land* separated from the waters, says St. Bonaventure, is a figure of Mary far removed from the deceptive, pestilential waters of worldly ideals and pleasures, from material sins or motions of sensual concupiscence in general, and this in accordance with a vow of strict virginity by which she had bound herself under the inspiration of the Most High, and she was the first of all maidens to pronounce such a vow.[7] Entirely disengaged from earth, she felt no desire to contract a worldly alliance. Happy in possessing the Lord for her portion, she knew no ambition for the dignity, the comforts or the resources conferred by matrimony and, like the solitary turtle-dove in the desert, she willingly embraced the lonely, hidden and dependent life recognized to be the virgin's peculiar inheritance. This perfect virginity of body and heart fitted her for union with her most

(6) As did Anna, the "prophetess," the daughter of Phanuel, who, after a marriage of only seven years, had served God as a widow up to her eighty-fourth year, "departing not from the temple, by fastings and prayers serving night and day" (Luke 2:36 ff.).

(7) "Fuit ergo beata Virgo Maria terra *aridissima* proprietate pro *incorruptione virginea,* in cuius figura dicitur Genesis primo: *Congregentur aquae, quae sub caelo sunt, in locum unum, et apparet arida. Et factum est ita. Et vocavit Deus aridam: terram.* Per *terram* sequestratam ab aquis intelligitur Virgo Maria elongata ab omnibus carnalibus et fluxibilibus concupiscentiis; quod quidem fuit per votum arctissimae virginitatis, cui se Virgo Maria divino instinctu totaliter mancipavit et ipsam inter alias prima expressit." *De Annuntiatione B. Virginis Mariae. Sermo III,* t.IX. 668b, 669a.

pure and most chaste heavenly Spouse, Who sings of her in the Canticle: "The flowers have appeared in our land. The time of pruning is come. The voice of the turtle is heard in our land" (Cant. 2:12). The turtle-dove is noted for its cleanliness; of all birds, it is the purest, the most chaste. The "voice of the turtle" is the vow of perfect chastity,—a sound first heard in the holy Virgin.[8] In answer to the call of her Spouse: "O my dove, . . . let me hear thy voice" (Cant. 2:14), Mary, with stainless heart, with faculty unimpaired, with mind unclouded and unsolicited by any promptings save those of grace, gave herself to her Creator without reserve and without recall "till the day break and the shadows retire" (Cant. 2:17). And the Spouse loved her, for she was the perfect Virgin, the only one who could offer a heart without stain, a heart purified and wholly dead to the world. As the Book of Canticles expresses it: "There are threescore queens . . . and young maidens without number. One is my dove, my perfect one is *but* one" (Cant. 6:7, 8).

The Perfect Wife

In apparent contradiction to Mary's perfect virginity as a woman consecrated to God, the fact remains, as the Gospel expressly tells us, that she was the wife of Joseph. Sprung from the seed of the great King David, Mary was, according to the testimony of tradition, the daughter of an aged couple then dwelling at Nazareth, a small town of Galilee, the poorest and most obscure district of Judea. In the absence of male offspring, her parents had affianced her to a young man of the same lineage, thus insuring the legal transmission of their property, according to the Jewish law which read: "All women shall take husbands of the same tribe that the inheritance may remain in the families" (Num. 36:8).

Jewish maidens were considered marriageable at the age of twelve years and six months, though the actual age of the bride varied with circumstances. The marriage was preceded by the betrothal, after which the bride belonged legally to the bridegroom, though she did not live with him until a year later, when the full marriage ceremony was performed. Until the marriage proper, all communication between the bride and her future husband was to be carried on through the medium of a friend deputed for the purpose, termed "the friend of the bridegroom" (cf. John 3:29),—a custom still in vogue in the unchanging East.

At the time of her espousal Mary was a mere child, at most fourteen years of age, perhaps younger. In view of her relationship to Elizabeth, the

(8) "Ideo idonea erat caelesti Sponso mundissimo et castissimo copulari. Propter quod Canticorum secundo: *Flores apparuerunt in terra nostra, tempus putationis advenit; vox turturis audita est in terra nostra.* Turtur est avis castissima, ideo in voce turturis designatur votum perfectissimae castitatis. Haec *vox audita est* in beata Virgine." *Ibid.*, 669a.

"daughter of Aaron" (Luke 1:5), the opinion grew that Mary was not of the house of David but rather a descendant of the sacerdotal tribe,—a deduction which called the legality of the marriage into question. St. Justin, who was born in Samaria A. D. 100, and was well acquainted with the traditions of Palestine, writes that Mary was of royal stock, descending in a direct line of ancestry from King David. On this question St. Augustine says: "One of David's sons, according to custom, married a wife from the sacerdotal line. Hence Mary belonged to both tribes and had her descent both in the royal and in the sacerdotal lines."[9] St. Bonaventure likewise holds that Mary was of sacerdotal lineage through her mother, of the royal race of David through her father. The not unfounded assumption that Mary was a so-called daughter of inheritance and therefore legally bound to offer her hand and fortune to her next kinsman, led to the espousal, and precisely with Joseph who was of the same descent and her next legal kinsman.[10]

Mary's virginity, and particularly her quality of virgin consecrated to God, could with good reason make it appear that her marriage to Joseph was not a true marriage. Here we may raise the fundamental inquiry: What precisely constitutes the essence of marriage? Is it the physical union of man and wife, or is union of wills sufficient? Marriage, says the Seraphic Doctor, is to be defined as the union of souls in bodies, for it takes place between persons of different sexes. Moreover, that union in which husband and wife form, as it were, a new complete whole, the union which constitutes the essence of marriage is neither the affection of souls nor the physical union of the sexes but a certain inviolable bond which cannot be destroyed despite changing affection or physical absence.[11] The essence of marriage consists in a certain union of wills whereby each party binds itself indissolubly to keep faith with the other. Therefore, the marriage of Joseph and Mary was a true marriage because the union attained its essential perfection; it was made with the consent of both.[12]

From what we have said it does not follow that a marriage between two

(9) *De diversis quaest.*, Lib.I. lxi.2. MPL 40. 49, 50.

(10) "Ulterius videtur, quod tali viro non debuit nubere: quoniam Virgo Maria erat cognata Elisabeth, quae erat uxor sacerdotis Zachariae, sicut dicitur Lucae primo; sed personae, quae erant de diversis tribubus, non debebant simul contrahere, sicut probatur per illud quod dicitur Numerorum ultimo: ergo cum Ioseph esset de tribu Iuda, ut patet in Matthaeo; videtur, quod male fecit beata Virgo, quod illi nupsit. . . . Ad illud quod obiicitur, quod fuit de genere sacerdotali; dicendum quod verum est ex parte matris, sed ex tribu David ex parte patris; et ideo ille nubere debuit et potuit etiam secundum Legem. Praeterea, puellae de genere sacerdotum sub illa lege non arctabuntur; nec etiam illae, ad quas non spectabat hereditas, propter hoc quod lex illa instituta fuit, ne confunderentur hereditates." *IV Sent.*, d. 30, a.1, q.2, concl., 5, t.IV, 709, 710. Cf. also Num 27:6; 36:6-12; Tob. 7:14; 6:11.

(11) "Matrimonium recte dicitur coniunctio maris et feminae. . . . Ad illud quod quaeritur, utrum sit corporum, an animorum; dicendum, quod animorum in corporibus, quia est coniunctio ratione utentium et habentium sexus distinctos; illa autem coniunctio, quae respicit *totum coniunctum* et est matrimonium essentialiter, non est affectio *animorum*, vel *approximatio corporum*, sed quoddam vinculum obligatorium, quod non perimitur, sive affectu, sive corpore separentur." *IV Sent.*, d.27, a.1, q.1, concl., t.IV, 676.

(12) "Item exemplo probatur: quia inter Mariam et Ioseph fuit matrimonium, et tamen non intervenit nisi consensus." *IV Sent.*, d.27, a.2, q.1, t.IV, 679.

persons who have resolved to live continently would not be a true marriage. Mary, though living continently with Joseph, was nevertheless his true spouse. Granted that spiritual companionship is attainable without conjugal intercourse, the question arises: How can a marriage which excludes the primary physical purpose of marriage, that is, the begetting of children, be a true marriage? It is a question of distinction between a right and the use of a right. The right to conjugal intercourse is essential for the validity of marriage; not so, however, the use of it. A man may acquire possession of a house without being obliged to occupy it. In like manner, two persons may acquire the right to conjugal intercourse without being obliged to make use of it. As St. Ambrose says: "It is the marital contract, not the destruction of virginity, that constitutes Matrimony."[13]

At the time when the Church was taking root in the Roman Empire, betrothal had lost much of the binding force which it possessed under the early Roman Law. At the present time, the ceremony of betrothal is united to that of marriage, but throughout the Middle Ages parents frequently betrothed sons and daughters as part of a family compact, while these were mere children. Even though in some cases the full ceremony of marriage was performed for the youthful pair, the rite, however, had the force of a mere betrothal and whatever the form of consent employed, it was considered as a consent *per verba de futuro*. Gratian and his followers through a wrong interpretation of Justinian's law considered betrothal equivalent to marriage. Consent *de futuro* has, they maintained, precisely the same value as consent *de praesenti,* both of them constituting a *matrimonium initiatum*. If a man swears that he will take a woman as his wife, he thereby marries her, though the marriage does not possess the sacramental character which renders it absolutely indissoluble. Following Hugh of St. Victor and Peter Lombard, the Seraphic Doctor refuses to attribute to betrothal the effects of Matrimony. In his treatment of the question, he employs terms which clearly indicate the essential difference between the pledges given at betrothal and marriage respectively. In both, the parties consent to take each other as husband and wife; but while the one is consent given in the present tense, the other is consent as regards the future. Betrothal is a mere promise; marriage is the fulfillment of the promise.[14] When the true meaning of Justinian's law was pointed out in the *Petri Exceptiones Legum Romanorum,* it was shown to be in perfect accord with this view.[15]

---

(13) "Cum enim initiatur conjugium, tunc conjugii nomen adsciscitur: non enim defloratio virginitatis facit conjugium, sed pactio conjugalis." *De Instit. Virg.*, n.41. MPL 16.331.

(14) "Nam per verba de futuro dicitur matrimonium *initiari,* per verba praesenti *ratificari,* sed per carnalem copulam habet *consummari.*" *Breviloquium* VI, 13, 1, t.V, 279a.

(15) Lib.iv, c.44: "Si quis ita jurat alicui mulieri: Ducam te uxorem, nondum est uxor. Sed si jurat ita: habebo te uxorem, uxor deinceps est, nec aliam ea vivente ducere potest, nisi juste matrimonium separetur." Cf. Appendix to vol. ii of von Savigny's *Geschichte des romischen Rechts im Mittelalter* (Heidelberg, 1816).

The view that declares that marriage is effected by consent and that consummation is not essentially requisite, is not merely in accordance with reason but in perfect harmony with Christian teaching. The Church has always held that the marriage of the Virgin Mary and Joseph, though one of perpetual continence, was nevertheless a true marriage. St. Augustine says it would be intolerable to say that the bond of marriage is dissolved because husband and wife agree to abstain from the exercise of marital rights.[16] St. Chrysostom, too, in his commentary on St. Matthew's Gospel known as *Opus imperfectum in Matthaeum,* states in precise terms: "Matrimonium non facit coitus sed voluntas."[17] Hugh of St. Victor likewise maintained that the holy couple were truly husband and wife[18] "since Holy Scripture proves this by its manifest authority and the Catholic religion confirms it by its testimony."[19] He then proceeded to explain how Mary could have given her consent to marry Joseph even while intending to preserve virginity,—an opinion stoutly contradicted by Gratian in his *Decretal,* published at Bologna about 1140. Probably one of the most decisive factors in the refutation of Gratian and his followers was the *Book of the Sentences,* a collection of theological and philosophical opinions, published by Peter Lombard about 1150, a part of the fourth section of which was devoted to the study of the relationship between Joseph and Mary. There Lombard fully agreed with Hugh of St. Victor and with St. Augustine in affirming that the mutual virginity of Joseph and Mary did not hinder the genuineness of their marriage, and by the logic of his arguments helped set aside the claims and citations made by Gratian. Since the *Book of the Sentences* was the standard theological textbook in the medieval universities and since the opinions it voiced were considered as general norms to be followed, Peter Lombard's defense of Joseph as the husband of Mary was propagated throughout all Europe and was made accessible to all scholars for four hundred years to come. With St. Bonaventure we accept the Lombard's teaching and look upon Mary as the true wife of Joseph and as such the ideal of those women who, acting under the inspiration of grace and with the consent of their husbands, choose to live in virginal wedlock.

---

(16) "Quibus vero placuit ex consensu ab usu carnalis concupiscentiae in perpetuum continere, absit ut inter illos vinculum conjugale rumpatur." *De Nupt. et Conc.,* lib.i, c.XI, MPL 44.420.

(17) C.xxvii,2. Cf. MPG 56.802.

(18) "Item, hoc ipsum expresse dicit Hugo in libro de Virginitate Mariae; et tamen ex consensu suo matrimonium contraxit: ergo non oportet in carnalem copulam consentire." *IV Sent.,* d.28, a.1, q.6, t.IV,695. For Hugh of St. Victor, cf. cap.1 and 4.

"Item, Augustinus dicit, et habetur in littera: 'Non dubium est, illam mulierem ad coniugium non pertinere, cum quo docetur commixtio sexuum non fuisse'." *IV Sent.,* d.26, a.2, q.3, t.IV, 669. Cf. also *IV Sent.,* d.26, c.6, t.IV, 660.

(19) *De B. M. Virginitate,* lib. epist. cap.1. MPL 176.857.

The Perfect Mother

Motherhood has been defined as the relation of the maternal principle to its offspring, a living being which is fashioned from its substance and with its help. Whether applied to the plant and animal kingdom or to mankind, it supposes an offspring which has the character of a self-sufficient and individual living being. Furthermore, it is not the body alone, nor the soul alone, but the new complete individual which is co-relative to the mother. It does not necessarily follow that the mother need be the total cause of her offspring, for what is true of the plant and animal kingdoms in this respect does not hold good for the human race. No human mother is the total cause of her child. Must a mother, to be a mother, give her child all the essential elements that make him what he is? If this were so, no mother could call herself the mother of her child, for in the natural order, a mother does nothing more than co-operate with the creative power of God. Not to mention the father's co-operation, it is not the mother who gives the child its most precious possession, its immortal soul, and therefore its spirituality, its personality, and self-sufficiency,—a circumstance which in no way detracts from the reality of her motherhood.

Motherhood is founded on the act of conception, a term which may be understood in either the active or the passive sense. Active conception is the parental act of generation, the preparation of the body for the infusion of the soul. Passive conception is the origin of the human being within the maternal womb. Passive conception is accomplished at the moment the intellectual soul is infused into the product of parental generation.

Mary was a true mother. Like every mother she co-operated with the creative power of God in the conception of her child. As to the manner of her co-operation, theologians of the Thirteenth Century held diverse opinions. There were those who maintained that the Virgin merely contributed the material for the production of the child, and these were the followers of Aristotle who regarded the mother as the material principle in the generation of the offspring and the male seed as the efficient and active principle.[20] According to this theory, the relation of the male seed to the seed of the woman is that of the artificer to the material with which he works, the woman's only function being to provide within her womb the material embodiment for the child and to nourish the newborn infant at her breast. All this the Virgin did, they maintain; truly, then, must she be called a mother, for she lacked none of the requirements of a mother in the procreation of her child.[21]

(20) "Primi, qui dicunt, quod cooperata fuit solum in materialis principii ministratione, moventur hac ratione: quia, sicut dicit Philosophus, mater in generatione prolis se habet sicut principium materiale, et semen viri sicut effectivum et operativum." *III Sent.*, d.4, a.3, q.1, t.III, 111ab.

(21) "Unde comparatur semen viri ad semen mulieris sicut artifex ad materiam, mulier vero non facit nisi materiam ministrare et exterius fovere. Et hoc totum fecit Virgo Maria; et ideo vere mater est appellanda, quia nihil ei defuit, quod spectat ad veram matrem in generatione prolis." *Ibid.*

But this opinion, says the Seraphic Doctor, stops short of the whole truth, first, because in procreation the mother possesses an active as well as a passive power, as is evident from the fact that the child often bears a closer resemblance to the mother than to the father. Therefore, when physiologists ascribe the active principle to the father, it is "by appropriation" that they must do so, that is, not exclusively but principally.[22] Futhermore, matter alone constitutes no bond of parentage, as is evident from the formation of woman from the side of man.[23] The mere contribution of matter does not entitle a woman to be called the mother of her child.

Thus does St. Bonaventure prove that Mary was a true mother, not in the sense that Aristotle and his disciples called a woman the mother of her child but in the true sense of the term. In forming her son's body Mary co-operated mainly by her natural activity just as every other mother co-operates in forming a human body. This co-operation consists, first, in the natural activity of the mother who prepares the formation of the human body even prior to the influence of an external principle which co-operates in procreation. For this formation she furnishes an organic seed susceptible of impregnation, a seed which needs only a fitting determination from without in order effectively to become a human body and thus to develop into a living fruit of the mother. The activity by which the mother at conception receives the impregnating influence, thus co-operating in the originating of the fruit, is fundamental and most important. There is, however, a secondary action, that of developing the child and bringing it into the world. Though this bearing, or preparing for the birth of the fruit, differs from the production in the strict sense, as regards both the father and the mother, yet it, too, is a productive action, for it includes a continuous communication of the substance of the mother to the fruit and together with the first, or fundamental action, forms the complete productive process natural to the mother. Mary, then, was a true mother. She generated her child by an active causality. She was no mere instrument but an integrating part in the work of generation. She functioned not as a mere corporeal receptacle but as an active principle and co-operatrix in the conception of her son.[24] It was not merely *in* her but *from* her that he took a body. Hers was the maternal womb from which he took flesh, as all children take flesh from their mothers; from her he derived his human powers and strength.

In rendering virginity fruitful in the person of Mary, the Almighty per-

(22) "Sed haec positio nimis parum dicit: primum, quia mater in generatione non solum habet potentiam *passivam*, sed *activam;* unde quandoque proles magis assimilatur matri quam patri. Unde quod dicunt physici intelligendum est per appropriationem." *Ibid.*, 111b.

(23) "Et sicut prius ostensum est, propter materiam solum non est appellanda mater, sicut patet in formatione mulieris de costa viri. *Ibid.*

(24) "Ergo si non solum habuit potentiam receptivam sed etiam generativam, non solum se habuit Virgo Maria per modum recipientis, sed per modum agentis et cooperantis." *III Sent.*, a.3, q.1, t.III, 110a.

formed a singular miracle, a twofold miracle, we may say, namely, in the *bestowal of power* and in the *operation of that power.* In the case of Sara and Elizabeth and other barren women who were rendered fruitful, there was a miracle only in the *restoration of the generative power* inasmuch as a barren woman was made fruitful but there was no miracle in the *working of the power,* because sterility and fruitfulness did not exist at the same time. Indeed, fruitfulness took away sterility. In this respect Mary was unique and singularly admirable; her fruitfulness did not rob her of her virginity nor did her virginity exclude fruitfulness.[25] As Virgin and Mother she stands alone. She was the first and only woman in all history to attain the glory of motherhood without losing her precious virginity.

Virgin Mother! Beautiful words, expressing a sublime and unique privilege, the glory of perpetual virginity joined with genuine motherhood, the one supplying the defect of the other. Virginity alone lacks something; there is an incompleteness about it,—a possibility unrealized, a faculty unused. Motherhood alone loses something; there is a surrender, an unflowering, a plucking of a blossom. In Mary we have both,—a virginity that never lacked anything, a motherhood that never lost anything. She is both Virgin and Mother,—a Virgin without the reproach of sterility; a Mother, but with the privilege of virginity. Therefore, Mary is perfect and complete and Mary the Virgin and Mary the Mother are interchangeable terms.

This is the prodigy we behold in Mary. She is both Virgin and Mother. The greatness of this prerogative, according to St. Bonaventure, is based on the threefold excellence of virginity: its inestimable *merit,* its ineffable *reward,* its priceless *worth* and *honor,*—its priceless worth, for it "is a treasure hidden in a field" (Matt. 13:44), more precious than all the world, nay, than a thousand worlds because "no price is worthy of a continent soul" (Ecclus. 26:20). The vow of chastity admits of no dispensation, for it has no equivalent in value; it is "ineffable," too sacred for expression. By it Man, who was created "a little less than the angels," rises above these celestial spirits in honor, for his state of life is more noble, more glorious than theirs.[26]

So speaks the Seraphic Doctor, turning back into the gloom of old the full light of revelation. But who taught thee, O prudent virgin, that virginity is pleasing to God? What page of the Old Testament exhorted thee, what ordinance counselled thee, what law commanded thee to lead on earth the

(25) "Unde duplex fuit hic miraculum, videlicet in *potentiae collatione,* et in ipsa *operatione.* In fecundatione autem mulierum sterilium, sicut Sarae et Elisabeth, solum fuit miraculum in *restitutione potentiae* in hoc quod est ibi sterilis fecundata, sed non fuit ibi miraculum in *exsecutione,* quia non simul mansit sterilitas et fecunditas, immo fecunditas abstulit sterilitatem. Hoc autemn fuit singulariter admirâbile, quod fecunditas Virginis Mariae non abstulit virginitatem, nec virginitas exclusit fecunditatem." *III Sent.,* d.4, a.3, q.2, t.III, 115ab.

(26) Cf. *supra,* p. 131, footnote 10.

life of angels? Or didst thou, too, belong to the New Law and could it have been a message which the finger of God had early written on thy heart?[27]

It would have been a *wonderful* privilege, says the Saint, if the Virgin had given birth to a mere man, a human being of the same nature as her own, but this privilege has been thrice magnified in Mary. To be a virgin and at the same time to become the mother of the most holy of men would in itself be a *great* honor. Inconceivably *greater* would be the honor of becoming the Mother of God. But greater than both and therefore *greatest* of all would be the privilege of becoming the Mother of the *Most Holy Man and God.* And this is the sublime and unique privilege which was Mary's,—not the mere glory of perpetual virginity joined with genuine motherhood but a prerogative as far above it as God is above man. Mary is the Mother of the God-Man, a dignity which exalts her far above every creature and places her in rank next to God Himself.[28] Her motherhood boundlessly surpasses all other motherhoods because her Offspring is divine and because the manner of His conception and birth was miraculous. Mary is the perfect Mother who brought forth in Bethlehem the Eternal Word, Our Lord and Saviour Jesus Christ.

(27) "Ad illud ergo quod obiicitur primo, quod non debuit *vovere,* quia hoc spectat ad Evangelium; dicendum, quod Virgo sanctissima non erat sub Lege. Nam quomodo sub Lege erat, quae Legis auctorem genuit? Et rursus, si illi *qui spiritu Dei aguntur,* non sunt sub Lege, cum haec esset plena Spiritu sancto, non pertinebat ad Legem, sed ad Evangelium, quod ab ipsa infantia in corde ipsius scripserat Dei digitus, ipse scilicet Spiritus sanctus." *IV Sent.,* d.30, a.1, q.2, t.IV, 710.

(28) "Super hanc est stella undecima, quae est, quod Mater Dei super praedictam stellam tanto est altior, quanto Deus homine est sublimior. Magnum enim esset, si purum hominem Virgo genuisset; unde haec gratiae excellentia tripliciter magnificatur. *Magnum* enim esset virginem et matrem sanctissimi *hominis* per se; infinitum autem *maius* esset esse matrem Dei per se; utroque maius, et ideo *maximum* inest esse matrem sanctissimi *hominis et Dei;* in ordine enim supremo sita est." *De Assumtione B. Virginis Mariae. Sermo VI,* t.IX, 706b.

Chapter II

THE VIRGIN MOTHER OF GOD

ON THE VERY DAY that Adam sinned and an angry and almighty voice split the boisterous storm clouds to chide the triumphant demon, God Himself linked Christ with Mary in the prophecy that has resounded down the avenues of time: "I will put enmities between thee and the woman, and thy seed and her seed. She shall crush thy head, and thou shalt lie in wait for her heel" (Gen. 3:15). According to God's own promise there was to be an irreconcilable enmity between the serpent and the woman. What woman? Obviously not Eve, nor any of her common daughters, for they were involved in the same doom. The one woman in all history to whom the glorious prophecy could apply, is plainly none other than Mary, the immaculate Mother of God. The crushing of the Evil One, to be sure, is the work of Christ, yet it is the work of Christ Who comes to us from His Mother, the Strong One who in her seed should conquer. She is the Woman of Promise whose Son is to crush the serpent's head, destroy the power of Satan, and restore man to the friendship of God.

This hope of a Redeemer Who would one day undo the harm they had done so heartened Adam and Eve as they began their years of penance, that it was stamped in the souls of all their descendants. Among the generations before the deluge it had been a revered and consoling tradition that after dreary reaches of time there would be found one of the race of Adam, a woman humble and sinless, whose privilege it would be to bring back to the world the light and life which it had lost. "To and fro like sparks among the reeds" (Wis. 3:7) ran the gladsome thought that gave courage and constancy to a fallen race,—the thought that from their progeny would arise a glorious Woman who would bring forth the Saviour of the world.

As time wore on and the consequences of original sin more and more disturbed their peace of soul, people began to sigh and weep for the coming of the Expectation of Nations.[1] Finally nearly eight hundred years before the first Christmas, began that amazing flood of prophecy concerning the Messiah, which raised the son of Amos above all his inspired peers and made of him an Evangelist rather than a Prophet. God Himself had appeared to

(1) "Rursus quoniam sublimitas remedii requirit, ut credatur fide firmissima et ametur caritate ardentissima tanquam mysterium secretissimum et saluberrimum; ideo congruentissimum fuit, ut ante Christi adventum praeirent multa testimonia Prophetarum, tam explicita in verbis quam implicita in figuris, ut multis et firmis testimoniis quod erat secretum fieret certum et indubitabile ad credendum; praeirent etiam multiplicia promissa et ardentissima desideria, ut promissum beneficium exspectaretur, exspectatum differretur, dilatum amplius desideraretur, et diu desideratum amaretur et gratiosius susciperetur et sollicitius servaretur." *Breviloquium,* IV, 4, t.V, 244b.

him in the majesty of His heavenly splendor and, sending a seraph to cleanse his lips with a burning coal, bade him go forth and cry to a people who would not hear. Bursting forth into impassioned prophecy, Isaias gave a definite sign of the coming of the Redeemer, saying: "The Lord himself shall give you a sign. Behold a virgin shall conceive and bear a son, and his name shall be called Emmanuel" (Isai. 7:14). For what other purpose would the prophet have called up the figure of this Maiden out of the dim, distant future and laid emphasis on her maidenhood, if not to distinguish the manner of her giving birth from the lot of all the mothers of Juda? It is a forecast of virgin motherhood, and the Virgin of Promise, whose virginity was not to be impaired by her maternity, is the Blessed Virgin Mary.

The connection of Emmanuel with the extraordinary divine sign which was given to the dark-hearted Achaz predisposes one to see in the child more than a common boy.[2] To him is ascribed the ownership of the land of Juda: "The stretching out of his wings shall fill the breadth of thy land, O Emmanuel" (Isai. 8:8). The government of the house of David is said to be on his shoulders, and he is described as being endowed with more than human qualities: "For a child is born to us, and a son is given to us, and the government is upon his shoulders, and his name shall be called Wonderful, Counsellor, God the Mighty, the Father of the world to come, and the Prince of Peace" (Isai. 9:6). Then comes the glorious prophecy which makes him of the seed of David: "And there shall come forth a rod out of the root of Jesse, and a flower shall rise up out of his root. And the spirit of the Lord shall rest upon him" (Isai. 11:1, 2). His advent shall be filled by the general signs of the Messianic era, and the remnant of the chosen people shall again be the people of God.[3]

Thus, as time passed on, the coming of the Saviour was foretold with ever-increasing clearness. He was to be of the race of Abraham, of the family of Jacob, of the tribe of Juda, of the seed of David,—prophetic words which bring tidings not only of the Messiah but also of Mary, His Mother, for her race and tribe and family were the same as His. While it is true that Our Lord Himself is primarily and especially foretold and prefigured by the Prophets, yet, running parallel to this mystic stream of prediction concerning the Messiah, there is another, which prepared men's minds for the coming of the wondrous virgin who was to be His Mother. The closeness of the ties between them was wonderfully revealed in the Oracles of God, so much so that wherever Jesus is clearly prefigured, we may confidently look for some promise of Mary. As we strain our eyes to the dim foreshadowings of the Ancient Law and the Messiah, Whose personality so beautifully colors its whole story, we unconsciously seek and not far from the side of the promised

(2) Cf. 4 Kings. 16:1-4 and 2 Par. 28:1-8.
(3) Cf. Isai. 11:3-16.

Redeemer invariably discern the pure and lovely presence of His Virgin Mother.

At last Daniel's prophetic seventy weeks of years had rolled by from the days of Nehemias' labors in rebuilding Jerusalem; the time marked out by so many prophecies arrived; the shadows of the Old Law disappeared and the fullness of time dawned on the world. St. Luke tells the story:

> "And in the sixth month, the angel Gabriel was sent from God into a city of Galilee, called Nazareth, to a virgin espoused to a man whose name was Joseph, of the house of David, and the virgin's name was Mary. And the angel being come in said unto her: Hail, full of grace, the Lord is with thee, blessed art thou among women. Who having heard, was troubled at his saying and thought with herself what manner of salutation this should be. And the angel said to her: Fear not, Mary, for thou hast found grace with God. Behold thou shalt conceive in thy womb and shalt bring forth a son, and thou shalt call his name Jesus. He shall be great and shall be called the Son of the Most High. And the Lord God shall give unto him the throne of David his father, and he shall reign in the house of Jacob forever. And of his kingdom there shall be no end. And Mary said to the angel: How shall this be done, because I know not man? And the angel answering said to her: The Holy Ghost shall come upon thee and the power of the Most High shall overshadow thee. And therefore also the Holy which shall be born of thee shall be called the Son of God. And behold thy cousin Elizabeth, she also hath conceived a son in her old age, and this is the sixth month with her that is called barren. Because no word shall be impossible with God. And Mary said: Behold the handmaid of the Lord, be it done to me according to thy word. And the angel departed from her" (1: 26-38).

With one stroke the Evangelist here confronts us with the mystery of a God-Man and the paradox of a Virgin Mother, for, like the *fiat lux* of Creation, Mary's *fiat* was operative in its direct effect. No sooner had she uttered the words, "Behold the handmaid of the Lord, be it done to me according to thy word," than the mystery of the Incarnation was wrought within her. In that instant the whole course of history was changed. The Messiah had come. The angel was gone. In Mary's womb "the Word was made flesh," and, as the angel had foretold, the Son of God became the Son of Mary.

There is nothing illogical in the thought of Mary's being the Mother of God, for to become the real Mother of God, it was not necessary for Mary to communicate to her Son a divine nature. There is a community of attributes of the Two Natures in Jesus Christ, not in the abstract (divinity and humanity), but in the concrete (God and man). The reason for this communication of idioms is found in the hypostatic union of the Two Natures, by which union the Son of God and the Son of Mary are only one Person.

This communication of idioms represents no effort to transform the divinity into a created being, but it is the only way in which the unity of the Divine Person can be safeguarded, for Christ reunited in His own Person those things which were proper to the divine nature and those things which were proper to the human nature.[4] It is obvious that she who was born in the course of the world's history in the same manner as other women have been born, is not the Mother of the Godhead which is from eternity, but neither is she the Mother only of the Manhood. She is the Mother of Jesus, Who, living from all eternity in the bosom of His Father, was in the fullness of time born of her at Bethlehem in the Human Nature which He deigned to unite inseparably to Himself. By His eternal procession from God the Father, Jesus is the true Son of God; by His birth in time from the Most Holy Virgin, He is the true Son of Mary. Jesus, however, is one undivided Person and therefore the Son of God is absolutely identical with the Son of Mary.

Mary is the Mother of God! Belief in this truth is the very heart of our religion, the touchstone and criterion of the Christian faith. It was for those who would make a distinction between the Everlasting Word of God and Jesus Christ the Son of Mary that St. John in his extreme old age wrote his Gospel and especially the opening passage: "In the beginning was the Word, and the Word was with God, and the Word was God. All things were made by Him, and without Him was made nothing that was made. And the Word was made flesh and dwelt among us" (cf. 1:1-14). This is the doctrine which Nestorius, Bishop of the great see of Byzantium, attacked when he declared that Mary was merely the Mother of Christ, and not truly the Mother of God,—a heresy which constituted a fundamental attack on the Divinity of Christ and which St. John Damascene, a true Doctor and lover of the Virgin, branded as false.[5] The General Council which convened at Ephesus in 431 deposed Nestorius and solemnly defined the truth that the title *Theotokos,* God-bearer, should be given to Our Lady, since through the operation of the Holy Ghost, she had conceived and given birth to God when He assumed Human Nature within her virginal womb. This proclamation of Mary's divine Motherhood assured for all time the safety of that precious truth of the Apostolic faith,—the true divinity and the true humanity of Christ.

---

(4) "Ad illud quod obiicitur, quod non est ei consubstantialis; dicendum, quod *mater Dei* dicitur non propter hoc, quod ipsa genuerit eum secundum divinam naturam, sed propter idiomatum communicationem et mysterii incarnationis expressionem et ipsius Virginis honorificationem. Unde ratio illa non valet: non est mater Dei secundum divinam naturam: ergo non est mater Dei; immo est ibi *consequens,* sicut si ita argueretur: hoc non praedicatur de illo alioque genere praedicandi." *III Sent.,* d.4, a.3, q.3, t.III, 116.

(5) Et propterea, quia beata Virgo illum concepit, qui non tantum dicendus est *Christus* propter unionem, sed etiam *Deus verus* propter aeternam generationem; *Dei genetrix* debet dici, ut ex ipso vocabulo honoretur, et impletatis error exstinguatur, qui dixit, Mariam concepisse purum hominem. Ad cuius erroris fomentum Nestorius, ut narrat Damascenus, verus doctor, voluit eam Christi genetricem, non *Dei genetricem* appellare, quasi purum hominem genuisset. Et ideo Damascenus, verus doctor et Virginis amator, docet nos vocabulum hoc effugere, non quia falsum, sed quia haereticus sub illo volebat occultare venenum. Unde Damascenus tertio libro, capitulo duodecimo: 'Christotocon, id est Christi genetricem, non dicimus Virginem; quoniam in destructionem Theotokos, id est Dei genetricis, vocis nequam et inquinatus Nestorius cum patre eius diabolo invenit'." *Ibid.,* 115b, 116a.

Because of the substantial union between Christ's human nature and His Divine Person, St. Bonaventure with the Damascene and all the Fathers and Doctors of the Church calls upon the faithful to invoke the Mother of the Lord in all reverence by that title which is justly and truly hers, *Dei Genetrix,* Mother of God.[6]

Mary's Physical Motherhood

Though the God-Man Who came to earth to redeem us might have appeared suddenly and miraculously in our midst, He chose to be born of an earthly mother, thus effecting His Incarnation and our Redemption through the medium of the holiest human relationship on earth—that of mother and child.

The mystery of the hypostatic union of the divine and human natures in the Person of the Eternal Word confirmed Mary in the title and rights of Mother of God. This in all truth she was, since she was the natural Mother of a Son Who was eternal God with the same certainty and truth as He was Man. Although she did not directly co-operate in the union of the Divinity with the Humanity, Mary did not on this account lose her right to be called Mother of the true God. Nor may the strictly literal meaning of motherhood be moderated as applied to divine maternity. In the generation and birth of the Incarnate Word, the arm of the Almighty selected and made use of all that substantially and unavoidably belongs to natural generation, so that the Word could truly call Himself conceived and engendered as a true Man born of the substance of His Mother ever Virgin. Mary fulfilled for her Divine Son all the functions that any mother fulfills for her child. She conceived Him in her womb, nourished the developing organism with her blood, brought Him forth into the world an individual of the human race, an individual as integrally human in His nature as any child ever born of woman.[7] And since her Son in His personality is not man but God, it follows that Mary is the Mother of God only insofar as she is the Mother of Christ.

What is the thing called life that enables a buried grain of wheat to sprout and grow and reproduce itself in scores of other grains, to which it transmits the same capacity to reproduce and multiply themselves? We see life all about us; learned men explain how it functions, and yet we have no slightest conception of what it is, except that it is a mysterious and invisible power beyond man's understanding. The life in the grain of wheat, which functions in accordance with "natural law," was placed there by the same power that created and ordained all things and is still creating mankind. Does Mary's

(6) "Concedendae sunt igitur rationes ostendentes, quod beata Virgo est Dei genetrix appellanda iuste et veraciter et devote." *Ibid.*, 116a.

(7) Cf. Matt. 1:18 ff. and Luke 2:5 ff.

conception of Christ seem a miracle? What of the millions of cenceptions that occur every year? How can two microscopic germs of life contain within themselves the foreordained qualities and capacities and the very destiny of the man they will become? With the evidence of God's illimitable power all about us, how strange that some should say: "This He cannot do."

Needless to say, the two different points of view concerning the mother's part in human generation contributed largely to the different aspects under which rival schools considered Mary's divine motherhood and her dignity as Mother of God.[8]

"Now the generation of Christ was in this wise," says St. Matthew. "When his mother Mary was espoused to Joseph, before they came together, she was found with child, of the Holy Ghost" (1:18). "She was found with child." Now a true mother co-operates in the generation of her child and since Mary was truly the Mother of Christ, so did she truly co-operate with the power of the Holy Ghost in His conception.[9] On this truth theologians are agreed. As to the manner of Mary's co-operation, however, there is a wide diversity of opinion among the Doctors of the Thirteenth Century. Some maintained that the Virgin co-operated as a *mere material principle,* her only function being to contribute the substance of the Body of Christ; others, that she co-operated not only in the *preparation of the matter* but also to a certain extent in the *infusion of the final form.* Still others held an opinion *midway* between the two.[10]

The first opinion, that advanced by the exponents of Aristotelian biology, St. Bonaventure rejects. By numerous proofs he supports his belief in Mary's active causality in the generation of Christ. Quoting St. John Damascene, he says: "After the consent of the Virgin, the Holy Ghost came upon her, according to the word of the Lord, purifying her and giving her the power to receive within herself the divinity of the Word, and at the same time to conceive Him according to the flesh."[11] If Mary had the power not only to receive the Word of God within her womb but also to conceive Him, it follows that she was no mere corporeal receptacle, no mere instrument but an active and co-operating principle, an integrating part in the work of genera-

(8) For the opinion of the Subtle Doctor on this point, cf. Duns Scotus, *Theologiae Marianae elementa,* edited by C. Balich, Sibenik in Jugoslavia, 1933, p. 89. *Ordinatio III,* d.4, q. un. in corp. Cf. also *ibid.* p. 93.111-112 and his reference to the same question in *Reportata Parisiensia* and in his *Lectura Completa,* also edited by C. Balich, p. 116-118. 273.

(9) "Item, vera mater cooperatur in filii generatione; sed beata Maria vere fuit Mater Christi: ergo vere fuit cooperata in conceptione virtuti Spiritus sancti." *III Sent.,* a.3, q.1, t.III, 110a.

(10) "Respondeo: Dicendum, quod absque dubio, cum Virgo Maria sit Mater Christi et vere ipsum concepisse dicatur, vere cooperata fuit Spiritui sancto in Filii sui conceptione. Et hoc communiter et generaliter tenent doctores theologiae. De *modo* autem cooperandi diversi sentiunt diversa. Quidam enim dicere voluerunt, quod Virgo Maria solum cooperata fuit *ministrando principium materiale.* Illi vero, quod cooperata fuit in *ultimae formae inductione* et in materiae *praeparatione,* quamvis non in tota operatione. Alii vero tenent *medium* inter utrumque." *III Sent.,* d.4, a.3, q.1, t.III, 111a.

(11) "Circa primum sic proceditur et quaeritur utrum in illa conceptione aliquid Virgo Maria fuerit Spiritui sancto cooperata in aliquo, mediante aliqua potentia. Et quod sic videtur: 1. Primo auctoritate Damasceni, quam ponit Magister in littera: 'Praevenit Spiritus sanctus in ipsam secundum verbum, quod dixerat Angelus ei, purgans eam et potentiam deitatis Verbi receptivam praeparans, simul autem et generativam'." *Ibid.,* 110a.

tion.[12] Again, the Antiphon "Genuit puerpera regem" is accepted and chanted by the Church as true Catholic doctrine. But *to generate* is to act; parental generation is the act of the generative power. Therefore in the conception of Christ, the generative power of the Virgin co-operated with the power of God.[13] On the other hand, had Mary not co-operated in the conception, her function would have been that of a purely material *cause* and she would, consequently, bear no more relationship to Christ than does man to the dust from which he was formed. But this is not true. Therefore Mary did co-operate in the conception of Christ.[14] And the Seraphic Doctor goes on to say that man contributed the material principle of woman when Eve was taken from his side but it does not follow that Adam can be called the father or the mother of the woman for the simple reason that he did not co-operate in her formation. But the Blessed Virgin bears the relationship of Mother to Christ. Therefore she not only prepared the substance of His Body but also co-operated in the infusion of the final form.[15] This does not mean that Mary concurred in the whole act of conception from its initial to its final stage, as some maintain,—an opinion which oversteps the truth inasmuch as it attributes to a creature powers which belong to the Creator alone.[16]

Thus, by the divergence of these two opinions, the one too narrow, the other too broad, we are directed to the path of truth, continues the Seraphic Doctor. The opinion that lies *midway* between the two seems best, namely, that the Blessed Virgin possessed a power given her by God by means of which she could contribute the material embodiment of the Child conceived within her womb. This matter was not the mere *material* principle of the passive power of generation but a self-sufficient matter, containing within itself everything necessary to effect its purpose, including the power to bring

(12) "Ergo si non solum habuit potentiam receptivam sed etiam generativam, non solum se habuit Virgo Maria per modum recipientis, sed per modum agentis et cooperantis." *Ibid.*

(13) "Item, hoc conceditur et cantatur ab Ecclesia tanquam verus et catholicus sermo: 'Genuit puerpera regem'; sed *generare* agere est et actio virtutis generativae: ergo videtur quod in illa conceptione generativa vis Virginis cooperata fuit divinae virtuti." *Ibid.*

(14) "Item, aut Virgo Maria cooperata fuit, aut non. Si *sic,* habeo propositum; si *non*: ergo habuit se solummodo sicut materia: ergo sicut nulla est affinitas hominis ad limum, unde formatus est, sic nec Mariae ad Christum. Sed hoc est falsum: ergo etc." *Ibid.*

(15) "Item, vir praebuit mulieri materiale principium, quando de eius costa formata est Eva; sed propter hoc ipsius mulieris non dicitur esse pater, aut mater, quia cooperatus non fuit in eius formatione; sed beata Virgo habitudinem matris habet ad Christum: ergo non solum praeparavit materiam, sed cooperata fuit ad inducendum formam." *Ibid.*

(16) "Et quoniam ista positio nimis parum dicit, ideo sunt alii, qui superaddunt et dicunt, quod non solum cooperata fuit Spiritui sancto *ministrando principium materiale,* sed etiam in *ultimae formae inductione.* Nam in *tota* operatione cooperari non potuit, quoniam formatio corporis instantanea, prout formatio comprehendit totam transmutationem, fieri non potest, nisi a virtute infinita. In ultimae autem formae inductione cooperari potuit, pro eo quod ultima forma in instanti potest induci a natura, vel a virtute creata; et ideo in hoc, in quo potuit, cooperata fuit Spiritui sancto potentia Virginis generativa, et pro tanto dicitur mater, quia operata fuit conceptionem et quantum ad *initium* et quantum ad *consummationem.* Sed haec positio nimis dicit: primum, quia eiusdem est *factum esse,* cuius est fieri; quodsi conceptionem *efficere* non est virtutis creatae, sed increatae, similter nec ipsum conceptum esse" *Ibid.,* 111b.

forth the Child.[17] This generative power of itself could attain the perfection of its act only by successive stages over a period of time and, since it ill became the Body of Christ to be formed by successive stages of development, the Holy Ghost by His infinite power brought that matter to a state of complete and perfect bodily organization at the very moment of its conception.[18]

Motherhood is founded on conception. If it could be proved that Mary conceived a mere man, even though this man was subsequently, before his birth, transformed into a God-Man, Nestorius would have been justified in denying her the title of Mother of God. It was to safeguard the dogma of the Hypostatic Union that the Church dogmatically defined the temporal coincidence of Christ's conception with the Hypostatic Union.[19] The conception of Christ, then, included three simultaneous events: (1) the formation of His human body from the maternal *ovum;* (2) the creation and infusion into that body of a spiritual soul; and (3) the Hypostatic Union of body and soul, as a unity, with the Divine Person of the Word. When Mary said: "Behold the handmaid of the Lord, be it done to me according to thy word," the mystery of the Incarnation was accomplished. From the fact that these three events occurred simultaneously, the medieval Scholastics, and St. Bonaventure was among them, concluded that the Body of Christ was informed by the spiritual soul from the first moment of its existence, and that it was at once complete and perfectly organized. The last-mentioned of these conclusions is based on the false Aristotelian theory that the human embryo is at first inanimate and is quickened by the spiritual soul only after it has reached a certain stage of physiological development. Since this principle was manifestly inapplicable to Christ, the Scholastics had recourse to a miracle and simply denied the existence of successive stages in the embryological evolution of the God-Man.[20]

With St. Augustine, the Seraphic Doctor adopted the view that the Body of Christ was perfectly organized from the first moment of its conception as the only one worthy of the *Word assuming* human nature, of the *power effecting* it, and of the *Virgin conceiving* the Word of God. It was fitting that the Word on becoming Man should assume not an incomplete but a complete

---

(17) "Et quoniam prima opinio parum dicit, et secunda multum excedit, suis obliquitatibus dirigunt nos in veritatis viam. Et propterea melius sentire videntur qui dicunt *medium* videlicet quod beata Virgo habuit virtutem sibi divinitus datam, per quam administraret materiam illi conceptui materiam, inquam, quae non solum habuit rationem *materiae* sive potentiae passivae, sed etiam *sufficientiam et virtutem* ad prolis productionem." *Ibid.*, 112a.

(18) Illa tamen virtus per se non poterat prodire ad perfectum actum nisi per successionem in tempore; sed quoniam non decebat, carnem Christi formari successive, sicut in praecedentibus ostensum est; ideo Spiritus sanctus sua infinita virtute produxit illam materiam ad actum completum." *Ibid.*

(19) Cf. Pohle-Preuss, *Christology*, pp. 166 *et sqq.* B. Herder Book Co., St. Louis, Mo. 1930.

(20) It is more in conformity with modern science to assume that the spiritual soul informs the human embryo from the moment of conception and gradually builds up the body and its organs, until the child becomes normally capable of living outside the uterus. Applying this principle to Christ, we maintain that Christ's spiritual soul was infused into the inchoate embryo at the moment of his conception. This interpretation makes the sacred humanity of our Lord subject to the ordinary laws of human development and makes Him like unto us in all things except sin (Heb. 4:15). Cf. Pohle-Preuss, *Mariology*, p. 12.

human nature, body and soul. And since the soul can inform only a complete and perfectly organized body, says the Saint, we must conclude that the Body of Christ was in a state of perfect organization from the first moment of its conception.[21] This opinion likewise is worthy of the *power effecting* the Incarnation, for there the Divine Power operated in a miraculous manner, and this is the miracle of all miracles that a woman should conceive a God. Therefore to show His wondrous power God, in a single instant, formed that Body which in the order of nature would have had to pass through successive stages of development.[22] This view is worthy, too, of the *Virgin conceiving* who, at the very moment of her consent, was filled with the Holy Ghost and became the Mother of God, as the angel had announced. And since Mary was the Mother of God only if God was united to the flesh which she had conceived, and since flesh could be united neither to God nor to the soul unless it was in a state of perfect organization, we must conclude that the Body of Christ was complete and perfectly organized from the very instant of its conception.[23] And surely it in no way derogates from the motherhood of the Virgin if God by His power hastened the embryological evolution of her child, a process which He accomplishes in other women by successive stages.[24] Indeed, the Virgin possessed not less power than any other woman, but, in truth, far greater, for hers was both a natural and a supernatural power in virtue of which she, of herself alone, was enabled to furnish the material embodiment of her child just as does a woman who has had intercourse with man. As a consequence, the whole substance of Christ was from His Mother. She is His only bond with the human race, the only human source of His earthly origin. Therefore, if we wish to speak and think aright, we must admit that the Virgin was the Mother of Christ in a truer sense than any other woman is the mother of her child.[25] By that same power conferred upon her, she nourished Christ during nine months within her womb, contributing to the same extent that other mothers contribute to the

(21) "Dicendum, quod absque dubio, sicut dicit Augustinus, corpus Christi ab instanti conceptionis habuit perfectionem organizationis. Et ratio huius sumi potest ex parte *Verbi assumentis,* et ex parte *virtutis efficientis,* et ex parte *Virginis concipientis.* Ex parte Verbi assumentis: quia non decebat Verbum assumere partem humanae naturae, ut esset homo *secundum quid,* sed totam humanam naturam, et ita carnem et animam, maxime cum anima det carni congruentiam, ut uniatur cum natura divina, sicut ostensum supra. Et quoniam anima non est nata uniri nisi carni formatae et organizatae, ideo in primo instanti conceptionis necesse fuit, corpus ad perfectionem organizationis perduci." *III Sent.*, d.3, p.2, a.3, q.2, t.III, 93ab.

(22) "Ratio etiam est ex parte *virtute operantis* quia ibi virtus divina operabatur mirabiliter. Hoc enim est miraculum miraculorum, quod femina concipiat Deum. Et ideo ad suae mirabilis potentiae ostensionem subito formavit illud corpus, quod natura potest formare nisi successive." *Ibid.*, 93b.

(23) "Ratio verum nihilominus est ex parte *Virginis concipientis,* quae statim, ut consensit, repleta fuit Spiritu sancto et Mater Dei effecta, iuxta illud quod Angelus annuntiabat. Et quoniam Mater Dei non erat, nisi Deus unitus esset carni, quam conceperat; et caro nec Deo nec animae congrueret uniri, nisi haberet membrorum distinctionem convenientem: hinc est, quod ab instanti conceptionis corpus Christi debuit in membrorum distinctione perfectum esse." *Ibid.*

(24) "Et per hoc in nullo Virgini derogatur, si Deus sua virtute acceleravit, quod in aliis mulieribus successive producit ad *esse.*" *III Sent.*, d.4, a.3, q.1, t.III, 112a.

(25) "Non enim fuit minor potentia in Virgine quam in alia muliere, immo multo maior, quia potentiam naturalem et supernaturalem habuit, per quam subministrare poterat materiam ipsa sola adeo, sicut mulier viro commixta; unde tota substantia Christi fuit de matre sua. Et ideo, si recte velimus sentire et loqui, veriori modo fuit Virgo mater Christi, quam sit aliqua mater filii sui." *Ibid.*

substance of their offspring, giving Him that secret service which all expectant mothers lavish upon their unborn.[26]

This characteristic of procreative activity whereby a certain part of the substance of the parent passes into the constitution of the offspring gives rise to an intimate bond between parents and offspring,—a bond far closer than any connection between cause and effect. By this closest of bonds Mary is related to her Son, insofar as He is Man. St. Augustine tells us that Christ Himself fashioned the body which He assumed from the flesh of the Virgin, while St. John Damascene says that Christ fashioned a living body from the most pure blood of the Virgin. Commenting on the words of the Damascene: *Copulavit sibi ex purissimis sanguinibus animatum carnem,* St. Bonaventure states that the term "pure blood" signifies the humors which are available for the formation of the body. This humor, or fluid, is sometimes called *flesh,* sometimes *blood,* sometimes a *seed,* according to the meaning one wishes to convey. As *blood,* it indicates the source from which it proceeds; as *flesh,* the substance formed from it; as *seed,* the form which it assumes. As regards the objection that flesh is more closely related to flesh, it is true as regards the species, but not as regards generation, for flesh is never changed into flesh unless it is first changed into bodily humors.[27] By her maternal co-operation Mary provides God with something more than a temple in which to dwell; she produces something with which He may clothe Himself personally, something which through its union with the Word of God becomes a part of God Himself. The Fathers and theologians often speak of the Second Person of the Blessed Trinity as descending into the womb of the Virgin and there fashioning the body which He assumed as "the divine seed." "Wisdom hath built herself a house," says the Book of Proverbs.

On the first Christmas night Mary gave birth to the Son of God. "And it came to pass that when they were at Bethlehem her days were accomplished that she should be delivered. And she brought forth her first-born Son, and wrapt Him up in swaddling clothes, and laid Him in a manger, because there was no room for them in the inn" (Luke 2:6, 7). Now the mystery "hidden from ages and generations" (Col. 1:26) was "manifested" on the earth when Shepherds and Kings, wise men from the gorgeous East and from the open fields, adored in a stable, a Babe wrapped in swaddling clothes, the Lord of all. "They found the Child," as Christians without number have

(26) "Unde et per illam virtutem ipsum in ventre per novem menses confovit." *Ibid.*

(27) "Item quaeritur de hoc dicit Damascenus: *Copulavit sibi ex purissimis sanguinibus animatum carnem.* Et hoc videtur, quod conceptus fuit Christus ex sanguine Virginis. Sed *contra* hoc est illud Augustini, quod sequitur, quod assumsit sibi carnem de carne virginis. Item proximior est caro carni quam sanguis: ergo prius debuit assumere carnem de carne quam de sanguine. Respondeo: Dicendum, quod purissimos sanguines intelligit humores, qui propinqui sunt ad corporis formationem, ex quibus caro Christi formata fuit. Ille autem humor aliquando vocatur *caro,* aliquando *sanguis,* aliquando *semen;* et hoc secundum diversam comparationem. *Sanguis* enim dicitur in comparatione ad illud, unde processit, *caro* in comparatione ad illud quod ex ipso fit; *semen* vero quantum ad forman, quam habet. Ad illud quod obiicitur, quod *caro* est carni propinquior; dicendum, quod verum est in via *speciei,* sed non in via *generationis,* quia caro nunquam convertitur in carnem, nisi prius convertatur in humorem. *III Sent.,* d.3, p.1, dub.3, t.III, 79b.

found Him since, "with Mary His Mother" (Matt. 2; 11; Luke 2:16). Here we find ourselves face to face with the very heart of Mystery, for when we behold the unveiled features of the Babe of Bethlehem, we are gazing in very truth upon the veiled majesty of God.

Although Mary was chosen to be His Mother, she made herself the humble handmaid and servant of the Lord, ministering to Him *faithfully, humbly* and *courageously,* as did Martha, the sister of Lazarus, in days to come. She was, therefore, prefigured by the good woman Abigail who, when she was sought by David in marriage, offered herself as a servant saying: "Behold, let thy servant be a handmaid, to wash the feet of the servants of my Lord" (I Kings 25:41). Such was the Virgin Mary through her wonderful humility, as she herself testifies: "He hath regarded the humility of his handmaid" (Luke 1:48). St. Augustine says: Everyone who is truly wise is convinced both by the evidence of her deeds and the unshaken truth of faith that Mary was the servant of Christ. Indeed, she proved herself the handmaid of the Lord; she bore Him in her womb, nourished Him with her milk and warmed Him in her arms. As the Gospel says, *she laid Him in a manger.* Fleeing the face of Herod, she carried Him into Egypt, and during all His infancy she guarded Him with a mother's tender care.[28]

With "the woman from the crowd," the Church proclaims the unchanging truth: "Blessed is the womb of the holy Virgin Mary which bore the eternal Son of the Father, and blessed are the breasts which nourished Christ Our Lord." As Moses was nursed not by an Egyptian, but by a Hebrew woman, his own mother, so was Christ nourished at the breast of Mary alone, as was prefigured in the Canticle: "Who shall give thee to me for my brother, sucking the breasts of my mother?" "Blessed is the womb that bore thee and the paps that gave thee suck" (Luke 11:27). Herein is contained the proof that the Virgin Mary is the true and perfect Mother of Christ. Not only did she bear Him but she also nourished Him; and as truly as she nourished Him, so truly did she bear Him. Herein, too, is refuted the wicked heresy of Manichaeus and others who deny the true humanity of Christ. In the presence of the blasphemous Jews, "the woman from the crowd" acknowledges the true Son of God and declares Him consubstantial with His Mother, for unless He and His Mother were one and the same flesh, to no avail would

(28) "Recte etiam in *ministrando* fuit Martha, quae Domino ministravit *fideliter* et *humiliter* et *viriliter*. Sic et Maria, cum esset Mater, fecit se ancillam et ministram, secundum illud supra primo: 'Ecce, ancilla Domini, fiat mihi secundum verbum tuum'. Unde designata fuit per illam bonam mulierem Abigail, quae, cum a David peteretur in coniugium, obtulit se administerium; primi Regum vigesimo quinto: 'Ecce, famula tua sit ancilla, ut lavet pedes servorum tuorum'. Talis fuit Virgo Maria prae nimia humilitate; unde de se ipsa dicebat: 'Respexit humilitatem ancillae suae'. Et hoc est quod dicit Augustinus: 'Mariam operis exhibitione et fidei rigidissima veritate ministram Christ fuisse, omnis, qui sane sapit, intelligit'. Absque dubio enim ministratrix ei exstitit, quae hunc in utero gessit partuque profusum aluit et fovit, atque, ut Evangelium ait, *in praesepio reclinavit* et a facie Herodis fugiens in Aegyptum accessit et omnem infantiam eius pio matris affectu et prosecuta." *Comment. in Evangelium Lucae,* C.X., t.VII, 276b.

the womb and the breasts of the Virgin be called blessed.[29] Faith in Christianity begins with faith in the truth that Jesus Christ, the Virgin's Son, is the Lord Our God. In His human nature He is as truly and really one substance with His human Mother, as in the Everlasting Trinity He is consubstantial with His Father in heaven. With deepest faith in her unspeakable dignity, let us, then, bow down and say:

"O Mary, Holy Mother of God, Who made thy womb His throne,
Mother of Christ,
Pray for us!"

Mary's Physical Virginity

Not only is Mary the Mother of God; she is the Virgin Mother of God, for, as St. Bernard says: "The only nativity worthy of God was that which made Him Son of the Virgin, as the only motherhood worthy of the Virgin was that which made her Mother of God."[30] Ordinarily we speak of virginity in its spiritual sense,—the abstention from all voluntary sexual pleasure, whether illicit, or licit, as in marriage. When we speak of Mary's virginity we include likewise that physical integrity which, in other women, may be lost in various ways and which is virtuously surrendered in the consecrated act of marriage. Even in this physical sense, Mary was a pure virgin, though she conceived and bore a Son. This inviolate virginity was purely miraculous, a concession to her who was to be the holy Mother of God.

Jesus Christ, the Son of God and the Son of Mary, was born miraculously, as we read in the Gospels of St. Matthew and St. Luke, outside the ordinary law of generation. The Holy Spirit, Who in the beginning "created heaven and earth out of the empty void" (Gen. 1:1, 2), made the Virgin Mary "conceive and bear a Son," as foretold by the prophet Isaias. Indeed, this was the sign by which the Jews of old were to recognize the Mother of the Messiah. "Behold a virgin shall conceive and bear a son" (Isai. 7:14). The virgin was to remain a virgin both in conceiving and in child-bearing; otherwise she would not have been given as a sign to the inhabitants of Jerusalem: "The Lord Himself shall give you a sign" *(ibid.)*. This wonderful event was

(29) "Nec tantum beatificat Virginem propter portationem, sed *ubera* propter lactationem, cum subdit: *Et ubera quae suxisti,* beata scilicet; ex quo datur intelligi, quod a solis uberibus Virginis beatissimae lactatus fuit. Quod designatum fuit in Moyse, qui lactari, ut dicitur, noluit a muliere Aegyptiaca; et ideo quaesita fuit mulier Hebraea, scilicet mater propria, sicut dicitur Exodi secundo. Haec autem designat Virginem Mariam, cuius ubera suxit Christus, secundum illud Canticorum octavo: 'Quis mihi det te fratrem meum sugentem ubera matris meae' etc. (Cant. 8.1). Ideo autem iunxit ista duo, ut ostenderetur Virgo Maria fuisse mater Christi vera et perfecta, quia non solum genuit, sed etiam educavit; et sicut vere educavit, ita vere genuit; et in hoc arguitur, ut dicitur in Glossa, impietas Manichaei et aliorum, qui dicunt, ipsum attulisse corpus aethereum. Unde Beda: 'Ex eodem fonte et lac nutriendis et semen procreandis pueris manat'. Ergo de semine Virginis, secundum physicos, potuit concipi qui de lacte eius potuit nutriri." *Ibid.,* C.XI, t.VII, 296b, 297a.

(30) *Super "Missus est,"* Hom. ii, I. MPL 183.61.

pointed out to Ezechiel in a glorious vision of the rebuilt temple. The Prophet beheld the Lord enter the temple by the gate which looks toward the East. In memory of this apparition, no man was to pass through the gate the Lord had entered; it was to remain closed forever. "And he brought me back to the way of the gate of the outward sanctuary, which looked towards the east," that is, to a consideration of the origin and Incarnation of the Son of God; "and it was shut" (Ezech. 44:1) through perfect virginal integrity. *This gate shall be shut* at the conception of the Lord; *it shall not be opened* at His birth; *and no man shall pass through it* by the exercise of marital rights; *because the Lord, the God of Israel, hath entered by it,*—a reference, no doubt, to Christ's miraculous conception within His Mother's womb.[31] Wherefore the Spouse, addressing the Virgin Mary, extols her purity in the Cantle of Canticles: "My sister, my spouse, is a garden enclosed; a garden enclosed, a fountain sealed up. Thy plants are a paradise" (Cant. 4:12, 13). The closed gate is the seal of purity, the integrity of her spotless flesh, for, far from being stained by bearing a Son, she was sanctified in conceiving Him. Thrice does the Prophet say, "the gate was shut"; thrice does the Spouse speak of the closed garden and fountain,—a figure which bears a striking analogy to the sacred womb of Our Lady, who remained a virgin unsullied *in the conception* of her Son, *at His birth,* and *for the remainder* of her life, a truth which confounds the heretics who said that after the birth of Christ, Mary "was known" by her husband.[32]

Mary was a pure Virgin before the birth of Christ and her virginity was not violated when she conceived her Divine Son. The conception of the Word Incarnate was miraculously virginal in that He was conceived without a human father. The germ in whose development and growth Mary cooperated was fecundated not by any human action but by the vital influence of the Holy Spirit.[33] As on the sixth day man was fashioned from the earth by the power and wisdom of the Divine Hand, says the Seraphic Doctor, so at length, when the fullness of time had come, at the beginning of the sixth age, the angel Gabriel was sent to a Virgin. And when the Virgin had given her consent to be the Mother of God, the Holy Ghost came upon her, like a

(31) "Viso de virginitate, sequitur videre de fecunditate; quae quidem respectu virginitatis fuit admirabilis.... Primo igitur fuit admirabilis propter concipientis integritatem; propterea dicitur Isaiae septimo: *Ecce, virgo concipiet,* ita quod simul sit *virgo* et *concipiens,* alioquin non *daretur in signum* habitantibus Ierusalem. Hoc mirabile ostensum fuit Ezechieli in descriptione templi, quadragesimo quarto: *Convertit me,* inquit, *ad viam portae sanctuarii exterioris, quae respiciebat ad orientem,* id est ad considerandum Filii Dei originem et incarnationem; *et erat clausa,* scilicet per omnimodam incorruptionem. Et reddit rationem: *Porta haec clausa erit,* scilicet in conceptu; *non aperietur,* scilicet in partu, *et vir non transibit per eam,* quantum ad matrimonii usum; *quoniam Dominus Deus Israel ingressus est per eam,* quantum scilicet ad conceptionis sacramentum." *De Annuntiatione B. Virginis Mariae, Sermo II,* t.IX, 663b.

(32) "Unde Sponsus Virginem Mariam alloquens Canticorum quarto dicit: *Hortus conclusus, soror mea sponsa; hortus conclusus, fons signatus; emissiones tuae paradisus.* Ter dicit clausionem ipsius, ut ostendat, quod incorrupta *in conceptu,* in *partu* et in *progressu,* contra haereticos, qui dixerunt, postea ipsam a viro fuisse cognitam." *Ibid.*

(33) "In Christo autem secus est; ipse enim neutro modo fuit propagatus, nec secundum propagationem legis naturalis nec secundum corruptionem libidinis; sed Spiritus Sanctus, adveniens in ipsam Virginem et ipsam fecundans...." *III Sent.,* d.15, a.1, q.3, t.III, 335a.

divine fire, inflaming her mind and purifying her flesh with the most perfect purity. And the power of the Most High overshadowed her, enabling her to bear the flame of love that leaped high in the holocaust of her heart. In that sacred moment, by the creative power of the Holy Ghost, a body was formed, a soul was created, and both were immediately and inseparably united to the Divinity in the Person of the Son, true God and true Man. O sublime mystery! in whose presence proud reason rebels, in whose belief divine faith bows down in humble adoration.[34]

The intercourse of man is, then, excluded in the conception of Our Blessed Lord, and the prophecy of Jeremias is fulfilled: "The Lord hath created a new thing upon the earth. A woman shall compass a man" (Jer. 31:22). The "new thing" created in woman is the body of the Lord, conceived within the Virgin without the co-operation of man.[35]

Mindful of the prophetic character of the history of the Old Testament, the clearness of which is attained only through the full light of revelation, the Fathers recognize with a special predilection, the miracles which prefigured the maternity and the inviolate virginity of the Mother of the Founder of the New Covenant. The revelation long since given by God to Moses in the burning thorn-bush which was not consumed (Exod. 3:2) was realized in Mary when "she was found with child, of the Holy Ghost",—an admirable "discovery," says the Seraphic Doctor, because it is the foundation and the consummation of all the marvels ever accomplished in the Old Testament in the time of the Law or in the time of grace.[36] Then it was "found that the rod of Aaron for the house of Levi, was budded" (Num. 17:8). Then, too, there came forth "a rod out of the root of Jesse" (Isai. 11:1). Nor does the one prophecy contradict the other, for Mary was of both sacerdotal and of royal descent.[37]

---

(34) "Denique, postquam venit plenitudo temporis, sicut homo sexta die conditus est de terra per divinae manus virtutem et sapientiam; sic in principio sextae aetatis, misso archangelo Gabriele ad Virginem, et Virgine praebente illi assensum, supervenit in eam Spiritus sanctus, sicut ignis divinus mentem eius inflammans carnemque ipsius perfectissima puritate sanctificans. Sed et *virtus eam obumbravit Altissimi,* ut tantum ferre posse ardorem; qua operante in instanti corpus fuit formatum, anima creata et simul utrumque Divinitate in persona Filii counitum, ut idem esset Deus et homo, salva utriusque proprietate naturae." *Lignum Vitae, De Mysterio Originis,* t.VII, 71ab.

(35) Referring to the prophecy of Isaias (7:14): *Ecce concipies in utero et paries filium,* St. Bonaventure says: "Et signanter dicit: *Ecce, concipies in utero,* ut ostendat, hoc ipsum esse magnum et mirum et novum, ut concipiat intra, nihil recipiendo ab extra; Ieremiae trigesimo primo: 'Novum fecit Dominus super terram: femina circumdabit virum.' " *Comment. in Evangelium Lucae* C.I, t.VII, 24.

(36) "Primo inventus est in *Nazareth in Maria,* ut conceptus; Matthaei primo: *Cum esset desponsata Mater eius Maria Ioseph, antequam convenirent, inventa est in utero habens de Spiritu sancto.* Et ista inventio est *admirabilis,* quia est fundamentum et consummatio omnium mirabilium, quae fuerunt tam in veteri Testamento in tempore Legis quam in tempore gratiae. Haec est prima visio, qua Moyses vidit *rubum ardentem, et non comburebatur,* Exodi tertio, hoc est fecundationem Virginis sine corruptione virginitatis per operationem Spiritus sancti." *Sermones de Tempore. Epiphania. Sermo III,* t.IX, 156b.

(37) "Item, Numerorum decimo septimo: *Invenit, germinasse virgam Aaron in domo Levi,* et hoc consummatum fuit in ista inventione; et Isaiae undecimo: *Egredietur virga de radice Iesse.* Nec contradicit huic quod praedictum est: *in domo Levi,* quia Maria fuit de tribu sacerdotali et regali." *Ibid.*

In another passage St. Bonaventure says that Mary's conception *without male seed* was prefigured in the miracle of the blooming rod of Aaron (Num. 17:5); "a flower shall rise up out of his root" (Isai. 11:1); her conception *without carnal desire,* in the burning bush, because "the bush was on fire and was not burned" (Exod. 3:2); her *childbirth without sorrow,* in the dew and fleece of Gedeon (Judges 6:37), for, as St. Jerome says, the fleece on the body of the sheep feels no suffering. Accordingly in the Divine Office for the feast of the Circumcision we find the words: "When thou wast born of a Virgin in a wonderful manner," then were the words of Scripture fulfilled: "He shall come down like rain upon the fleece."[38]

There were two precepts of the ancient law concerning the birth of first-born sons. One was that the mother should remain in retirement for forty days, after which time she should go to the temple to be purified. The other required the parents of the first-born to take him to the temple, and there offer him to God. The Law of Moses prescribed: "If a woman having received seed shall bear a man child, she shall be unclean seven days . . . and she shall remain three and thirty days in the blood of her purification" (Lev. 12:2, 4), that is, forty days in all. Although Mary was not bound by the law of purification, since she was always a virgin, yet she wished to go, like other mothers, to be purified and at the same time to obey the second precept, to present and offer her Son to the Eternal Father: "And after the days of her purification, according to the Law of Moses, were accomplished, they carried Him to Jerusalem to present Him to the Lord, as it is written in the law of the Lord: Every male opening the womb shall be called holy to the Lord" (Luke 2:22, 23). Here the Evangelist seems to put Mary on a level with ordinary mothers. As a matter of fact, he is merely citing a provision of the Mosaic Law which was made for mothers in general, not for the exceptional mother. In the law of purification what is the meaning of the addition, *suscepto semine,* if the Author of the law thought not of "the Woman," who, since she conceived and gave birth without the aid of man, remained pure? If the Lawgiver is wise, asks St. Bonaventure, why does he add what anyone at all knows? If there is not some woman who can bear a male child without having received a seed, why does he say, *if she has received a seed?* But if there is a woman who can bear a male child without having received a seed, speak, O Judean, and tell who that woman is. She is none other than the glorious Virgin; she in truth was undefiled, for she conceived of the Holy

(38) "Et nota, trium praecedentium triplicem praecessisse figuram: quia *sine virili semine,* in virga Aaron, quae floruit, Numerorum decimo septimo; Isaiae decimo: 'Flos de radice eius ascendet' etc.; quia *sine libidine,* in rubo et igne, Exodi tertio, quia rubus ardebat et non comburebatur; quia *partus sine dolore* designatur in rore et vellere Gedeonis, Iudicum sexto. 'Vellus enim, ut dicit Hieronymus, cum sit de corpore, nescit tamen corporis passionem'; et ideo in Psalmo: 'Descendet sicut pluvia in vellus'." *Comment. in Evangelium Lucae* C.I, t.VII, 25a.

Ghost.[39] Since the physiological suppositions did not exist, surely the Blessed Virgin was exempt from the law of purification. Nevertheless, Mary fulfilled the ordinance with a perfection peculiar to herself. Though she had given birth to her Son without detriment to her virginity, she submitted to the ceremony, thus assimilating herself in public estimation with ordinary mothers and carefully concealing the secret of her miraculous virginity. "Truly, O Blessed Virgin," says St. Bernard, "in you there is no reason for purification nor any need of it. But did your Son have any need of circumcision?" To the pure Mother of God may be addressed the words which King Assuerus spoke to Esther: "This law is not made for thee, but for all others" (Esther 15:13).[40]

The same may be said of the provision of the Mosaic Law whereby "every male opening the womb shall be called holy to the Lord," for it is written: "Sanctify unto me every firstborn that openeth the womb among the children of Israel" (Exod. 13:2). This requirement, like the law of purification, evidently, did not apply to the Virgin Mary, who was a "closed gate" (Ezech. 44:2) before, after, and at the birth of Christ.[41] "Who is this gate but Mary?" says St. Ambrose. "She was a 'closed gate' because she was a virgin. Mary is the gate through which Christ came into this world when He issued forth by a virginal birth, without loosing the bars of virginity. The pure enclosure remained unsullied; the seal of integrity was kept inviolate. . . . A good gate is Mary, who was closed and was not opened. Through her passed Christ, but He opened not."[42] And the Seraphic Doctor: "From the womb of her to whom it was said: 'The Holy which shall be born of thee shall be called the Son of God' (Luke 1:35), came forth a Child of noble race, leaving her virginal seal unbroken."[43]

---

(39) "Dicit: *secundum Legem Moysi;* scriptum fuit *in Lege Moysi:* Mulier, si suscepto *semine, peperit masculum immunda erit septem diebus et manebit in sanguine purificationis suae triginta diebus;* et sunt quadraginta dies in universo. Dicit: *si suscepto semine* etc.; si sapiens legislator, quare addidit, quod quilibet scit? Si nulla est mulier, quae possit parere masculum sine suscepto semine, quare dicit: *si suscepto semine etc.?* Si vero aliqua mulier possit parere masculum non suscepto semine, dic tu, Iudaee, quae est illa? Non est haec nisi Virgo gloriosa; ipsa enim non fuit immunda, quia de Spiritu sancto concepit. Igitur quantum ad Mariam, Lex Moysi non fuit ei obligatoria per necessitatem, sed per mysterium." *De Purificatione B. Virginis Mariae, Sermo I,* t.IX, 635a.

(40) "Bernardus: . . . 'Vere, o beata Virgo, non habes causam, nec tibi opus est purificatione. Sed nunquid filio tuo opus erat circumcisione'? Unde potest dici quod dixit Assuerus Esther, decimo quinto: 'Non propter te, sed pro omnibus lex ista posita est'." *Comment. in Evangelium Lucae* C.II, t.VII, 56.

(41) "Tertio, quantum ad *mandatum scriptum,* subditur: *Sicut scriptum est in lege Domini,* quia omne masculinum, adaperiens vulvam, sanctum Domino vocabitur; Exodi decimo tertio: 'Sanctifica mihi omne primogenitum, quod aperit vulvam in filiis Israel, tam de hominibus quam de iumentis'. Sed illud non videtur conveniri virgini Mariae, quae est porta clausa ante partum et post partum et in partu. Et ideo potest dici, sicut supra dictum est de lege purificationis." *Ibid.*

(42) "Quae est haec porta nisi Maria? Ideo clausa, quia virgo. Porta igitur Maria, per quam Christus intravit in hunc mundum, quando virginali fusus est partu et genitalia virginitatis claustra non solvit. Mansit intemeratum septum pudoris et inviolata integritatis duravere signacula. . . . Bona porta Maria, quae clausa erat et non aperiebatur, transivit per eam Christus, sed non aperuit." *De Instit. Virg.,* c.VIII, n.52. MPL 16.334.

(43) "Nam de eius utero infans nobilissimi generis prosiluit, iuxta illud: 'Quod enim nascetur ex te Sanctum vocabitur Filius Dei, 'salvo tamen signaculo virginali'." *De Assumtione B. Virginis Mariae. Sermo II,* t.IX, 692b.

Thus, the virginal conception of Christ is consummated by His virginal birth. Mary's supernatural conceiving is followed by a miraculous child-bearing. If her conceiving was like the Father's conceiving, so must her child-bearing resemble the eternal procession of the Son from the Father. In the brightness which streams forth from the light, a brightness born with the light and yet not identical with it, St. Bonaventure sees the spotless generation of the Son from the Father, consubstantial with the Father, yet both distinct Persons of one and the same God. Contemplating the glorious birth of the Incarnate Word Who came forth from Mary's womb without impairing the integrity of the Virgin, the Church sings: "O rising sun, brightness of the light eternal!" (Rom. Brev., Antiph. at Magnificat, Dec. 21).[44] And such a birth was befitting Christ, of Whom St. Paul says: "In him we have redemption and remission of sins, Who is the image of the invisible God, the first-born of every creature" (Col. 1:14, 15). Wherefore, as He is the firstborn of the Father, so, too, is He the firstborn of His Mother; as He is the Only-begotten of His Father, so is He the Only-begotten of His Mother. "And we saw His glory, the glory as it were of the Only-begotten of the Father" (John 1:14).[45]

The virginal conception of Christ was highly appropriate in view of the chief purpose of the Incarnation, which was the regeneration of the human race. Christ came that He might take away the sins of the world; yet a natural conception would make Him guilty of the sin He came to destroy. The problem confronting the Second Person of the Blessed Trinity in becoming man was how to become man without becoming sinful man, that is, man-infected by the sin to which all flesh is heir. He had to be a true man in order to suffer for man, but He could not be a sinful man if He was to redeem man from sin. Original sin can be transmitted only by the natural mode of sexual generation, according to the law of concupiscence, that is, by the commingling of male and female, because this is the way in which all children of Adam come into being. If a man, therefore, though a descendant of Adam, were not born *ex semine Adae,* he would not be subject to original sin. God could become man by being born of woman; He could be sinless man, without original sin, by dispensing with man as the principle of generation, in other

(44) "Oritur splendor ex luce ita, quod connaturalis est luci, nec tamen dicimus, quod lux sit splendor, et e converso. Per hunc modum est Filius a Patre, ut sit consubstantialis Patri, sed tamen nec Filius est Pater, nec Pater est Filius, sed idem ipsum unus, quod alius. Et ideo gloriosam illam nativitatem recolens Ecclesia canit: 'O oriens! splendor lucis aeternae'." *Sermones de Tempore. Vigilia Nativitatis Domini. Sermo XII,* t.IX, 100a.

(45) "Talis partus decebat Christum, de quo ad Colossenses primo: "In ipso habemus redemptionem et remissionem peccatorum, qui est imago Dei invisibilis primogenitus omnis creaturae'; unde sicut est primogenitus Patris, ita etiam primogenitus Matris; sicut etiam unigenitus Patris, ita unigenitus Matris; Ioannis primo: 'Vidimus gloriam eius, gloriam quasi Unigeniti a Patre' etc." *Comment. in Evangelium Lucae.* C.II, t.VII, 46b.

words, by being born of the chaste womb of a virgin.[46] In the conception of her Son, the power of God entered the womb of Mary as serenely enriching and undamaging as a thought enters the mind. In the birth of Mary's Son, the Son of God left her womb, leaving the seals unbroken, with the same divine ease with which He left the tomb on Easter morn, the stone still sealed; with which He came to His Apostles in the Upper Room, the doors being locked.

Mary's Son was the Eternal Son of God. For many reasons it was fitting that He should take flesh from woman alone: first, to preserve the dignity of His Mother, who in conceiving the Son of God, did not lose the sublime honor of virginity;[47] secondly, to preserve the honor of His Father, for Christ had a Father in His eternal generation, and since His Father fully sufficed for Him in heaven, He came to earth to seek not a father but only a mother, for a child deriving his existence from two fathers would be the true son of neither and the first father would, in a way, be dishonored. It was beneath the dignity of the Eternal Father to share His parenthood with mortal man.[48] It was fitting, thirdly, that Christ should take flesh from woman alone for the completion and perfection of the whole as regards the possible modes of bringing human beings into existence, for there is a fourfold mode of generation: namely, from man and woman, from neither man nor woman, from man without woman, and from woman without man. The first three ways had already been exemplified; the first, in the natural birth of children; the second, in the production of Adam; the third, in the production of Eve. It remained for Christ to furnish an example of the fourth mode, which He would not have done if He had been conceived in any other way.[49] The fourth reason was to make manifest a corresponding congruity between the Fall and its reparation, for just as the Fall was brought about by both sexes, having been begun by the woman and consummated by the man, so would it be in the reparation. The Woman by believing and conceiving would in

(46) "Illud autem intelligitur traduci *secundum legem concupiscentiae,* in cuius procreatione concurrit foeditas delectationis carnis ex parte viri generantis et mulier concipientis. Neutrum horum fuit in generatione Christi. Nam conceptio eius *mirabilis* fuit et supra virtutem naturae; non enim fuit ex virili semine, pro eo quod caro eius concepta fuit sola ex muliere. Fuit etiam praeter *legem concupiscentiae,* quia non intervenit delectatio ex commixtione sexus; conceptus enim fuit ex castissimis Virginis visceribus." *III Sent.,* d.3, p.2, a.2, q.2, t.III, 89a.

"Possemus autem hoc exponere de Christo, qui solus evasit a corruptione concupiscentiae originalis, qui solus fuit 'inter mortuos liber'." *Comment. in Ecclesiasten,* C.VII, t.VI, 63a.

(47) "Sed tamen non fuisset ita congruum, sicut nunc; et hoc multiplici ratione congruentiae, ob quam magis decebat, ut carnem sumeret de sola muliere. Prima est servandam *dignitatem Matris* quae ob conceptionem Filii Dei non amisit privilegium virginitatis." *III Sent.,* d.12, a.3, q.2, t.III, 272b.

(48) "Secunda est propter servandam *honorificentiam Patris;* Christus enim secundum generationem aeternam habebat patrem; et cum ille plene sibi sufficeret in caelis, non venit in terris patrem quaerere, sed solum matrem, ne duobus patribus filius existens neutrius esset filius plene, et sic iniuria primo patri quodam modo fieret." *Ibid.*

(49) "Tertia est propter complendam perfectionem universitatis in modis educendi hominem in *esse:* quia, cum esset quadruplex modus educendi hominem in *esse,* scilicet de viro et muliere, nec de viro nec de muliere, de viro sine muliere, et de muliere sine viro; tres primi praecesserant; et ideo non restabat, nisi ut Deus quartum modum adderat; quod non fecisset, si alio modo conceptus esset." *Ibid.*

secret begin the overthrow of Satan whom her Son would later conquer in open warfare on the gibbet of the cross.[50]

Let us, then, invoke Our Blessed Lady, saying:
"Hail, Holy Virgin of Virgins!
Thou untarnished corner of earth, thou bush that burneth not!
Hail, thou who hast taken away our curse!
Mother Inviolate,
Pray for us!"

* * *

When the Son of God undertook the redemption of mankind and willed to be born of a Virgin Mother, He did not need the agency of any human father, real or apparent. Yet, for reasons of His own He decreed that the Woman who was to be His Mother should be married to a man whose name was Joseph, and this despite the fact that she had already consecrated herself to God by a vow of virginity. To slur over this important fact, for fear that it may occasion a revision of the lofty conception we have formed of the Virgin Mother of God, is to attempt to belittle the works of God and to destroy the beautiful synthesis, the perfect harmony and symmetry of the finished design woven from the threads of apparent contradiction.

We must always remember that there was a real marriage between Mary and Joseph and that Joseph is in a real and true sense called the husband of Mary, as St. Matthew notes: "Jacob begot Joseph, the husband of Mary" (1:16). Mary was the true and genuine wife of Joseph. We do not say this to the prejudice of the Virgin but in all reverence, for we cannot deny that a true marriage existed between Mary and Joseph since Sacred Scripture explicitly says so and all the Saints are agreed on this point.[51] On the other hand, our faithful love and reverence for the Virgin do not permit us to think that her most blessed, most pure and innocent soul had the faintest intention of accomplishing the activity of marriage by carnal means, nor does the Seraphic Doctor believe that Mary ever wavered, even slightly, in her virginal resolution. Indeed, he says, we must be most careful not to lessen the honor of Our Lady but to keep it unsullied even at the risk of our lives.[52]

As distant as earth from heaven were the thoughts of the Virgin from the

(50) "Quarta ratio propter *correspondentiam congruitatis* lapsus et reparationis, ut, sicut lapsus est factus in utroque sexu, sed primo in muliere est inchoatus et in viro consummatus; sic esset in reparatione, ut mulier credendo et concipiendo inciperet diabolum superare in abscondito, et post eius filius in manifesto eum vinceret in duello, scilicet in crucis patibulo." *Ibid.*

(51) "Haec autem sine praeiudicio dicta sint, maxime propter reverentiam Virginis; non enim possumus negare, quin inter Mariam et Ioseph fuerit verum coniugium, cum hoc dicat Scriptura evangelica, et Sancti omnes in hoc consentiant." *IV Sent.*, d.28, a.1, q.6, t.IV, 697. Cf. Matt. 1:18 *et sqq.* and Luke 1:27 *et sqq.*

(52) "Rursus, pietas fidei et reverentia Virginis non patitur nos sentire, ipsius beatissimam et purissimam et integerrimam animam ad opus carnis fuisse aliquantulum inclinatam; nec credo, ipsam in dubio se super hoc posuisse. Si quis tamen aliter dicat, dum tamen Virgini non faciat iniuriam, non est magna vis facienda. Cavendum est enim diligenter, ut honor Dominae nostrae in nullo ab aliquo minuatur, qui etiam in periculo capitis debeat integer custodiri." St. Bonaventure, *ibid.*, 697.

plans the Most High had for her, for indeed the ultimate reason of her espousal was found in a divine direction. A light which never before shone upon the mothers of Israel had discovered to her the value of perpetual continence and she had resolved never to know man. But God, Who had inspired Mary to remain a virgin, now showed her clearly and unmistakably that she should also become espoused to Joseph. She who had consecrated her virginity to God was now commanded to join herself in earthly wedlock; the Bride of the Most High was to be counted the bride of mortal man. We may easily imagine that Mary, following the common custom of the Israelites in the selection of the marriage state, was instigated thereto by her relatives. Judging from her character, it may be assumed as certain that she would yield to such a direction of her kin, if it were favored by a legal provision, for then she might hope that God, Who directed her upon this twofold path, would also point out to her the union of the same. Implicitly trusting divine guidance, Mary acceded to the wishes of her parents, confident that her vow would be kept, even in her married state. The Virgin was pure and chaste, says St. Bonaventure, but she was also obedient. That she might better practice this virtue, the Lord willed that she should be married to Joseph, that she should be subject to him and obey him as her husband.[53] The Seraphic Doctor goes on to say that there was no risk or imperfection involved in Mary's conduct, for she had been assured either by divine inspiration or by angelic revelation of the continence of Joseph. Concerning herself, who had never experienced even the least sting of the flesh, she had no misgivings. Therefore, she could marry without the least imperfection or risk; in fact, she was in conscience bound to do so, since God so inspired her.[54]

Mary gave her consent to the matrimonial union, says St. Bonaventure, but not to the carnal union. Hugh of St. Victor likewise expressly states that although Mary entered the marriage state of her own free will, she did not thereby necessarily consent to the carnal union.[55] There are some, continues the Saint, who maintain that consent to carnal intercourse is an *absolute* requisite for the contraction of a true marriage. These theologians say that the Virgin Mary consented to the carnal union but that she did so without sin, however, as she had not taken a vow but had merely resolved to preserve

(53) "Virgo erat pura et munda; et fuit etiam obediens, quam etiam ut melius servaret obedientiam, voluit Dominus, ut esset desponsata ut ei esset subdita et obediret sicut suo viro." *Sermones de Sanctis. De Sancto Marco Evangelista,* t.IX, 522b.

(54) "Ad illud quod obiicitur de *periculo* et *imperfectione,* dico, quod Virgo certificata fuit vel inspiratione divina, vel revelatione angelica de ipsius sancti Ioseph continentia; et ipsa de se certa erat, quae nullum omnino carnis stimulum sentiebat: et ideo sine omni imperfectione et periculo nubere poterat et debebat, quoniam Deus sic inspirabat." *IV Sent.,* d.30, a.1, q.2, t.IV, 710b.

(55) "Item, in distinctione trigesima dicitur: 'Consensit Maria in copulam maritalem, sed non in copulam carnalem.' Item hoc ipsum expresse dicit Hugo in libro *de Virginitate Mariae;* et tamen ex consensu suo matrimonium contraxit: ergo non oportet in carnalem copulam consentire." *IV Sent.,* d.28, a.1, q.6, t.IV, 695.

her virginity.[56] But this opinion belittles the glorious Virgin, for, although it excuses her from guilt, it detracts from the glory of her virginity, robbing her of the right to be called Virgin of all virgins. This opinion, so offensive to our minds and ears, has received the suitable disapprobation of Hugh of St. Victor.[57]

Here a question arises concerning St. Augustine's statement: "Entrusting herself to Divine Providence, the Blessed Virgin consented to the carnal union," which would seem to imply the blasphemous thought that the Virgin had lost at least the integrity of her resolution. However, the objection continues, the Saint seems to contradict himself, for just previously he had said that "Mary consented to the conjugal companionship of her husband, but not to carnal union with him." St. Bonaventure resolves the difficulty by explaining that St. Augustine did not mean to imply that the Virgin consented to the carnal relationship, for in the opinion of the Seraphic Doctor, the Virgin herself never willed such a union nor did God so inspire her, but that she consented to the conjugal companionship or to the union through which offspring is begotten, but not unconditionally so.[58] There are ways of escape, not known to all, but to spiritual souls,—ways known to the glorious Virgin, we are sure, and in all probability to Joseph, too.[59] So when St. Augustine says that the Blessed Virgin consented to the carnal union, we must understand that she agreed to the physical surrender characteristic of the carnal union, only on the condition, however, that it would be pleasing to God. Mary contracted the matrimonial union; the rest, namely, the activity of her marriage, the operation whereby it would in some manner attain its purpose, she entrusted to the arrangement of Divine Providence, always believing that God would keep her without stain and, as in the case of St. Cecelia nearly three hundred years later, her trust was not in vain.[60]

---

(56) "Respondeo: Dicendum, quod quorundam opinio fuit, quod ad hoc, quod contrahatur matrimonium, necesse est *absolute* consentire in copulam carnalem. Et dicunt hi, quod beata Virgo . . . consensit, tamen sine peccato . . . quia non voverat, sed tantum proposuerat." *Ibid.*

(57) "Sed haec opinio iniuriam facit Virgini gloriosae, quia, quamvis excuset a culpa, minuit tamen virginitatis eius gloriam, ut iam non debeat Virgo super omnes virgines nuncupari; quod noster refugit animus pariter et auditus. Unde haec opinio satis convenienter a magistro Hugone reprobatur." *Ibid.*, 695b, 696.

(58) "Item quaeritur de hoc quod dicit: *Committens se divinae dispositioni consensit in carnalem copulam:* ergo videtur, quod saltem fuerit mente corrupta; quod dicere est blasphemia. Item, videtur sibi contradicere, quia paulo ante dicit: 'Consensit Maria in maritalem societatem, sed non in carnalem copulam': ergo falsum dicit nunc. Respondeo: Dicendum, quod illud verbum Augustini intelligitur, non quia Virgo consenserit, ut ipsam cognosceret, quia nunquam credo hoc ipsam voluisse, nec Deum hoc sibi inspirasse; sed consensit in coniugalem societatem sive in mutuam corporum potestatem, quae ordinata erat ad copulam carnalem, non tamen ordinatione necessaria." *IV Sent.*, d.30, dub. 5, t.IV, 713a.

(59) "Ad illud quod obiicitur, quod conditio illa impedit; dicendum, quod verum est, contra collationem mutuae potestatis; in consensu enim in copulam coniugalem datur potestas petendi debitum, licet non teneatur ad statim, sed viam habet, per quam evadere possit; quae etsi non erat nota omnibus, erat tamen nota spiritualibus mentibus; sicut certum est nobis de gloriosa Virgine et probabilius praesumitur de Ioseph, quoniam hoc non est iuris positivi, sed magis iuris divini." *IV Sent.*, d.28, a.1, q.6, t.IV, 696b.

(60) "Ad illud quod obiicitur, quod dicit Augustinus, quod consensit in copulam carnalem; dicendum, quod illud intelligitur, quia consensit in mutuam corporum *potestatem*, quae ad carnalem copulam ordinatur, non tamen de necessitate; et beata Virgo in illam mutuam corporum *potestatem* absolute consensit, residuum vero, scilicet *ordinationem in actum*, divinae dispositioni commisit, credens semper, quod Dominus ipsam servaret sine macula. Exemplum est de beata Caecelia." *Ibid.*

Mary, as we have said, had learned by divine inspiration, or perhaps from the lips of Joseph himself that he would never take advantage of the rights to which his marriage entitled him, that she would find in Joseph's virginity a reflection of her own. She knew, too, that, if necessary, she could make known her vow which he was bound to respect, for even the Old Testament acknowledged a dedication to God: "The man who shall have made a vow, and promised his soul to God, shall give the price according to estimation" (Lev. 27:2).[61] Even though we wish to define the conjugal union as the mere physical union of the sexes, we can say that the Blessed Virgin consented to the union, as do all women who take the marriage vows. Marital rights were transferred from one to the other, as in every real marriage, but it is not essential for validity that these rights be used. Even though the glorious Virgin gave her consent to the marriage contract, she was certain that she would never consummate her marriage. This she knew from the revelation of the Holy Ghost, or from Joseph's assurance on this point, or because she was thinking of making known her vow, which she was bound to keep according to the precept of the Old Law which reads: "Vow ye, and pay to the Lord your God" (Ps. 75:12). But heretofore no one had the courage to vow virginity.[62] Though married, Our Lady preserved her virginity till death, and the same is true of Joseph who, as St. Jerome remarks, "was Mary's protector rather than her husband, and like her, he led a celibate life."[63]

The Virgin was "espoused to a man whose name was Joseph" (Luke 1:27). The Evangelist mentions the name of the man, says St. Bernard, not because he was the husband of Mary, but because he was "a just man" who would prove a trustworthy witness of the virginity of his spouse. Joseph was "a just man" who would esteem Mary's chastity and be a witness of it, a man who would pay her the tribute accorded the valiant woman of Sacred Scripture: "Her husband, and he praised her" (Prov. 31:28).[64] These words give us a true insight into the character of Joseph; he knew the holiness of his spouse and loved her for it. But now Mary had a secret from Joseph, but it was God's secret and she waited for Him to tell it. When Mary's approach-

(61) "Quoniam igitur beata Virgo divina inspiratione noverat, vel fortassis ipsius Ioseph relatione, quod nunquam vellet uti eius corporis potestate, sed eius custodire virginitatem; ideo potuit et debuit ei committere sive dare. Sciebat etiam, quod si vellet exigere, quod posset publicando votum contraire; et sic patet illud." *Ibid.*, 696a.

(62) "Si ergo volumus istam mutuam corporum *potestatem* vocare *copulam coniugalem;* sic beata Virgo consensit in copulam, ut omnes nubentes. In matrimonii autem *consummatione* omnino transfertur potestas, ita quod nec voto privato nec solemni possit petenti debitum adversari. Unde gloriosa Virgo matrimonium consensit *contrahere,* sed certa fuit, quod nunquam matrimonium consummaret, et hoc scivit Spiritus sancti revelatione vel Ioseph relatione, vel quia considerabat de voti publicatione; quia in Lege praeceptum erat servare, sed nullus fuerat ausus hoc vovere." *Ibid.*, 696b.

(63) "Mariae custos potius fuit quam maritus; relinquitur, virginem eum mansisse cum Maria." *De Perpetua Virginitate B. Mariae adversus Helvidium,* n. 9, MPL 23. 213.

(64) "Ostenditur etiam probata, cum dicit: *Desponsatam viro, cui nomen erat Ioseph* etc., ut scilicet 'Ioseph, vir iustus,' secundum quod dicitur Matthaei primo, esset testis castitatis ipsius, secundum illud Proverbiorum ultimo: 'Et vir eius laudavit eam.' Bernardus: '*Virum* nominat, non quia maritus, sed quia homo virtutis et iustus erat'; et ideo fuit testis legitimus." *Comment. in Evangelium Lucae* C.I., t.VII, 21b.

ing motherhood took on the appearance of circumstantial evidence which seemed to compromise her honor, Joseph was cast into perplexity, as the Evangelist says:

> "Whereupon Joseph her husband, being a just man and not willing publicly to expose her, was minded to put her away privately. But while he thought on these things, behold the angel of the Lord appeared to him in his sleep, saying: Joseph, son of David, fear not to take unto thee Mary thy wife, for that which is conceived in her, is of the Holy Ghost. And she shall bring forth a son. And thou shalt call his name JESUS, for he shall save his people from their sins. Now all this was done that it might be fulfilled which the Lord spoke by the prophet, saying: *Behold a virgin shall be with child and bring forth a son, and they shall call his name* EMMANUEL, which being interpreted is, *God with us*" (Matt. 1:19-23).

What did Divine Providence intend by directing Joseph to conceive the thought of separating himself from his wife? To this Sacred Scripture gives a clear answer: Joseph himself is to be the unsuspecting witness of the virginal birth of Christ, of His conception by the Holy Ghost, and of the fulfillment of the words of Isaias. The Virgin Birth was proved, as alone it could be proved, by the word of the Mother. It was confirmed, as alone it could be confirmed, by the word of the husband. Besides, St. Matthew attains another purpose; he establishes the descent of Jesus from David: "Jacob begot Joseph, the husband of Mary, of whom was born Jesus, who is called Christ" (1:16).[65] Through her marriage to Joseph, Mary's lineage was established and the genealogy of Christ certified through His putative father. Only thus, according to the law of the period, could Christ be a legitimate son of David, and so fulfill the prophecies concerning the Messiah. As foster father of Jesus Christ, Joseph provides the legal ancestry of the Redeemer; he was truly "the husband of Mary," and, consequently, the adoptive and legal father of Jesus. As such, he enjoyed all the rights and prerogatives of a true father, including the privilege of naming the child. The Evangelist gives us the pedigree of Joseph rather than that of Mary to conform to the custom of the Hebrews, who in their genealogies took no notice of women, but as they were near akin, the pedigree of the one showed that of the other.[66]

The house of David had a glorious destiny; it was the family preserved by the providence of God for nearly a thousand years to culminate in the Messiah, the Son of God made man. David had the honor of being the ancestor of Mary, the Mother of God, and the title of her Divine Son was "Son of

(65) For the genealogy of Christ, cf. Matt. 1: 1-16.

(66) "Sed hoc videtur, quod genealogia sequens nihil faciat ad Christum secundum veritatem. Ad quod respondet Beda secundum Hieronymum, quod non est consuetudinis Scripturarum, ut mulierum in generationibus ordo texatur; deinde et Ioseph et Mariam ex eadem tribu dicit esse generatos, unde ex Lege tenebatur eam accipere ut propinquus. Cuius etiam signum est, quod simul in Bethlehem censentur, sicut habetur supra secundo. Et ideo generationis series in uno pertinet ad alium." *Comment. in Evangelium Lucae* C.III, t.VII, 85b.

David." Thus the royal family of David is the most glorious in the world. Humble and obscure, as she was, Mary was yet greater than the greatest of her ancestors, for she became the Mother of Christ. Contrary to all Jewish custom, St. Matthew mentions in his genealogy the mother Mary, and adds, "of whom was born Jesus, who is called Christ." Only a parent in whose veins the blood of David flowed could really transmit the royal blood to a son, and thus fulfill in a satisfactory manner the prophecy that the Messiah was to be born of the seed of David. Joseph's descent from David is indisputable, but he was not the real parent of Jesus. Hence, it is essential that Mary, the only human parent of Jesus, should be a Davidite. St. Paul expressly states that Jesus was "of the Seed of David, according to the flesh" (Rom. 1:3). Mary, like Joseph, was a member of the royal line of David, the house wherein was to be fulfilled the Lord's promise to the powerful King: "The Lord hath sworn to David, and he will not make it void. Of the fruit of thy womb I will set upon thy throne" (Ps. 131:11). St. Bernard says: "Both were of the house and family of David, but the truth which the Lord swore to David was fulfilled in the one; the other, namely, Joseph, merely shared a knowledge of the truth and was a witness to it."[67] Joseph served pre-eminently as an unimpeachable witness of the inviolate virginity of his spouse.

The Saints give various reasons why Mary should be married, despite the fact that she had already consecrated her virginity to God. St. Bonaventure gives three reasons why God willed Mary's marriage: first, on account of its symbolism; secondly, that scandal might be avoided; thirdly, to keep secret the hidden designs of God.[68] First, on account of the symbolism of the marriage. Mystically, the marriage of Joseph and Mary prefigured the union of Christ with His Church. The Church, the spiritual spouse of Christ, is both virgin and mother. The Church deserved a worthy symbol but it could be found only in a woman who was at one and the same time both Virgin and Mother. Therefore, if the Virgin was to be a perfect and expressive symbol of the Church, it was necessary that she likewise be espoused.[69] And St. Augustine says: "The greatest mystery was prefigured in the Virgin, for as the Virgin Mary gave birth to Christ in the flesh, so was the Virgin Church to give birth to Christ spiritually.[70] The second reason which St. Bonaventure

(67) "Ostenditur etiam *promissa* in hoc quod dicit: *De domo David;* quod refertur ad Virginem et Ioseph, quia uterque de semine David, cui facta erat repromissio in Psalmo: 'Iuravit Dominus David veritatem et non frustrabitur eam; de fructu ventris tui' etc. Bernardus: 'Ambo erant de domo et familia David; sed in altera completa est veritas, quam iuravit Dominus David, altero tantum teste et conscio,' scilicet ipse Ioseph." *Comment. in Evangelium Lucae* C.I., t.VII, 21b.

(68) "Non solum autem conveniens fuit, ut voveret, sed etiam ut *nuberet,* triplici ex causa: primo propter *significationem,* secundo propter *infamiae vitationem,* tertio propter *divini consilii occultationem.*" *IV Sent.*, d.30, a.1, q.2, t.IV, 709b.

(69) "Propter *significationem,* quia Ecclesia est spiritualis sponsa et virgo et mater, hoc significari debuit; et nulla alia ad hoc significandum idonea fuit, nisi haec quae simul fuit Virgo et mater: et ideo, ut perfecte *significaret,* debuit etiam desponsari." *Ibid.*

(70) "Augustinus: 'Mysterium maximum praecessit in Virgine, ut sicut illa Virgo Deum peperit carnaliter, sic virgo Ecclesia pareret Christum spiritualiter'." *Sermones de Tempore. Vigilia Nativitatis Domini. Sermo XI,* t.IX, 98b.

discerned in the espousal was God's care to safeguard Mary's honor and that of her Divine Son. The honor of Our Lady and of the Holy One Who was to be born of her imperatively required that she should be married before the Annunciation. As St. Bernard says: "If Mary had not been married, everyone would have believed her guilty of fornication and Christ would have been despised as a child of adultery. In order to keep His Mother beyond all suspicion and shadow of dishonor and to preserve His own good name before the world, it was preferable that Christ, for the time being, be looked upon as a child of lawful wedlock."[71] In the words of St. Ambrose: "The Lord preferred that some people should doubt His own origin rather than His Mother's honor."[72] "He well knew the delicate modesty of the Virgin as well as the insecure reputation of virginal honor."[73] Without her marriage, the visible signs of her pregnancy would have aroused the suspicions of the Jews and caused a public scandal. And if the Virgin and her Son were branded with infamy, the Pharisees would find therein a semblance of excuse for themselves and infamous women would have a veil for their guilt.[74] Because of the espousal, they could not allege the excuse that the Virgin of virgins herself allowed ill-repute to befall her. Thirdly, in her espousal, the Lord had given Mary a faithful companion to conceal the secret designs of God from the enemy and to execute with deep wisdom the secret work of the Redemption of man. In this way, Satan was excluded from the celestial secrets, because, as St. Bernard says: "What men knew could not be concealed from the devil." In this case, Satan could not learn of the designs of God *from men,* nor could he know them *of himself,* for he was kept at a distance from the Virgin.[75] In addition to these three reasons for Mary's marriage, St. Bonaventure, in another passage, says that Joseph was to be Mary's *protector in time of need,* a source of consolation to the Virgin during their sojourn in Egypt, a constant loving guardian of the Child and His Mother.[76] And again, he says that God willed that Mary should marry the villager Joseph because *he was poor;* that Christ came to confound the proud and, therefore, He preferred to be called "the carpenter's son" rather than the son of a King. O admirable and truly wonderful mystery, revealed to

(71) "Secunda ratio est propter *infamiae vitationem:* quia, ut dicit Bernardus, omnes credidissent, quod esset fornicaria; et 'non decebat, hoc credi de Matre Dei nec etiam de Christo, quod esset natus ex adulterio; tolerabilius autem fuit ad tempus credi, quod esset natus ex coniugio'." *IV Sent.,* d.30, a.1, q.2, t.IV, 709.

(72) *De instit. virg.,* c.vi, n.42. MPL 16. 331.

(73) *Idem, In Lucam* 2.1. MPL 15.1633.

(74) "Si enim Virgo fuisset infamata et Filius eius, tunc color excusationis Pharisaeis esset relictus, et velamen ipsis mulieribus infamibus." *IV Sent.,* d.30, a.1, q.2, t.IV, 709b.

(75) "Tertia ratio est propter *consilii divini occultationem,* ne adversario notum fieret consilium Dei. Hoc autem occultatum fuit adversario per hunc modum, quia, sicut Bernardus dicit, 'non poterat latere diabolum quod scirent homines'; unde *per homines* scire non potuit, nec *per se,* quia a Virgine procul repellebatur." *Ibid.,* 709b, 710a.

(76) ". . . propter *obsequii opportunitatem,* ut esset Virgini peregrinanti in Aegyptum in solatium et Proli et Matri in familiare obsequium." *Vigilia Nativitatis Domini. Sermo XI,* t.IX, 98b.

some but hidden in darkness from others![77] The Almighty intended to conceal for a time the miraculous conception and birth of Jesus Christ, and for this end to veil the mystery under the solemn rites of marriage. For thirty years Mary concealed the virgin birth, oft repeating to herself the words of Isaias: "My secret to myself, my secret to myself" (Isai. 24:16).

O Mary, Mother Most Chaste,
Thou whose secret leaves us silent,
Pray for us!

* * *

> *Filiae Jerusalem, quid me admiramini? Divinum est mysterium hoc, quod cernitis."* Daughters of Jerusalem, why look ye so wonderingly upon me? The mystery which you see is of the Godhead.

As we ponder the motherhood of Mary, we, too, look wonderingly upon her whom the Church invokes as "Mother Most Admirable." In her virginal childbearing is reflected the perfect working of Divine Power, for there was due perfection in the *Offspring,* in the *conception itself,* and in the *Virgin's power to conceive.* Since the *Offspring* was to be perfect, there took place at the very instant of conception not only the formation of His human Body from the maternal ovum and the creation and infusion of a spiritual soul into that Body but also the Hypostatic Union of Body and Soul with the Divine Person of the Word. Christ was a God-Man.[78] Since there was to be due perfection in the *conception itself,* it was fitting that the fourth mode of generation be exemplified in the birth of Christ, namely, that He be born of woman without male seed by the power of the Most High.[79] Since there was to be due perfection in the *Virgin's power to conceive,* there was in the conception of the Son of God the concurrence of an *innate or natural power,* an *infused power,* and an *Uncreated Power.* The *natural* reproductive power of the Virgin prepared the material; the *infused* power, the spiritual soul, informed the Body of Christ; and the *Uncreated* Power in a single instant brought that Body to a state of perfect organization.[80] By conceiving the

(77) "... *ratione pauperitatis.* Christus enim super omnia venerat confundere superbiam, et ideo maluit vocari fabri filius quam regis. O admirabile mysterium! Et vere mirabile, quod ex una parte se manifestat et ex altera se celat." *Ibid.,* 98b, 99a.

(78) "Postremo, quoniam est a primo principio reparante modo completissimo; hinc est, quod in conceptione completio debita fuit in *prole,* fuit in *conceptu,* fuit et in *virtute concipiente.* Quia completio debita debuit in *prole,* hinc est, quod in instanti conceptionis non tantum fuit seminis, decisio, verum etiam consolidatio, configuratio, vivificatio per animam et deificatio per Deitatem unitam; ut sic Virgo Dei Filium vere conciperet propter unionem carnis ad Deitatem, mediante spiritu rationali, per quam tanquam per medium congruentiae caro erat idonea ad unionem." *Breviloquium,* Pars IV, Cap. III, t.V, 243b, 244a.

(79) "Quia vero completio debita debuit esse in *conceptu;* cum ex quatuor modis tres modi producendi hominem praecessissent: primus nec de viro nec muliere, sicut in Adam; secundus de viro sine muliere, sicut in Eva; tertius de muliere et viro, sicut in omnibus concupiscibiliter natis: decuit, ad completum universi quartum modum introduci, qui scilicet esset de muliere sine semine virili per virtutem summi operatoris." *Ibid.,* 244a.

(80) "Quia vero completio debita debuit esse in *virtute;* hinc est, quod in conceptione Filii Dei simul concurrit virtus *innata,* virtus *infusa* et virtus *increata:* virtus *innata* materiam praeparavit, virtus *infusa* purificando segregavit, virtus *increata* subito perfecit quod non poterat a virtute creata nisi successive fieri." *Ibid.*

Son of God without the concurrence of man and being made fruitful by the Holy Ghost, the Virgin Mary became a Mother in the most perfect and complete sense of the term. Because the love of the Holy Ghost burned in the heart of the Virgin with a flame unparalleled and unique, the power of the Holy Ghost accomplished wonderful things in her flesh, divine grace sometimes *inciting,* sometimes *helping,* sometimes *ennobling* nature as that miraculous conception required.[81] Only perfect God could become perfect Man. It was Mary's privilege to give Our Lord a human body at its best,—the perfect vehicle. As the Word Incarnate possessed from the first moment of His conception all His perfections excepting those connected with His bodily development, His Mother is rightly said to "compass a man." No need to point out that such a condition of a newly conceived child is rightly called "a new thing upon the earth," for the Mother of Christ differed from other mothers in this, that her Child, even while within her womb, possessed all those properties which constitue real manhood. This truly is wonderful, but far more wonderful the thought that within a single instant there came to dwell within the Virgin's womb perfect God and perfect Man,—a breathtaking thought which made St. Ambrose exclaim: "Indeed the grace of the Holy Spirit knows no slow working."[82]

"The Lord hath created a new thing upon the earth. A woman shall compass a man" (Jer. 31:22). The amazing conception of Christ, long since foretold by the Prophet, makes Mary our "Mother Most Admirable." In all previous ages, says St. Bonaventure, it was a new and unheard of thing that the conception of a child should mean not the reception and development of a seed but the perfect and unimpaired enclosure of a man,—a man certainly not only as regards sex, but also as regards wisdom and power.[83] Announcing this "new thing" to Mary, the angel in confirmation pointed out an extraordinary event, namely, the conception of a child by a woman who had been barren: "And behold thy cousin Elizabeth she hath also conceived a son in her old age; because no word shall be impossible with God" (Luke 1:36, 37). Elizabeth's conception of the Baptist was not a "new thing," because Sara, a barren and aged woman, had already conceived her son Isaac (cf. Gen. 11:30 and 21:1-3). It was, however, an astonishing thing, outside all laws of nature. But all things are possible

(81) "Et sic beatissima Virgo Maria mater fuit completissimo modo, ipsum Dei Filium concipiendo absque viro, fecundante Spiritu sancto. Quia enim in mente Virginis amor Spiritus sancti singulariter ardebat; ideo in carne eius virtus Spiritus sancti mirabilia faciebat, gratia scilicet partim *excitante,* partim *adiuvante,* partim *elevante* naturam, iuxta quod conceptus ille mirabilis exigebat." *Ibid.*

(82) "Hoc re vera mirabile, sed mirabilius ultra modum, quod sine temporis intervallo perfectus Deus, perfectus homo in ipsa conceptione fuit in Virginis utero; . . . unde Ieremias: *Creavit Dominus novum super terram: femina circumdabit virum,* virum certe non tantum sexu, sed sapientia et virtute. Ambrosius: 'Nescit tarda rerum molimina Spiritus sancti gratia'." *De Annuntiatione B. Virginis Mariae. Sermo I,* t.IX, 658ab.

(83) "Tertio fuit admirabilis propter conceptionis *novitatem,* quam novitatem admirabilem praevidit Ieremias trigesimo primo: *Creavit Dominus novum super terram: Femina circumdabit virum.* Hoc, inquam, est novum et omnibus retroactis temporibus inauditum, ut ipsa Prolis conceptio esset non seminis coagulatio et susceptio, sed viri perfecti scientia et virtutibus perfecta et integra circumvallatio." *De Annuntiatione B. Virginis Mariae. Sermo II,* t.IX, 664a.

with God,—the great as well as the small, the new as well as the extraordinary, but the greater and more extraordinary the happening, the more astonishing and wonderful it becomes.[84] For a Virgin to conceive a God is the miracle of all miracles. Of all events of all times the overwhelming mystery of the conception of the Son of God has in itself most reason for wonder. "From time unending," says St. Bernard, "it has not been heard that a woman has been at one and the same time a mother and a virgin. And if you consider whose Mother she is, where does your admiration of her high dignity carry you, if not to the conviction that you can never admire her sufficiently?" And he adds: "But what wonder if God, Who is 'wonderful in His saints' (Ps. 67:36), has shown Himself more wonderful still in His Mother?" Venerate, then, O wives, integrity of flesh in corruptible flesh. And you, O holy virgins, venerate fruitfulness in a virgin. O all men, imitate the humility of the Mother of God. O ye holy angels, who adore the Virgin's Child, *our* King as well as yours, the Redeemer of our race, the Restorer of your city, honor the Mother of your King."[85]

Mary's child-bearing, like her conception, was supernatural and miraculous. She is "Mother Most Admirable", for in her is reversed the curse pronounced against Eve in the beginning: "In sorrow shalt thou bring forth children" (Gen. 3:16). Every childbirth means suffering; Our Lady alone knew not the labor of a woman in travail. "O truly unheard of miracle," says St. Bernard. "He was conceived without shame, He was born without sorrow."[86] There were no attendants at the birth of Christ. Sacred Scripture says: "She brought forth her first-born son and wrapped him up in swaddling clothes and laid him in a manger" (Luke 2:7).

In her *painless child-bearing,* Mary enjoyed a wonderful privilege, a threefold privilege, in fact, corresponding to a threefold pain: the pain of *loss,* the pain of *need,* the pain of *sin* and its punishment; and this threefold pain comes to every mother, whoever she may be, the Blessed Virgin alone

(84) "Hoc novum Angelus annuntians Mariae, ostendit aliquid rarum ad confirmationem, scilicet sterilis conceptionem, cum dixit ad Virginem: *Ecce, Elisabeth, cognata tua, et ipsa concepit filium in senectute sua; quia non erit impossibile apud Deum omne verbum.* Hoc non erat novum, quia Sara sterilis et senex conceperat, sed tamen mirum erat; et tamen bene erat possibile Deo magnum sicut parvum, novum sicut rarum, licet, quanto aliquid sit maius et rarius, et tanto sit mirabilius." *Ibid.,* 664ab.

(85) "Unde inter omnia opera Dei conceptionis sacramentum plus habet in se rationem admirationis; et hoc est quod beatus Bernardus dicit: 'A saeculo non est auditum, ut mater simul aliqua esset et virgo. O si et, cuius mater est, attendas! Quo te tua super eius mirabili celsitudine ducit admiratio? Nonne ad hoc, ut videas nec satis posse mirari'? Et postea subdit: 'Et quid mirum, si Deus, qui *mirabilis* legitur et dicitur *in Sanctis suis,* mirabiliorem se exhibuit in Matre sua?' Veneramini ergo, coniuges, in carne corruptibili carnis integritatem; miramini etiam vos, sacrae virgines, in Virgine fecunditatem; imitamini, omnes homines, Dei Matris humilitatem; honorate, sancti Angeli, vestri Regis Matrem, qui nostrae adoratis Virginis Prolem, ipsum utique nostrum pariter ac vestrum Regem, nostri generis Reparatorem, vestrae civitatis Instauratorem." *Ibid.,* 664b.

(86) "O nova vere miracula! Conceptus fuit sine pudore, partus sine dolore. Mutata est in Virgine nostra maledictione Evae; peperit enim filium sine dolore etc." Bernard., *In Vigilia nativ. Domini, sermo 4.* n.3. MPL 183. 101. Cf. St. Bonaventure, t.VII, footnote 1, p. 46.

"Et quia conceptum sine libidine sequitur partus sine parturitione et dolore." *Comment. in Evangelium Lucae* C.I., t.VII, 24a.

excepted.[87] A mother's pain of *loss* is threefold: in conception she loses her *virginity;* after conception she loses her *physical loveliness and grace;* at the birth of her child, she loses the *companionship* of men. But this Mother in conceiving was endowed with *purity,* a purity second only to the purity of God; after conception she was endowed with *beauty* and grace so dazzling that Joseph could not bring his eyes to rest upon her; at the birth of her Babe, she had the *companionship* of the angels and of God himself, as Gabriel said: "The Lord is with thee."[88] The pain of *need* in other mothers is likewise threefold: in the act of conception, they need a *husband;* after conception, they need *rest;* at the birth of the child, they need an *attendant.* But this Mother Mary conceived with the help of the *Holy Ghost;* after the conception of her child, she did not wish to be ministered to but *she herself* went *to minister,* as St. Luke says: "And Mary rising up in those days went into the hill country" (1:39); at the birth of Jesus, the *angels* were her only attendants.[89] Mothers likewise experience a threefold pain of *sin: concupiscence* in the act of conceiving, *heaviness* in carrying the child, and *sorrow* in giving it birth. But this Mother Mary conceived without *concupiscence;* she carried a Precious Burden without *feeling its weight;* she brought forth her child without *sorrow.* Concerning the first, Isaias says: "Behold a virgin shall conceive" (7:14); concerning the third: "Before she was in labor, she brought forth."[90] There was no sorrow at the birth of Christ, only joy for the Virgin who with Habacuc could say: "I will rejoice in the Lord, and I will joy in God my Jesus" (Hab. 3:18), as it is written in the Book of Proverbs: "Let thy father and thy mother be joyful, and let her rejoice that bore thee" (Prov. 23:25). Truly the Maiden was glad at the birth of her Child; she experienced the greatest possible joy, inviting others to rejoice with her in the words which the Church sings in her person: "Rejoice with me, all ye who love God, because, although I was a little maid, I was pleasing to the Most High and brought forth from my womb both God and Man."[91]

(87) "Nona stella . . . est, quando haec Mater *genuit sine vae.* Et haec quoque praerogativa triplex est. Est enim triplex vae: vae *damni,* vae *indigentiae,* vae *culpae* et poenae; et quaelibet istarum triplex est in qualibet matre, excepta beata Virgine." *De Nativitate B. Virginis Mariae. Sermo I,* t.IX, 706a.

(88) "Vae *damni* matris triplex est: perdit in conceptu *virginitatem;* post conceptum corporis *venustatem;* in partu, hominum *societatem.* Haec autem mater in conceptu accepit *puritatem,* qua sub Deo nequit maior intelligi; post conceptum, multam *pulcritudinem,* quod eam Ioseph non poterat intueri; in partu Angelorum et Dei *societatem* habuit; unde Gabriel: *Dominus tecum. Ibid.*

(89) "Vae quoque *indigentiae* in matribus aliis triplex est: in conceptu indigent *mare;* post conceptum, *quiete;* in partu, *obstetrecatione.* Haec autem concepit, Spiritu *sancto* cooperante; post conceptum noluit ministrari, sed *ministrare* ivit; Lucae primo: *Exsurgens Maria ivit in montana;* in partu, Angelis obsequentibus, pariebat." *Ibid.*

(90) "Item, vae *culpae* in matribus est triplex: *libido* in concipiendo, *congravitas* in portando, *dolor* in pariendo. Haec autem concepit sine *libidine,* gravida (erat) sine *gravamine,* peperit sine *dolore.* De primo, Isaias: Ecce, virgo concipiet; de (tertio), Isaias: *Antequam parturiret, peperit." Ibid.*

(91) "Nam ipsa sine tristitia parturivit: unde ipsa potuit dicere illud Habacuc tertio: *Ego autem in Domino gaudebo et exsultabo in Deo Iesu meo;* et Proverbiorum vigesimo tertio: *Gaudeat pater tuus et mater tua, et exsultet quae genuit te.* Re vera gaudebat Puella pariens et congratulabatur quam plurimum, ceteros ad secum gratulandum invitans, secundum quod in persona eius cantat Ecclesia: 'Congratulamini mihi, omnes, qui diligitis Dominum, quia cum essem parvula, placui Altissimo et de meis visceribus genui Deum et hominem'." *In Nativitate Domini. Sermo III,* t.IX, 111b.

Though an inviolate Virgin, our "Mother Most Admirable" was fecund with the most perfect fecundity. Hence the Spouse in the Canticle sings: "Thy plants are a paradise" (4:13), and this by reason of her perfect fecundity, in which there was no defect or failure, no impurity, no sorrow, as in Eve's conception of children. No trace of pride in Mary, no sin, only unparalleled humility, most fruitful integrity, most joyful happiness. Therefore she is worthy of all praise and admiration. "O happy Mary," exclaims St. Bernard, "who lacked neither humility nor virginity; whose matchless virginity, fecundity did not defile but rather enhanced; whose singular humility, fruitful virginity did not take away but brought to light; whose altogether incomparable fecundity, both virginity and humility attended. Mary's virginity, her humility, her fecundity, which of these is not wonderful, incomparable, unique? Indeed, as you ponder them, it is a wonder if you do not hesitate in your choice of the one most worthy of admiration. Undoubtedly, all three taken together are to be preferred to any single one of these prerogatives and to have possessed them all is incomparably better and more blessed than to have possessed any single one of them."[92]

Hail, thou, the beginning of the miracles of Christ!
Mother Most Admirable,
Pray for us!

* * *

Mary's motherhood is admirable on account of the *eternity of the Child* conceived. With the Church we sing:

"Genuit puerpera Regem, cui nomen aeternum, et
gaudia matris habens, cum virginitatis honore,
nec primam similem visa est, nec habere sequentem."

"She was in labor and brought forth the King whose name is eternal; she had the happiness of a mother together with the honor of virginity; she was seen to have no equal before or since." In Mary's motherhood, natural causality effected its supreme achievement. By the exercise of her natural powers, under the influence of God's omnipotence, she brought forth the most noble fruit of nature and of supernature, the very crown of creation, the Son of God and the Wisdom of the Father Who of Himself in the Proverb says: "I was set up from eternity, and of old before the world was made.

(92) "Et in hoc tamen valde mirabile, quod sic clausa, et tamen fecunda erat fecunditate summa; unde dicit: *emissiones tuae paradisus*, propter fecunditatem perfectissimam, in qua nihil defectionis, nihil impuritatis, nihil erat tristitiae, sicut fuit in conceptione Evae; nihil erat ibi superbiae, nihil vitiositatis, sed totum erat eximiae humilitatis, fecundissimae integritatis et iucundissimae felicitatis; et ideo omni laude et admiratione dignum. Unde Bernardus: 'Felix Maria, cui nec humilitas defuit nec virginitas; et quidem sigularis *virginitas*, quam non temeravit, sed honoravit fecunditas; et nihilominus specialis humilitas, quam non abstulit, sed extulit fecunda virginitas; et incomparabilis prorsus fecunditas, quam virginitas simul comitatur et humilitas. Quid horum non mirabile? Quid non incomparabile? Quid non singulare? Mirum vero, si non haesitas in eorum ponderatione, quid tua iudices dignius admiratione; nisi quod indubitanter horum singulis praeferenda sunt simul iuncta, et incomparabiliter excellentius est atque felicius omnia percepisse quam aliqua'." *De Annuntiatione B. Virginis Mariae Sermo II,* t.IX, 663b, 664a.

The depths were not as yet, and I was already conceived" (Prov. 8:23, 24). If He was conceived from eternity, how could He be conceived toward the end of ages by the Virgin Mary? If He was eternal, He was as a consequence immutable, therefore incomprehensible, therefore interminable. But how could the Interminable One be conceived by a *young* maiden? How could the Incomprehensible One be conceived by a *little* maiden? How could the Immutable One be conceived by a *frail* and *delicate* maiden? And yet so wondrous and so great a Son did Mary conceive according to the testimony of the angel who said to her: "Behold thou shalt conceive in thy womb and shalt bring forth a son," and the angel went on to describe Him: "He shall be great" in His boundlessness and "He shall be called the Son of the Most High" by reason of the immutability of His Being and "of His kingdom there shall be no end" by reason of His interminability.[93]

Wherefore in this conception Divine Majesty is wonderfully humbled and virginal humility is wonderfully exalted. As St. Bernard says: "Admire the one and the other and choose the one which you admire more, the loving condescension of the Son or the unexcelled dignity of the Mother. Both are stupendous; both, wonderful. That a God should be subject to a woman,—O humility unprecedented! That a woman should be the origin of a God,—O sublimity unshared!"[94] And then, expressing astonishment at the Child Whom Mary conceived within her womb, he exclaims: "There, indeed, the long is made short; the wide, narrow; the high is brought low; and the depths are made level. There is seen a Light that shines not; a Word which is speechless; there Water thirsts and Bread is hungry. There, if you take heed, you can see Might in subjection, Wisdom instructed, Power upheld and, lastly, a God, nursing at the breast but refreshing the angels, weeping in the crib but consoling the afflicted."[95]

In Mary, God's power stands out against the background of human weakness. Her womb was the great meeting-place of things infinitely far apart. There God became man; the Creator, a creature; Immensity became little-

(93) "Secundo fuit admirabilis propter *Concepti aeternitatem;* Conceptus enim erat Deus, Dei Filius et Sapientia, quae de se dicit Proverbiorum octavo: *Ab aeterno ordinata sum et ex antiquis, antequam terra fieret. Nondum erant abyssi, et ego iam concepta eram.* Si ab aeterno fuit concepta, quomodo concipi potuit in fine saeculorum a Virgine Maria? Si enim aeterna erat, ergo immutabilis, ergo incomprehensibilis, ergo interminabilis. Quomodo ergo Interminabilis concipi potuit a iuvencula? Quomodo Incomprehensibilis a parvula? Quomodo Immutabilis a fragili et tenella? Et tamen talem et tantum concepit, secundum testimonium angelicum; Lucae primo, inquit Angelus ad Virginem: *Ecce, concipies in utero et paries Filium* etc.; et post describit eum: *Hic erit magnus,* scilicet incomprehensione; *et Filius Altissimi vocabitur* suae essentiae immutabilitate; *et regni eius non erit finis,* sua interminabilitate." *Ibid.*, 644a.

(94) "Unde in hoc conceptu est divina Maiestas mirabiliter humiliata, et virginalis humilitas mirabiliter exaltata. Unde Bernardus: 'Mirare utrumlibet et elige, quid amplius mireris, sive Filii benignissimam dignationem, sive Matris excellentissimam dignitatem! Utrimque stupor, utrimque miraculum: et quod Deus feminae obtemperet, humilitas absque exemplo; et quod Deo femina principetur, sublimitas sine socio'." *Ibid.*

(95) "Et post, idem ostendens mirabile, dicit: 'Porro, ibi agnoscitur longitudo brevis, latitudo angusta, altitudo subdita, profunditas plana. Ibi cognoscitur lux non lucens, verbum infans, aqua sitiens, panis esuriens. Videas, si attendas, potentiam regi, sapientiam instrui, virtutem sustentari, Deum denique lactentem, sed Angelos reficientem, vagientem, sed miseros consolantem'." *Ibid.*

ness; the Word, a speechless child; the Eternal became temporal, as St. John says: "The Word was made flesh" (1:14).[96] He Who formed the womb was formed in the womb, as foretold in the Psalms: "Glorious things are said of thee, O city of God" (Ps. 86:3). "Man is born in her, and the Highest Himself hath founded her" (Ps. 86.5), for which reason Mary is "an admirable instrument, the work of the Most High" (Ecclus. 43.2).[97] He Who contains all things is Himself contained within her womb. Therefore to her the Church sings: "He whom the heavens could not contain rested in thy bosom.[98] Jesus was the long-awaited Messiah, the glorious heir of all the regal splendor of Israel, the very Son of God Who "shaped the suns and marked their ways upon the ancient deep," and Mary is His Mother. She herself is a creature and her Creator becomes her Child. Who but Dante could tell the mystery?

O Virgin Mother, daughter of thy Son!
Created beings all in lowliness
Surpassing, as in height above them all;
Term by the Eternal Counsel pre-ordained;
Ennobler of thy nature, so advanced
In thee, that its great Maker did not scorn
To make Himself His own Creation.

O holy Virgin, Mother of Our Creator,
Pray for us!

* * *

Because she is the Mother of the Creator, Mary embodies the perfect type of created personality. If Our Lord Jesus Christ, the Creator, is the embodiment of all conceivable perfection in His Sacred Humanity, must not Mary the Virgin be the perfect *creature,* God's ideal of perfect womanhood in its exquisite realization in the most holy Mother of God? With the exception of her Divine Son, "the first-born of every creature," with Whom, of course, she cannot be compared, Mary is undoubtedly the loveliest flower that ever bloomed on earth, the only blossom that opened perfectly to the sun and we are wholly justified in greeting her as *Mystical Rose.*

Artists who, like Janssens, have painted Christ and His holy Mother with faces identical, have the approval not only of theology but of biology as

(96) "Primum es coniunctio infinite distantium. Deus enim ibi factus est homo; Creator, creatura; immensus, parvus; Verbum, infans; aeternus, temporalis, secundum illud Ioannis primo: 'Et Verbum caro factum est'." *Comment. in Evangelium Lucae* C.XI, t.VII, 296b.

(97) " 'Gloriosa dicta sunt de te, civitas Dei'; et post: 'Homo natus est in ea, et ipse fundavit eam Altissimus.' De hoc potest exponi illud Ecclesiastici quadragesimo tertio: 'Vas admirabile opus Excelsi'." *Ibid.*

(98) "Tertium miraculum, quia qui continet omnia continetur in ventre isto; ille ibi capitur, 'quem totus non capit orbis.' Unde cantat Ecclesia: 'Quia quem caeli capere non poterant tuo gremio contulisti'." *Ibid.*

well. Born of His Virgin Mother, Christ bore no impress of an earthly father. In a sense unique in history, Mary could say that her Son was bone of her bone, flesh of her flesh and, looking on her Child, she could see in His Face a masculine reflex of her own exquisite beauty. Though we have no authentic portrait or reliable description of Our Lady, we cannot doubt her physical loveliness. Theologians teach that the Saviour had a perfect human body. In that case, His Mother was perfect, too,—the feminine counterpart of His masculine loveliness. Since Christ, the most "beautiful above the sons of men" (Ps. 44:3), derived His body solely from hers, we may be sure that her body and features, reflected and in a sense repeated in Him, were exquisitely beautiful. Mary must have been as beautiful in body and soul as God Himself could make her. Descended from a long line of kings, a scion of the most illustrious family in Israel, she possessed a natural distinction, a personal charm, and spiritual loveliness which made her unique in history's long parade of women. "Blood will tell," and the blood-strain in David's progeny was clearly revealed in the nobility of her bearing, in her poise and gesture, in her voice, her manner, the expression of her countenance. Truly "to the manner born," she was endowed with a natural grace but far more with an inner beauty such as earth could never breed nor the things of earth beget,—a grace which came from looking into the face of God and yielding herself unreservedly to the will of Him Who holds the world within the hollow of His Hand. Hers is a radiant beauty, not the hard cold brilliance of the sterile diamond but the soft, graceful loveliness of the fecund rose. She "was exalted . . . as a rose plant in Jericho" (Ecclus. 24:18). Pure and fruitful at the same time, she unites within herself all that attracts, all that touches the heart of man,—virginal integrity and a mother's love. "There shall come forth a rod out of the root of Jesse, and a flower shall rise up out of her root" (Isai. 2:1). The *rod* is Mary; the *flower is* Mary's Christ Whom "she budded forth as the rose planted by the brooks of waters" (cf. Ecclus. 39:17). As Dante sings:

> "Here is the Rose
> Wherein the Word Divine was made Incarnate."

The unique beauty of the rose,—its velvety texture, its delicate coloring, its perfect symmetry, the harmonious arrangement of its petals around the center of the flower; in a word, the splendor of order is emblematic of the moral beauty of Mary. As St. Bonaventure says, from the time of her birth all through her life, Mary was the Mystical Rose of this world,—the dazzling white Rose of chastity or perpetual purity, the budding Rose of consecrated devotion, the adorning Rose of perfect reverence, the fragrant

Rose of heavenly sweetness, the deep-red Rose of burning love, the life-giving Rose of heavenly intercession, the full-blown Rose of unbounded pity.[99]

O Lady all-beautiful, Mystical Rose,
Pray for us!

(99) "Fuerunt autem Christus nascens et Mater Virgo pariens *lilium* et *rosa* huic mundo, quia a nativitate per omne tempus fuerunt instar lilii et rosae *candidissimi* castitate sive puritate perpetua; . . . *Virentissimi* sive florentissimi devotione votiva; . . . *Ornatissimi* religione perfecta; . . . *Fragrantissimi* suavitate caelica; . . . Rubentissimi caritate flammea; . . . *Medicinalissimi* intercessione superna; . . . Expansissimi pietate continua; . . ." *Sermones de Tempore. In Nativitate Domini. Sermo XII,* t.IX, 117b.

Chapter III

THE BRIDE MOTHER OF CHRIST

GOD'S PURPOSE IN BECOMING MAN was not to call the human race in a truer sense His own but rather to remove the barriers between the Creator and the creature and to open the floodgates of His grace. God became man that man might become like God. In taking a human body He contracted a holy marriage with the human race through which man may ascend to God's kingdom and become partaker of His divine nature. "Go forth, ye daughters of Sion, and see King Solomon in the diadem wherewith his mother crowned him in the day of his espousals, and in the day of the joy of his heart" (Cant. 3:11). *Go forth, ye daughters of Sion,* from disfiguring sin, *and see the King* of Kings, the true Solomon, the Saviour, Christ Incarnate, *in the diadem* of original innocence *wherewith his mother,* the Virgin Mary, *crowned him,* conceiving Him by the power of the Holy Ghost *on the day of his espousals* with the human race, which as a collective unity was wedded and joined to the Word of God as a bride with the Bridegroom by an indissoluble bond in the virginal womb by a chaste and benevolent love with unspeakable happiness and overflowing joy.[1] The nuptial chamber in which God contracted this holy marriage with the human race was the pure womb of the Virgin Mary. There was consummated the union of Divinity with Humanity and, consequently, of Christ with His Church, as St. Paul says: "This is a great sacrament, but I speak in Christ and in the church" (Eph. 5:32).[2]

Christ built for Himself a marriage chamber, says the Seraphic Doctor, that in a virginal womb He might espouse human nature, thus bringing to pass what David had foretold in prophetic vision: "He hath set his tabernacle in the sun, and he as a bridegroom coming out of his bride chamber, hath rejoiced as a giant to run his course" (Ps. 18:6). "He hath set his tabernacle in the sun," that is, in the Blessed Virgin, rightly called the *sun*

(1) "Primo *coronavit eum Mater Virgo Maria carneo diademate* originalis innocentiae in conceptione, secundum quod dicitur Canticorum tertio: *Egredimini et videte, filiae Sion, regem Salomonem in diademate, quo coronavit eum mater sua in die desponsationis et laetitiae cordis eius. Filiae Sion, egredmini,* a deformitate peccati, *et videte regem* regum, verum Salomonem, salvatorem, Christum incarnatum, *in diademate,* originalis innocentiae, *quo coronavit* eum *Mater sua,* Virgo Maria, virtute Spiritus sancti eum concipiendo, *in die desponsationis,* humanae naturae, quae in unitate personae copulata est et coniuncta Dei Verbo ut sponsa sponso vinculo indissolubili, in utero virginali et amore pudico et benevolo cum laetitia inenarrabili et gaudio magno." *Dominica in Palmis. Sermo II,* t.IX, 244a.

(2) "Has nuptias fecit Deus Pater, secundum quod dicitur Matthaei vigesimo secundo: 'Simile est regnum caelorum homini regi, qui fecit nuptias filio suo'. Hae nuptiae celebratae sunt in thalamo uteri virginalis; Psalmus: 'In sole posuit tabernaculum suum, et ipse tanquam sponsus procedens de thalamo suo'. Ibi consummatus est matrimonium inter divinam et humanam naturam et inter Christum et Ecclesiam per consequens, secundum illud ad Ephesios quinto; loquens Apostolus de matrimonio dicit: 'Sacramentum hoc magnum est, ego autem dico, in Christo et in Ecclesia'." *Comment. in Evangelium Lucae* C.XIV, t.VII, 362b.

because she was clothed with Christ and filled with the light of eternal brightness, as the Apocalypse says: "A woman clothed with the sun and the moon beneath her feet" (Apoc. 12:1). Clothed with the sun, Mary had the moon beneath her feet because of her *purity,* and "being compared to light she is found before it" (Wis. 7:29).[3] And "as a bridegroom" He came forth from the marriage chamber of the Virgin's womb in which God was united with human nature, His bride, and kissing and embracing her, He took her to Himself in bonds of closest wedlock,—a union clearly prophesied in the Book of Genesis: "Isaac brought Rebecca into the tent of his mother, and took her to wife" (24:67). Isaac is a type of Christ; Rebecca, to whom Isaac brought rich gifts, "vessels of silver and gold, and garments" (Gen. 24:53), is human nature which received so rich a dowry in its espousal; Sara is the Virgin Mary, the Mother of the true Isaac, Christ. Into this tent of Sara, namely, the Virgin's holy womb, the Son of God ushered the human race that He might wed her, Our Creator thus becoming the Brother of us all and the Blessed Virgin becoming the *Mother* of all Saints. Blessed the day on which all these things took place, because through the Virgin Mary, God became our *Father;* the Son of God, our *Brother.*[4] Therefore, St. Bernard, addressing the Virgin, says: "All generations shall call thee blessed, for to all generations thou hast brought life and glory. In thee the angels have found everlasting joy; the just, grace; sinners, pardon. Deservedly do the eyes of every creature turn towards thee, for in thee and through thee and by thee, the bountiful Hand of the Almighty has created anew all that He had created."[5]

Mary's relation to the Bridegroom is much closer than that which binds Him to His other children, for it rests on the natural basis of Motherhood, which of itself supposes a correspondingly greater content of grace. Mary is the Bride of the Incarnate Word in a sense altogether unique and sublime. There is only one Lord Jesus Christ, only one Mother of God. They stand apart from all the world besides. The union existing between them is

(3) "In quo statuit sibi *cubiculum nuptiale* et hoc quidem fecit, ut humanam naturam sibi in virginali utero desponsaret, quod praevidens in Spiritu, dicebat prophetica certitudine Propheta David: *In sole posuit tabernaculum suum. In sole,* dicit, id est in beata Virgine, quae recte sol dicitur, quia amicta fuit sole et impleta lumine claritatis aeternae, secundum illud Apocalypsis duodecimo: *Mulier amicta sole et luna sub pedibus eius,* propter munditam; nam ipsa *luci comparata purior invenitur,* Sapientiae septimo." *De Annuntiatione B. Virginis Mariae. Sermo IV,* t.IX, 672ab.

(4) "Et post subditur: *tamquam sponsus,* quia Virginis uterus thalamus fuit, in quo naturae humanae coniunctus est Deus, et eam deosculans, nuptiali est sibi foedere copulatus. Hoc bene figuratum fuit Genesis vigesimo quarto: *Introduxit eam in tabernaculum Sarae, matris suae et accepit eam uxorem.* Quid per *Isaac* autem intelligitur nisi Christus; quid per *Rebeccam* autem, quae *multum accepit,* nisi humana natura, quae multum accepit dotis in hac desponsatione; quid per *Saram* nisi Virgo Maria, quae Mater fuit veri Isaac, intelligitur? In hoc Sarae tabernaculum, id est sacrosanctum uterum, introduxit Dei Filius humanam naturam, ut eam sibi desponsaret, et omnium Creator noster fieret *frater,* et beata Virgo efficeretur omnium Sanctorum *mater.* Benedicta sit dies, in qua omnia haec facta sunt, quia per Virginem Matrem Deus effectus est noster *pater;* Dei Filius, noster *frater.*" *Ibid.,* 672b.

(5) "Ideo Bernardus loquens ad Virginem: *"Beatam te dicent omnes generationes,* quae omnibus generationibus vitam et gloriam genuisti. In te enim Angeli laetitiam, iusti gratiam, peccatores veniam invenerunt in aeternum. Merito te respiciunt oculi totius creaturae, quia in te et per te et de te benigna manus Omnipotentis quidquid creaverat recreavit'." *Ibid.*

a supernatural, total union, a union not only of mind and heart but also of very flesh and blood,—the spiritual union of two lovers as Bride and Bridegroom, the physical union existing between the Mother and her Child. Mary is both Mother and Bride of the Incarnate Word. Christ is not only Man but the Eternal King Who by His own Hand while His Mother was on earth moulded her soul for her eternal destiny as Queen in His Kingdom. The realization of this supreme reality opens to our gaze a vista of transcendent loveliness and awe-inspiring majesty. As God had given Eve to the first Adam, so in the very heart of the human race, He created Mary to be His Son's all-pure and holy Bride. To her He addressed His appeal, and at her Willing *fiat,*—a sound most sweet to men, to angels, and to the Spouse Himself, He raised up the lowly Bride to the status of the Bridegroom, making her stand beside Him, we may say, never for a moment forgetting the infinite abyss between Christ, anointed with Godhead, and Mary, the maid of Nazareth. Like Esther of old who found favor with King Assuerus, the head of the whole monarchy, and was taken in marriage to become his bride and queen, Mary, a lowly little maiden, was prepared in time, exalted among her people and taken in marriage by the Most High King, that she might become the Mother of God.[6]

Mary, then, had no chance place in the Divine Dispensation. From the beginning she was high in the councils of God, the predestined Mother of the Son predestined. In the dim distant stretches of eternity, when God, the Father, Son, and Holy Ghost decreed to create the world and, foreseeing the fall of Adam, to redeem the human race by the Son's becoming Man, in that incomprehensible, eternal instant, God's eye rested lovingly on the little maid of Nazareth and chose her out of millions to be the Mother of the Messiah. "The Lord possessed me in the beginning of his ways, before He made anything from the beginning. I was set up from eternity, and of old before the world was made. The depths were not as yet, and I was already conceived" (Prov. 8:22-24). In the beginning, before He formed any ideal in His mind, because He desired to create paths and to open ways in His Mind for the communication of the Divinity, God decreed, as a beginning, the formation of the Humanity of the Word Who was to be the highway by which other creatures might come to the Father.[7] Joined with this decree was that of His most holy Mother, the *Vessel of Honor,* through

(6) "Nam Esther interpretatur *praeparata in tempore* vel *exaltata in populo,* et fuit uxor Assueri regis, qui fuit princeps totius monarchiae; et cum esset parvula, facta est regina, et significat beatam Virginem, quae fuit *praeparata* in tempore et *exaltata* in populo et assumta est connubium summi Regis, ut Mater fieret Dei." *De Assumtione B. Virginis Mariae.* Sermo IV, t.IX, 695b.

(7) "As the Word and only-begotten Wisdom of the Father and as the God-Man, He is the source of all knowledge of God and of all salvation. Whoever desires to return to the Father must return by and through Him." Cf. *St. Bonaventure's De Reductione Artium ad Theologiam, A Commentary with an Introduction and Translation* by Sister Emma Thérèse Healy, St. Bonaventure, N. Y. 1939, pp. 201, 202; second edition, pp. 157, 158.

"And Jesus saith to him: I am the way . . . No man cometh to the Father but by me" (John 14:6).

whom His Divinity was to enter the world,—the "vessel of election," foreseen from the eternal ages of the Divinity, by the Beings which alone are ancient, the Indivisible Trinity. Even then was Mary stamped and delineated in the Mind of the Eternal Artificer and possessed of the inseparable embraces of His love. Truly, then, to her may be applied the words which the Lord addressed to Jeremias: "Before I formed thee in the bowels of thy mother, I knew thee" (Jer. 1:5), for God knew Mary not only through the knowledge of predestination but also through the inspired announcements of the prophets who for five thousand years from the beginning of the world until her birth foretold her coming.[8]

Before Abraham, therefore, before Creation itself, had the Almighty selected the virgin through whom the Word was to be generated in the flesh. "And the creator of all things commanded and said to me; and he that made me rested in my tabernacle and he said to me: Let thy dwelling be in Jacob and thy inheritance in Israel, and take root in my elect" (Ecclus. 24:12, 13). And when the fullness of time was come, Mary "took root in an honorable people" (Ecclus. 24:16) and became a child of Israel, a true daughter of Adam, and she was called *Mary,*—a name not found on earth nor invented by the mind or will of man but a name that came from heaven and was given to the Virgin by divine ordinance. This sweet and lovely name was destined for her, says the Seraphic Doctor, for Mary means "Star of the Sea." Mary is the Star promised by the prophet Balaam when he said: "A star shall rise out of Jacob, and a sceptre shall spring up from Israel" (Num. 24:17). Mary is "as a morning star in the midst of a cloud" (Ecclus. 1:6). Speaking in her name, St. John says: "I am the root and stock of David, the bright and morning star" (Apoc. 22:16).[9] Lineage, which meant so much to others, meant nothing to Mary. It was not her ancestors, illustrious though they were, who ennobled her, but she who ennobled them. Her nobility depended on an order of excellence which was the pure reversal of all that had gone before. Mary is a beginning, not an end; she is the *Morning Star*. When she is first mentioned by name, it is not in connection with her forbears but with the Son together with Whom she existed in the mind of God before the day-star. She is "Mary, of whom was born Jesus, who is called Christ" (Matt. 1:16), the only one through whom Christ had any juridic title to the throne of David and the promise made to Abraham. As Cardinal Newman well says: "When she appears in the darkness, we know that He is close

(8) "Unde sibi competit quod dicit Dominus ad Ieremiam: *Priusquam te formarem in utero, novi te,* non solum congnitione praedestinationis, sed multiplicis praenuntiationis; ab initio (enim) mundi usque ad suum ortum fuit praenuntiata per quinque millia annorum, antequam nasceretur." *De Purificatione B. Virginis. Sermo II,* t.IX, 641b.

(9) "Ostenditur etiam praenominata in hoc quod dicit: *Et nomen Virginis Maria. Maria* enim stella maris interpretatur, et sic ostenditur impleta illa prophetia Balaam; Numerorum vigesimo quarto: 'Orietur stella ex Iacob, et surget virga de Israel'; Ecclesiastici quinquagesimo: 'Quasi stella matutina in medio nebulae'; Apocalypsis ultimo: 'Ergo sum radix et genus David, stella splendida et matutina'." *Comment. in Evangelium Lucae* C.I. t.VII,, 21b, 22a.

at hand." The morning heralds the sun. After night's darkness, when its luster pierces the clouds, we know that day is near. So after the fall of Adam, when the brightness of God's presence was withdrawn from the earth and men's minds and souls were darkened, the Virgin loomed on the horizon, the Star of Morning ushering in the dawn of Redemption, the dawn of the "true light that enlighteneth every man that cometh into the world" (John 1:9).

O Mary, Morning Star,
Pray for us!

Mary's Spiritual Virginity

With the exception of the union existing between the Sacred Humanity and the Godhead, we can conceive no closer association of the finite with the Infinite than that which was to exist between Christ and His Blessed Mother. What bodily integrity, what spiritual perfection did not this most intimate alliance postulate of the holy Mother of God! If, as Tertullian says, God fashioned the primeval clay for the creation of Adam "with Christ in view," what of her from whose substance Christ Himself was to be, not remotely, but immediately and directly formed? First of all, it was morally necessary that she be a consecrated virgin. This by divine decree she had been from the beginning. Now through her vow and her own will she was to enter subjectively into the relationship of the Bride of God.

"The marriage of the Lamb is come," says St. John in the Apocalypse, "and his wife hath prepared herself and it is granted to her that she should clothe herself with fine linen, glittering and white" (19:7, 8). The innocent *Lamb* was to have a wife like to himself in all things. Therefore, she must be pure and innocent. Such a Bride was Mary, as the Bridegroom Himself testifies in the Canticle: "Thou art all fair, O my love, and there is not a spot in thee" (Cant. 4:7).[10] Like the young women sought for the King, she was a virgin and beautiful (Esth. 2:2), pure within and without, immaculate in body and soul.[11]

St. Bonaventure assigns three reasons why Mary should be a consecrated virgin: first, that she might be *a most worthy dwelling-place* of God, for, since "Wisdom is the brightness of eternal light and the unspotted mirror"

(10) "Candor *innocentiae* virginalis designatur in candore *vestis;* de qua, Apocalypsis decimo nono: *Uxor Agni praeparavit se. Et datum est illi, ut cooperiat se byssino splendenti et candido. Agnus* innocens non debet habere *uxorem* nisi similem sibi per omnia, ergo agninam et innocentem; et talis fuit beata Virgo; de qua, Canticorum quarto: *Tota pulcra es, amica mea, et macula non est in te." De Assumtione B. Virginis Mariae. Sermo V,* t.IX, 699ab.

(11) ". . . virginitas *immaculata,* quae scilicet est mentis et corporis; et de hac potest intelligi illud in figura Esther secundo: *Quaerantur regi puellae virgines ac speciosae,* Illae quidem sunt *virgines speciosae,* id est plenae speciei, quae non habens maculas nec interius, sicut virgines sola carne, nec exterius, sicut virgines sola mente, sed illae quae ad imitationem Virginis Mariae sunt mente et corpore immaculatae." *De Annuntiatione B. Virginis Mariae. Sermo II,* t.IX, 663a.

into which "no defiled thing cometh" (Wis. 7:25, 26), it was fitting that He should be conceived by a Mother undefiled both in actuality and in resolute will, and in the vow of virginity, there is perfect integrity of will.[12] It was fitting that Mary should make a vow of virginity, secondly, that she might be for her sex *a model of absolute virginity,* for, as God the Father proposed Christ as an example or model for men, so did He propose His Mother as a model for women, and since the vow of virginity is especially worthy of imitation and praise, without doubt it was fitting that she be consecrated by such a vow.[13] It was fitting that Mary make a vow of virginity, thirdly, that she might be invested with *every privilege of nobility and sanctity without exception.* May it never be said that any other virgin surpassed the Blessed Mary. Indeed, "the Highest Himself hath founded her" (Ps. 86:5); He has adorned her with every privilege of grandeur and dignity, that she, whom He loved more than all other maidens, might be holier and more lovable than all other women combined. Predestined as she was to be the Mother of God, she deserves to this very day to be loved and praised beyond all other Saints. Therefore, the Holy Ghost, Who would inspire other maidens to make the vow of virginity, did not withhold this privilege from Mary.[14]

From the very depths of her soul, Mary had given herself to the Bridegroom with a virginal surrender that was perfect and complete. She, in return, was to be adorned with many privileges, the first of which was to be her perfect *conformity* to the likeness of the Lamb, Who in His own adorable yet human self combines all conceivable holiness and perfection. She was to "follow the Lamb whithersoever He goeth" (Apoc. 14:4), walking behind Him in the straight and narrow way of perfect *continence.* And that there might be no dissimilarity between Himself and her, she was, in proof of her perfect love, to follow Him in the *patient endurance* of suffering, for "the Lord hath trodden the winepress for the virgin daughter of Juda" (Lam. 1:15).[15] Mary was to enjoy, secondly, the unique privilege

---

(12) "Primo namque decuit, Virginem virginitatem *vovere* triplici ratione. Prima est, ut esset Dei decentissimum habitaculum. Quia enim *sapientia candor est lucis aeternae et speculum sine macula, quam nihil inquinatum incurrit;* decebat, ut ex Matre incorrupta et re et voluntate firma conciperetur; perfecta autem incorruptio voluntatis in voto consistit virginitatis." *IV Sent.*, d.30, a.1, q.2, t.IV, 709b.

(13) "Secunda ratio est, ut esset mulieribus totius *virginitatis exemplum.* Sicut enim Deus Pater Christum viris proposuit in exemplum sic eius Matrem in exemplum proposuit mulieribus; et quoniam hoc est maxime imitandum et laudandum, scilicet votum virginitatis, absque dubio in illa esse debuit." *Ibid.*

(14) "Tertia ratio est, quia debebat in ea esse omnis *nobilitatis et sanctitatis privilegium.* Absit enim, quod aliqua alia virgo beatam Mariam excellat; immo, Altissimus, qui fundavit eam, omnis dignitatis privilegio adornavit, ut, sicut ipse eam prae ceteris adamavit, sic ipsa omnibus esset sanctior et amabilior universis. Unde circumscripta maternitate Dei, adhuc ipsa prae ceteris Sanctis debet amari et laudari; et ideo Spiritus Sanctus, qui aliis inspiravit virginitatis votum, ab ea non retinuit celatum." *Ibid.*

(15) "Haec autem virginitas immaculata fulget *multis privilegiis,* quorum, primum est perfecta *conformitas* imitationis Agni Apocalypsis decimo quarto: *Hi sunt, qui cum mulieribus non sunt coinquinati,* in carne; Virgines enim sunt, scilicet mente; *hi sequuntur Agnum, quocumque ierit,* per omnimodam conformitatem continentiae. Et ut nihil eis desit, facit Dominus, quod sequantur per conformitatem *patientiae* in signum perfectae amicitiae; unde Threnorum primo; *Torcular,* scilicet passionis, *calcavit Dominus virgini, filiae Iuda,* eam ad aemulationem provocando, ut imitetur." *De Annuntiatione B. Virginis Mariae. Sermo II,* t.IX, 663a.

of *living in closest intimacy with her Spouse,* whose heart she rejoiced, as Isaias had foretold: "The young man shall dwell with the virgin, and the Bridegroom shall rejoice over the Bride" (Isai. 62:5).[16] Mary was to enjoy a third privilege, namely, that of *sharing the full and exultant joy of the Holy Spirit,* for she was the Virgin of Virgins. "After her shall virgins be brought to the king. With gladness and rejoicing they shall be brought into the temple of the king" (Ps. 64:15, 16). "And their soul shall be as a watered garden" (Jer. 31:12) through perfect grace, "and they shall be hungry no more" *(ibid.)* through concupiscence. "Then shall the virgin rejoice in the dance" *(ibid.*:13) through the exultation of the Holy Spirit, and this is true joy, for it is inward as well as outward, as Ecclesiasticus says: "There is no pleasure above the joy of heart" (30:16).[17] And so, resplendent with the glorious privileges of virginity, Mary was joined to the bountiful Christ, Who in a wedlock of perfect love gave her every gift.[18]

O Mary, Holy Virgin of Virgins, Bride inviolate,
Vessel of Honor,
Pray for us!

* * *

The story of Genesis points to the failure of the purpose of life through the corruption of a woman. Mary stands as the symbol of the restoration of this lost purpose through the sanctification of a woman. Eve, the first woman, the feminine principle of things, had failed and now the medium, the receptacle, was to be rehabilitated in Mary. She is the human organ chosen by the Holy Ghost for the Incarnation and the central figure in this miracle of love, a "Spiritual Vessel," the work of the Most High, a Vessel admirable in its *material,* its *outward form,* and its *contents,* for its material was wondrously *precious;* its *outward appearance,* wondrously *beautiful;* its contents, wondrously *rich.*[19]

The Vessel was *precious,* for it was of *gold,* "a massy vessel of gold, adorned with every precious stone" (Ecclus. 50:10). In the *vessel* we see a susceptibility to grace; in the *gold,* the pricelessness of love; in its *massive-*

(16) "Secundum privilegium est praecipua *familiaritas cohabitationis Sponsi;* Isaiae sexagesimo secundo: ***Habitat enim iuvenis cum virgine,*** **id est Christus, filius Virginis;** ***et gaudebit sponsus super sponsam,*** **id est Christus super animam sanctam sibi copulatam."** ***Ibid.***

(17) "Tertium privilegium est plena *iucunditas exsultationis* Spiritus sancti; propter quod dicitur in Psalmo: *Adducentur regi virgines post eam;* Ieremiae trigesimo primo: *Erit anima eorum quasi hortus irriguus,* per gratiam perfectam, *et ultra non esurient,* per concupiscentiam; *tunc laetabitur virgo in choro,* per Spiritus sancti exsultationem, . . . Et haec est laetitia magna, quia intus et extra, et *non est oblectamentum super cordis gaudium." Ibid.*

(18) "Et quoniam tot refulget privilegiis, ideo copulanda est Christo Largitori, qui omnia dedit perfecti amoris desponsatione; et hoc desiderabat Apostolus secundae ad Corinthios undecimo: *Despondi enim vos uni viro virginam castam exhibere Christo,* ubi consistit omnis perfectio et meritum." *Ibid.,* 663b.

(19) *"Vas admirabile, opus Excelsi,* Ecclesiastici quadragesimo tertio. In verbo isto ostenditur valde *admirabilis,* et per consequens plurimum *commendabilis* Imperatrix totius creaturae, quae quidem in sua nativitate fuit *vas admirabile;* sed certe ideo, quia *opus Excelsi.* . . . Fuit autem puella regia *vas admirabile* ratione *materiae,* ratione *formae,* ratione *rei contentae.* Ratione materiae fuit vas mirabiliter *pretiosum;* ratione formae fuit vas mirabiliter *speciosum;* sed ratione rei contentae vas mirabiliter copiosum." *De Nativitate B. Virginis Mariae. Sermo IV,* t.IX, 713b, 714a.

ness, the strength of endurance, all of which were verified in the Virgin Bride. Of her love, Hugh of St. Victor says: "Because the love of the Holy Ghost burned singularly in her heart, the power of the Holy Ghost worked wonders in her flesh. And since the love of her heart was unshared by any human creature, the operation of the Spirit of Love in her flesh had no precedent."[20] Mary is wondrously precious because she is a *brightly shining* vessel, "being an instrument of the armies on high, shining gloriously in the firmament of heaven" (Ecclus. 43:9) and all the while illumining by her brilliance the whole Church of God. Truly, at her coming, "to the Jews a new light seemed to rise" (Esth. 8:18).[21]

Mary was a Vessel of surpassing *beauty,* a precious vessel bright with jewels, whose loveliness attracted the Son of the Heavenly King, as the Psalmist had foretold: "The King shall greatly desire thy beauty" (Ps. 44:12).[22] As on a royal table there are many precious vessels but one of such outstanding beauty that the others seem insignificant in comparison, so on the table of the Eternal King were many precious vessels, all of which seemed to lose their luster when placed beside the wondrous vessel destined for the lips of the Most High King. "Gold cannot equal it" (Job 28:17), and, as St. Jerome says: "As in comparison with God no man is good, so in comparison with His Mother, no woman is perfect, however outstanding in virtue she may be."[23] The surpassing beauty of the "Spiritual Vessel" is evident, secondly, in the complacency of the Maker, for the work merited the approval of the Eternal Potter. "And I went down into the potter's house, and behold he was doing a work on the wheel. And the vessel was broken which he was making of clay with his hands, and turning he made another vessel, as it seemed good in his eyes to make it" (Jer. 18:3, 4). The potter is Our Creator. Wherefore man is, as the prophet says, "as clay in the hand of the potter" (*ibid.* 6). The "work done on the wheel" is the human race built on the inconstancy of human nature, a vessel of clay, and it *was broken* by the sin of the first man, *and turning he made another vessel,* namely, the

(20) "Secundo, quia fuit *aureum;* Ecclesiastici quinquagesimo: *Quasi vas auri solidum, ornatum omni lapide pretioso.* In *vase* vero, gratiae susceptibilitas; in *auro,* amoris pretiositas; in *soliditate,* tolerantiae strenuitas; quae omnia fuisse in virginali thalamo comprobatur. Nam de *amore* eius Hugo de sancto Victore: 'Quia in corde eius amor Spiritus sancti singulariter ardebat, ideo in carne eius virtus Spiritus sancti mirabilia faciebat. Et cuius dilectio in corde eius non habuit socium, eius operatio in carne illius non habebat exemplum'." *Ibid.,* 714a.

(21) "Tertio, quia fuit *luminosum;* Ecclesiastici quadragesimo tertio: *Vas castrorum in excelsis, in firmamento caeli resplendens gloriose.* In firmamento caeli Maria resplenduit, dum sua claritate totam Dei Ecclesiam illustravit, iuxta illud Esther octavo: *Iudaeis nova lux oriri visa est* etc. Quod de ipsa convenientissime potest dici." *Ibid.*

(22) "Secundo, ratione *formae* fuit vas mirabiliter *speciosum;* unde de ipsa speciositate ait Bernardus: 'Virgo regia, gemmis ornata virtutum geminoque, scilicet mentis pariter et corporis, decore fulgida, caelestium civium in se provocavit aspectum, ita ut et Regis animum in sui concupiscentiam inclinaret et caelestem nuntium ad se ad supernis adduceret'." *Ibid.,* 714ab.

(23) "Huius speciositas in tribus potest manifestissime deprehendi, scilicet ex decore *praeeminentiae.* Sicut enim est in mensa regia, quod multa sunt vasa pretiosa, sed unum est ad os regis deputatum, speciosius ceteris, cuius comparatione pulcritudo aliorum videtur quam plurimum obscurari; sic in mensa Regis aeterni multa sunt vasa pretiosa, comparata tamen isti vasi mirabili, ad os summi Regis deputato, videntur amittere claritatem. Ideo dicitur: *Non adaequabitur ei aurum;* et Hieronymus; 'Sicut in comparatione Dei nemo bonus, sic in comparatione Matris eius nulla invenitur perfecta, quamvis virtutibus eximia comprobetur'." *Ibid.,* 714b.

glorious Virgin, *as it seemed good in his eyes to make it.*[24] She was not merely an ornamental vessel to be set up and admired as a thing of beauty but a practical, useful vessel well suited for the service of God, as the prophet Baruch says: "It is better to be a profitable vessel in the house, with which the owner thereof will be well satisfied" (6:58), and "I think of Mary on high," says St. Anselm. "God, Who made all things, made Himself from Mary, and thus re-made all things which He had made."[25]

The Vessel was wondrously *rich* in its contents, for it was filled to the brim and overflowing with the *salt of discretion,* the *manna of refreshment,* and the *oil of gladness,*—three substances, the respective significations of which are attributes of the rational, the concupiscible, and the irascible power of the soul.[26] The Vessel was filled, first with the *salt of discretion,* as is figuratively expressed in the Fourth Book of Kings: "Bring me a new vessel, and put salt into it" (2:20). The new vessel was the virginal womb, bright in its pristine purity. Into that vessel was put the *salt of discretion,* when at the announcement of the Angel Gabriel, the Wisdom of God the Father came down into the Virgin's womb.[27] The Vessel was filled, secondly, with the *manna of refreshment.* "Take a vessel and put manna into it," says the Book of Exodus (16:33). These words can be addressed to the Holy Ghost by Whose operation the Word of God containing the reward of eternal refreshment and life came down to the Virgin's bosom.[28] The Vessel was filled, thirdly, with the *oil of gladness.* That Vessel full of gladness could not come into the Synagogue of the Old Law to restore to life mankind long dead in sin, as is pointed out in the Fourth Book of Kings, where the wife of the prophet, pouring oil at his command, said to her son: "Bring me yet a vessel. And he answered: I have no more. And the oil stood" (4:6). But, indeed, *when* the abundance of grace and *the fullness of time was come* in which

(24) "Secundo potest comprehendi ex operis *complacentia;* Ieremiae decimo octavo; *Descendi in domum figuli, et ecce, ipse faciebat opus suum super rotam. Et dissipatum est vas, quod faciebat e luto manibus suis; conversusque fecit illud vas alterum, sicut placuerat in oculis eius. Figulus* est Creator noster; unde ibidem dicitur: *Sicut lutum in manu figuli; et opus factum super rotam* est genus humanum super vertibilitatem naturae constitutum; *fractum est* autem per peccatum primi hominis; sed *conversus fecit vas alterum,* Virginem scilicet gloriosam, *sicut placuit in oculis eius." Ibid.*

(25) "Tertio potest deprehendi ex multiplici cum apta et utili *convenientia;* Baruch sexto: *In vase utili gloriabitur qui fecit illud.* Anselmus: 'In sublimi contemplor Mariam. Deus, qui omnia fecit, ipse se ex Maria et sic omnia, quae fecerat, refecit'." *Ibid.*

(26) "Tertio, ratione rei contentae fuit vas mirabiliter *copiosum;* fuit enim contentivum *sale discretionis, manna refectionis* et *oleo exsultationis.* In *sale* namque discretio, in *manna* refectio, in *oleo* exsultatio datur intelligi, quorum primum pertinet ad vim rationabilem; secundum, ad concupiscibilem; sed tertium, ad irascibilem." *Ibid.*

(27) "Primo fuit contentivum *sale discretionis,* iuxta illud quod figurate dictum est quarti Regum secundo: *Afferte mihi vas novum et mittite in illud sal. Vas novum* fuit uterus virginalis, novitatis retinens puritatem. In istud vas fuit missum *sal discretionis,* cum in Virginis uterum, nuntiante Gabriele Archangelo, descendit Sapientia Dei Patris." *Ibid.*

(28) "Secundo fuit vas contentivum *manna refectionis;* Exodi decimo sexto; *Sume tibi vas unum et mitte ibi manna.* Verbum potest esse ad Spiritum sanctum, cuius operatione descendit in Virginis gremium Dei Verbum aeternae refectionis praemia contentivum." *Ibid.*

God sent His Son (Gal. 4:4), a Vessel was carved by the Hand of Wisdom and filled with the oil of gladness for all who would partake thereof.[29]

O Mary, Spiritual Vessel, Vessel of manna divine,
Cause of our joy,
Pray for us!

* * *

Rejoice, O Mary, "for thou hast found grace with God" (Luke 1:30); indeed, a threefold grace, says St. Bonaventure,—the grace of *election,* as did Moses, to whom the Lord said: "I know thee by name, and thou hast found favor in my sight" (Exod. 33:12); the grace of *perfection,* as did Noe, of whom Sacred Scripture says: "Noe found grace before the Lord. Noe was a just and perfect man; he walked with God" (Gen. 6:8, 9); the grace of *espousal,* that she might become the Spouse of God and the Mother of God's Son. Therefore she was prefigured by Esther, whom "King Assuerus loved more than all the women, and she had favor and kindness before him above all the women. And he set the royal crown on her head, and made her queen" (Esth. 2:17).[30] If the wonderful mystery of the King is to be measured by His own greatness, is it not fitting that the Woman, in whose womb He was to become Man, should be adorned with the plenitude of His treasures,—treasures far surpassing those which King Assuerus heaped upon the gracious Esther (Esth. 2:9)? If grace is bestowed in proportion to the office one is destined to fulfill, what graces do we think the Lord would refuse to the Woman who was to give Him birth by the splendid prodigy of her fruitful virginity? Would He not surround her birth and every phase of her life with the most glorious privileges? Would He not bestow upon His Mother and His Bride a rich dowry of beauty and splendor, of rarity and preciousness, of grace and sanctity?

"Hail, full of grace!" said the Angel of the Annunciation. We read in Sacred History that many servants of God were full of grace. But how much more abundant was Mary's fullness of grace than that of all the saints united! The stars in the firmament are full of light, and yet what is their combined light in comparison with the light of the full moon when she sails majestically

(29) "Tertio fuit vas contentivum *oleo exsultationis.* Istud vas plenum laetitia non poterat invenire synagoga, quemadmodum signatum fuit quarti Regum quarto; ubi quaedam de uxoribus Prophetarum, infundens oleum iuxta verbum Prophetae, per quam synagoga datur intelligi, dixit filio suo: *Affer mihi adhuc vas. Et ille respondit: Non habeo;* sed certe, cum *venit* abundantia gratiarum et *plenitudo temporis* in quo *misit Deus Filium suum,* fuit vas incisum manu Sapientiae et *prae participibus suis oleo exsultationis* repletum, cuius nos faciat participes Mater totius bonitatis, quae in suo Filio iucundatur aeternaliter sine fine." *Ibid.,* 714b, 715a.

(30) "Et rationem reddit: *Invenisti enim gratiam apud Deum,* gratiam scilicet *electionis,* sicut Moyses; Exodi trigesimo tertio: 'Invenisti gratiam apud me, et te ipsum novi ex nomine'; sic dicitur Virgini Mariae. Gratiam etiam *perfectionis,* sicut Noe; Genesis sexto: 'Noe invenit gratiam coram Deo'; et paulo post: 'Noe vir iustus atque perfectus cum Deo ambulavit'. Gratiam *desponsationis,* ut fieret sponsa Dei et mater Filii Dei; Esther secundo: 'Habuit Esther gratiam et misericordiam coram Assuero super omnes mulieres, et posuit diadema regni in capite eius'." *Comment. in Evangelium Lucae* C.I., t.VII, 23b.

in all her fullness through the solemn hours of night? We read that Stephen was full of grace and that the Apostles were *filled* with the Holy Ghost, but like the bright orb of light, Mary surpasses all grace-favored souls in the fullness of grace from heaven, for within her stainless body was to dwell the fullness of Divinity, the Word made Flesh.[31] "The more closely one approaches a principle of any kind," says St. Thomas, "the more one participates in the effect flowing from that principle. . . . Now Christ is the principle of grace; as God He is its author; as man, its instrument. . . . But the Blessed Virgin was nearest to Christ in His Humanity, because He assumed His human nature from her. Consequently, she must have received from Him a greater fullness of grace than any other creature."[32]

Holy Mary, holy Mother of God, holy Virgin of Virgins! Mary was always holy. As man is man and angel is angel, Mary was always her holy self, an order and hierarchy set apart, the *Virgo Singularis,* created and sanctified for a destiny unique. The Fathers of the Greek and Latin Church extol her as "all-holy, a miracle of grace, holier and purer than the angels," and justly so, for even before becoming the Mother of God, Mary was full of grace,—endowed not merely with the extrinsic graces proper to her state of life but with a full measure of sanctifying grace, which precedes the grace of vocation, strictly so-called, by way of preparation and endowment. Not without reason does the angel greet her as *full of grace,* says the Seraphic Doctor, for at his coming, Mary was full of a sevenfold grace.[33] First, she was full of *sanctifying* grace, a superabundance of holiness which was hers from the beginning,—a grace which sanctified not only the soul but also the flesh of the Virgin, that with it she might clothe the Eternal Word. For this initial sanctification, we have no standard of comparison. "Indeed, the Mother of the Lord was holy before she was born," says St. Bernard. Grace issued forth to meet her at the very threshold of her existence. And again: "I think that such fullness of grace descended upon her that it not only sanctified her very entrance into life but thereafter kept her free from sin." The reason for this full and perfect holiness is assigned by the Prophet when he says: "Holiness becometh thy house, O Lord, unto length of days" (Ps. 92:5).

---

(31) "Plenitudo *excellentiae* reperitur in beatissima *Virgine,* cui dictum est Lucae primo: 'Ave, gratia plena' quam plenitudinem tractans, beatus Bernardus ait: 'Legimus Stephanum plenum gratia, Apostolos *repletos* Spiritu sancto, sed longe dissimiliter in Maria. Non enim habitavit in eis plenitudo Divinitatis corporaliter, quemadmodum in Maria'." *Coll. in Ioannem* Cap.I, Coll.3, t.VI, 538b. *Acts* 6:8: "And Stephen, full of grace and fortitude, did great wonders and signs among the people." *Acts* 2:4: "And they were all filled with the Holy Ghost."

(32) "Quanto aliquid magis appropinquat principio in aliquo genere, tanto magis participat effectum illius principii. . . . Christus autem est principium gratiae, secundum divinitatem quidem auctoritative, secundum humanitatem vero instrumentaliter. . . . Beata autem virgo Maria propinquissima Christo fuit secundum humanitatem, quia ex ea accepit humanam naturam. Et ideo prae ceteris maiorem debuit a Christo gratiae plenitudinem obtinere." *Summa Theol.,* III, q.27, a.5

(33) "Hoc autem salutionis exordium, . . . cum sit compendiosum, ets tamen sententiosum; non enim sine causa Virginem salutatam vocat Archangelus Gabriel *gratia plenam.* Fuit enim Virgo Maria septiformi plenitudine plena." *De Annuntiatione B. Virginis Mariae Sermo V,* t.IX, 678a.

The Lord, says David, sanctified his habitation *in the morning early;* that is, from the beginning of her life (Ps. 45:56). And St. Anselm says: "It was altogether fitting that this Virgin, to whom God was to give His only Son, should be adorned with a purity that would surpass the purity of all men and angels and be second in greatness only to that of God. "A holy and shamefaced woman is *grace upon grace*" (Ecclus. 26:19). Mary was not only *grace,* but she was *grace upon grace,* for she was full of sanctifying grace.[34] Because she was to be the Mother of God, her sanctity was already so eminent that an angel fresh from the dazzling holiness of the heavenly court cried out his homage as a representative of the angelic world to his Queen: "Hail, full of grace; full of the beauty and holiness that is God!" Well might he so exclaim, for not even in heaven had he seen a created holiness like to that now revealed to him. With the angel, then, let us say: "Hail, full of grace," for in these words so brief, so full of meaning, Mary's troubadour has taught us how to greet her.[35]

Mary was full, secondly, of *fortifying* grace,—a grace to strengthen and support her lest she fail in the hour of trial. Rightly to her, then, may be applied the words: "A gracious woman shall find glory" (Prov. 11:16). A woman full of the grace of fortitude in battle *shall find* the *glory* of praise and renown in victory. But *who shall find this valiant woman* (Prov. 31:10), who will crush the head of the hostile serpent of old?" The angel found her in the Woman whom he greeted, for she it was who crushed Satan's head with the strength of her foot and destroyed every wicked heresy. She is the hope of the race promised in the Garden of Eden when God said to the serpent: "I will put enmities between thee and the woman, and thy seed and her seed. She shall crush thy head, and thou shalt lie in wait for her heel" (Gen. 3:15). Mary was to have "enmity" with the devil, an enmity that could mean only one thing, that he, the very power of sin, should find in her no harborage, no welcome, no point of entry, no slightest claim. Therefore, Mary alone can boast: "My heart doth not reprehend me in all my life" (Job 27:6) and in a celebrated passage St. Augustine says that speaking of Mary, he would make no mention of sin, for the honor of the Lord Whom she merited for her Son, and through Whom she had the grace

(34) "Plena etenim fuit gratia sanctificante. . . . *Gratia super gratiam, mulier sancta et pudorata. Mulier sancta,* per purgationem mentis, et *pudorata,* per incorruptionem carnis, antonomastice est Virgo Maria, de qua Bernardus ad Lugdunenses scribit: 'Fuit quippe Mater Domini ante sancta quam nata'; nec tantum sancta fuit, sed etiam pudorata; unde idem Bernardus subiungit: 'Puto, quod copiosior gratia sanctificationis in eam descenderit, quae non tantum eius sanctificaverit ortum, sed et vitam ab omni deinceps peccato custodiret immunem.' Rationem autem huius plenae et perfectae sanctificationis assignat Propheta in Psalmo, cum dicit: *Domum tuam decet sanctitudo, Domine, in longitudinem dierum.* Et propterea Anselmus dicit: 'Decebat, ut illius hominis conceptio fieret de Matre purissima ea puritate, qua maior sub Deo nequit intelligi.' Et ideo non tantum dicitur gratia, sed *gratia super gratiam,* pro eo, quod plena fuit gratia sanctificante. Dicamus ergo cum Angelo: *Ave, gratia plena." Ibid.*

(35) "Salutans igitur Virginem Mariam, dicit Angelus: *Ave, gratia plena.* . . . Hoc autem salutationis exordium, quamvis sit breve, est tamen utile, quia datur nobis in eo forma salutandi Virginem; cum sit compendiosum, est tamen sententiosum. *Ibid.*

to conquer sin in every way."[36] It was fitting, says St. Bonaventure, that she who was to take away our shame, should conquer the devil completely, leaving him not a modicum of victory.[37] Mary was free from all sin, mortal as well as venial,—a special privilege granted to her alone. "If we say we have no sin, we deceive ourselves and the truth is not in us" (I John 1:8), but the Virgin Mary was pre-redeemed and completely filled with singular grace, so that she already possessed the fruit of her womb, Whom she had not yet borne, the Lord of the universe. By this prerogative, Mary surpassed human nature in excellence; indeed, the angelic nature, too, for she possessed a human nature and led an angelic life.[38] Mary's sinlessness must be understood in the sense in which the Fathers of the Church define it, not as a divine attribute nor a result of the beatific vision but as a state of free will; it consists in her freedom from every inclination to evil and a fullness of grace for good.[39] This fullness of grace did not dispense with her personal efforts; she was not like the inanimate works of God, glorious and beautiful without any merit of her own. Mary was an intelligent moral being, free to choose the good and to reject the evil. Her sinlessness rests upon the grace of divine motherhood. The honor bestowed upon her is all gratuitous in origin, yet, as always, glory is founded on merit. By her correspondence with one grace, Mary merited another, and so increased in holiness like all the saints of God. Because she was to be the Advocate of sinners, the glory and crown of the just, the Spouse of God, the abode of the Three Persons of the Blessed Trinity, and the special resting-place of the Son, sin had no place in her.[40] She was a vessel filled with God's grace without any leakage or diminution of capacity; she is uniquely "our tainted nature's solitary boast." With the angel, then, let us bow down and say:

Hail, full of grace!
Mother Undefiled,
Pray for us!

(36) "Plena etiam fuit gratia *fortificante* ad fulcimentum infirmitatis poenae, ne unquam posset superari in tentatione; unde sibi recte competit illud Proverbiorum undecimo: *Mulier gratiosa inveniet gloriam. Mulier,* inquam, plena gratia fortitudinis in pugna, *inveniet gloriam* laudis et honoris in victoria. Sed hanc *mulierem fortem quis inveniet,* quae caput conterat inimici et serpentis antiqui? Hanc invenit Angelus salutando; sola enim haec est, quae fortitudine pedis contrivit caput diaboli et interemit universam haereticam pravitatem. Unde ipsa sola potest gloriari, quod ipsam *non reprehendat cor* eius *in omni vita* sua. Et propterea Augustinus: 'Cum de peccatis agitur, de sola Matre Domini nullo modo haberi volo mentionem'." *Ibid.*, 678ab.

(37) "Congruum etiam erat, ut beata Virgo Maria, per quam aufertur nobis approbrium, vinceret diabolum, ut nec ei succumberet ad modicum." *III Sent.*, d.3, p.1, a.2, q.1, t.III, 73a.

(38) "Possunt etiam . . . praerogativa intelligi, singularitates collatae beatissimae Virgini, quibus super omnem aliam puram creaturam singulariter est coronata. Quarum prima est *immunitas,* a peccato videlicet, quod nunquam mortaliter nec venialiter peccavit. . . . Ioannes ait: *Si dixerimus, quoniam peccatum non habemus, ipsi nos seducimus, et veritas in nobis non est.* Illa autem Virgo singulari gratia praeventa est atque repleta, ut ipsa haberet *ventris sui fructum,* quem ab utero non habuit, universitatis Dominum. Per hanc ergo praerogativam transcendit naturam (humanam), immo et angelicam, quia naturam habuit humanem et angelicam vitam." *De Assumtione B. Virginis Mariae. Sermo VI,* t.IX, 702a.

(39) "Beatissima igitur Virgo excessit utramque, quia *lucrari* et mereri. *Lucrari* potuit, eo quod viator fuit; *perdere* non potuit, quia peccare non potuit. Quod peccare non potuit, sane intelligendum est, ut ita dicat statum liberi arbitrii, sicut sancti Patres dicunt *non peccare posse,* scilicet ut dicat remotionem omnis dispositionis vel inclinationis ad malum et plenitudinem gratiae ad bonum." *Ibid.*

(40) "Quoniam igitur beata virgo Maria advocata est peccatorum, gloria et corona iustorum, sponsa Dei et totius Trinitatis triclinium et specialissimum Filii reclinatorium; hinc est quod speciali gratia Dei nullum in ea peccatum habuit locum." *III Sent.*, d.3, p.1, a.2, q.1, t.III, 73.

Mary was full, thirdly, of *perfecting* grace, the grace which supplies for any natural deficiency, leaving in her no empty void, but filling every crevice of her soul so that she could say in the words of St. Paul: "By the grace of God I am what I am, and his grace in me hath not been void" (I Cor. 15:10); in other words: "The Lord has given me my natural existence,—a gift which He has completed and perfected by fullness of grace."[41] Therefore Mary could say that grace in her *has not been void,* for she was filled to capacity. The angel had declared her "full of grace." What, then, could be added to that plenitude? Nothing, according to our way of thinking; yet, in the judgment of God, she had then imbibed but the mere rudiments of that science of the saints in which she was afterwards to attain such pre-eminence. Wherefore St. Bernard ponders the question: "Who shall call her void, whom the angel greets as 'full of grace'?" Nor is this all, for he adds that the Holy Ghost shall come upon her. What does this mean if not that at the present coming of the Holy Ghost she was "full of grace" for herself; that at His coming down from above, she would be full to overflowing for us? Therefore, the Blessed Virgin possessed graces far exceeding those given to all other creatures. With Solomon, then, we can truly say: "Many daughters have gathered together riches, thou hast surpassed them all" (Prov. 31:29) and with the angel let us greet her: "Hail, full of grace!"[42]

No gorgeous gown or lifted throne betrayed the majesty of Mary's rank, for the grandeur of the royal house of David was now on the wane, but she was full of an *adorning* grace,—an embellishment worthy of the daughter of kings.[43] Unmarred by imperfection, she stood forth as the pride of the whole creation, the most noble ornament of the universe. "Hail, full of grace," said the angel, as if to call attention to her gracious loveliness, for like Esther, "she was exceeding fair, and her incredible beauty made her appear agreeable and amiable in the eyes of all" (Esth. 2:15).[44] She was agreeable and fair not only in body but also in mind, for "favour is deceitful and beauty is vain; the woman that feareth the Lord, she shall be praised" (Prov. 31:30). Mary's external beauty was but the radiance of the fullness of grace which adorned her soul. And since she was beautiful within and without, the Divine

(41) "Plena etiam fuit gratia *consummante* ad supplementum defectabilitatis naturae, ut nulla remaneret in ea vacuitas indigentiae, sed recte posset dicere illud primae ad Corinthios decimo quinto: *Gratia Dei sum id quod sum, et gratia eius in me vacua non fuit,* quasi dicat: ipse Dominus dedit esse naturae, et illud consummavit et perfecit per plenitudinem gratiae." *De Annuntiatione B. Virginis Mariae. Sermo V,* t.IX, 678b.

(42) "Et ideo dicit: *non fuit vacua,* quia omnino fuit repleta. Unde Bernardus: 'Quis vacuam dixerit, quam salutat Angelus gratia plenam? Neque hoc solum, sed adhuc quoque in eam superventurum asserit Spiritum sanctum. Ad quid, nisi, ut adveniente iam Spiritu sancto, plena sibi; eodem superveniente, nobis quoque fieret superplena'? Unde ipsa habuit gratiam consummatissimam super omnes. . . . Propter quod recte sibi possumus dicere cum Salomone, Proverbiorum trigesimo primo: *Multae filiae congregaverunt divitias, tu supergressa es universas,* et cum Angelo salutare: *Ave." Ibid.*

(43) "Plena nihilominus gratia *decorante* ad ornamentum honestatis vitae, ut nihil appareat in ea reprehensibile, et rectissime possit de ipsa dici quod dicitur de Esther." *Ibid.,* 679a.

(44) "Ut ergo ostendat eam *amabilem gratiositate,* dicit: *Ingressus Angelus ad eam, dixit: Ave, gratia plena.* Et ideo bene per Esther designata est, de qua Esther secundo dicitur, quod erat formosa valde et incredibili pulcritudine, omnium oculis gratiosa et amabilis videbatur." *Comment. in Evangelium Lucae* C.I., t.VII, 22b.

Bridegroom, praising her, says: "Thou art all fair, O my love, and there is not a spot in thee" (Cant. 4:7). "All fair," re-echoes St. Bernard, "because most beautiful in outward appearance, wholly undefiled in body, most holy in soul."[45] And St. Jerome: "If you study her carefully, you will find that there is no virtue, no beauty, no innocence, no glory which does not shine forth in her." "She was resplendent with many meritorious virtues, purer than the driven snow by the gifts of the Holy Ghost, showing forth in all things the simplicity of a dove."[46] In the words of St. Bernard: "The royal Virgin, adorned with the jewels of virtue and resplendent with twin beauty of body and soul, renowned in heaven above for her surpassing loveliness and holiness, so drew to herself the gaze of the denizens of heaven that she turned the mind of the King Himself in desire of her and brought down His heavenly messenger from above.[47] The gracious Virgin so touched the heart of God that He came down naturally, as it were, to be united to her in love, and the dazzled angel could find no other words than these with which to greet her: "Hail, full of grace!"

Fifthly, Mary was full of the grace of *espousal* for a union of divine intimacy in which she was joined in the bonds of closest wedlock with the King, as was long foretold: "She was brought to the chamber of Assuerus, the tenth month, which is called Tebeth, in the seventh year of his reign. And the king loved her more than all the women, and he set the royal crown on her head, and made her queen" (Esth. 2:16, 17). That Esther, who *was brought to the chamber of Assuerus,* is the Virgin Mary when through intimate love she arrived at a union of divine familiarity. Wherefore St. Jerome says: "The grace of the Holy Ghost so completely filled Mary's soul, the love of God so wholly consumed her, that there remained in her no blemish to defile her affection, only continuous ardor and the fullness of an overpowering love." Therefore not only is she said to have had grace but to have had it *above all the women* because in tender intimacy with God she surpassed them all, and this to such an extent that St. Bernard in admiration exclaims: "How familiar you have become with Christ, O Lady, how very close, nay, how intimate you have deserved to become! What great grace you have found with Him! He abides in you and you abide in Him; you vest Him, and you are vested by Him; you clothe Him with a robe of stainless

(45) "*Gratiosa* erat et *formosa* non tantum corpore, sed etiam mente, quia *fallax gratia et vana est pulcritudo; mulier timens Dominum ipsa laudabitur.* Et quoniam pulcra erat intus et extra, ideo dicitur Canticorum quarto: *Tota pulcra es, amica mea, et macula non est in te;* quod exponens Bernardus de Virgine dicit: 'Tota pulcra, quia facie pulcherrima, corpore integerrima, spiritu sanctissima'." *De Annuntiatione B. Virginis Mariae. Sermo V,* t.IX, 679a.

(46) "Et hoc ipsum Hieronymus: 'Si diligentius inspicias, nihil virtutis est, nihil speciositatis, nihil candoris et gloriae, quod ex ea non resplendeat.' 'Erat enim multis candidata meritorum virtutibus et dealbata nive candidius Spiritus sancti muneribus, simplicitatem columbae in omnibus repraesentans'." *Ibid.*

(47) "Et idem: 'Virgo regia, gemmis ornata virtutum, geminoque mentis pariter et corporis decore praefulgida, *specie sua et pulcritudine sua* in caelestibus cognita, caeli civium in se provocavit aspectus, ita ut et Regis animum in sui concupiscentiam inclinaret et caelestem nuntium ad se de supernis attraheret'." *Ibid.*

flesh; He clothes you with the glory of His majesty." How truly is it said, comments the Seraphic Doctor, that the King "set the royal crown on her head."[48]

Mary was full, sixthly, of *fecundating* grace for a conception of virginal integrity, that she might conceive without the least taint of sin. Wherefore the angel said to her: "Thou hast found grace with God. Behold thou shalt conceive in thy womb and shalt bring forth a son and thou shalt call his name Jesus" (Luke 1:30, 31). Mary, indeed, was full of grace,—grace which filled "not only her soul, but also her womb." "Truly full," says St. Jerome, "for to others it is offered in drops, but upon Mary the fullness of grace poured itself out all at once to the last drop." And St. Bernard: *"Mary has chosen the best part,—the best,* indeed, for conjugal fecundity is good, virginal chastity is better, but best of all is virginal fecundity or fruitful virginity. This is the unique privilege of Mary; it shall not be given to another, for *it shall not be taken away from her* (Luke 10:42). And again: "The inviolate, chaste, and undefiled womb of Mary, like a pasture land of never-failing fruitfulness, brought forth a Flower, Whose beauty knows no corruption, Whose glory never fades." Contemplating the fullness of Mary's virginal fruitfulness, let us say with the angel: "Hail, full of grace!"[49]

Mary was full, lastly, of grace *overflowing* for the advancement of man's salvation, that there may be no one who "can hide himself from her heat" (Ps. 18:7). Mary was "full of grace," for in her was to lie hidden the Treasure of Grace, according to the words of Ecclesiasticus which are applicable to her: "In me is all grace of the way and of the truth; in me is all hope of life and of virtue. Come over to me, all ye that desire me, and be filled with my fruits" (24:25, 26). "In me," she says, "is all grace of the way and of truth," and truly so, for she was to bring forth the Word made Flesh, the Word Who is the Only-begotten of God the Father, "full of grace and truth"

(48) "Plena etiam fuit gratia *desponsante* ad contubernium familiaritatis divinae, per quam assumeretur in vinculum indissolubilis copulae, ut ipsi possit recte aptari illud reginae Esther, sponsae Assueri, de qua Esther secundo: *Ducta est Esther ad cubiculum regis Assueri mense decimo, qui vocatur Tebeth, septimo anno regni eius.* Et adamavit eam rex plus quam omnes mulieres habuitque gratiam et misericordiam coram *eo super omnes mulieres, et posuit diadema regni in capite eius. Esther* ista Virgo Maria est, quae *ducta est ad cubiculum Assueri,* quando per intimum amorem pervenit ad consortium divinae familiaritatis. Unde Hieronymus: 'Totam impleverat Spiritus sancti gratia, quam totam incanduerat divinus amor, ita ut in ea nihil, esset mendanum, quod violaret affectum, sed ardor continuus et ebrietas profusi amoris.' Unde non tantum dicitur habuisse gratiam, sed etiam *super omnes mulieres,* quae prae ceteris Deo familiarior est effecta, secundum quod dicit Bernardus: 'Quam familiaris Christo facta es, Domina, quam proxima, immo quam intima fieri meruisti! Quantam invenisti gratiam apud eum! In te manet et tu cum eo; et vestis eum, et vestiris ab eo; vestis eum substantia carnis, vestit te ille gloria suae maiestatis.' Et propterea recte dicitur in praemisso verbo: *posuit diadema regni in capite eius." Ibid.*

(49) "Plena fuit etiam gratia *fecundante* ad conceptum integritatis virgineae, ut conciperet sine omni corruptione; unde sibi dicit Angelus, Lucae primo: *Invenisti gratiam apud Dominum. Ecce, concipies in utero et paries Filium et vocabis nomen eius Iesum.* Haec vere fuit gratia plena, quae 'non tantum mentem, verum etiam ventrem implevit.' Unde Heieronymus: 'Vere plena, quia ceteris per partes praestatur, Mariae vero se totam infudit simul gratiae plenitudo.' Et Bernardus: *'Optimam partem elegit sibi Maria. Optima* plane, quia bona fecunditas coniugalis, melior autem castitatis virginalis, prorsus autem optime est fecunditas virginea, seu fecunda virginitas; Mariae privilegium est, non dabitur alteri, quia non auferetur ab ea.' Et idem: 'Inviolata et casta et integra Mariae viscera tanquam pascua aeterni vigoris florem protulere, cuius pulcritudo non videat corruptionem, cuius gloria in perpetuum non marcescat.' Et propter plenitudinem fecunditatis virgineae debemus dicere: *Ave." Ibid.,* 679b.

(John 1:14). With the angel, then, let us bow down and greet her: "Hail, full of grace overflowing!"[50]

Holy Mary,
Holy Mother of God,
Holy Virgin of Virgins,
Pray for us!

* * *

Then to show that the Virgin was *most venerable by reason of the high honor to be conferred upon her,* the angel, not like an angel addressing a woman but with the deference of a courtier addressing his Queen, exclaimed: "The Lord is with thee." He spoke clearly and distinctly as if to emphasize the excellent and singular manner in which the Lord was soon to be with her,—in His own tabernacle, as it were. The Lord is and ever has been with Mary by the fullness of His grace; now He is to be with her by His corporeal presence, assuming human flesh in her chaste womb, so that she could in all truth say in the words of Ecclesiasticus: "He that made me rested in my tabernacle" (24:12). "The Lord is in His holy temple," says the Psalm (10:5). "The Most High has sanctified his own tabernacle. God is in the midst thereof, and it shall not be moved" (Ps. 45:5, 6). St. Bernard, paraphrasing the words of the angel, says: "The Lord is with thee. Thou shalt become the Mother of Him Whose Father is God; the Son of His Father's love will be the crown of thy chastity,—an inestimable dignity exalting thee above every creature, whose queen thou shalt be, as the Psalmist foretold: "The queen stood on thy right hand" (Ps. 44:10).[51] In echo to the angel's greeting, let us address her, "Hail, Lady, hail, our earthly queen!"

Virgin Most Venerable,
Pray for us!

* * *

"Blessed art thou among women," continued the angel, thus bringing to fulfillment the words of Ecclesiasticus: "In the multitude of the elect she shall have praise, and among the blessed she shall be called blessed" (24:4). "Blessed among women was Jahel" (Judges 5:24); blessed was Ruth, whose lowly serviceableness drew from Booz the words: "Blessed art thou of the

---

(50) "Plena postremo fuit gratia *redundante* ad profectum salutis humanae, ut nemo sit, *qui se abscondat a calore eius,* secundum quod de ipsa potest exponi illud Ecclesiastici vigesimo quarto: *In me gratia omnis viae et veritatis, in me omnis spes vitae et virtutis. Transite ad me, omnes, qui concupiscitis me, et a generationibus meis implemini. In me,* inquit, *omnis gratia viae et veritatis,* quia Verbum genuit incarnatum; Verbum, inquam, unigenitum Dei Patris, *plenum gratiae et veritatis;* . . . Recte igitur dici potest: *Ave, plena gratia redundante. Ibid.*

(51) "Ut autem ostendat *venerabilem ex dignitate* addit: *Dominus tecum;* discretive dictum est, quia excellenti et singulari modo, tanquam in proprio tabernaculo; Ecclesiastici vigesimo quarto: 'Qui creavit me requievit in tabernaculo meo'; Psalmus: 'Dominus in templo sancto suo,' hoc est in Virginis utero; et rursus: 'Sanctificavit tabernaculum suum Altissimus, Deus in medio eius, non commovebitur.' Bernardus: 'Dominus tecum; illius eris mater, cuius est Deus pater; Filius paternae caritatis erit corona tua castitatis'; ex quo super omnes sortiris inaestimabilem dignitatem, et propterea regina dicitur in Psalmo: 'Astitit regina a dextris tuis'." *Comment. in Evangelium Lucae* C.1, t.VII, 22b, 23a.

Lord, my daughter" (Ruth 3:10). Blessed was Abigail, whose prudence made David exclaim: "Blessed be thou, who has kept me from revenging me with my own hand" (I Kings 25:33). "Blessed was Judith to whom Ozias, the prince of the house of Israel, said: Blessed art thou, O daughter, by the Lord the most high God, above all women upon the earth" (Judith 13:23). Thus, in type and figure, the Elect Woman of the Ages shines forth from the Inspired Word of God. In these holy Jewish women, Sacred Scripture gives us foreshadowings of the Woman who was to bring forth the Eternal King. Among these women and above them all was the Virgin Mary blessed. She was the glory of her sex in whom all the blessings bestowed upon the holy women of Israel found their perfection and fulfillment.[52]

O Mary, blessed beyond compare, Virgin Most Renowned,
Pray for us!

* * *

"The Lord is with thee, blessed art thou among women." The angel's greeting was highly complimentary, disturbingly so, in fact, for the Evangelist says that the Virgin "having heard, was troubled at his saying and thought with herself what manner of salutation this should be." And this was great prudence, for it contained the depth of wisdom of which Sacred Scripture says: "To think therefore upon her is perfect understanding" (Wis. 6:16). When "Daniel, whose name was Baltasser," was bidden to interpret the King's dream, he "began silently to think within himself for about one hour and his thoughts troubled him" (Dan. 4:6). So, too, was Mary troubled, not so much at the brilliant intelligence of the angel but rather concerning her virginal innocence. She knew not the angel, nor the cause of his coming, nor the meaning of his words, for they were heavy with mystery. St. Bernard says that Mary was troubled, but not unduly disturbed. In the words of the Psalm she could say: "I was troubled, and I spoke not. I thought upon the days of old, and I had in my mind the eternal years" (Ps. 76:5, 6).[53]

Mary had meditated much upon the prophecies; she had learned from the Holy Scriptures that the time foretold for the coming of the Messiah had arrived; that Daniel's prophetic seventy weeks of years had now rolled by;

---

(52) "Completum est etiam in Maria illud Ecclesiastici vigesimo quarto: 'In multitudine electorum habebit laudem et inter benedictos benedicetur.' 'Benedicta in mulieribus Iahel.' Benedicta fuit Ruth, Ruth tertio: Benedicta es a Domino, filia.' Benedicta Abigail, primi Regum vigesimo quinto: 'Benedicta tu, quae prohibuisti me hodie, ne me mea manu ulciscerer.' Benedicta Iudith, decimo tertio: 'Benedicta es tu, filia, a Domino Deo excelso prae omnibus mulieribus super terram.' Inter has mulieres et super has mulieres benedicta est virgo Maria, quia illae benedictiones impletae sunt in hac." *Ibid.*, 29b.

(53) "In *cogitatu* laudatur *prudentia,* cum dicitur: *Et cogitabat, qualis esset ista salutatio;* et hoc erat magna prudentia, continebat enim profunditatem sapientiae, de qua Sapientiae sexto: 'Cogitare de illa sensus est consummatus'; unde Danielis quarto: 'Daniel, cuius nomen Balthassas, coepit intra semetipsum tacitus cogitare quasi una hora, et cogitationes eius conturbabant eum.' Cogitationes autem Virginis, etsi turbarent propter pudorem innocentiae, non tamen perturbabant propter splendorem intelligentiae. Bernardus: 'Turbata est, sed non perturbata; immo secundum illud Psalmi: *Turbatus sum et non sum locutus, sed cogitavi dies antiquos*' etc." *Ibid.*, 23b.

that already, according to the prophecy of Jacob, the sceptre of Juda had passed into the hands of Herod, a strange king, and she well knew that a virgin was to be the mother of the Messiah. When she heard the praises of the angel offered to herself, did she not perhaps suspect that she herself might be that chosen Mother of God? Evidently not, her only reaction was one of fear. With Job she could say: "I was troubled at his presence, and when I consider him I am made pensive with fear" (Job 23:15). Mary was troubled, as was Esther in the presence of the King to whom she said: "I saw thee, my lord, as an angel of God, and my heart was troubled for fear of thy majesty" (Esth. 15:16).[54] "And the angel said to her: Fear not, Mary, for thou hast found grace with God." Then in a few words Gabriel announces to Mary that she will become a mother and he reveals to her the name, the mission, and the glory of her Son.

> "Behold thou shalt conceive in thy womb and shalt bring forth a son, and thou shalt call his name Jesus. He shall be great and shall be called the Son of the Most High. And the Lord God shall give unto him the throne of David his father, and he shall reign in the house of Jacob forever. And of his kingdom there shall be no end" (Luke 1:31-33).

The angel was offering Mary the motherhood of the Messiah,—a proposal which she was free to accept or reject. To become the mother of the greatest and holiest Son of David, nay, Son of the Most High, a King Whose coming her whole nation had ardently awaited and desired! It was a thought overwhelming to her humility, confusing to her virginity.

There have been moments in history when the destiny of nations hung upon the decision of an individual but there has never been a choice so fraught with importance as that involved in the *fiat* of the Handmaid of the Lord. Hers was a decision which could halt the course of events and take it up again in the stream of a new destiny. Instead of being at once carried away with excessive joy at the prospect of the magnificent future opening out before her, Mary wisely and prudently reflects. What superb calm in the demeanor of the ingenious Virgin! What a searching look she casts upon God, as with perfect composure she carries on a conversation with the heavenly messenger, expressing her only doubt in the query: "How shall this be done, because I know not man?" (Luke 1:34). Mary hesitates not from unwillingness but from perplexity. "I know not man," that is, "I have taken a vow not to know man. I am a virgin in mind, and flesh, and firm resolve." And in truth, Mary was, like Rebecca, "an exceeding comely maid, and a most beautiful virgin, and not known to man" (Gen. 24:16). And being a

(54) "In *affectu* commendatur *verecundia,* cum dicitur: *Turbata est in sermone eius,* scilicet ex verecundia. . . . ut posset dicere spiritus eius illud Iob vigesimo tertio. 'A facie eius turbatus sum, et considerans eum, timore sollicitor.' Exemplum huius Esther, penultimo: 'Vidi te, domine, quasi Angelum Dei, et turbatum est cor meum prae timore gloriae tuae'." *Ibid.,* 23ab.

virgin, she was thinking, as the Apostle says, not on the things of the world but "on the things of the Lord that she might be holy in body and in spirit" (I Cor. 7:34). Since Mary was resolved not to know man, it was not at all unreasonable for her to ask concerning the manner in which she would conceive a child, that she might give her consent, if it were possible for her to have virginity and motherhood at one and the same time.[55]

"How shall this be done, because I know not man?" What delicate purity, lofty faith, and heroic strength stand out in these first words of the Blessed Virgin that the evangelists have given us!—words worthy of the Mother of God. "How shall this be done?" Nicodemus had asked the Lord the same question, when he heard the words: "You must be born again" (cf. John 3:1-7). And when the same Archangel Gabriel told Zachary that his wife Elizabeth would bear him a son, Zachary doubted and asked for a sign that he might believe: "Whereby shall I know this? For I am an old man, and my wife is advanced in years" (Luke 1:18). Mary did not ask, "How shall I know this?" as did Zachary, in a spirit of disbelief, but, "How shall this be done?" in momentary anxiety for her virginity. Was her conception to be carnal or spiritual, or miraculous and unique? It was a reasonable question, well becoming the maiden's age and sex, and it was asked in a thoroughly justified curiosity with a view to consent, according to the words of the Proverb: "Let thy eyelids go before thy steps" (Prov. 4:25).[56]

Hail, thou depth beyond sounding!
Virgin Most Prudent,
Pray for us!

* * *

Since her hesitation proceeded from reason directing her aright, Mary deserved a satisfying answer and the angel proceeded to assure her that her virginity, far from being an obstacle, fitted most marvelously into the divine plan. "And the angel answering, said to her: The Holy Ghost shall come upon thee and the power of the Most High shall overshadow thee" (Luke 1:35). And in paraphrase St. Bonaventure adds: "You will be made

(55) *"Rationem moventem* tangit, cum dicit: Quoniam virum non cognosco, id est, non cognoscituram propono, et ita sum virgo mente et carne et proposito, ut sibi recte competat illud Rebeccae, Genesis vigesimo quarto, quod erat 'puella decora nimis virgoque et incognita viro.' Et secundum Apostolum, primae ad Corinthios septimo, iam non cogitabat, quae carnis erant, sed 'quae Domini sunt quomodo esset sancta et corpore et spiritu'; et ideo non irrationabiliter quaerebat, quomodo debeat prolem concipere, quae non proponebat virum cognoscere, ut, si posset esse, quod haberet simul virginitatem et fecunditatem, tunc consensum praeberet." *Ibid.*, 24b, 25a.

(56) *"Dixit autem Maria ad Angelum.* Introduxit prius Evangelista Angelum narrantem; subiungit his prudentissimam *Virginem percunctantem;* in qua percunctatione tria nobis explicantur, scilicet *dubitatio conveniens, ratio movens* et *solutio satisfaciens. Conveniens dubitatio* notatur, cum dicitur: *Quomodo fiet istud?* Cum enim triplex sit concipiendi modus: unus carnalis, alius spiritualis et tertius admirabilis et singularis; quaero, quo istorum modorum fiat? Nicodemus sic quaerebat a Domino, cum audiret, quod oporteret, eum renasci denuo; Ioannis tertio: 'Quomodo, inquit, possunt haec fieri'? Et nota, quod non quaerit modum *sciendi* sive signum, quod fidem faciat, sicut Zacharias, qui punitus fuit, supra eodem: 'Unde hoc sciam? Ego enim sum senex, et uxor mea processit in diebus suis'; sed quaerit modum *fiendi,* ut consentiat, secundum illud Proverbiorum quarto: 'Palpebrae tuae praecedant gressus tuos'." *Ibid.*, 24b.

fruitful without defilement; you will conceive without carnal desire; you will bear a child without sorrow, for you will bear him not from male seed but by the power of the Holy Ghost. That you may not feel the heat of concupiscence, "the power of the Most High shall overshadow thee," that the words sung of thee in the Canticle might be fulfilled: "I sat down under his shadow, whom I desired" (Cant. 2:3).[57] When Gabriel had given to Mary the solution of her difficulty, and had explained to her the process by which this sublime mystery was to be accomplished, the Virgin believed, she desired it, and she acquiesced at once.[58] "And Mary said: Behold the handmaid of the Lord. Be it done to me according to thy word" (Luke 1:38),— evidence at once of the *humility* which disposed her for the reception of the grace of becoming the Mother of God, the *love* which accomplished it, and the *faith* which was manifested in her words.[59] "Be it done to me according to thy word,—the language, as St. Bernard says, of perfect love and surrender. "Be it done,"—words, not of doubt, but of longing desire, words of acquiescence and affection, prayerful words which voice her love, her humility, her unquestioned belief,—the sweetest sound ever heard by men, by angels, and by the Spouse Himself. The sound He longed to hear when He said in the Canticle: "Let thy voice sound in my ears, for thy voice is sweet and thy face comely" (Cant. 2:14), was the sound of Mary's voice when she said to the angel: "Be it done unto me according to thy word."[60]

Of Mary God asked a blind faith. It seems almost a miracle that the idea of Virgin Birth should have entered the mind of a simple Galilean maid. Though the prodigies of His omnipotence which the Most High was about to display in her favor exceeded the limits of Mary's comprehension, the words which she addressed to the angel show that she immediately submitted her reason to the supreme wisdom of Him Who is Sovereign Truth and Infinite Power and unhesitatingly believed His words, "for with the heart, we believe unto justice, but with the mouth, confession is made unto salvation" (Rom. 10:10). "I have believed," says the Psalm, "therefore have I spoken" (115:10). "And Mary said: Behold the handmaid of the Lord. Be

(57) "Et quoniam dubitatio sua rationem habebat recte moventem; ideo meruit *responsionem satisfacientem*, quae notatur ibi: *Et respondens Angelus dixit ei: Spiritus sanctus* superveniet in te, et virtus Altissimi obumbravit tibi; quasi dicat Angelus: quaeris, quomodo concipies? Ad hoc respondeo, quod fecundaberis sine corruptione, concipies sine libidine, partes sine dolore, quia non ex virili semine, sed ex Spiritus sanctus virtute. . . . Non etiam erit *libido,* quia *virtus Altissimi obumbrabit tibi,* scilicet ne sentias aestum concupiscentiae, secundum illud Canticorum secundo: 'Sub umbra illius, quem desideraveram, sedi'." *Ibid.*, 25a.

(58) "De modo incarnationis hoc tenendum est, quod Angelo nuntiante beatissimae Virgini Mariae mysterium incarnationis perficiendum in ipsa, Virgo credidit, appetiit et consensit." *Breviloquium IV*, C.III, t.V, 243a.

(59) "Hunc autem consensum describit debite et ordinate factum: quia ex *humilitate praedisponente* et *caritate perficiente* et *credulitate pronuntiante.*" *Comment. in Evangelium Lucae* C.I, t.VII, 26a.

(60) "Postremo subditur *consensus perfectus ex caritate,* cum dicitur: *Fiat mihi secundum verbum tuum.* 'Fiat, ut dicit Bernardus, est *desiderii signum,* non dubitationis indicium'; etiam est *signum assertionis,* . . . et iterum *affectionis,* . . . et potest esse *orationis* ut sic sit *desideratorium,* quia ex caritate; *oratorium,* quia ex humilitate; *assertorium;* ex credulitate. Haec est vox dulcissima hominibus, Angelis et ipsi Sponso. Hanc petebat in Canticorum secundo: 'Sonet vox tua in auribus meis; vox enim tua dulcis, et facies tua decora'; quod facit, cum dixit Angelo: *Fiat mihi secundum verbum tuum.*" *Ibid.*, 26b.

it done to me according to thy word." Of this word of faith, St. Paul says: "The word is nigh thee, even in thy mouth and in thy heart. This is the word of faith which we preach" (Rom. 10:8). Because Mary conceived the word of faith in her heart, she conceived the Son of God in her womb.[61]

O Mary, Virgin Most Faithful,
Pray for us!

* * *

It was Mary's love which prompted her to acquiesce to the angel's appeal. Wherefore the words spoken of Wisdom and her lover are applicable to her: "And she will meet him as an honorable mother, and will receive him as a wife married of a virgin (Ecclus. 15:2). The angel was urging Mary to accept the fruitfulness and dignity of motherhood, the purity of her virginity remaining unsullied, and since both these offers implied sincere love, out of the sincere love which filled her heart, not forced or allured but consenting of her own free will, Mary accepted the proposal of the angel. And since the Holy Ghost is All-holy Love, the sincere love in the Virgin's heart disposed her to receive Him, that of Him she might conceive a perfectly immaculate Son.[62] Just as a woman conceives through love and desire of her husband and in close union with him, so did the Blessed Virgin by the *uniqueness of her love* conceive God of God, for which reason she is said to have *conceived of the Holy Ghost.*[63] Hugh of St. Victor says: "Mary conceived of the Holy Ghost, not because she received the seed of her child from the substance of the Holy Ghost, but because by the force of divine love and the operation of the Holy Ghost, she supplied from her own virginal flesh the natural substance of the Divine Child to be born of her. Because the love of the Holy Ghost burned singularly in her heart, the power of the Holy Ghost worked wonders in her flesh; because the Holy Spirit possessed the undivided love of

---

(61) "Introducitur ergo primo *pronuntiatio ex credulitate,* cum dicitur: *Dixit autem Maria ad Angelum.* Quia enim Angeli credidit esse verum, ideo dat expresse responsum consentaneum; ad Romanos decimo: 'Corde creditur ad iustitiam, ore autem confessio fit ad salutem'; et in Psalmo: 'Credidi, propter quod locutus est.' *Dixit;* de hoc verbo fidei dicitur ad Romanos decimo: 'Prope est verbum in ore tuo et in corde tuo, hoc est verbum fidei, quod praedicamus.' Quia ergo corde concepit verbum fidei, ventre concepit Filium Dei." *Ibid.,* 26a.

(62) "Propter *sinceritatem dilectionis,* quae disponebat ipsam ad angelicae persuasionis *assensum;* unde sibi competit illud Ecclesiastici decimo quinto, quod dicitur de sapientia et eius amatore: *Obviabit illi quasi mater honorificata, et quasi mulier a virginitate suscipiet illum.* Persuadebat namque Angelus, ut, salva puritate virginitatis, consentiret in fecunditatem et dignitatem matris; et quia haec duo faciunt ad sinceritatem dilectionis, ideo Virgo Maria propter sincerissimum amorem, quo plena erat, non compulsa, non tracta, sed mera voluntate consentiens, Angelo suadenti *obviavit* quasi *mater honorificata* in salutatione angelica, *et quasi mulier a virginitate suscepit illum,* quia sic consensit, quod haberet filium, ut tamen nullo modo vellet cognoscere virum, cum dixit: *Ecce, ancilla Domini, fiat mihi secundum verbum tuum.* Et haec fuit *dispositio* summa et immediata ad conceptum, quia Spiritus sanctus amor est sanctissimus, ideo sinceritas amoris in corde Virginis disponebat ad ipsum suscipiendum, ut de ipso conciperet Filium omnino immaculatum; et hoc est quod dicit ei Angelus: *Spiritus sanctus superveniet in te, et virtus Altissimi obumbravit tibi. De Annuntiatione B. Virginis Mariae. Sermo II,* t.IX, 660b.

(63) "Illud enim quod maxime praeparavit Virginem ad Filii Dei conceptionem, fuit amor divinus. Unde quemadmodum mulier concipit per viri delectationem et ipsius adhaesionem, quae est cum desiderio et amore virtutis generativae; sic beata Virgo propter *amoris singularitatem,* singulariter concepit Deum ex Deo; et ideo concepisse dicitur *de Spiritu sancto. III Sent.,* d.4, a.1, q.1, t.III, 99a.

her heart, His operation in her flesh had no precedent."[64] Mary's union with her Divine Son was a total union; her maternity was spiritual as well as physical. She enjoyed the closest possible intimacy with her Spouse, conceiving Him in her heart before she conceived Him in her womb.

In the Incarnation Mary's virginity was not violated by her motherhood, but it received a new consecration and her sanctity and holiness were augmented. In that sacred moment we venerate the holy Virgin as *Mother Most Pure,* for she was endowed with peerless purity, a perfection which she had attained by four gradual stages of development: first, by her *sanctification in the womb of her mother;* secondly, by *the practice of virtues;* thirdly, *in the overshadowing of the Holy Ghost;* fourthly, *in the conception of the Son of God.* In the first stage Mary was purified because there remained in her no inclination to sin. In this respect she excelled all others sanctified in the womb, as is evident in the Precursor of Jesus, of whom St. Matthew says: "There hath not risen among them that are born of women a greater than John the Baptist" (11:11). Although sanctified in the womb of St. Elizabeth, he fled into the desert "lest he stain his life by a fault of the tongue." In the second stage Mary was purified, not indeed by withdrawal from sin but by drawing near to the Most Pure by an ever-increasing growth in holiness. She was purified still more in the third stage when the Holy Ghost with the water of His blessing and the oil of sanctification consecrated her in the Holy of Holies as the living temple of the Word, into which the High Priest would one day enter "in the year of goodness" (Ps. 64:12). In the fourth stage, the Majesty of God entered the temple.[65] In the first stage of purification there was conferred upon the Virgin the perfection of the sacraments; in the second stage, the perfection of the virtues and the beatitudes; in the third, the perfection of the gifts; in the fourth, the perfection of the fruits. Sacred Scripture bears witness to Mary's ever-increasing purity. Of the first degree, the Canticle says: "Thou art all fair, O my love, and there is not a spot in thee" (Cant. 4:7). *Thou art all fair,* unstained by original sin; *and there is not a spot in thee,* unstained as thou art by actual sin, mortal or venial. Of the second degree of her purity, again the Canticle says: "How beautiful art

(64) "Magister Hugo de virginitate Mariae: 'Concepit Maria de Spiritu sancto, non quod de substantia Spiritus sancti semen partus acceperit, sed quia per amorem et operationem Spiritus sancti ex carne Virginis divino partui naturae substantiam ministravit. Nam quia in corde suo amor Spiritus sancti singulariter adrebat, ideo in carne eius virtus Spiritus sancti mirabilia faciebat. Et cuius dilectio in corde illius non suscepit socium, eius operatio in carne illius non habebat exemplum'." *De Annuntiatione B. Virginis Mariae. Sermo II,* t.IX, 661a.

(65) "Secunda stella est praerogativa, quae est *puritas in summo,* quae in beatissima virgine quadrupliciter fuit secundum quatuor gradus, quorum primus *sanctificatio in utero* fuit, secundus, *virtutum exercitatio;* tertius, in *Spiritus sancti obumbratione;* quartus, in *Filii Dei conceptione.* In primo gradu purgata fuit, quia nulla in ea inclinatio ad aliquod peccati remansit, in quo et alios omnes sanctificatos in utero superavit; nam remansit ad minus inclinatio et dispositio ad peccatum veniale, ut patet in Ioanne Baptista, quo nemo *inter natos mulierum maior surrexit,* qui, licet sanctificatus in utero, tamen postmodum fugit in desertum, 'ne levi posset maculare vitam crimine linguae.' In secundo gradu purgata fuit non per *recessum* ab impuro scilicet, sed per *accessum* ad magis purum et ad summum purum. Similiter in tertio, quando Spiritus sanctus aqua suae benedictionis et chrismate sanctificationis dedicavit ipsam in Sanctam sanctorum, in quam intrare debuit summus pontifex semel in *anno benignitatis.* In quarto ingressa est maiestas Dei in templum."*De Assumtione B. Virginis Mariae. Sermo VI,* t.IX, 702b.

thou, my love, how beautiful art thou; besides what is hid within" (4:1). How beautiful in thy works through charity! How beautiful in thy body through chastity, *besides what is hid within,* in thy heart through humility! Of the third degree of Mary's purity the Psalm says: "The Most High has sanctified his own tabernacle" (Ps. 45:5) and St. Luke: "The Holy Ghost shall come upon thee" (1:35). Isaias had said: "There shall come forth a root out of the rod of Jesse, and a flower shall rise up out of his root, and the spirit of the Lord shall rest upon him" (11:1, 2), and, indeed, upon her, too. In the fourth degree of Mary's purification, that is, in the conception of the Son of God, there is a union of our humanity with the Divinity of Christ, as symbolized in every Holy Mass by the mixture of the water and the wine. Concerning this degree, Ezechiel says: "The majesty of the Lord went into the temple by the way of the gate that looked to the east" (43:4 and 43:2), and the earth grew resplendent with the majesty of God. Do we wonder, then, at the brilliant splendor of Mary, in whom was encased the Light of the whole world, of all things celestial and supercelestial? Mary was then so resplendent with sanctity that Joseph could not bring his gaze to rest upon her, and this is not strange, for the eye of the owl cannot look at the Sun in his chariot. At the conception of Christ, all the radiance of the Eternal Sun was in the Moon, Mary. Then, truly, was there an eclipse of the Sun, an emptying of the Deity. Concerning this last degree of Mary's purity, this purest of purity, St. Anselm says that God's holy Mother shone with a purity second only to the purity of God.[66]

O Mary, Mother Most Pure,
Pray for us!

* * *

We are awed by the splendor of the magnificent temple which Solomon, the wisest of the ancient kings, erected to the Most High God. Surely it was a House of Gold, for "there was nothing in the temple that was not covered with purest gold." The oracle or Holy of Holies, the house before the oracle, the altar, the two winged cherubim, the floor of the house, within and without, were all overlaid with gold" (III Kings 6:20-30). "The altar of gold,

(66) "In primo gradu purificationis confertur beatissimae Virgini perfectio *graduum sacramentalium;* in secundo, perfectio *virtutum* et *beatitudinum;* in tertio, *donorum;* in quarto, perfectio *fructuum.* De primo, Canticorum quarto: *Tota pulcra est, amica mea,* ab originali, *total pulcra,* ab actuali mortali, *et macula,* venialis peccati, *non est in te.* De secundo, in eodem: *Quam pulcra est, amica mea, quam pulcra es! absque eo quod intrinsecus latet; quam pulcra* in *opere* per caritatem, quam pulcra in *corpore* per castitatem; *absque eo quod intrinsecus latet,* in *corde per humilitatem.* De tertio gradu puritatis, Psalmus: *Sanctificavit tabernaculum suum Altissimus;* et Lucae primo: *Spiritus sanctus superveniet in te;* Isaiae undecimo: *Egredietur virga de radice Iesse; et requiescet super eum Spiritus Domini;* haud dubium, quin et super eam. De quarto gradu, Ezechiel, ut si aliquod vas contineret aquam et vinum sine medio impermixta: *Maiestas Domini ingressa est templum per viam portae quae respiciebat ad orientem;* et tunc terra resplenduit a praesentia maiestatis Divinitatis; nec mirum, si resplenduit, in qua lux omnium caelestium et supercaelestium est inclusa. Unde Ioseph ipsam respicere non potuit; nec mirum, quia solem in rota oculus noctuae intueri non valuit. Cyclus enim solis in luna fuit; unde tunc vere eclipsis solis fuit, exinanitio Deitatis. De hac, inquam, purissima puritate dicit Anselmus, quod 'ea puritate nitebat, qua sub Deo nequit maior intelligi'." *Ibid.,* 702b, 703a.

the table of gold, golden candlesticks, lamps of gold and golden snuffers, and pots, and fleshhooks, and bowls, and mortars, and censers, of most pure gold. And the hinges for the doors of the inner house of the Holy of Holies, and for the doors of the house of the temple were of gold" (III Kings 7:48-50),—everything was of gold, for nothing could be too rich or magnificent for the House of God.

When the Word of God took flesh of the Virgin and dwelt within her breast, Mary became the living temple of the Most High, the Mystic House of Gold, a temple which the adorable Trinity deigned to beautify with all the gracious gifts of heaven and earth, for she was the beloved Daughter of the Father, the Mother of the Only-begotten Son, and the Spouse of the Holy Ghost. The Triune God dwelt within the Virgin's womb, the glorious temple of God *fashioned* by Divine Power, *adorned* by Divine Wisdom, *dedicated* by Divine Grace, and *filled* with the Divine Presence. The building or exquisite workmanship of this living temple is ascribed to the power of the Father; its adornment, to the wisdom of the Son; its dedication, to the grace of the Holy Ghost; the filling of the temple, to the presence of the Incarnate Word, for although Mary was the magnificent abode of the Three Persons of the Most Blessed Trinity, she was in a very special sense the Temple and dwelling-place of the Incarnate Word.[67]

O Mary, Mystic House of Gold, thou temple of the incarnate God,
Pray for us!

* * *

Note that the temple of the virginal womb was dedicated by God in holiness. Indeed, "the Most High hath sanctified His own tabernacle" (Ps. 45:5), and truly of Mary may we say: "Holy is thy temple, wonderful in justice" (Ps. 64:5). The temple which was Mary, like the magnificent temple of Solomon, was built in perfect proportion and symmetry. She was "wonderful in justice," for she was the great meeting-place of faith and reason, of a mother and a virgin, of God and man,—the first in her *mind,* the second in her *flesh,* the third in her *Child.*[68]

"Holy is thy temple." Dionysius defines holiness as "freedom from all sin

(67) "Secundum *allegoriam* vero nomine templi datur intellgi *uterus Virginis,* in quo tota Divinitas corporaliter habitavit; et ideo recte dicitur Dei templum *fabricatum* divina potentia, *adornatum* divina sapientia, *dedicatum* divina gratia et *adimpletum* divina praesentia. Debetur enim huius templi fabricatio potentiae Patris; adornatio, sapientiae Filii; dedicatio, gratiae Spiritus sancti; adimpletio, praesentiae Verbi incarnati. Cum enim sit 'totius Trinitatis nobile triclinium,' est tamen Verbi incarnati speciale templum et hospitium." *De Purificatione B. Virginis Mariae. Sermo IV,* t.IX, 651a.

(68) "De templo *uteri virginalis* nota, quod fuit a Deo *dedicatum in sanctificatione,* quando scilicet 'sanctificavit tabernaculum suum Altissimus,' sicut dicitur in Psalmo. Tunc enim potuit dici: 'Sanctum est templum tuum, mirabile in aequitate.' Et re vera in hoc templo mirabilis fuit adequatio, quando convenerunt fides et ratio, mater et virgo, Deus et homo: primum in *mente,* secundum in *carne,* tertium in *prole.*" *Collationes in Ioannem* Cap.II. Coll.X, t.VI, 548b.

and unalloyed goodness." To speak of holiness, then, is to speak of purity.[69] By her fullness of grace and freedom from sin, Mary became the "Mirror of Justice,"—the stainless, spotless mirror that perfectly reflected the light of God. By heritage of birth, Jesus resembled Mary. She was His only parent, His only bond with the human race. His Flesh was hers alone. She alone nourished Him. Jesus and Mary, then, we may suppose, looked very much alike. In a sense, the one was the reflection of the other. Christ was the physical reflection of Mary, or, reversing the process, we may say with equal truth that Mary was the spiritual reflection of Christ. Of which was Dante thinking when he said:

Now raise thy view
Unto the visage most resembling Christ.

If holiness consists in a likeness of Christ, then no soul was ever so like the soul of Christ as was that of His immaculate Mother. Mary's soul is a mirror, not flawed or broken or covered with spots but Christlike, a shining mirror of all holiness.[70] "She is the brightness of eternal light, and the unspotted mirror of God's majesty, and the image of his goodness" (Wis. 7:26). "Holy is thy temple, wonderful in justice."

O Mary, Mirror of Justice,
Pray for us!

* * *

Our Lady is Wisdom's fairest shrine, for she is the Mother of the Eternal Wisdom of the Father. "Wisdom hath built herself a house," says the Book of Proverbs (9:1). What did she not know of God in whom the Wisdom of God lay hidden and in whose womb He fitted for Himself a body?[71] Mary surpassed all others in wisdom because her intimate union with Christ was the sum and measure of her enlightenment. Quoting St. Bernard, the Seraphic Doctor says: "Mary penetrated the deepest abyss of divine wisdom, that is, as far as the condition of a creature permits; she seemed immersed in that 'light inaccessible'."[72] Even in this life she enjoyed perfect contemplation of God and possessed in mind and heart the sublimest secrets of heaven. She knew the mystery of the Incarnation by which she became the living temple of the Deity,—an ineffable mystery over which the Virgin draws a veil of secrecy at the moment it is accomplished within her. Who but Mary alone,

(69) "Dionysius dicit, quod 'sanctitas est ab omni contamine munda et sincera bonitas'; igitur non est aliud loqui de sanctificatione quam de purificatione." *De Purificatione B. Virginis Mariae. Sermo II,* t.IX, 641a.

(70) "Fuit enim in ea omnis sanctificationis *receptaculum mundum* ex gratiae divinae plentitudine; fuit omnis sanctificationis *speculum praeclarum." Ibid.*, 641b.

(71) "Ex illa autem carne sapientia Patris, scilicet ipse Filius Dei, aedificavit sibi corpus immaculatum, et illud corpus univit sibi et animae rationali." *III Sent.*, d.15, a.1, q.3, t.III, 335a.

(72) "Maria Virgo hac sapientia fuit plena, secundum quod dicit Bernardus: 'Maria profundissimam divinae sapientiae penetravit abyssum, ut, quantum de creatura credi fas est, illi luci inaccessibili videatur immersa'." *De Nativitate B. Virginis Mariae. Sermo V,* t.IX, 717b.

who most happily deserved to experience the mystery, could grasp by the understanding or discern by reason how that Splendor Inaccessible could pour Himself into the Virgin's womb and how she could bear the Inaccessible to come to her and dwell within her as in a cloud, His greatness and majesty concealed? And perhaps it was for this reason that the power of the Holy Ghost *overshadowed her,* that the great mystery of the Incarnation which the Holy Trinity wished to accomplish in the Virgin might be known to her alone whose privilege it was to experience it. By thus overshadowing her, the Power and Wisdom of God, concealing His secret designs from others, revealed them to the Virgin alone. In the words of St. Bernard: "So great a mystery can be taught only by the Giver of the gift; it can be learned only by the recipient."[73]

In this prerogative, namely, this supernatural knowledge of matters of faith, Mary excels the Prophets. Wherefore she knew how to answer the question of the Prophet who asked "Who shall declare his generation?" (Isai. 53:8). Who, indeed, if not she who gave him birth? Mary could declare the generation of Christ, and in fact she did declare it to St. Luke, who wrote it down at her dictation, describing it in detail. In this knowledge she excelled John the Baptist who was "a prophet and more than a prophet" (Matt. 11:9), for she knew how to "loose the latchet of her Son's shoe,"—a thing which the Baptist knew not how to do. In this supernatural knowledge, she likewise excels the angels. Hence she can answer the question which puzzled them: "Who is this that cometh from Edom, with dyed garments from Bosra, this beautiful one in his robe, walking in the greatness of his strength?" (Isai. 63:1). Mary knew who He was, for it was she who made for Him "the robe of divers colors flowing to His feet" (cf. Gen. 37:3). This supernatural knowledge was not a transitory knowledge bestowed only for a time and on particular occasions, not the knowledge of ecstasy but a continuous, untroubled knowledge well suited to the throne of God and the resting-place of the Trinity. Like the blessed angels who surround the throne of God, Mary, even in this life, enjoyed the most exalted degree of contemplation, and this in a sublime manner without any withdrawal of her affections but with all the powers of her soul rendered Godlike in their operations. Let it not be said that Christ was nearer to any one in this life or better known

(73) "Quarta stella sive praerogativa est *perfecta Dei in via contemplatio* et mysterii incarnationis cognitio, quorum utrumque habuit in via, quamvis non de via. . . . Quis enim, excepta illa quae hoc sola in se felicissime meruit experiri, intellectu capere, ratione discernere possit, qualiter splendor ille inaccessibilis virgineis visceribus se infuderit, et ut illa inaccessibilem accedere ad se ferre potuisset, de portiuncula eiusdem corporis, cui se animatae contemperavit, reliquae massae umbraculum fuerit? Et fortasse propter hoc maxime dictum est *obumbrabit tibi,* quia res nimirum in sacramento erat, ed quod sola per se Trinitas in sola et cum sola Virgine voluit operari, soli datum est nosse, cui datum experiri." Et infra: 'Illum modum, quo, de Spiritu sancto concipies, *Dei virtus et sapientia Dei,* Christus, sic in suo secretissimo consilio obumbrando conteget et occultabit, quatenus sibi tantum notus habeatur et tibi; ac si Angelus respondeat Virgini: Quid a me quaeris quod in temetipsa experieris? Scies et feliciter scies, sed illo doctore, quo et auctore.' Et infra: 'Non potest doceri nisi a donante, et non potest addisci nisi a suscipiente." *De Assumtione B. Virginis Mariae. Sermo VI,* t.IX, 703b, 704a.

by any one than He was by His Mother. As a proof of this fact, all things that have been written of Wisdom in the Book of Ecclesiasticus are read and explained of Our Lady. This supernatural knowledge of hers the Lord wished to express by the figure of the Ark of the Covenant in which were enclosed the two tables of the law which God had given to Moses on Mt. Sinai and a golden pot of manna, as if to say: "Whatever wisdom or relishable knowledge there is, all this has been preserved in my Mother, who 'kept all these words, pondering them in her heart'."[74]

Hail, thou throne of the Sovereign King!
Seat of Wisdom,
Ark of the Covenant,
Pray for us!

* * *

"But Mary kept all these words, pondering them in her heart." Behold the habitual attitude of Mary's soul, the natural outcome of her love, that *perfection of charity,* which determined the direction of her thoughts, the center of her interests, the destination of her affections. As the Canticles tell us, Mary was full of charity and love. In her were concentrated the pure white flames of every affection which could glow within a woman's heart,—the deepest *natural* love, the most ardent *acquired* love, the most perfect *gratuitous* love, all three burning with the greatest intensity and uniting to form one overpowering love, the like of which could be experienced by no other individual.[75] The greatest *natural* love is the love of a mother for her son, as is pointed out in the Second Book of Kings, where David mourns the death of his brother Jonathan: "I grieve for thee, my brother Jonathan, exceeding beautiful and amiable to me above the love of women. As a mother loveth her only son, so did I love thee" (1:26). Now the Blessed Virgin

---

(74) "Et patuit, quod habuit perfectam Dei contemplationem et incarnationis cognitionem. Et haec praerogativa tres includit excellentias: prima est, quod excellit in hac praerogativa Prophetas, scilicet in cognitione; unde ipsa scivit solvere quaestionem Prophetae, qui quaesivit: *Generationem eius quis enarrabit?* cum responderi potest: Certe illa quae genuit. Illa enim enarrare potuit, et sicut enarravit Lucas, qui enarrat eam et describit. Secunda excellentia est, quod excellit in hac cognitione Ioannem Baptistam, qui fuit *propheta et plus quam propheta.* Unde ipsa scivit *dissolvere corrigiam calceamenti* Filii eius, quod nescivit Ioannes Baptista. Terta excellentia est, quod in hac cognitone antecellit Angelos; unde scit etiam solvere quaestionem eorum, quam quaerunt: Quis est iste qui venit de Edom? etc. Quis esset hic, illa scivit, quae ei tunicam talarem polymitam fecit. Notandum autem, quod haec cognitio *temporalis* non fuit, id est ad tempus collata et particularis vel non modum raptus, sed continua et per modum quietis, sicut decebat vere thronum Dei et triclinium Trinitatis. Unde et proprietas Thronorum ei maxime convenit proprie. . . . Secundum hunc modum, credo, quod summam contemplationem habuit in via, et hanc sublimiter et sine (affectionum) abstractione, sed omnes potentiae eius deiformes factae sunt in operationibus suis. Absit enim, quod unquam alicui in via familiarior fuerit vel notior quam Matri suae. In cuius rei argumentum omnia, quae scripta sunt de sapientia in Ecclesiastico, universa leguntur et exponuntur de Domina nostra; quod et Dominus exprimere voluit in figura, quando librum et mannam reponi fecit in arca, quasi dicat: Quidquid est saporis vel sapidae cognitionis, hoc totum reservatum est in Matre mea, quae *conservabat omnia verba haec, conferens in corde suo.*" *Ibid.*, 704ab.

"*Arca foederis Domini* est beata Virgo, in qua omnia arcana sunt recondita." *Sermones de Tempore. Feria Sexta in Parasceve. Sermo II,* t.IX, 263b.

(75) "Quinta stella est *perfectio caritatis;* in Canticis vidimus eam plenam caritate et dilectione, quae plenitudo constat in tribus. Habuit enim summam dilectionem *naturalem,* summam *acquisitam,* summam *gratuitam,* et unamquaque in summo et ex his tribus unam summam, cui in creaturis impossible est similem reperiri." *De Assumtione B. Virginis Mariae. Sermo VI,* t.IX, 704b.

had this love in the highest degree, for never did any mother love her son so dearly as Our Lady loved hers, and with a natural love. Now the nature of love is the nature of fire; the more it is scattered and divided, the less intense it is; the more concentrated it is, the stronger it becomes. All other mothers who had sons and "knew" their husbands had a divided love. Then, too, mothers sometimes had other sons and daughters, and so their love, being divided, was lessened for each individual child. This Mother alone had no husband; she had no other son or daughter; therefore her whole heart with all its natural affection she poured out on her Only-begotten Son. Hence Mary experienced the most intense natural love in the highest degree.[76] The greatest *acquired* love is the love of a bride for her spouse and that love the Virgin Mary had for her Son in the highest possible degree. Now if virgins are the spouses of Christ, the Virgin of Virgins was the most perfect Bride of the Spouse; not only did she "follow the Lamb whithersoever he goeth" (Apoc. 14:4), but the Lamb likewise followed her.[77] The greatest *gratuitous* love is charity, which love Mary possessed in the highest degree, for she was full of *charity* and *love*,—of *charity* for God, of *love* for her neighbor. And thus Mary united within herself these three great loves and of them formed one immense love,—a thing which she alone could do, for every other mother loves her son and she loves her God. In the one love, if it is a natural one, is the love of her son; in the other, the love of God. But this Mother of God alone had for her God the same love which she had for her Son, for her Son was her God. This love is the perfection of charity, whose mystery we can hardly hope to gauge.[78]

O Mary, Mother Most Amiable,
Pray for us!

* * *

It was this triple love burning in Mary's heart and focusing its combined flames on her Son and her God, that made Mary keep all these words, pondering them in her heart. The first words she heard of Jesus, the revelation

---

(76) "Summus amor *naturalis* est matris ad filium, iuxta illud: *Super amorem mulierum* etc. Hunc amorem habuit beatissima Virgo in summo; nunquam enim mater aliqua tantum amabat filium suum, quantum Domina nostra delexit suum et naturali dilectione. Natura enim amoris natura est ignis, qui, quanto plus spargitur et dividitur, tanto amplius minuitur, et quanto plus adunatur, tanto plus augmentatur. Omnes enim aliae matres, quae filios habuerunt, et viros cognoverunt, et sic divisum amorem habuerunt. Praeterea, matres et aliquando plures filios habuerunt vel filias, et sic amor divisus in singulis minuitur. Haec sola mater virum non habuit, filium vel filiam aliam non habuit; unde totum cor suum cum omni naturali virtute sua in suum Unigenitum transfudit; et sic habuit naturalem dilectionem summam in summo." *Ibid.*

(77) "Summa dilectio *caquisita* est ea quae est sponsae ad sponsum, et illam habuit Virgo Maria ad Filium suum in summo. Si enim virgines sponsae Christi sunt, ergo Virgo virginum sponsa erat summa Sponsi, quae non tantum *Agnum,* sed et ipsam *Agnus, quocumque ierat, sequebatur.*" *Ibid.*

(78) "Summus amor *gratuitus* caritas est, quam habuit etiam in summo. Plena enim, ut dictum est, fuit *caritate* et *dilectione: caritate* ad Deum, *dilectione* ad proximum. Et sic ista tria coniunxit summa, et sic unum summum fecit ex his; quod nunquam alia creatura facere potuit. Quaecumque enim alia creatura diligit filium suum et diligit Deum: in alia (dilectione) si sit naturalis dilectio filii; in alia, Dei; haec autem Mater Dei sola eandem dilectionem, quam habuit ad Filium suum, habuit ad Deum suum, quia Filius eius, Deus eius; et sic patet, quod in eadem fuit caritatis perfectio." *Ibid.*

of His coming, Mary kept in her heart and they blossomed forth into the *Magnificat,* that glorious song of praise and of gratitude, of prophecies and promises fulfilled. The angel of the Incarnation disturbed her; the angels of of Bethlehem, whose message came to her through the shepherds, left her pondering. She had been brought into physical, living contact with her God, but more than that, and affecting her more profoundly, was the intimate, loving contact of her soul with God. Mary's union with Christ was a *total* union, perfect and complete, spiritual as well as physical. She had received Christ in the nuptial chamber of her womb; she had nourished Him with her blood and fed Him at her breast; she had watched over His growing years and carefully supplied His every want but more than that, she had received Him in the chamber of her heart by constantly listening to His words, by believing in Him and loving Him, by ever striving to become more and more like Him. And St. Augustine says, her maternal relationship would have been of no avail to Mary if she had not borne Christ more happily in her mind than she had borne Him in her womb.[79] Of all creatures Mary was physically nearest to Christ because she was His Mother according to the flesh. But it was not that physical intimacy, almost unbelievably close though it was, but rather her spiritual resemblance to Christ, the supernatural affinity which made her mind and heart one with His, that constituted her real title to grandeur.

It was to His Mother, we may believe, that Christ alluded when He made answer to "a certain woman from the crowd," who "lifting up her voice, said to Him: Blessed is the womb that bore three and the breasts that nourished thee. But He said: Yea, rather blessed are they who hear the word of God and keep it" (Luke 11:27,28). Not contradicting the woman but enlarging upon her statement, Jesus says in effect: "Blessed not only the womb that bore me, the Word made Flesh, but even *more blessed* she who receives the word spoken by me." Mary was *blessed* because she bore Christ in her womb, but even *more blessed* because she bore Him perfectly in her heart. As St. Augustine says: "Mary was more blessed in conceiving the faith of Christ than she was in conceiving the flesh of Christ." And blessed, indeed, is everyone who hears and obeys. "If you know these things, you shall be blessed if you do them," says St. John (13:17). And St. James: "Be ye doers of the word and not hearers only" (1:22). Indeed, "blessed are they who hear the word of God and keep it." Thus, in the Gospel story, Our Lord took occasion to praise a nobler motherhood than that of flesh and blood, a motherhood in which His own Mother Mary was without a peer. Since her

(79) "Sive, quia hic agitur de duplici Christi susceptione: *corporali* et *spirituali: corporali* a Martha in hospitio domus exterioris; *spirituali* a Maria in hospitio domus interioris. Et haec duplex susceptio perfectissime fuit in Maria, quae ipsum suscepit in *thalamo corporis,* aluit et nutrivit et educavit et sedulo ministravit; suscepit etiam in *thalamo cordis* ipsum videndo, credendo, amando, imitando.... Unde Augustinus: 'Materna namque propinquitas nihil Mariae profuisset, nisi felicius ipsum mente quam carne gestasset'." *Comment. in Evang. Lucae X,* t.VII, 276a.

motherhood implies the most vivid bridal relation of Mary to God, we can easily understand the utterances of the Fathers in which the physiological side of the motherhood and Mary's union of love with God are so compared that the latter is invariably looked upon as the more sanctifying good. As St. Augustine says, union of minds and hearts is holier than union of bodies.[80]

On another occasion when Our Lord was preaching, He was interrupted by the announcement: "Behold, thy Mother . . . stands without, seeking thee. But he answering him that told him, said: Who is my mother and who are my brethren? And stretching forth his hand toward his disciples, he said: Behold my mother and my brethren. For whosoever shall do the will of my Father that is in heaven, he is my brother, and my sister, and mother" (Matt. 12:47-50). The meaning is unmistakable. There is such a thing as spiritual maternity, bonds other than those of flesh and blood. I acknowledge as my brethren, my sister, my mother those alone who do the will of my Father; I admit no other union with men than a union based on divine grace. Knowing that Mary had ever perfectly fulfilled the will of God, Jesus, though apparently assigning her a subordinate rank among His disciples, was in reality loudly proclaiming her as His Mother, pronouncing the highest encomium upon her, strongly expressing His love for her, and clearly testifying to the intimacy of her spiritual union with Him.

Mary's Spiritual Motherhood

Ordinarily a mother does not share, except from afar, in the lifework of her son. She accompanies him to the threshold of life and there relinquishes him to his wife, his helpmeet. Mary, however, was privileged to remain with Christ as His Helpmeet, His Bride, the Eve of the New Covenant, and to play a woman's part in the work of Redemption whereby children of grace are born to the heavenly Father. In the Garden of Eden, at the side of the first Adam, stood a mother who would bring forth children unto woe. At the side of Christ stands a mother who with Him will bring forth children unto redemption. For this special task and life's work, the riches of her bridal dowry and her anticipated and perfect redemption had perfectly prepared her. Her destiny is best described in the words in which God Himself referred to the first Eve: "Let us make him a helpmeet like unto himself" (Gen.

(80) "Tertio vero quantam ad *approbationem laudis expressae* subdit: At ille dixit: *Quin immo beati, qui audiunt verbum Dei*. Hoc non dicit adversando, sed potius superaddendo, quasi dicat: non solum *beatus* venter, qui portavit me, Verbum caro factum, verum etiam *beatior* qui suscipit verbum a me prolatum. Unde et Maria non tantum *beata* fuit, quia Christum gestavit in carne, verum etiam *beatior,* quia perfectissime gestavit in mente, secundum quod dicit Augustinus: 'Beatior fuit Maria concipiendo fidem Christi quam carnem Christi'. Beatus est enim omnis, qui audit et obedit, secundum illud Ioannis decimo tertio: 'Si haec scitis, beati eritis, si feceritis ea'. Et deo subdit: *Et custodiunt illud;* et ideo Iacobi primo: "Estote factores verbi et non auditores tantum'. In quo verbo Christus noluit, laudari mere cognationem *carnalem* per se; nam ita dicitur Iudaeis supra tertio: 'Nolite dicere: Patrem habemus Abraham' etc.; sed *spiritualem,* quia sanctior est copula mentium quam corporum." *Comment. in Evangelium Lucae* C.XI, t.VII, 297a.

2:20), for it was of Mary that the words were prophetically spoken and it was in her that they found their fulfillment.[81] It is only in sharing the *work* of her Divine Spouse that the holy Mother of God stands forth in the full glory of her character as Bride of the Incarnate Word.

The doctrine of Mary's co-operation in the work of Redemption is implicit in the fundamental dogma of her virginal Motherhood. Chosen to be the Mother of God, Mary was thereby destined to be associated with Him in the work of redeeming the human race. Though her consent was the work of divine grace with which Mary fully co-operated, we cannot minimize the merit attached to the freedom of her choice. This is the reason why the Fathers delighted in beholding Mary as the New Eve. They did not speak of the Blessed Virgin as the mere physical instrument of Our Lord's taking flesh, but as an intelligent responsible cause of it, her faith and obedience being accessories to the Incarnation, and gaining it as her reward.

In the mystery of the Redemption St. Bonaventure finds an amazing parallel running in inverse order to the Fall, a remarkable antithesis which serves to throw the role of Mary into strong relief. As the human race had fallen through the *suggestion of the devil* and the *consent of the woman* whom he had deceived, and through *propagation according to the law of concupiscence* transmitting original sin to the offspring, so it was fitting, says the Saint, that in the restoration there should be a *good angel* proposing good and a *Virgin full of faith* consenting to the good proposed, and *the love of the Holy Spirit* sanctifying her and making her fruitful for a conception without sin, that thus "contraries by contraries might be compensated." And so just as a woman deceived by an angel of darkness and known and corrupted by man in concupiscence, transmitted to all her descendants sin, disease, and death, so now a woman instructed by an angel of light, sanctified and made fruitful by the Holy Ghost, free from all corruption of mind as well as of body, brought forth a Child Who would give to all those who would come to Him grace, health, and life.[82] By giving herself to God in obedience and faith, Mary, the Virgin pure and undefiled, paved the way for our salvation and in all truth became the "Cause of Our Joy."

When Gabriel proposed the Divine Motherhood to the Virgin, he painted no grandiose picture of the Son Who was to be born of her. On the contrary,

---

(81) ". . . sed novit ab ipsa adiuvari, ut adimpleretur quod de eo prophetice dictum fuit, Genesis secundo: *Faciamus ei adiutorium simile sibi." De Assumtione B. Virginis Mariae. Sermo VI,* t.IX, 704b.

(82) "Quoniam ergo incarnatio est a primo principio reparante modo congruentissimo; et congruus modus est, quod medicina ex opposito respondeat morbo, et reparatio lapsui, et remedium nocumento; cum genus humanum lapsum fuerit per *diabolicam suggestionem* et per *consensum mulieris* deceptae et per *generationem concupiscentialem,* transfundentem originale in prolem: oportuit, quod e contrario hic esset *Angelus bonus* suadens bonum, *et Virgo credens* et consentiens in bonum suasum, et *caritas Spiritus sancti* sanctificans et fecundans ad conceptum immaculatum; ut sic 'contraria contrariis curarentur'. Ac per hoc, sicut mulier, per diabolum decepta et per virum concupsicibiliter cognita et corrupta, transfudit in omnes culpam, morbum et mortem; sic mulier, per Angelum erudita et per Spiritum sanctum sanctificata et fecundata, absque omni corruptione tam mentis quam corporis prolem generaret, quae omnibus ad ipsam venientibus daret gratiam, sanitatem et vitam." *Breviloquium,* Pars IV, Cap. III, t.V, 243b.

he portrayed Him as the Saviour, the expected Messiah, the Eternal King of regenerated mankind. He was to be called Jesus, Saviour,—a name which expresses His destiny as well as His mission, for the saviours are the crucified. Upon the commission of God, the Angel extended to Mary the invitation to become the Mother of the Saviour. Too deeply versed in the spiritual meaning of the prophecies not to know that the Messiah was to be "a man of sorrows" (Isai. 53:3), "a worm and no man, the reproach of men and the outcast of the people" (Ps. 21:7), Mary was not taken by surprise when she pronounced her glorious *fiat,* "Be it done unto me according to thy word."

In accepting the title proposed to her by the angel, Mary stood in need of a fund of heroism, generosity, and courage, and she was not found wanting. She is the Valiant Woman whom Solomon commends for her dauntless courage when he asks: "Who shall find the valiant woman?" Not in despair does he ask, but confidently. Who, then, shall find her? Eternal Wisdom Himself, Who "reacheth from end to end mightily and ordereth all things sweetly" (Wis. 8:1), He shall find her and send to her the "friend of the Bridegroom." Gabriel, the Archangel, is sent to find the valiant woman. Undoubtedly the King wished to repose in her as in a safe abode, for which reason she must be valiant, for it is written that "threescore valiant ones of the most valiant of Israel surrounded the bed of Solomon" (Cant. 3:7). The Bride of the King must be a valiant woman, ever ready to obey the dictates of the natural law and the commandments of God, ever invincible to attack from without. "Strength and beauty are her clothing" (Prov. 31:25). As the body is adorned by its raiment, so is the soul adorned with fortitude. Fortitude is the raiment of the glorious Virgin. Wherefore the prophet says: "Arise, arise, put on thy strength, O daughter of Sion, put on the garments of thy glory" (Isai. 52:1).[83] Without hesitation, Mary executed the ringing command. Her answer was clear, definite, fearless, complete: "Behold the handmaid of the Lord. Be it done unto me according to thy word."

St. Bernard says: "If our salvation and the salvation of the whole world, if the restoration of innocence is to be placed in the hands of a woman, a valiant woman must be found, one who will be equal to the task," and he adds: "Not from earth, nor from the near heaven but from the end of heaven is his going out" (cf. Ps. 18:7). "Far and from the uttermost coasts is the

(83) "Primo, dico, commendatur a *spiritualis fortitudinis robore,* cum dicit: *Mulierem fortem quis inveniet?* Quaerit non desperando, sed confidendo. Quis igitur inveniet? Certe ille qui *attingit a fine usque ad finem;* ipse inveniet eam et misit ad eam paranymphum, id est Gabrielem Archangelum. Gabriel interpretatur *fortitudo Dei* et ipse missus est ad inveniendum *fortem mulierem*. Absque dubio Salomon in ea voluit requiescere tanquam in loco securo: sed hoc non potuit esse, nisi esset fortis, quia dicitur in Cantico, quod ante *lectum Salomonis ambiunt sexaginta fortes*. Salomon interpretatur *rex desiderabilis;* lectum eius ambiunt sexaginta fortes . . . Quantum aliquis est fortis et expeditus secundum dictamen legum et praeceptorum decalogi; tunc est fortis, ita quod ab exteriori laedi non potest. Unde in Proverbiis: *Fortitudo et decor indumentum eius*. Sicut corpus ornatur ex habitu, ita ornatur anima ex fortitudine; ideo dicitur indumentum *animae;* nec solum fortitudo est indumentum animae, vel *Virginis gloriosae* . . . Unde Isaias: *Consurge, consurge, filia Sion; induere vestimentis gloriae tuae." De Donis Spiritus Sancti. Collatio V. De Dono Fortitudinis,* t.V, 479b, 480a.

price of her" (Prov. 31:10). This is the price of which the Apostle says: "You are bought with a great price. Glorify and bear God in your body" (I Cor. 6:20). How great that price is the Apostle Peter tells: "You were not redeemed with corruptible things, as gold or silver, . . . but with the precious Blood of Christ, as of a lamb unspotted and undefiled" (I Pet. 1:18, 19). Behold the great price by which the whole world and the whole human race were to be redeemed! And since it was impossible for one man to make satisfaction for all men, and for a mere creature to atone for an insult offered to God, the price had to be both human and divine. Where shall that price be found? Certainly nowhere except in the womb of the glorious Virgin, that the words of Isaias might be fulfilled: "Behold a virgin shall conceive and bear a son, and his name shall be called Emmanuel" (7:14), "God with us." It was fitting that the Virgin have only God for a Son; that God have only a Virgin for His Mother. That price could be found only in the Virgin. "Far and from the uttermost coasts is the price of her," for therein is the Highest joined with the lowest, the First, with the last. *Far* is the price by which the whole human race is redeemed. Because the *lowest* is redeemed, the price is the *Most High;* because man, the *last* of creation, is redeemed, the price is the *First Beginning* of all things.[84]

It is an article of faith that Christ came to us by the Immaculate Virgin; to her we owe Our Saviour. Within her sacred womb she conceived the God-Man. She alone furnished the Flesh and Blood, the twin matter of sacrifice, the price of our Redemption. He was "bone of her bone and flesh of her flesh," for she was the one and only principle of His Humanity. The Blood which flowed in the Circumcision, in the Praetorium, and on Calvary had once flowed in her veins. She had supplied, too, the first substance of the Body which was torn in the scourging and nailed to the Cross. "Go forth, ye daughters of Sion, and see the King in the diadem wherewith his mother crowned him" (Cant. 3:11). That diadem is nothing else but the Humanity of Christ, says the Seraphic Doctor, for as a diadem encircles the heads of kings, so was Christ encircled by that most pure flesh in the womb of the most holy Virgin who wrapped Him 'round with that stainless flesh when

(84) "Hoc non habeo ex me, sed Bernardus dicit: 'Si nostra et omnium salus, si innocentiae restitutio posita est in manu mulieris, necesse est, ut fortis mulier quaeratur, quae ad tantum opus est necessaria'; et subdit: 'Non de terra, non de caelo propinquo, sed a summo caelo egressio eius'. '*Procul* igitur et de ultimis finibus pretium eius'. Hoc est pretium, de quo dicit Apostolus: *Empti estis pretio magno; portate et glorificate Deum in corpore vestro.* Quo pretium illud sit magnum, dicit Apostolus Petrus: *Non corruptibilibus auro vel argento redempti estis de vana vestra conversatione paternae traditionis, sed pretioso sanguine quasi Agni immaculati et incontaminati.* Hoc debuit esse pretium magnum, quo redimi debebat totus mundus et totum genus humanum; quia homo satisfacere non potuit, quia nullus homo potuit valere omnes homines, nec creatura aliqua. Nihil fuit sufficiens ad redimendum totum genus humanum, nisi haberet humanam et naturam super omnem creaturam; ergo oportuit, quod haberet naturam divinam et humanam. Illud pretium ubi invenietur? Certe nusquam nisi in utero Virginis gloriosae. Unde Isaias: *Ecce, Virgo concipiet et pariet filium, et vocabitur nomen eius Emmanuel. Emmanuel* interpretatur *nobiscum Deus.* Non decebat Virginem habere filium nisi Deum, nec Deum habere matrem nisi Virginem. Pretium illud non potuit inveniri nisi in Virgine. *Procul et de ultimis finibus* est, quia in ipso coniunctum est *summum* cum *infimo, et primum* cum *ultimo.* Pretium illud *procul* est, quo redimitur totum genus humanum; quia redimitur *infimum,* ideo est *summum;* quia redimitur *ultimum,* ideo est *primum.* Homo inter creaturas ultimo creatus est." *Ibid., Coll. VI. De Dono Fortitudinis,* t.V, 484a.

He was formed from her most pure and virgin blood by the operation of the Holy Ghost. Significantly does Sacred Scripture say *his mother,* for His Father had already crowned Him with the diadem of an everlasting kingdom. Now His Mother has crowned Him with the diadem of a temporal kingdom, namely, His all-pure and adorable flesh.[85] St. Paul once said to the Hebrews: "But Christ, being come a high priest of the good things to come, by a greater and more perfect tabernacle, not made by hand, that is, not of this creation, neither by the blood of goats or of calves, but by His own blood, entered once into the Holies" (9:11, 12). Christ, our High Priest, entering into the Holy of Holies," comments St. Bonaventure, "passed through the womb of the Virgin, where he received the pontifical robe, and from thence to the gibbet of the Cross on which He offered the most holy victim and thereby brought us into a covenant with God." Commenting further on the passage, the Seraphic Doctor says that the Apostle here stresses two points: the dignity of the virginal womb in the words "by a greater tabernacle"; the excellence of Christ's oblation on the Cross in the words "by His own Blood," for it was within the womb of the Virgin that Christ assumed the gleaming white and crimson robe of His adorable Flesh and Blood which He offered in sacrifice on Calvary.[86]

On Calvary Mary completed her life's work by sharing in the work of greatest love,—the redemption of the human race through suffering. That it was a work of the greatest love is seen from the testimony of Christ Himself: "Greater love than this no man hath, that a man lay down his life for his friends" (John 15:13). The Father of mercies knew that Christ *accomplished* the Redemption out of mercy towards mankind but He also knew that He was *helped* by the Mother of mercy, that the words prophetically spoken of Him in the Garden of Eden might be fulfilled: "Let us make him a helpmeet like unto himself" (Gen. 2:18). It is no mere paradox that the deepest happiness is often conjoined with the most poignant suffering. Even human love, if it be pure and unselfish, love worthy of the name, means sacrifice, and in sacrifice there is hidden joy. This mysterious union of joy and sorrow finds its highest expression in Our Lord Himself, Whose human

(85) "Sequitur: *in diademate, quo coronavit eum mater sua.* Diadema illud non est nisi humanitas Christi. Sicut enim diadema circumcingitur capitibus regum, sic ipse Christus fuit circumdatus illa beatissima carne in ventre Virginis sacratissimae, quae circumgyravit illam carnem mundissimam, quando de purissimis et virgineis sanguinibus sive humoribus suis generatus est Christus operatione Spiritus sancti. Dicit autem signanter *mater sua,* quoniam Pater coronavit eum diademate regni aeterni, sed mater Virgo coronat diademate temporalis regni, scilicet carnis mortalis mundissimae et venerabilis." *Sermones de Tempore. In Nativitate Domini. Sermo XIX,* t.IX, 121ab.

(86) "De quo assumsit sibi *ornamentum sacerdotale,* ut cum illo introiret in Sancta; unde ad Hebraeos nono: *Christus assistens pontifex noster futurorum bonorum per amplius et perfectius tabernaculum non manufactum, id est non huius creationis, neque per sanguinem hircorum aut vitulorum, sed per proprium sanguinem introivit semel in Sancta.* Christus, *pontifex* noster, introiens *in Sancta,* transivit per uterum Virginis, in quo accepit pontificalem stolam, et per patibulum crucis in qua obtulit sanctissimam hostiam et per hoc Deo nos confoederavit. Haec duo tangit Apostolus in (illa) auctoritate: quantum ad dignitatem uteri virginalis dicit: *per amplius tabernaculum;* quantum ad excellentiam oblationis crucis dicit: *per proprium sanguinem.* Ibi enim vestimentum candidum et rubicundum, quod in utero Virginis sumsit." *De Annuntiatione B. Virginis Mariae. Sermo IV,* t.IX, 673ab.

soul, even in the hour of its utmost dereliction, enjoyed unutterable bliss. And as her Son experienced the deepest joy and the deepest sorrow on the Cross and through the Cross, so Mary His Mother experienced the deepest *joy* and the deepest *sorrow* beneath the Cross and near the Cross. Christ experienced in its most poignant form the *natural sorrow* which accompanies death; he experienced, too, the deepest *spiritual joy* over the redemption of the human race. Of the first, the prophet Jeremias said: "O all ye that pass by the way, attend, and see if there be any sorrow like to my sorrow" (Lam. 1:12). The most convincing proof of the second,—that bloody sweat, "trickling down upon the ground" (Luke 22:44), undeniable evidence not of fear but of love, for fear constrains the heart, retards the flow of blood and restricts the breathing, leaving the bodily extremities cold and bringing terror and dread; but joy expands the soul, makes the blood course through the veins, opening the pores, and warming the extremities. From these facts we may naturally gather that the bloody sweat was proof of the ineffable joy which our Saviour experienced in the knowledge that He redeemed us in the most loving manner conceivable. Our Lady, likewise, experienced the deepest *natural sorrow* out of love for her Son, Whose death she beheld before her eyes; she experienced the deepest *spiritual joy* in the knowledge that One born of her had redeemed the human race with so great manifestation of love. Of the first, St. Luke says: "And thy own soul a sword shall pierce" (2:35); of the second, St. Ambrose remarks: "Mary *stood* near the Cross to await, not the sufferings of her Son, but the salvation of the human race."[87]

Hail, thou that didst dry the tears of Eve!
Mother of Our Redeemer,
Pray for us!

* * *

On Calvary Mary proved herself a "Singular Vessel of Devotion." Let us

(87) "Sexta stella est actus *excellentissimae caritatis communicatio*, quae fuit redemptio generis humani per passionem; quem actum gloriosissimum et summae caritatis demeruit, ipso attestante, qui ait: *Caritatem nemo habet maiorem* etc. (Hunc) novit Pater misericordiarum, sive Mater misericordiae *exercere*, utpote effectum summae misericordiae; sed (ille) ab ipsa *adiuvari*, ut adimpleretur quod de eo prophetice dictum fuit, Genesis secundo: *Faciamus ei adiutorium simile sibi*. Ipsa enim ad similitudinem Filii sui sub cruce et iuxta crucem habuit summum *gaudium* et summum *dolorem*, sicut Filius in cruce et per crucem. Summum habuit *dolorem naturalem* de morte et summum *gaudium rationale* de humani generis redemptione. De primo, Threnorum primo: *O vos omnes, qui transitis per viam*. De secundo argumentum efficacissimum, *sudor* ille *sanguineus, decurrens in terram*, qui non tam ex timore quam ex amore processit. Timor enim cor constringit, sanguinem et spiritum retrahit, extrema corporis frigida relinquit, tremorem et horribilationem efficit; gaudium autem aperit spiritum et sanguinem per corpus diffundit, poros aperit, extremitates calefacit. Ex his naturaliter colligi potest, quod sudor ille sanguineus ineffabilis gaudii argumentum fuit, quod Redemptor noster habuit super eo, quod amicabilissimo modo, qui excogitari poterat, nos redemit. Similiter et Mater benedicta summum habuit *dolorem naturalem* ex dilectione Filii pro morte, quam praesens aspexit; summam *dilectionem rationalem* super eo, quod ille qui de ea natus est, tanta caritatis ostensione humanum genus redemit. De primo, Lucae secundo: *Tuam ipsius animam pertransibit gladius*. De secundo Ambrosius (dicit), quod 'stabat iuxta crucem, non ut dolorem Filii, sed ut salutem generis humani exspectaret'." *De Assumtione B. Virginis Mariae. Sermo VI*, t.IX, 704b, 705a.

hear something of her devotion, says St. Bonaventure, for she is our hope, this valiant and loving woman, who in mysterious union with Christ as He enacted the drama of His redemptive love, offered the price of our Redemption in *loving reverence for God,* in *loving compassion for Christ,* and in *loving pity for the world,* especially for the whole body of Christians.[88]

Valiant and loving, Mary paid that price, first, in *loving reverence for God.* Full of reverence and zeal for the restoration of His honor, with courage surpassing that of Anna, the mother of Samuel, who offered her son to the service of the Lord, or that of the poor widow who cast into the treasury "two brass mites, all the living that she had, this Woman, the glorious Virgin, so full of mercy, so loving and devoted to God, offered her whole substance, her dear and only Son, to satisfy the inexorable justice which demanded so noble a victim.[89]

Valiant and loving, the Blessed Virgin, paid the price, secondly, in *loving compassion for Christ.* In St. John we read: "A woman, when she is in labor, hath sorrow, because her hour is come" (16:21). A woman hath sorrow when she is about to bring forth her child. Mary experienced no sorrow before the birth of Christ, because she did not conceive in sin, as did Eve, to whom a curse was given, but she suffered deepest anguish when she brought us forth at the foot of the Cross. Then, indeed, were fulfilled the words of Simeon: "And thy own soul a sword shall pierce" (Luke 2:35). Other women suffer physical sorrow, but Mary, the sorrow of compassion and of love.[90] Her feelings at that moment surpass the comprehension of mortal mind; she endured the agonies of a spiritual death, incomparably more terrible than those of corporal dissolution. It was then she uttered the groans she had not known at the birth of Jesus. She suffered a martyrdom of love, and the words of the Psalm were fulfilled: "The iron pierced her soul" (104:18). As the Damascene says: "The sorrow which she escaped at childbirth, Mary endured at the time of the Passion." She saw the sacred side of Jesus pierced with a lance, but Jesus was already dead and the pain

---

(88) "Audiamus aliquid de pietate eius. Haec est spes nostra, quae persolvit pretium istud, ut pia pietate *venerationis divinae;* secundo, *pietate compassionis ad Christum;* et tertio, pietate *miserationis ad mundum,* et praecipue ad populum christianum." *De Dono Fortitudinis Coll. II,* t.V, 486b.

(89) "Primo, dico, persolvit pretium istud fortis et pietate *venerationis divinae.* . . . Et beata Virgo est venerativa et restaurativa honoris Deo subtracti, et mater consentiens, quod Christus in pretium offerretur. Ergo laudabitur. Laudata fuit Anna, quia obtulit Samuelem. Laudatur vidua paupercula, quia totum, quod habuit; sed haec mulier, scilicet Virgo gloriosa, misericordiosissima, pia et Deo devota obtulit totam substantiam suam. . . . Beata Virgo solvit pretium illud fortis et pia pietate venerationis divinae." *Ibid.,* 486b, 487a.

(90) "Secundo persolvit pretium illud Virgo gloriosa, fortis et pia pietate *compassionis ad Christum.* Dicitur in Ioanne: *Mulier, cum parit, tristitiam habet, quia venit hora eius.* Propter parturitionem habet mulier dolorem, scilicet antecedentem ad partum. Sed beata Virgo non habuit dolorem antecedentem partum; quia non concepit ex peccato, sicut Eva, cui maledictio data est; sed habuit dolorem post partum. Unde peperit, antequam parturiret. In cruce parturivit; unde in Luca: *Et tuam ipsius animam pertransibit gladius.* In aliis mulieribus est dolor corporis, in ista est dolor compassionis et caritatis." *Ibid.,* 487a.

wounded only the Mother's heart which was then, in truth, pierced through. Because she suffered anguish of soul, says St. Jerome, Mary was more than a Martyr.[91] Let us compassionate Our Lady as she compassionated her dearly beloved Son and say to her:

"O Mary, Queen of Martyrs,
Pray for us!"

* * *

Valiant and loving, the Blessed Virgin paid the price of our salvation, thirdly, in *loving pity for the world,* and especially for the whole body of Christians. "Can a woman forget her infant, so as not to have pity on the son of her womb? And if she should forget, yet will I not forget thee," said Isaias (49:15), expressing the undying love of Christ and His Blessed Mother for souls. And here we are given to understand that the whole body of Christians has been brought forth from the womb of the glorious Virgin,—a mystery prefigured in the formation of the first woman from the side of man. The Book of Genesis tells us: *Then the Lord cast a deep sleep upon Adam, and when he was fast asleep, he took one of his ribs and built it into a woman, and he brought her to Adam. And Adam said: This now is bone of my bones, and flesh of my flesh; she shall be called woman, because she was taken out of man.* And the Lord said: *Wherefore a man shall leave father and mother* and sons and daughters, *and shall cleave to his wife* (Gen. 2:21-24). And the Apostle said: *This is a great sacrament, but I speak in Christ and in the Church* (Eph. 5:32). "Why," queries the Seraphic Doctor, "did God take a rib from Adam while he slept? Could He not have done it if he were awake?" "This," continues the Saint, "is a solemn and mysterious symbol of the formation of the Church from the side of Christ as He fell asleep in death on the Cross. The water and blood which flowed from the pierced side of Christ are symbols of the two sacraments, Baptism and Holy Eucharist, by which the Church is reborn. Eve was formed from the rib of Adam to whom she was joined in wedlock. As man was formed from the virgin earth, so Christ, from the Virgin Mary. And as woman was formed

---

(91) "Quantum ad *martyrium compassionis maternae* dictur: Et tuam ipsius animam *pertransibit gladius,* id est tui ipsius, gladius compassionis; unde sibi competit illud Psalmi: 'Ferum pertransivit animam eius'. Damascenus: 'Dolores, quos pariens effugit, tempore passionis sustinuit'. Et Bernardus: 'Dum perforatur lancea ille tuus Iesus, omnium quidem, sed specialiter *tuus;* **ipsius** animam non gladius pertransivit, quia iam ille exspiraverat, sed tuam, unde te plus quam Martyrem praedicamus'. Et Hieronymus: 'Quia mente passa est, plus quam Martyr fuit'. Unde, quia ipsa veraciter diligebat, ex affectu intimo vehementer compatiebatur." *Comment. in Evangelium Lucae* C.II, t.VII, 61b.

from the side of Adam as he lay in sleep, so from the side of Christ as He hung in the sleep of death upon the Cross was formed His Spouse, the Church. And as Abel and his descendants were formed from Adam and Eve, so the whole body of Christians from Christ and His Church. And as Eve is the mother of Abel and us all, so do all Christians have the Virgin as their Mother. "O what a loving Mother we have," says St. Bonaventure. Taking her as our model, let us imitate her love[92] and say:

"O Mary, Our Mother, Singular Vessel of Devotion,
Pray for us!"

* * *

The Church, like her prototype Mary, is a Virgin-Mother;[93] like her she is the spouse of the Holy Ghost,—a virgin spouse of amazing vitality and fecundity. She regards herself and the elect as children of the heavenly pair, Christ and Mary. As a natural mother gives her child flesh and blood and makes him a man, Mary gives him the grace of her Crucified Son and makes him a Christian. In the order of grace, she is the Christian's Mother, strictly so-called, for she bore the Whole Christ,—not only Jesus, the Head of the Mystical Body, but also each one of us, His living members. She who was Mother of the Head according to the flesh is spiritually mother of the members. In becoming the Mother of God, Mary became the Mother of all His creatures.[94] Pope Pius XII, in his Encyclical on the Mystical Body, emphasizes this truth: "Thus she who corporeally was the Mother of our Head, through the added title of pain and glory became spiritually the Mother of all His members."

The mission which Jesus and Mary began at Bethlehem had its consumma-

(92) "Tertio persolvit beata Virgo pretium illud sicut mulier fortis et *pietate miserationis ad mundum,* et specialiter ad populum christianum. Isaias: *Nunquid oblivisci potest mulier infantem suum, ut non misereatur filio uteri sui? Et si illa oblita fuerit, ego tamen non obliviscar.* Hoc dicitur de Christo. Et potest intelligi hic, quod totus populus christianus de utero Virginis gloriosae sit productus; quod significatur nobis per mulierem de latere viri formatam, quae significat Ecclesiam. Unde in Genesis: *Immisit Dominus soporem in Adam; cumque obdormisset tulit unam de costis eius et fecit mulierem et adduxit eam ad Adam.* Et dixit Adam, quod esset *virago, quia de viro sumta est. Hoc,* inquit, *os ex ossibus meis, et caro de carne mea.* Et dixit Dominus: *Propter hoc relinquet homo patrem et matrem* et filios et filias, *et adhaerebit uxori suae.* Et Apostolus dixit: *Sacramentum hoc magnum est; ego autem dico, in Christo et in Ecclesia.* Et quare, eo dormiente, tulit unam de costis eius? Nonne potuit facere hoc, ipso vigilante? Hoc est mysteriale. Nunquid formata est Ecclesia de latere Christi, donec Christus obdormivit in cruce? Et de latere eius refluxit sanguis et aqua, id est Sacramenta, per quae renascitur Ecclesia. De costa Adae formata est Eva, quae ei copulata est in coniugium. Sicut homo formatus est de terra virginea, sic Christus de Virgine gloriosa. Et sicut de latere Adae dormientis formata est mulier, ita Ecclesia de Christo in cruce pendente. Et sicut de Adam et Eva formatus est Abel et successores sui, sic de Christo et Ecclesia totus populus christianus. Et sicut Eva mater est Abel et omnium nostrum, ita populus christianus habet matrem Virginem. O quam piam matrem habemus! Configuremus nos matri nostrae et sequamur eius pietatem. *De Dono Fortitudinis Coll. II,* t.V, 487ab.

(93) "Propter significationem, quia Ecclesia est spiritualis sponsa et virgo et mater, et hoc significari debuit." *IV Sent.,* d. 30, a.1, q.2, t.IV, 709b.

(94) "Item, ex hoc quod Virgo Maria effecta est Mater Dei, est effecta mater omnium creaturarum." *III Sent.,* d.9, a.1, q.3, t.III, 205a.

tion on Calvary. There men found the source of life. There, too, Mary's spiritual maternity found its final fulfillment. St. John says:

> "Now there stood by the cross of Jesus, his mother and his mother's sister, Mary of Cleophas, and Mary Magdalen. When Jesus therefore had seen his mother and the disciple standing whom he loved, he saith to his mother: Woman, behold thy son. After that, he saith to the disciple: Behold thy mother" (19:25-27).

The words of the dying Christ include something more than a mere commendation of Our Lady to the care of the beloved disciple. The occasion was too important and the hour too solemn for an interpretation such as this. St. John represented the unit of divine Mystical filiation; he was the type and figure of all mankind redeemed by the Blood of Christ. "Woman, behold thy son!" What a strange Annunciation, this proclamation to Mary of the maternity of men! How unlike the Annunciation of her Divine Maternity! The exultant joy of her first Motherhood has given way to the intolerable anguish of the second. Now no angel, but the sweet human voice of Christ Himself proclaims to her the message of her selection as Mother of the Church. In the first Annunciation, the angel addressed her as "Mary"; now her own Son calls her "Woman," not because she has ceased to be His Mother but because her Motherhood has been widened and expanded, made spiritual and universal. When Mary heard the word of Christ: "Woman, behold thy son," she beheld not only the faithful disciple standing near her beneath the Cross, but all those who in every age and clime would call her Mother.

And this is the glory of Mary. She has a double maternity, two Motherhoods which are essentially and causally interwoven in the divine plan. She is the physical Mother of God and the *spiritual* Mother of men. As our first mother Eve has begotten us all for this world, so has Our Lady begotten us all for Heaven. "Come over to me, all ye that desire me, and be filled with my fruits," she says in the words of Ecclesiasticus (24:26). "With my fruits," she says, because she gave birth to One *in the flesh,* but the whole human race she brought forth *spiritually*. Hence the Holy Spirit inspired the Evangelist to write: "Mary brought forth her first-born Son" (Luke 2:7), because after she gave birth to her Son Jesus in the flesh, she gave birth to us all in her heart. Therefore Isaias in wonderment exclaimed: "Shall the earth bring forth in one day? Or shall a nation be brought forth at once? Who ever heard such a thing?" (66:8). Hence Mary's excellence is threefold: She is the Mother of all *things spiritual* and she is the Mother of the *earthly creation* and she is the Mother of the *angels' restoration,* as St. Bernard implies in his beautiful invocation: "Deservedly, O Lady, do the eyes of every creature look to thee, through whom and in whom and for whom the all-merciful Hand of God has created anew His whole creation." Solomon's praise of Wisdom for the innumerable riches that came to him through her hands may be our praise of Mary, for she is "that wisdom who went before me," that is, she rejoiced in all these things, "and I knew not that she was the mother of them all" (Wis. 7:12).[95]

O Mary, Our Mother, Mother of Divine Grace,
through whom creation is renewed,
Help of Christians,
Pray for us!

* * *

On Pentecost when the Holy Ghost descended to form the Mystical Body, Sacred Scripture tells us that the Apostles "were persevering with one mind in prayer with the women, and Mary the Mother of Jesus" (Acts 1:14). Tradition and art have always represented Mary in the midst of the Apostles receiving tongues of fire and being filled with the Holy Ghost,—a favor which came to her not so much for her own sanctification which was already sealed, as to consecrate her as the Mother of Christ's Mystical Body. Around her, from whom God had taken to Himself a human body, the infant Church, His Mystical Body, was to take shape and form. Mary was now Mother of the faithful not only by the appointment she received when she stood near the Cross of her Son, but by consecration in her sublime office as Queen of the Apostles and Evangelists and as the organ of the Christian dispensation of truth and grace in a sense truly unique. Surrounding the holy Virgin were the men who had been with Our Lord from His baptism by John until the day He ascended into heaven. All were qualified to aid in the collection of the mysteries into one common deposit of the faith. Some could testify to one thing; some, to another, but not one of them could testify to the fundamental mystery of them all, the mystery of the Divine Incarnation. Joseph's earthly days were ended. Simeon and Anna had long since gone to their rest. Mary, and Mary alone could transmit to the Apostles the marvels of the Infancy, Elizabeth's testimony to Our Saviour at the Visitation, the glorious prophecy of the *Magnificat;* the holy Christmas

(95) "Duodecima stella est, quod non tantum est ipsa Mater Dei carnalis, (sed etiam) hominum *spiritualis;* sicut Eva omnes nos genuit mundo, sic Domina nostra omnes nos genuit caelo; unde Ecclesiasticus: *Transite ad me, omnes, qui concupiscitis me, et a generationibus meis implemini. Generationibus* dicit, quia unum genuit *carnaliter,* omne tamen genus humanum genuit *spiritualiter.* Unde proprie dicitur in Luca: *Maria* genuit *Filium suum primogenitum,* quia, licet unum genuit carnaliter, nos omnes genuit spiritualiter. Unde exclamat admirando Isaias, ultimo: *Nunquid parturiet terra in die una?* Aut parietur gens simul? Quis audivit unquam talia? Unde haec excellentia triplex est: est enim omnium *mater spiritualium* et est mater *machinae mundialis* et est mater *angelicae reparationis.* Unde Bernardus: 'Merito igitur, O Domina, ad te respiciunt oculi universae creaturae, per quam et in qua et ex qua benignissima Dei manus quidquid creavit recreavit'. Et hoc (est) quod dicitur Sapientiae septimo: *Antecedebat me ista sapientia,* id est, delectabatur in omni; *et ignorabam quoniam bonorum omnium mater est." De Nativitate B. Virginis Mariae. Sermo I,* t.IX, 706b.

night; the worship of the Magi, the Presentation of the Infant Saviour in the Temple and Simeon's prophecy; the Wisdom of the Child Jesus confounding the Doctors in the Temple; and, lastly, the humble subjection of the Saviour during the first thirty years of His life. Of all these truths Mary is the sole witness. St. Luke, who reveals them all in detail, wishes to emphasize the fact that Mary is his authority. Three separate times he tells us that "His Mother kept all these things in her heart." Thus it is from the words of Our Lady and under her dictation, so to speak, that the Evangelists wrote their account of the Annunciation and of the birth of Our Saviour.[96] Without this testimony the whole chain of Christian evidence would have remained inconclusive. Thus the Faith which the Apostles preached depended, in the final analysis, on the simple declaration of Mary. Because they were convinced of her holiness they could supplement their own testimony with hers and offer her unattested words as sufficient human warrant for the whole dispensation. The extraordinary reverence with which she was held in the Pentecostal Church continues to this day in the veneration of true believers. Without shedding her blood for Christ, Mary confessed His faith by the exercise of heroic virtues and the eminent holiness of her life. She is "Queen of Confessors," for whoever confesses Christ confesses Him on the word of His Mother, and whoever accepts her word pays tribute to the sanctity which made her an Apostle to the Apostles and an Evangelist to the Evangelists.

O Mary, Queen of Apostles,
Queen of Confessors,
Pray for us!

(96) Cf. *supra,* p. 230, footnote 74.

Chapter IV

QUEEN OF HEAVEN AND EARTH

FIFTEEN YEARS HAD PASSED since Mary strained her eyes to catch one last glimpse of the beatified countenance of her Son, as the cloud on Olivet enveloped Him and hid Him from her sight. The Church in the hands of St. Peter was now sufficiently strong to dispense with her physical presence but not with her motherly care and protection, which she would continue from heaven. For Mary there remained only death,—the passing from earthly life to heavenly blessedness out of sheer longing for her Beloved.

As to the time and circumstances of Mary's death, Sacred Scripture is silent. Though denied by some theologians, the reality of Our Lady's death has been a matter of common belief from primitive times,—a belief which rests on a universal law from which not even the God-Man Himself was exempt. "Thou shalt die the death," God had said in Eden, but these were only words to our First Parents till the day when Eve held the lifeless body of Abel in her arms and wondered what strange thing had happened to her boy. From that day the realization of death has gone shuddering through all mankind. Since Christ Himself had died for the salvation of the world, it was fitting that Mary, too, should die.[1] But death is one thing, decomposition another. Christ proved His power over death's corruption beyond a shadow of a doubt in His own resurrection. The stainless flesh, the diadem of original innocence with which His earthly Mother first crowned Him in His conception, the flesh which *mater synagoga,* the Jewish assembly, crowned with the thorny crown of sorrow and ignominy in His Passion, that same flesh *Mother Divine Justice* crowned with a splendid diadem of honor and glory in His resurrection.[2] If the Body of Jesus, the Sanctuary of the Divinity, rose triumphant over death, we may be sure that the virginal body of Mary, who conceived and gave birth to the God-Man, was likewise preserved from the corruption of the tomb. She is the Mystic Ark of the Covenant, framed according to the design of God "of setim wood," (Exod. 25:10), a hard, durable, incorruptible wood symbolic of Mary's complete and inviolate virginity of body. Nothing is more just than that our flesh should become the prey of worms, for it is the "flesh of sin," but the glorious Virgin who in life and in the conception of her Child was undefiled with the corruption of

(1) "Ad illud quod obiicitur, quod potuit mori; dicendum, quod non est simile, pro eo quod non fuit decens, Filium Dei habere matrem immortalem, cum ipse esset mortalis." *III Sent.,* d.3, p.1, a.2, q.3, t.III, 78b.

(2) "Honoravit Christum sive coronavit, primo Mater Virgo Maria carneo diademate originalis innocentiae in conceptione; secundo, *mater synagoga* spineo diademate doloris et ignominiae in passione; tertio, *mater divina iustitia* splendido diademate honoris et gloriae in resurrectione." *Sermones de Tempore. Dominica in Palmis. Sermo I,* t.IX, 244a.

concupiscence, was rightly exempt from the corruption, the ashes, and worms of the tomb.[3] That pure and heavenly flesh which in this life knew no corruption, was, like the sun, raised high above the changing and corruptible spheres of this world and given a lofty position in the skies.[4] From the pure body of His Blessed Mother, Christ withheld the effects of death, so that she, His Bride and His Mother, who had shared with Him every joy and sorrow of this earthly life might share with Him the beautiful privilege of being with Him body and soul in heaven. There are no relics of Mary. She is altogether heavenly. In the Nativity, she brought Christ, Body and Blood, Soul and Divinity, to earth. In her Assumption, the roles are reversed. Christ took His blessed Mother, body and soul, into heaven and clothed her with an incorruptibility like His own. The fate of the ark whose final "resting place" is in the temple of heaven (cf. Apoc. 11:19) typifies Mary's bodily "assumption." Now glorified in triumph with the King, this heavenly pair manifests the perfect accomplishment of the Redemption, and with the Fathers we quote the Psalm: "Arise, O Lord, into thy resting place; thou and the ark which thou hast sanctified" (131:8).

The doctrine of the Assumption lifts our eyes from things of earth to the sight of the purest of women conquering death, rising above earth in a glow of unearthly beauty and moving straight into the arms of Christ the King. If Our Lord wished the ark of the covenant to be conducted with great pomp into the city of David—"and David and all the house of Israel brought the ark of the covenant of the Lord with joyful shouting and with sound of trumpet" (II Kings 6:15),—with what splendor and glorious pomp did He ordain that His Mother should enter heaven! The Book of Kings says: "And the king arose to meet her, and bowed to her, and sat down upon his throne. And a throne was set for the king's mother, and she sat on his right hand" (III Kings 2:19). Here are enumerated the four honors bestowed upon Mary at her entrance into heaven.[5]

The first honor was her meeting with the Most High King, for we firmly

(3) "Est igitur Maria primo arca testamenti quantum ad *fabricam,* quia *materiae imputribilis* per integritatem carnis, secundum illud Exodi vigesimo quinto: *Arcam de lignis setim compingite* mihi; Glossa: 'Ligna setim levia et imputribilia, parum a qualitate albae spinae distant'; in quo datur intelligi integritas gloriosae Virginis, quae ipsam *levem* fecit exonerando a pondere carnalitatis, et *imputribilem* sequestrando a contagio corruptionis, quae quidem est in opere carnis. Quid enim aliud est virginitas quam quaedam imputribilitas? . . . Unde a concupiscentia nati sunt putridi; Iob decimo septimo: *Putredini dixi: Pater meus es* etc.; unde nos tanquam putridi et putrefacti merito corporaliter incineramur. Sed gloriosa Virgo Maria, sicut vivendo et concipiendo non putruit per corruptelam concupiscentiae actualis; sic moriendo et exspirando non putruit per poenam incinerationis et vermis; et hoc quidem convenientissimum erat integerrimis et incorruptis visceribus uteri virginalis." *De Nativitate B. Virginis Mariae. Sermo V,* t.IX, 715b.

(4) "Tertio etiam habet sol *sublimitatem in situ* propter permanentiam incorruptibilem; quia enim corpus incorruptibile est de se, ideo elevatur super omnes sphaeras corruptibiles et elementares. In quo beata Virgo soli similis est, quia . . . gratiam, quem semel accepit, nunquam amisit, sed semper in ea incorruptibiliter permansit; unde sublimitatem in situ habuit, quia per gratiam perfectivam tota fuit caelestis." *De Nativitate B. Virginis Mariae. Sermo II,* t.IX, 710b.

(5) *"Surrexit rex in occursum matris adoravitque eam, positusque est thronus matri regis, quae sedit ad dexteram eius,* tertii Regum secundo. . . . Quatuor honores describuntur in verbis propositis, quibus hodie Mater Dei, Maria, in sua assumtione, fuit solemniter honorata." *De Assumtione B. Virginis Mariae. Sermo III,* t.IX, 693b.

believe without the shadow of a doubt that the Virgin was met at the threshold of heaven not only by the King, but by the whole celestial court in solemn procession. First in full flight come the Angels to see their Queen; the Patriarchs traverse the heavens to behold their daughter; the Apostles in a body run to see their teacher and their guide; the Martyrs hasten to behold their counselor; the matrons, wives, mothers, and widows come to behold their companion and their sister; the virgin-nuns assemble to greet their standard-bearer and Superioress. Truly in Mary were fulfilled the words of *Ecclesiasticus:* "And my abode is in the full assembly of the saints" (24:16), and those spoken of Judith of old for "all ran to meet her from the least to the greatest. And lighting up lights they all gathered round about her" (Judith 13:15, 16).[6] But all the reverence of these creatures is as nothing in comparison with the surpassing honor which the Creator Himself bestows upon her. The whole Trinity comes to meet her, the Spouse of chaste love, the Palace of holy indwelling, the Workshop of wondrous operation. The Father recognized in the Blessed Virgin, the house of His Majesty, as Isaias had foretold: "I will glorify the house of my majesty" (Isai. 60:7). The Son recognized in her the source of His Humanity or abasement; the Holy Ghost, the sanctuary of His goodness, into which most plentifully and without measure He had poured the treasures of His grace. But as regards Christ, her Son, the words mean exactly what they say: "The king rose to meet his mother." Rising from His throne, He incited the whole court of heaven to pay her homage. Hence, St. Bernard, comparing the Ascension of Christ and the Assumption of His Mother, says that the former was attended by more power and majesty; the latter, by more glorious splendor and pomp. "The angels alone came to meet the Redeemer, but the Blessed Virgin went to glory accompanied by the Lord of glory Himself, and by all the blessed company of angels and saints."[7]

The second honor which Jesus paid to Mary was the reception full of sweetness and reverence, as indicated in the words, "He bowed to her."

(6) "Primus ergo honor est *obviatio summi Regis.* Omnino enim credendum est et nullatenus dubitandum, quin hodie solemni processione obviatum sit Virgini ascendenti non solum a *Rege,* verum etiam a tota *curia caelesti.* Praevolant Angeli videre dominam suam; desiliunt Patriarchae videre filiam suam; occurrunt Apostoli videre magistram suam; accelerant Martyres videre exhortatricem suam; irruunt maritatae et viduae aspicere sociam et sororem suam; confluunt consorores videre praelatam et abbatissam suam, ut iustificetur illud Ecclesiastici vigesimo quarto: *Et in plenitudine Sanctorum detentio mea;* et quod legitur Iudith decimo tertio: *Concurrerunt ad eam omnes a minimo usque ad maximum. Et ascendentes luminaria congregaverunt circa eam universi." Ibid.*

(7) "Verum quidquid reverentiae ipsae conferant creaturae, nihil est comparatione superexcellentis honoris, quem confert ei Creator. Occurrit enim tota Trinitas. . . . Tota siquidem beata Trinitas te cognovit, Maria, *sponsam* castae dilectionis, *aulam* sanctae inhabitationis, *officinam* mirae operationis. Vel distinctive dicamus: Cognovit beatam Mariam Pater domum suae maiestatis; Isaiae sexagesimo: *Domum maiestatis meae glorificabo;* recognovit Filius principium suae humanitatis sive humilitatis; recognovit Spiritus sanctus sacrarium suae bonitatis, in quo plenissime et absque mensura charismata condidit gratiarum. . . . Sed de Christo, Filio eius, proprie intelligitur quod dicitur: *Surrexit rex in occursum matris.* Exsiliens enim de solio suo totam imperii machinam in Matris obsequium movit. . . . Et propterea dicit beatus Bernardus, comparando ascensionem Christi et ascensionem Matris, quod illa potentior maiestate, sed ista solemnior invenitur, his verbis: 'Attolle, inquit, oculos ad assumtionem Virginis et, salva Filii maiestate, invenies occursum huius pompae non mediocriter digniorem. Soli quippe Angeli Redemptori occurrere potuerunt, Matri vero caelorum palatia penetranti Filius ipse, cum tota curia tam Angelorum quam iustorum solemniter occurrens, evexit eam ad beatae consistorium sessionis'." *Ibid.,* 694a.

What are you doing, Lord? Do you, the true Lord to Whom every creature should bow, bow to a woman? "I bow to her," He says, "for two things make her adorable to me, namely, her motherhood and her humility. Her motherhood was unique; her humility incomparable. Does a son violate the law if he venerates his mother? No, indeed, because the eternal law orders that the natural law be observed, not disregarded." Jesus, therefore, venerates His Mother, not as a common, ordinary mother, but as a Mother of singular *sufficiency,* singular *grandeur,* and singular *love,*—of singular *sufficiency,* because without admixture of male seed, she of herself alone was equal to the task, the Holy Ghost in wondrous manner bestowing upon her the power to conceive Him; of singular *grandeur,* because of all mothers she alone gave birth to a God and after childbearing remained a virgin; of singular *devotion* and care, because she was the most loving, the most solicitous of mothers.[8] God reverenced His Mother, secondly, on account of her *humility,* for He Himself has said: "He who humbles himself shall be exalted" (Luke 14:11). Mary not only humbled herself but in her humility she abased herself to the lowest depths, completely effacing herself in that profound abyss. Now in her Assumption, God not only raised her up among the Saints but He extolled her far above the Saints and as a final honor, He bowed to her in person. "He bowed to her," giving proof to the world of the great honor which is due a mother from her son, just as Joseph's embrace when at the Angel's bidding "he took unto him his wife" (Matt. 1:24), was an example of the love which is due an earthly spouse from her spouse. Now, indeed, "from the chamber of women," that is, from the Church Militant, Mary, like Esther, "was brought to the chamber of the King" (Esth. 2:16), to Whom with the Psalmist, she could say: "Thou hast held my right hand and in thy will thou hast led me and with glory received me" (Ps. 72:24).[9]

Significantly of Mary does Sacred Scripture say: "My abode is in the full assembly of the saints," for, in the words of St. Bernard, "she lacked not the faith of the Patriarchs, the hope of the Prophets, the zeal of the Apostles, the constancy of the Martyrs, the fortitude of the Confessors, the chastity of the

(8) "Secundus honor fuit in illa *receptione* plenitudo *dulcedinis* et *reverentiae,* pro qua dicitur: *et adoravit eam.* Quid facis, Domine? Tu verus Dominus ab omnibus adorandus mulierem adoras? Adoro, inquit, quoniam (eam) mihi duo faciunt adorandam, scilicet ratio *maternitatis* et meritum *humilitatis.* Nam et *maternitas* in ea fuit singularis et *humilitas* incomparabilis. Nunquid, si filius matrem adorat, contra iura facit? Non, quia lex aeterna ordinem naturalem observari iubet, non perturbari. Adorat ergo Iesus matrem non qualemcumque, sed matrem singularis *sufficientiae,* singularis *magnificentiae,* singularis *diligentiae.* Fuit, inquam, singularis *sufficientiae,* quia sine virilis seminis mixtione ad hoc opus suffecit, Spiritu sancto virtutem conceptivam ei mirabiliter tribuente. Fuit iterum singularis *magnificentiae,* quia nulla mater Deum genuit praeter ipsam et post partum virgo permansit. Fuit etiam mater singularis *diligentiae* et curae, quia nulla mater tam dilexit et sollicita fuit." *Ibid.,* 694ab.

(9) "Ulterius debebatur hic honor merito *humilitatis,* de qua ipse Dominus dicit: *Qui se humiliat exaltabitur.* . . . Maria non solum se humiliat, sed in humilitate se profundat et in ipsa profunditate se inanit et in nihil redigit, ut de se nihil sentiat praeter nihil; et Deus non solum exaltat eam inter Sanctos et magnificat super Sanctos, sed ultimato honore corporaliter eam adorat. . . . Sicut haec littera *adoravit* demonstrat magnum honorem, qui debetur matri a filio, ita littera Iosephi, quae dicit: amplexatus est eam, ostendit amorem, qui debetur sponsae a sponso. Tunc enim de triclinio feminarum, id est Ecclesia militante, traducebatur ad cubiculum Assueri, ita ut ei conveniat illud Psalmi: *Tenuisti manum dexteram meam, et in voluntate tua deduxisti me et cum gloria suscepisti. Ibid.,* 694b.

Virgins, the fecundity of the married, or even the purity of the angels."[10] If it is true that God rewards according to merit, it is equally true that Mary who excelled angels and men in merit, has been exalted above them all in glory. As a sign of her dignity, the Lord Himself shared with her all the honor given to Himself on earth. He gave her beautiful feasts, one for each season of the year, as if to say: "Serve my beloved Mother throughout the year, as you serve Me." And as if this were not enough, He gave to her one day out of every seven, that Sabbath day which He especially loved, of which significantly He says: "Remember that thou keep holy the Sabbath day" (Exod. 20:8), and the following day He set aside for His own especial worship. And as if this were not yet enough for His love, He entitled His Mother as well as Himself to daily veneration, appointing certain hours during the day and even during the night for her honor. And so the Lord shared all things with His Blessed Mother to show that He exalted her above every creature.[11]

O Mary, thou exalted one, whom no mortal man can reach,
Virgin Most Venerable,
Pray for us!

* * *

Mary was exalted not only spiritually but in reality in her Assumption, as is said of Esther: "And on the third day she laid away the garments she wore, and put on her glorious apparel" (Esth. 15:4). "And going in she passed through all the doors in order, and stood before the King, where he sat upon his royal throne, clothed with his royal robes and glittering with gold and precious stones" (Esth. 15:9). The *doors* of Assuerus, that is, of supreme blessedness, are the doors which the Lord enumerates in the Gospel of St. Matthew: "Blessed are the poor in spirit, for theirs is the kingdom of heaven. Blessed are the meek, for they shall possess the land. Blessed are they that mourn, for they shall be comforted. Blessed are they that hunger and thirst after justice, for they shall be filled. Blessed are the merciful, for they shall obtain mercy. Blessed are the clean of heart, for they shall see God. Blessed are the peacemakers, for they shall be called the children of God" (5:3-9). Thus does the Evangelist enumerate the doors through which the Blessed Virgin passed, as her deeds testify. The seventh door, "Blessed are the

(10) "*In plenitudine,* inquit, *Sanctorum, detentio mea,* Ecclesiastici vigesimo quarto, Bernardus: '*Merito in plenitudine Sanctorum detentio eius,* cui non defuit fides Patriarcharum, spes Prophetarum, zelus Apostolorum, constantia Martyrum, sobrietas Confessorum, castitas Virginum, fecunditas coniugatorum, nec etiam puritas Angelorum'." *De Assumtione B. Virginis Mariae. Sermo IV,* t.IX, 698b.

(11) "Inde huius excellentiae est signum, quod etiam Dominus omnem honorem suum, quem in terra habuit, ei communicavit. Unde quatuor festa eius in quatuor anni partibus distincta dedit, quasi dicat: sicut per totum (annum) servitis mihi, servite meae dilectissimae Matri. Et quasi hoc non sufficeret, in qualibet septimana ei unum diem dedit, Sabbatum illum, quem maxime dilexit; de quo signanter ait: *Memento, ut diem Sabbati sanctifices,* et sequentem suo cultu specialiter mancipavit. Sed (quasi) nec adhuc sibi sufficeret, quin, sicut se ipsum, sic et Matrem suam quotidiano servitio manciparet, horis distinctis, diurnis et nocturnis etiam honorari ordinavit; et sic omnia secum communicavit in signum, quod ipsam super omnem creaturam exaltaverit." *De Assumptione B. Virginis Mariae. Sermo VI,* t.IX, 705ab.

peacemakers, for they shall be called the children of God," is that peace which is no longer a *door,* but a *place of abode* and a *throne* on which to rest. At the first door dwell the Confessors; at the second, the Martyrs; at the third, the Prophets; at the fourth, the Patriarchs; at the fifth, the Apostles; at the sixth, the Virgins and Angels. The application is self-evident. The Most Blessed Virgin, "flowing with delights, leaning upon her beloved" (Cant. 8:5), mounting upward, passed through each of these doors in order, rose above all the choirs of Angels, each choir greeting her with shouts of acclamation as she passed: "With thy comeliness and thy beauty set out. Proceed prosperously and reign" (Ps. 44:5). Thus with her Son exalted above every creature, Mary took her place at her Son's throne, "and a throne was set for the king's mother and she sat on his right hand" (III Kings 2:19). Now what other woman has been thus exalted above every creature?[12]

O Mary, Queen of Confessors, Queen of Martyrs, Queen of Prophets,
Queen of Patriarchs, Queen of Apostles, Queen of Virgins,
Queen of Angels, Queen of Peace,
Pray for us!

* * *

"A throne was set for his mother." This is Mary's third honor,—her glorious enthronement. And since her throne is of the same height as the throne of the Eternal King, to say that "a throne was set" is the same as to say that "the King married her and made her queen" (Esth. 10:6). For the three virtues which flourished in her in an eminent degree, Mary is given a throne of threefold beauty. For her *chastity,* is set "a great throne of ivory overlaid with finest gold" (III Kings 10:18); for her *poverty,* which sought the things of heaven rather than those of earth, a throne bejeweled with richest sapphires of heavenly blue, as foretold by the prophet: "And above the firmament was the likeness of a throne, as the appearance of the sapphire stone" (Ezech. 1:26); for the *humility* which kept her hidden and concealed, she is given a throne bright and shining as the sun, "a throne as the

(12) "Quod (non) tantum rationabiliter, sed realiter in assumtione ipsius factum est, sicut (dicitur) Esther decimo quinto: *Die tertio circumdata est* Esther *gloria sua* etc.; et post pauca: *Ingressa igitur cuncta per ordinem ostia, stetit contra regem, ubi ille residebat super solium regni sui, indutus vestibus regiis auroque fulgens et pretiosis lapidibus. Ostia* Assueri, id est beatitudinis, sunt ostia, quae enumerat Dominus in Matthaei quinto: *Beati pauperes spiritu* etc.; et sic enumerat ibi ostia, quae pertransivit beata Virgo, sicut planum est de factis eius. Septimum, videlicet: *Beati pacifici* etc., haec pax est, quae non iam est *ostium,* sed *sedes* et *thronus,* in qua quiescunt. Apud primum ostium habitant Confessores; apud secundum, Martyres; apud tertium, Prophetae; iuxta quartum, Patriarchae; iuxta quintum, Apostoli; iuxta sextum, Virgines et Angeli. Haec quoque adaptatio per se patet cuique. Beatissima Virgo, *deliciis affluens, innixa super dilectum suum,* ascendens per haec ostia, singula *per ordinem* intravit, omnia agmina Angelorum transcendit, singulis, cum pertransiret, succlamantibus: *Intende, prospere procede et regna;* et sic cum Filio suo super omnem (creaturam) in throno sui Filii consedit; et *positus est thronus matri regis, quae sedit ad dexteram eius*. Quae enim alia sic super omnem creaturam est exaltata?" *Ibid.*

sun before me" (Ps. 88:38). Thus honored, Mary reigns in triumph on a throne of imperishable beauty.[13]

"Hasten," said the Spouse to the Virgin as she was departing from this world, "hasten with joy to your heavenly home, for thou shalt be crowned with a glorious crown, by which thou shalt be as the Eternal Father in Majesty," according to the words of Isaias: "And thou shalt be a crown of glory in the hand of the Lord and a royal diadem in the hand of thy God" (Isai. 62:3). Highest of all in glory, in the very hand of God, as it were, Mary shines forth as a model of divine union and burning love. Hence she sits as Queen of Heaven at the right Hand of the Eternal King. "The queen stood on the right hand in gilded clothing," and she was crowned with a crown in all things like the crown of the Eternal King, of Whom it is said: "O Lord, thou hast crowned him with glory and honor" (Ps. 8:6).[14] The brightness of her crown is the brightness of her Only-begotten Son, as St. John says in the Apocalypse: "A great sign appeared in heaven, a woman clothed with the sun, and the moon under her feet, and on her head a crown of twelve stars" (12:1). Shining brightly in Mary's crown are twelve stars, for it is written: "They that instruct many to justice shall shine as stars for all eternity" (Dan. 12:3). The twelve Apostles, then, who spread the light of faith, now shine as twelve stars in glory. And because the Virgin herself instructed the Apostles in the mystery of the Incarnation and enlightened them by the revelation of so great a "mystery hidden from eternity in God" (Eph. 3:9), all the radiance of the Apostles' crowns and of the whole Church Triumphant shines brightly in the Virgin's starry crown.[15] As "star differeth from star in glory" (I Cor. 15:41), so, too, the Saints, the full assembly of those saved from the four quarters of the globe and crowned by faith in the Blessed Trinity. They are "the four and twenty ancients" who "cast their crowns before the throne" (Apoc. 4:10), the twelve Patriarchs symbolizing

---

(13) "*Positus est thronus matri eius. Hic est tertius honor dignissimae inthronizationis.* Et cum *thronus* sit aeternae regalis celsitudinis, nihil aliud est dicere:*Positus est thronus,* quam: *rex accepit uxorem et voluit esse reginum,* et merito . . . Istis ergo tribus virtutibus, quae in ipsa eminentius floruerunt, triplex respondet mirabilis thronus. Nam *castitati* respondet thronus de ebore, quem rex Salomon varie adornavit, ut legitur tertii Regum decimo; *paupertati,* quae caelestia, non terrena sectatur; respondet thronus *sapphirinus,* qui caelestis coloris est; Ezechielis primo: *Quasi aspectus lapidis sapphiri similitudo throni;* humilitati vero, quae se abscondit et obumbrat, respondet thronus *solaris* et lucidus; de quo Psalmus: *Thronus eius sicut sol in conspectu meo.* In his omnibus durantibus in perpetuum coronata triumphat." *De Assumtione B. Virginis Mariae. Sermo III,* t.IX, 694b, 695a.

(14) "Festina namque quia coronaberis corona gloriosa, per quam efficieris conformis malestati Patris aeterni, secundum illud Isaiae sexagesimo secundo: *Eris corona gloriae in manu Domini et diadema regni in manu Dei tui.* Ipsa namque, in gloria prae ceteris excelsior, quasi *in manu Dei* ostenditur ad exemplum unionis et accensionis desiderii. Unde ipsa tanquam regina caeli sedet ad dexteram Regis aeterni, secundum illud Psalmi: *Astitit regina a dextris tuis in vestitu deaurato,* et coronata est corona consimili coronae Regis aeterni; de quo, in Psalmo: *Gloria et honore coronasti eum, Domine."* *De Assumtione B. Virginis Mariae. Sermo VI,* t.IX, 699b, 700a.

(15) "Coronaberis etiam corona *luminosa,* per quam conformaberis claritati Unigeniti, secundum illud Apocalypsis duodecimo: *Signum magnum apparuit in caelo: Mulier amicta sole, et luna sub predibus eius, et in capite eius corona stellarum duodecim;* quia scriptum est Danielis duodecimo: *Qui ad iustitiam erudiunt multos quasi stellae fulgebunt in perpetuas aeternitates;* et tales fuerunt duodecim Apostoli; et ideo in gloria sunt sicut duodecim *stellae.* Sed quia Virgo ipsos Apostolos erudivit mysterium incarnationis et illuminavit eos per revelationem tanti *sacramenti absconditi a saeculis;* ideo omnis luminositas coronae apostolicae et totius Ecclesiae triumphantis quasi coercervatur in lumine coronae virginalis." *Ibid.,* 700a.

the saints of the Old Law; the twelve Apostles, all those of the New. All without exception, realizing that they have been crowned by God and His Blessed Mother, cast their crowns at the feet of Mary as she reigns upon her throne.[16]

O Mary, Queen of Heaven, crowned with stars by the hands of Christ,
Queen of All Saints,
Pray for us!

* * *

Reign on, great Queen. Draw the bright mantle of thy motherhood 'round thee; fix the starry diadem on thy head and from thy lofty throne, devote thyself to the consummation of thy task. Thy royalty shall be to thee no sinecure; thou hast us and a whole world to save.

"And she sat on his right hand." Enfolded in the mantle of her motherhood, the unbelievable motherhood where the love she had for her own flesh and blood and the love she had for her God were identified physically in the one Person of her Divine Son, Mary is enthroned close beside the King. She is the Mediatress of our salvation; not, indeed, Mediatress of justice, but of grace and intercession, as St. Bonaventure says: "Our first Advocate is Christ; our second Advocate is the Holy Spirit; our third Advocate is the Most Blessed Virgin. She is our Advocate of *intercession,* our powerful Mediatress with our great Mediator, Jesus Christ. That she might have greater influence with the Judge, she bears the feminine sex. She is the Queen long foretold in the person of Esther, at whose sight the King's heart 'changed to mildness' " (Esth. 15:11).[17] She it was who furnished the gleaming white and crimson robe of His adorable Flesh and Blood which He offered in sacrifice on Calvary. This robe the Lord willed to assume in the tabernacle of the Virgin's womb, that He might not have to stand alone as Advocate before the face of His Heavenly Father but might have at His side the most pure Virgin, that through two persons who cannot possibly be rejected, namely, the Son and the Mother, "we may have the strongest comfort, we

(16) "*Stellae duodecim* Sanctos significant; primae ad Corinthios decimo quinto: *Sicut stella a stella differt in claritate;* Daniel: *Fulgebunt in perpetuas aeternitates.* Duodecim stellae universitatem Sanctorum significant, utpote qui in quatuor partibus mundi, fide sanctae Trinitatis coronati, salvantur. Quod in capite eius corona stellarum duodecim esse dicitur, nihil aliud est, quam omnes Sancti coronas ei ascribendo ipsam coronant, per quam post Deum se esse coronatos recognoscunt, sicut Ioannes vidit Apocalypsis quarto, quod *viginti quatuor seniores mittebant coronas suas ante thronum.* Per hos viginti quatuor seniores intelligitur universitas Sanctorum: per *duodecim Patriarchas,* universitas veteris Testamenti; per duodecim *Apostoles,* novi Testamenti. Omnes ergo Sancti coronas suas *ante pedes sedentis in throno mittunt,* quia omnes se a Deo et a Matre sua, quae per thronum intelligitur." *Ibid.*, 710b, 702a.

(17) "Primus advocatus Christus est. . . . Secundus advocatus est Spiritus sanctus. . . . Tertius advocatus est beatissima Virgo. Haec est advocata ad *intercedendum,* quae, ut magis moveat iudicem, femineum praefert sexum. Haec est illa Esther, ad cuius aspectum 'convertitur cor regis in mansuetudinem', secundum quod figuratum est Esther decimo quinto. Haec est illa, cui canit Ecclesia: 'Eia ergo, advocata nostra'." *Comment. in Ioannem Cap. XIV. Coll. LIII,* t.VI, 603a.

who have fled for refuge to hold fast the hope set before us" (Heb. 6:18.)[18] "Do you not know," says St. Bernard, "that you have sure access to God when you have the Mother before the Son, the Son before the Father? In your behalf, the Mother shows the Son her heart and breast; the Son shows the Father His pierced side and wounds. I think there can be no refusal where there are so many proofs of love." With the utmost confidence, then, O my soul, say with St. Anselm: "O Lady, if through thee thy Son has become my Brother, hast not thou through that same Son became my Mother? Therefore 'I will be glad and rejoice in thee' (Ps. 9:3), for whatever the judgment concerning me, it will rest on the decision of my Mother and my Brother."[19]

"And she sat on his right hand," first, because of the *intimate love which bound them heart to heart,* for as there were no barriers between the heart of the Virgin and that of her God, so were there no barriers between the Queen's throne and that of the King, to Whom with Esther, Mary could say: "Thou knowest that thy handmaid hath never rejoiced, since I was brought thither unto this day, but in thee, O Lord, the God of Abraham" (Esth. 14:16-18).[20] Thus Our Lady sits at the right hand of Christ Who will not let us escape the throbs of His merciful love but draws us by an argument that even our blindness cannot reject,—the argument of a mother's heart. She is a Queen, not of justice, intent upon the punishment of the guilty, but a Queen of Mercy, solely intent upon compassion and pardon for sinners. Therefore Holy Church bids us invoke her: "Hail, holy Queen. Mother of Mercy, our Life, our Sweetness, and our Hope!" "These two things have I heard, that power belongeth to God, and mercy to thee, O Lord" (Ps. 61:12) says the holy King David. This kingdom of heaven, consisting of justice and mercy, the Lord has divided. The kingdom of justice He has reserved for Himself; the kingdom of mercy He has granted to Mary, ordaining that all the mercies which are dispensed to men should pass through her hands and should be bestowed according to her good pleasure.[21] "Thy neck is as a tower of ivory," says the Psalm (86:2).

---

(18) "Ibi enim vestimentum candidum et rubicundum, quod in utero Virginis sumsit. Hoc autem vestimentum voluit Dominus sumere in tabernaculo uteri virginalis, ut non solum ipse esset advocatus, sed etiam ipsa, ut per duas personas, quas impossibile est repelli, Filium scilicet et Matrem, *fortissimum solatium habeamus, qui confugimus ad tenendum propositam spem, ad Hebraeos sexto." De Annuntiatione B. Virginis Mariae. Sermo IV*, t.IX, 673b.

(19) "An ignoras, quod secundum Bernardum 'securum habes accessum ad Deum, ubi Matrem habes ante Filium, Filium ante Patrem? Mater pro te ostendit Filio pectus et ubera, Filius Patri latus et vulnera. Puto, quod nulla potest ibi esse repulsa, ubi tot sunt caritatis indicia.' . . . Dic igitur, o anima, magnam in ipsam habens fiduciam: 'O Domina, si tuus Filius per te factus est frater meus, nonne tu per ipsum facta es mater mea? *Exsultabo* igitur et *laetabor in te,* quia quidquid iudicabitur de me, pendet ex sententia Matris et Fratis mei.' Haec Anselmus." *Soliloquium* C.1, t.VIII, 37b.

(20) *"Et sedit ad dexteram eius.* Hic est quartus honor: *immediata locatio circa Regem.* Et sunt ad hoc tres rationes: prima est immediatio amoris cordis ad cor. Sicut enim nihil fuit medium inter cor Virginis et Deum, ita nihil medium inter thronum et thronum; Esther decimo quarto: *Tu scis, quod nunquam laetata sit ancilla tua usque in praesentem diem nisi in te, Domine, Deus Abraham." De Assumtione B. Virginis Mariae. Sermo III,* t.IX, 695a.

(21) "Sextam divisionem fecit cum Filio, cum quo divisit regnum caelorum, cuius duae erant partes, *iustitia* et *misericordia.* Beata Virgo optimam sibi elegit, quia facta est regina misericordiae, et Filius eius remansit rex iustitiae." *Ibid., Sermo VI,* t.IX, 703b.

O Tower of Ivory, pure and strong,
Mystic neck through which life-giving graces
flow from Christ Who is the Head, into His Mystical Body,
Pray for us!

* * *

"And she sat on his right hand," secondly, that she might make *frequent intercession for sinners.* Now a person holding the office of intercessor and mediatress must not sit far away but must assist near at hand, draw near, side by side, as it were, nay more, she must keep very close, in fact, ear to ear, lest perchance a cruel sentence might be pronounced against her clients and in case it should be pronounced, she must be there to see that it is not carried out. You have the example of Esther, to whom the king said: "What is thy petition, Esther?" (Esth. 7:2) and immediately at her word, the cruel sentence of death was revoked, the enemy Aman was hanged, rivals were destroyed, and the people set free. For this reason Mary is said to be "terrible as an army set in array" (Cant. 6:3) in bringing help to the world and in conquering demons.[22] "Thy neck is as the tower of David, which is built with bulwarks; a thousand bucklers hang upon it, all the armour of valiant men" (Cant. 4.4). Like that mighty tower which was the defense and ornament of Jerusalem, Our Lady is the invincible defense of the kingdom of Christ on earth, doing battle with the demons who assail it.[23] She is the Woman who crushed the serpent's head, the Mother of Him Who freed us from the bondage of sin and "delivered us from the servitude of corruption, into the liberty of the glory of the children of God" (Rom. 8:21).[24]

O Tower of David, glory and invincible fortress of the Church,
Help of Christians, Refuge of Sinners,
Pray for us!

* * *

"And she sat at his right hand," thirdly, because the *headship* which Adam held among men and Eve among women to sit at the right hand of God, that is, in the possession of better things, was transferred to Christ and Mary,

(22) *"Et sedit ad dexteram eius.* Secunda ratio est *frequenter interpellandi* pro peccatoribus. Habentem enim interpellatricis et reconciliatricis officium non oportet longe sedere, sed prope assistere et quasi lateraliter appropinquare, immo auriculariter cohaerere, ne forte contra suos commendatores crudelis dictetur sententia, et si dictata fuerit, irritetur. Habes exemplum Esther septimo: *Quae est petitio tua, Esther?* et statim ad verbum eius crudelis sententia revocatur, suspenditur hostis, perduntur aemuli, populus liberatur. Ideo dicitur Canticorum sexto *terribilis* esse *ut castrorum acies ordinata* ad succurrendum mundo et daemones expugnandos." *De Assumtione B. Virginis Mariae. Sermo III,* t.IX, 695a.

(23) "Recte Virgo Maria in suscipiendo Christum fuit *castellum turribus virtutum munitum* et elevatum; cuius prima turris fuit *fortutido districtionis,* de qua Canticorum quarto: "Sicut turris David collum tuum, quae aedificata est cum propugnaculis, mille clypei pendent ex ea', quia Virgo Maria nullo vitio potuit superari." *Comment. in Evangelium Lucae* C. XI, t.VII, 276ab.

(24) "Unde Christus ipse fuit nostra liberatio, qui nos liberavit a servitute peccati et liberavit *a servitute corruptionis in libertatem gloriae filiorum Dei.* Et ratione huius dicitur Virgo Maria liberatrix captivorum." *De Annuntiatione B. Virginis Mariae,* t.IX, 665a.

His Mother, for as the former were the destroyers of the human race, so the latter were the restorers. Hence we read in the Book of Esther: "Let another, that is better than her, be made queen in her place" (Esth. 1:19).[25]

As the Eve of the New Covenant, Mary sat at the right hand of Christ "in the possession of better things," namely, her fullness of grace,—grace so wonderful that we can conceive no greater grace; grace so inclusive that no good thing was lacking to her; grace so abundant that, filling all things, she herself remained full. First *Mary could receive no greater grace* because next to being God, there is no greater good than to be the Mother of God. Secondly, *no good thing was lacking to her,* and this we are told in the tenth chapter of St. Luke: "Mary hath chosen the best part" (10:42). This Virgin Mother not only chose the best things, but she chose the best part of the best things and St. Bonaventure mentions seven of the good things of heaven and of earth of which Mary chose the best part. The first of these good things, Mary shares with all, for there are two ways along which man journeys to eternal life,—the *active* and the *contemplative.* The part of those following the *active* way is good; the part of those following the *contemplative* way is better but the best part is the part of those following both paths, combining the active life with the contemplative, and this part the Most Blessed Mary chose. Hence she is typified by both Martha and Mary, as our Lord Himself pointed out when He said: "Mary hath chosen the best part." If He had wished merely to express the excellence of the contemplative life over the active life, Christ would have said: "Mary hath chosen the better part." The use of the word *best* points out a very special prerogative of Mary,—her perfection in both the active and the contemplative life. The second good thing which Mary enjoys she likewise shares with *all,* for there are three states in which men lead a holy life: *the married state, the state of widowhood,* and *the state of virginity.* The part of the married woman is *good;* the part of the widow is *better,* and the part of the virgin is *best,* and this part the Blessed Virgin Mary hath chosen. "Mary hath chosen the best part" both in quality and in quantity, because she possessed them all; she led the life of a married woman, of a widow, and of a virgin. Now the third good thing which Mary enjoyed she shares with *virgins and mothers.* The part of mothers is *good,* because they have fecundity; the part of virgins, *better,* because they have virginal dignity, but again the Most Blessed Virgin "hath chosen the best part," for she had both the fecundity of a mother and the dignity of a virgin. The fourth good thing Mary shares with *God* and with *creatures.* The part of creatures, who have the Lord Jesus Christ as their *God,* is *good;* the

(25) "Et *sedit ad dexteram eius.* . . . Tertia ratio est, quia *patriarchatus,* quem habuisset Adam in numero virorum et Eva in numero feminarum, ut sederet ad dexteram Dei, id est *in potioribus bonis,* translatus est ad Christum et Mariam, Matrem eius, quia, sicut illi fuerunt peremptores humani generis, ita isti fuerunt reparatores. Unde legitur Esther primo: *Detur regnum illius alteri, quae melior illa sit." De Assumtione B. Virginis Mariae. Sermo III,* t.IX, 695a.

part of God the Father Who has Him for a *Son* is *better;* but Mary "hath chosen the best part"; she has Him both as her *God* and her *Son.* The fifth good thing Mary shared with the *Holy Ghost,* for the Holy Ghost proceeded from the Son, but the Son did not proceed from the Holy Ghost; the Blessed Virgin proceeded from the Son, and the Son proceeded from her. The sixth good thing Mary shared with her *Son,* with Whom was divided the Kingdom of Heaven, and of which there are two parts—*justice* and *mercy*. Again the Blessed Virgin "hath chosen the best part" because she became the *Queen of Mercy* while her Son remained the *King of Justice;* and mercy is better than justice because, as the Apostle says, "mercy exalteth itself above justice" (James 2:13), and God's tender mercies are over all his works" (Ps. 144:9). The seventh good thing, Mary likewise shared with her *Son,* for the Son "sitteth at the right hand of the Father" (Mark 16:19) in the more desirable good things of the Father, and "the queen stood on the right hand of her Son" (cf. Ps. 44:10) in the more desirable good things of the Son and, of all desirable good things, this desirable good thing is the best. Again "Mary hath chosen the best part" and it is evident that *no good thing was lacking to her.*[26]

Mary sat at the right hand of Christ, her hands full to overflowing with an abundance of grace. She is the "little fountain" spoken of in the Book of Esther which "grew into a very great river, and abounded into many waters" (11:10).[27] Bedewed with the morning gifts of her Spouse at the very dawn of her existence, Mary "grew into a great river" with the influx of additional graces received in her conception of the Son of God and "was turned into the light and into the sun" with the final and crowning grace of her glorification

---

(26) "Tertia stella est *plenitudo gratiae,* quae in tribus quoque consistit: primum, quia *plus concipere non potuit;* secundum, quia *nullum bonum defuit;* tertium, quod ita effluxit, quod omnia replens, *plena remansit. Plus capere non potuit,* quia post *esse* Deum nullum bonum fuit maius quam esse Matrem Domini. Et de hoc dicitur in Lucae primo: *Ave, gratia plena. Nullum bonum defuit,* et hoc dicitur in Lucae decimo: *Maria optimam partem elegit.* Primam divisionem fecit universorum cum *omnibus.* In hominibus enim duae erant partes bonae, scilicet *activa* et *contemplativa.* Bona est pars *activorum,* melior *contemplativorum,* sed optima, quae habuit utrumque simul; et hanc elegit beatissima Maria. Unde significatur per Martham et Mariam, quod et Dominus ipse innuit, dicendo: *Optimam.* Si enim non voluisset nisi contemplativam activae praetulisse, dixisse debuisset: Maria *meliorem* elegit partem; dicendo vero *optimam,* de ipsa specialiter intelligitur, quod in utraque vita perfecta fuit.—Item, et aliam divisionem habuit cum *omnibus.* Triplex enim erat bona vita in hominibus: *coniugatae, viduae* et *virginalis. Bona* est pars coniugatorum; *melior,* viduarum; *optima,* virginum; et hanc elegit beata Virgo Maria, et sic *elegit optimam* qualitate et quantitate, quia hos omnes status habuit.—Tertiam divisionem fecit cum *virginibus* et *matribus. Bona* enim fuit pars matrum, quia habuerunt fecunditatem; *melior,* virginum, quia habuerunt dignitatem virginalem; sed iterum beatissima Virgo *optimam partem elegit,* quae habuit et matris fecunditatem et virginis dignitatem.—Quartam divisionem fecit cum *Deo* et *creaturis.* Bona fuit pars creaturarum, quae Dominum Iesum Christum habuit *Deum; melior fuit pars* Dei Patris, qui habuit eum *Filium: optimam* ergo partem elegit quae eum et *Deum* et *Filium* habuit.—Quintam divisionem habuit cum *Spiritu Sancto.* Spiritus enim sanctus procedit a Filio, sed non Filius a Spiritu sancto; sed beata Virgo procedit a Filio, et Filius ab ipsa.—Sextam divisionem fecit cum *Filio,* cum quo divisit regnum caelorum, cuius duae erant partes, *iustitia* et *misericordia.* Beata Virgo optimam sibi elegit, quia facta est *regina misericordiae,* et Filium eius remansit *rex iustitiae;* et melior misericordia quam iustitia, quia *superexaltat misericordia iudicium,* et *miserationes eius super* omnia opera eius.—Item, septimam divisionem fecit cum *Filio;* Filius enim sedet ad dexteram Patris in potioribus bonis Patris; et *regina astat a dextris* Filii; Glossa: Scilicet 'in potioribus bonis' Filii; sed inter potiora potius hoc est optimum: ergo optimam partem elegit sibi Maria. Et sic patet, qualiter nullum bonum sibi defuerit." *De Assumtione B. Virginis Mariae. Sermo VI,* t.IX, 703ab.

(27) "Tertium, in quo consistebat plenitudo, fuit, quod ita *effluxit,* quod omnia *replet,* et tamen *plena* remansit. Unde fuit haec plenitudo *fontis,* qui superplenus effluxit; unde Esther undecimo: *Fons parvus crevit in fluvium maximum* etc." *Ibid.,* 703b.

in heaven.[28] Knowing that she is overflowing with grace, she invites us all to partake of her fullness. As St. Jerome says: "The holy Virgin Mary is the help of the whole world and the ready protection of those who watch at her gates; she is the Refuge of Christians and of all who have recourse to her; she is the Comfort of the afflicted and the Way for all those who have wandered from the path; she is the redemption of captives and the Mediatress of all with God." And St. Bernard: "Of her fullness, all receive." Let us therefore have recourse to her according to the admonition of the same Bernard who says: "Let human frailty hasten to Mary. In her you will find no harshness, no severity, no austerity, no bitterness. She is all-sweet and gracious, all-merciful and mild, offering milk and wool to all."[29] Mary's mercy is the mercy of a mother: tender, patient, forgiving, boundless, understanding. It flows freely to every child of hers, no matter how low his spiritual estate. To the captive she gives redemption; to the sick, restoration to health; to the sorrowful, consolation; to the sinner, pardon; to the just, grace; to the angels, joy; to the Three Persons of the Ever Blessed Trinity, glory; to the Person of the Son, the estate of His human flesh, "that there may be no one who can hide himself from her heat" (Ps. 18:7).[30] Rightly, then, may we greet her:

"Hail, full of grace overflowing!"
Mother of Divine Grace, Mother Most Merciful, Help of Christians,
Health of the Sick, Refuge of Sinners, Comfort of the Afflicted,
Pray for us!

* * *

Because she is the Mother of God, Mary is all-powerful, "Suppliant Omnipotence," we may call her, for the omnipotence that is God's by essence is made graciously over to the service of her love. It was at her request that Christ anticipated His public mission and worked His first miracle at the wedding feast of Cana. When the Kings from the East came to offer gifts to their new-born King, "they found the child," as Christians have found Him since, "with Mary his mother" (Matt. 2:11). If we wish to find Christ, says

(28) "Et describitur nobis hic sub metaphora *fontis* et *fluvii, solis* et *lucis,* in quibus laudatur a plenitudine omnium bonorum; et proponitur nobis sub metaphora *fontis* ratione gratiae *acceptae* in sua origine; sub metaphora *fluvii,* ratione gratiae *superadditae* in conceptione Filii Dei; sub metaphora *solis* et *lucis,* ratione gratiae *consummatae* in eius glorificatione. Primum notatur, cum dicit: *Fons parvus;* secundum notatur, cum dicit: *crevit in fluvium maximum;* et tertium, cum dicit: *et in lucem solemque conversus est.* Hodie est dies consummationis gloriae eius." *De Assumtione B. Virginis Mariae. Sermo IV,* t.IX, 696a.

(29) "Et ideo sciens, se habere gratiam redundantem, omnes invitat ad suam plentitudinem. Unde Hieronymus: 'Universale auxilium et praeparata protectio ad eam vigilantium, Christianorum quoque refugium ad eam concurrentium et consolatio tribulatorum, errantium via et redemptio captivorum est sancta Virgo Maria et mediatrix omnium apud Deum.' Et Bernardus: 'De plenitudine eius accipiunt universi.' Et propterea confugiendum est ad ipsam, secundum quod ipse Bernardus hortatur: Quia ad Mariam trepidet humana fragilitas. Nihil in ea durum, nihil in ea asperum, nihil austerum, nihil amarum; tota dulcis et suavis, tota misericors, omnibus offerens lac et lanam'." *De Annuntiatione B. Virginis Mariae. Sermo V,* t.IX, 679b.

(30) "Et ideo Bernardus loquens de ipsa: 'De plenitudine eius acceperunt universi: captivus redemptionem, aeger curationem, tristis consolationem, peccator veniam, iustus gratiam, Angeli laetitiam, denique tota Trinitas gloriam, Filii persona carnis humanae substantiam, ut non sit *qui se abscondat a calore eius*'." *De Annuntiatione B. Virginis Mariae. Sermo IV,* t.IX, 673a.

St. Bonaventure, we must first draw near to Mary, for of her the Angel said: "Thou hast found grace with God" (Luke 1:30). She is that Esther whom the king "loved more than all the women, and she had favor and kindness before him above all the women" (Esth. 2:17). "Let us go therefore with confidence to the throne of grace, that we may obtain mercy and find grace in seasonable aid" (Heb. 4:16).[31] Let us hail her, then, as "Virgin Most Powerful" and with the immortal Dante sing:

So mighty art thou, Lady, and so great,
That he who grace desireth, and comes not
To thee for aidance, fain would have desire
Fly without wings. Not only him who asks
Thy bounty succors; but doth freely oft
Forerun the asking.

* * *

In her "is all grace of the way and of truth" (Ecclus. 24:25). She is the Mother of Good Counsel, who will direct us aright, for she is filled with the grace of the Holy Spirit, and enlightened by the splendor of His wisdom. Even in this world, she enjoyed perfect contemplation of God and an understanding of the deepest mysteries of faith. Mary was not present at the Transfiguration nor did our Lord appear to her after His resurrection from the dead, for she needed no instruction in the faith. She possessed a knowledge of all secrets, as was evident at the marriage feast of Cana. Knowing beforehand what her Son wished to do, she said to the waiters: "Whatsoever he shall say to you, do ye" (John 2:5).[32] In these few words of Our Lady we have the sense and the summary of her advice to us as Our Mother of Good Counsel. Her counsel to us will always be the counsel of Cana, but the counsel of Cana made clear for us in our own difficulties, our own sorrows, and our own joys. Let us, then, go to her and say:

"Virgin Mother, Lady of Good Counsel,
Sweetest picture artist ever drew,
In all my doubts I fly to thee for guidance,
Mother, tell me, what am I to do!"

* * *

In her "is all hope of life and of virtue" (Ecclus. 24:25). She is the

(31) "Matthaei secundo: 'Et intrantes domum, invenerunt puerum cum Maria, matre eius, et procidentes adoraverunt eum, et apertis thesauris suis, obtulerunt ei munera, aurum, thus et myrrham.' In hoc etiam instruimur, ut, si Christum volumus invenire, primus ad Mariam debeamus accedere; de ipsa enim dicitur supra primo: 'Invenisti gratiam apud Dominum.' Ipsa ergo invenit gratiam et misericordiam coram Assuero 'super omnes mulieres', sicut dicitur Esther secundo. Et ideo 'accedamus cum fiducia ad thronum gratiae, ut misericordiam consequamur et gratiam inveniamus in auxilio opportuno'." *Comment. in Evangelium Lucae* C.II, t.VII, 52b.

(32) "Quarta stella sive praerogativa est *perfecta Dei in via contemplatio* et mysterii incarnationis cognitio, quorum utrumque habuit in via, quamvis non de via; et huius argumentum (est), quod nullam postmodum factam ipsi legimus revelationem. Unde nec transfiguratione interfuit, nec aliqua ei post resurrectionem facta fuit apparitio, quia in fide instrui non indiguit, quae omnium secretorum semper conscia fuit, ut patuit in *nuptiis*. Ideo, quando praescia, quid Filius facere voluit, dixit ministris: *Quodcumque dixerit vobis, facite.*" *De Assumtione B. Virginis Mariae. Sermo VI*, t.IX, 703b.

"Morning Star" which leads us to Christ, as foretold in the Book of Numbers: "A star shall rise out of Jacob and a sceptre shall spring up from Israel, and shall strike the chiefs of Moab" (Num. 24:17). Mary is the star of unfailing virtue who struck the *chiefs of Moab,* namely, the demons or the seven capital sins. She is the star that led the Magi to Christ.[33] Shining high in the heavens, her silvery rays still pierce the gloomy darkness of this world to guide and direct our course into the port of salvation. Of herself she said: "I am the root and stock of David, the bright and morning star" (Apoc. 22-16). "I love them that love me, and they that in the morning early watch for me shall find me" (Prov. 8:17). The Angel of the Annunciation called her by the beautiful name of "Mary." Since she is the "Comforter of the Afflicted," St. Bernard admonishes: "In dangers, in troubles, in doubts, think of Mary. Call upon Mary. Let her name be ever on your lips, her love ever present in your heart, and that you may obtain the suffrage of her prayers, do not lose sight of her unparalleled virtues."[34] "When tossed by storms and tempests on this life's shoals, fix your eyes on the star, call upon Mary! When overwhelmed by the waves of pride, ambition, calumny, and jealousy, look at the star, call upon Mary. When anger, avarice, the allurements of the flesh have shattered the frail bark of your soul, look at the star, call upon Mary. When troubled by the enormity of your sins or confounded by the guilt of your conscience, when on the verge of despair's abyss, lift up your eyes to Mary. As long as you follow her, you cannot stray from the path; as long as you pray to her, you cannot lose hope; as long as you think of her, your course is sure. You cannot fall when she sustains you; you have nothing to fear when she protects you. With her as guide, you will not grow weary; if she favors the voyage, you will reach the harbor in safety."[35]

O Mary, Our Mother, Morning Star,

Pray for us!

* * *

Especially appropriate to her dignity is Mary's title "Gate of Heaven," for no one enters heaven except through her and no grace has ever come from heaven except through her hands. It is only through faith in the Son of God made Flesh of the Virgin Mary that anyone has entered or will enter

(33) "Secundo est stella superior, quae est Virgo beata, *deducens* nos ad Christum; de qua stella intelligitur quod dicitur in libro Numerorum, ubi dicitur: *Orietur stella ex Iacob, et consurget virga ex Israel et percutiet duces Moab.* Beata Virgo dicitur *stella,* quia habuit virtutem stabilem et inconcussam; per *Moab* intelliguntur voluptuosi. *Duces Moab* sunt daemones, vel peccata capitalia. Ista stella *percussit duces Moab,* id est septem peccata capitalia. . . . Ista stella *percussit duces Moab* et deduxit ad Christum Magos." *Sermones de Tempore. Epiphania. Sermo I,* t.IX, 150b.

(34) "*Sicut abundant passiones Christi in nobis,* ita et per Christum abundat consolatio nostra. Et ratione huius Virgo Maria dicitur et est *consolatrix miserorum;* unde Bernardus: 'In periculis, in angustiis, in rebus dubiis Mariam cogita, Mariam invoca. Non recedat ab ore, non recedat a corde, et ut impetres orationis eius suffragium, non deseras conversationis exemplum'." *De Annuntiatione B. Virginis Mariae. Sermo II,* t.IX, 664b, 665a.

(35) "Unde Bernardus: 'In periculis, in angustiis, in rebus dubiis . . . etc.' et post: 'Ipsam sequens non devias, ipsam rogans non desperas, ipsam cogitans non erras, ipsa tenente, non corruis, ipsa protegente, non metuis, ipsa duce, non fatigaris, ipsa propitia, pervenis'." *De Nativitate B. Virginis Mariae. Sermo II,* t.IX, 710b, 711a.

heaven; it is only through Mary that grace comes to us from heaven. Hence Our Lord never receives anyone except through her mediation. Mary is a gate which swings both ways, up to heaven, and down to earth. As regards the first, the Book of Wisdom says: "All good things came to me together with her" (7:11); as regards the second: "And I knew not that she was the mother of them all" (Wis. 7:12): Mary, then, is the Gate of Heaven, but how can this be, since Our Lord says: "I am the door"? "By me, if any man enter in, he shall be saved. And he shall go in and go out, and shall find pastures" (John 10:9). This is not a contradiction, explains St. Bonaventure, the *gate* is at the *door* or entrance of heaven, as is signified in the description of Solomon's temple with its two doors, both of which opened at the same time: "And two doors of fir tree, one on each side. And each door was double, and so opened with folding leaves" (III Kings 6:34). But what kind of gate is Mary? In the Apocalypse St. John saw twelve gates (Apoc. 21:12), all leading back to the Gate which is Mary, because through it run an approach and entrance from every part of the world. Deservedly is Mary called the Gate because both by her example and the help of her intercession she leads souls to heaven. She is the *Beautiful Gate of the Temple* (Acts 3:10) of Light *"which looks toward the east"* (Ezech. 44:1), a gate easy of access and most alluring to all who pass her way. "Come over to me, all ye that desire me, and be filled with my fruits (Ecclus. 24:26). Thus does the glorious Virgin by her charm and winning ways attract souls "to the banquet of the Lord."[36] Why, O Lady, do we say that the whole world is full of thy blessings? They penetrate the depths of earth, they rise to the heights of heaven, for through the fullness of thy grace, those in this world below rejoice that they have been delivered; those in the world above rejoice that they have been restored, and thus the Blessed Virgin has become the Queen of the whole universe. Let all, therefore, praise her; in her honor let every knee be bowed, "of those that are in heaven, on earth and under the earth" (Phil. 2:10), for her blessings flow abundantly upon all.[37] If Jesus is King of the whole world, then Mary is its Queen,—Queen not only of earth but also of heaven, to which her power extends. Let all greet her, then, in the

(36) "Octava stella est *appropriatio dignitatis,* quae dicitur *porta caeli;* et hoc est, quod nisi per ipsam nullus intrat caelum, sed nec unquam aliquid gratiae egressum est de caelo, quia sine fide Filii Dei incarnati ex Maria Virgine nunquam aliquis intravit vel intrabit in caelos, nec sine hac aliquid gratuitum unquam exivit de caelo. Unde Dominus nunquam recipit (aliquem), nisi ipsa mediante. Propter primus dicitur Sapientiae septimo: *Venerunt mihi omnia bona pariter cum illa.* Propter secundum, ibidem: *Ignorabam, quoniam horum omnium mater est.* Haec est ergo *porta caeli;* sed qualiter hoc, cum Dominus dicat: *Ego sum ostium?* etc. Sed nec est contradictio, quia *porta* est in *ostio,* sicut significatum fuit in templo, ubi erant duo ostia, quae simul aperiebantur. Sed qualiter haec *porta* est? Ioannes in Apocalypsi vidit duodecim portas, sed omnes illae portae reducuntur ad istam portam, quia ista ex omni parte mundi apportabat et importabat; et hoc merito et exemplo et inercessionis auxilio. Unde ipsa est veri *templi speciosa porta* lucis quae respicit ad *orientem,* porta *pervia* et invitans omnes transeuntes, dicens: *Transite ad me, omnes, qui concupiscitis me* etc., id est attrahens et invitans sicut vinum dominicum." *De Assumtione B. Virginis Mariae. Sermo VI,* t.IX, 705b, 706a.

(37) " 'Cur loquor, Domina, beneficiis tuis plenum esse mundum? Inferna penetrant, caelos superant; per plenitudinem enim gratiae tuae et quae in inferno erant se laetantur liberata, et quae super mundum sunt se gaudent restaurata.' Et ideo beata Virgo omnium regina facta est.—Omnes ergo eam laudent, in eius honorem *omne genu flectatur, caelestium, terrestrium et infernorum,* quia beneficia eius in omnes redundant." *De Annuntiatione B. Virginis Mariae. Sermo IV,* t.IX, 673a.

words of St. Anselm: "O Woman wondrously unique, and uniquely wonderful, through whom all things are renewed, earth's wrongs are righted, demons are crushed, men are saved, and Angels' ranks made whole!"[38]

O Mary, Our Queen,
resurrection of the fallen,
Gate of Heaven,
Pray for us!

* * *

So far does the grandeur of the glorious Virgin transcend our human understanding, so far does her glory outstrip our poor powers of expression that the Holy Spirit Himself Who filled her with His gifts, speaking now through the Prophets, now through the Doctors of the Church, now in words clear and simple, now in figures and metaphors, has placed His own praise of this glorious Lady on our lips. We have already referred to the passage in which He unfolds the fullness of her grace: "A little fountain grew into a very great river, and abounded into many waters; the light and the sun rose up, and the humble were exalted" (Esth. 11:10). And again in the Book of Esther we read: "The little fountain which grew into a river, and was turned into a light, and into the sun, and abounded into many waters, is Esther, whom the king married, and made queen" (10:6). Though the words are spoken of her forerunner and prototype, who of old found favor with King Assuerus, the head of the whole kingdom, and was taken in marriage to become his bride and queen, they have a peculiar application to the lowly little maiden who was prepared in time, exalted among her people and taken in marriage with the Most High King, that she might become the Mother of God.[39] In the words of Pope Benedict XV of revered memory: "Mary is the beautiful Esther whom the sovereign King of kings so loved, that, for the salvation of her people, he not merely gave her half of his kingdom, but raised her up to be his consort in power and majesty." Seated on the right hand of her Son, she shines in an ocean of light, in the full maturity of her grace and beauty, in the consummation of her glory. An extraordinary thing that a fountain should be turned into a light and not at all according

(38) "Si David, princeps, Mater Domini non erat ancilla, sed domina et regina, domina utique omnium, non solum terrestrium, sed et caelestium, ad quae se extendit ipsius imperium. Et ideo Anselmus: 'O femina mirabiliter singularis et singulariter mirabilis! per quam omnia renovantur, inferna remediantur, daemones conculcantur, homines salvantur, Angeli redintegrantur!' " *Ibid.*

(39) *"Fons parvus crevit in fluvium maximum, et in solem lucemque conversus est et in aquas plurimas redundavit; Esther est, quam rex accepit uxorem et voluit esse reginam.*

Carissimi! gloriosae Virginis excellens sublimitas adeo transcendit capacitatem humanam, ut non sufficiant verba ad eius explicationem; et ideo Spiritus sanctus, qui eam replevit charismatibus virtutum, ipse Spiritus sanctus loquens per Prophetas et alios sacrae Scripturae doctores, laudat ipsam multipliciter, non solum per verba expressa, sed etiam per figuras et metaphoras. Unde et verbum istud, licet dictum sit de Esther, multo tamen eximius et plenius, visum interius, exponitur de beata Virgine, quia Esther figuram gerit beatae Virginis tam ratione nominis quam ratione rei. Nam Esther interpretatur *praeparata in tempore* vel *exaltata in populo,* et fuit uxor Assueri regis, qui fuit princeps totius monarchiae; et cum esset parvula, facta est regina, et significat beatam Virginem, quae fuit *praeparata* in tempore et *exaltata* in populo et assumta est in connubium summi Regis, ut Mater fieret Dei." *De Assumtione B. Virginis Mariae. Sermo IV,* t.IX, 695b.

to nature that one of the material elements should be changed into a heavenly body, but it is the way of grace in the glorification of the Virgin: "A great sign appeared in the heaven: a woman clothed with the sun, and the moon under her feet, and on her head a crown of twelve stars" (Apoc. 12:1).[40] Having been God's spotless Mother on earth, she now shines in purest light as the benign Queen of Heaven. She is "clothed with the sun," for the brightness of God shines 'round her; beneath her feet rests the changeful moon, a symbol of the vicissitudes of this fleeting world. She is crowned, not as the queens of earth with a diadem of perishable gold, but with the stars, unchanging, everlasting.

Surrounded by all the glories of the heavens, Mary outshines these masterpieces of God's material creation in the brightness and splendor of her presence. "She is more beautiful than the sun," for of all creatures she is most like the Source and Fountain-head of all beauty, the Beauty ever ancient, ever new; "and above all the orders of the stars," that is, above all the Saints who shine in glory. "Being compared to the light, she is found before it" (cf. Wis. 7:29), for enlightened by Divine Wisdom above all the saints, she has illumined the whole world by the light of her grace.[41] As the sun in the high heavens shines upon the whole world with unfailing splendor, so does the glorious Virgin Mary illumine the whole Church and the whole world, as Ecclesiasticus says: "The sun giving light hath looked upon all things, and full of the glory of the Lord is His work" (42:16). Since she lights up the whole world with her rays, Mary with Wisdom "who praiseth herself" can say: "I made that in the heavens there should arise a light that never faileth. I dwelt in the highest places, and my throne is in a pillar of a cloud" (Ecclus. 24:6,7). As St. Jerome says: "If you study her very closely, you will find that there is no virtue, no beauty, no splendor and glory which does not shine forth in her." Like a light on a candlestick placed high where all can see, this Exalted Woman shines upon all with the light of Eternal Wisdom which is in her, as Tobias had foretold: "Thou shalt shine with a glorious light, and all the ends of the earth shall worship thee" (Tob. 13:13).[42] Mary's light is the light of God, the pure and unchanged ray of

(40) Cf. *supra*, p. 251, footnote 15.

(41) "*Est enim haec speciosior sole et super omnem dispositionem stellarum, luci comparata, invenitur prior,* Sapientiae septimo. In verbis istis Imperatrix gloriosa, super choros supernorum civium sublimata commendatur a Spiritu sancto quantum ad assumtionem suam commendatione perfecta; commendatur autem quantum ad tria, quae aliquam nobilem dominam excellentissime commendabilem reddunt, quae quidem sunt *perfecta speciositas, superexcellens nobilitas* et *sapientiae claritas.* Quantum ad perfectam speciositatem commendatur hic, cum *sole speciosior* nuncupatur; quantum ad excellentem *nobilitatem,* cum *stellis* omnibus, id est universis Sanctis, sublimius et altius collocatur; sed quantum ad sapientiae *claritatem,* cum *luci* aeternae sapientiae *comparata,* propius omnibus creaturis dicitur illustrata." *De Assumtione B. Virginis Mariae. Sermo II,* t.IX, 691a.

(42) "Secundo, propter *refulgentiam inerrabilem;* ideo enim sol in altissimis collocatur, ut cetera mundi corpora ab ipso illustrentur. Talis fuit gloriosissima Virgo Maria, quae illustrat totam Ecclesiam et machinam mundanam; propter quod Ecclesiastici quadragesimo secundo: *Sol illuminans per omnia respexit, et gloria Domini plenum est opus eius.* Ipsa namque Virgo Maria ad modum solis radiis eius perlustrat universa; unde sibi competit illud Ecclesiastici vigesimo quarto: *Ego feci in caelis, ut oriretur lumen indeficiens;* et ideo subdit: *Ego in altissimis habitavi, et thronus meus in columna nubis.* Illustrat enim suis exemplis omnia tanquam lucerna super candelabrum mundi posita; unde Hieronymus: 'Si diligentius respicias, nihil virtutis, nihil speciositatis, nihil candoris et gloriae, quod non in ea resplendeat'." *De Nativitate B. Virginis Mariae. Sermo II,* t.IX, 710b.

the Light that "enlighteneth every man that cometh into this world," but it is reflected from the will, the feelings, the emotions of the most perfect, the most womanly of all women, the Woman best suited to interpret the Christian character for her own sex. In her character of Virgin and Mother, Mary shines forth as the glory of all women and as a magnificent and convincing proof of the ennoblement which is theirs by reason of the Incarnation of the Son of God.

This masterpiece of God's creation, adorned with all the qualities and virtues which distinguish her sex, St. Bonaventure presents to the minds and hearts of all women as the Exemplar best suited to convey to them the dignity of their nature and their functions. "As the sun when it riseth to the world in the high places of God, so is the beauty of a good wife for the ornament of her house" (Ecclus. 26:21). The Christian ideal has two perfect models,—the one, the great original of all holiness and justice, God Himself Who became man and walked amongst us, that from His example we might see and hear and understand the dignity of our human nature; the other, Mary, a mere creature like ourselves, a woman chosen and approved by God Himself and endowed with all the excellencies peculiar to her sex, who would shine forth not only as the perfect image of the Word made Flesh but also as a Guide and Model whom all women within the meet sphere of their womanhood could follow in her imitation of the Man-God. As the sun, the most excellent of all material bodies, enhances the beauty of the physical universe by its rays, so does the Blessed Virgin, the most excellent member of the Church Militant and even of the Church Triumphant, shine forth as the ornament and glory of her sex. Not only is she a good woman, but she is the best of all women, for she is endowed with every quality which could redound to the praise and perfection of a good woman according to the metaphor of the material sun and its likeness to the Eternal Sun of Justice. As the sun in the heavens has the power to *purify, illumine,* and *perfect* all things, and to *diffuse its rays* over the whole earth, so a perfectly good woman, such as was the Virgin Mary, was found to be endowed with a fourfold kind of grace corresponding to the four properties just mentioned, for the Virgin Mary was *virtuous, beautiful, gracious,* and *dutiful.*[43]

---

(43) "*Sicut sol oriens mundo in altissimis Dei, sic bonae mulieris species in ornamentum domus suae.* Consideranti mihi excellentiam Virginis gloriosae respectu universalis Ecclesiae, nulla occurrit similitudo nobilior quam illa quam ponit Ecclesiasticus in verbo praemisso. Sicut enim sol praecellit et decorat corpora totius machinae mundialis, sic beata Virgo praecellit et decorat membra totius Ecclesiae militantis et etiam triumphantis, et hoc, quia ipsa est mulier, non tantum bona, sed etiam optima, pro eo quod nihil deest ei de eo quod facit ad commendationem et perfectionem bonae mulieris, secundum metaphoram solis materialis et imitationem Solis aeterni. Sicut enim sol habet virtutem *purgativam, illuminativam, perfectivam* et sui per omnia *diffusivam;* sic mulier perfecte bona, qualis fuit Virgo Maria, quadriformi genere gratiae invenitur repleta. Virgo namque Maria fuit mulier *virtuosa, speciosa, gratiosa et officiosa* iuxta proprietates praedictas." *De Nativitate B. Virginis Mariae. Sermo III,* t.IX, 712a.

Mary was a *virtuous* woman. Hence she was prefigured by Ruth, to whom her kinsman Booz said: "All the people that dwell within the gates of my city, know that thou are a virtuous woman" (Ruth 3:11). Indeed the Virgin Mary was a woman of *virtue,* first, on account of the *holiness of her renunciation:* "Now therefore pray for us, for thou art a holy woman, and one fearing God" (Judith 8:29). Mary was *holy* by freedom from all impurity of the flesh, *god-fearing* by her avoidance of all impurity of mind. Hence she was free "from all defilement of the flesh and of the spirit," thus perfecting her sanctification in fear of God, according to the admonition of St. Paul: "Let us cleanse ourselves from all defilement of the flesh and of the spirit, perfecting sanctification in the fear of God" (II Cor. 7:1).[44] Mary was a woman of *virtue,* secondly, on account of the *rectitude of her choice.* "As everlasting foundations upon a solid rock, so the commandments of God in the heart of a holy woman" (Ecclus. 26:24), because, according to St. Matthew, "everyone that heareth these my words and doth them shall be likened to a wise man that built his house upon a rock" (7:24). Such a woman, without doubt, was the Virgin Mary.[45] Mary was a woman of *virtue,* thirdly, on account of her *fortitude in suffering.* "Who shall find the valiant woman?" (Prov. 31:10). This valiant woman was the Virgin Mary, whose unfailing constancy made her especially pleasing to God, as Ecclesiasticus says: "A virtuous woman rejoiceth her husband" (26:2).[46] Virtuous souls who wish to follow Mary as their model must begin their sanctification by contempt of all earthly possessions and by freedom from all carnal desires, and this by embracing the cross. Then they must grow in holiness by observance of the commandments and by zeal for the divine law. Having observed these, they can very easily attain the constancy of fortitude. On the other hand, if we love the things of earth and are not zealous for the law of God, it is impossible to be brave and patient in suffering.[47]

Mary was a *beautiful* woman, hence she was prefigured by Abigail: "Abigail was a prudent and comely woman" (I Kings 25:3). Like Judith, she was *comely,* first, on account of the *honor of her deeds.* "There was not such

(44) "Fuit namque mulier *virtuosa,* unde designata fuit per Ruth; Ruth tertio: *Scit omnis populus, qui habitat intra portas urbis meae, mulierem te esse virtutis. Mulier* namque *virtutis,* fuit Virgo Maria: primo, propter *sanctitudinem in respuendis;* Iudith octavo: *Nunc ora pro nobis, quoniam mulier sancta es et timens Deum; sancta,* per sequestrationem ab omni immunditia carnis, et *timens Deum,* per elongationem ab omni immunditia mentis; et sic munda erat *ab omni inquinatione carnis et spiritus,* ac per hoc perficiebat sanctificationem in timore Dei, iuxta documentum Apostoli, secundae ad Corinthios septimo: *Mundemus nos ab omni inquinamento carnis et spiritus, perficientes sanctificationem in timore Dei." Ibid.*

(45) "Secundo, propter *rectitudinem in eligendis;* Ecclesiastici vigesimo sexto: *Fundamenta aeterna supra petram solidam, et mandata Dei in corde mulieris sanctae,* quia, secundum quod dicitur Matthaei septimo, *omnis, qui audit verba mea haec et facit ea, assimilabitur viro sapienti, qui aedificavit domum suam supra petram.* Talis, non est dubium, fuit Virgo Maria." *Ibid.,* 712ab.

(46) "Tertio, propter *fortitudinem in sustinendo;* Proverbiorum ultimo: *Mulierem fortem quis inveniet?* Haec mulier Virgo Maria fuit, quae propter multam constantiam singulariter placuit Deo; Ecclesiastici vigesimo sexto: *Mulier fortis oblectat virum suum." Ibid.,* 712b.

(47) "Iuxta hanc formam, si virtuosi esse volumus, necesse est, ut incipiamus a sanctitudine per contemptu omnium mundanorum et sequestrationem omnium carnalium desideriorum, et hoc per amplexum crucis, et post transeamus ad rectitudinem per observantiam mandatorum et zelum divinae legis. Quibus habitis, facile est pervenire ad constantiam fortitudinis, alioquin, si terrena diligimus et legem divinam non zelamus, impossibile est, quod in passionibus fortes et patientes simus." *Ibid.*

another woman upon earth in look, in beauty, and in sense of words" (Judith 11:19), for she was so honorable in word and deed that the most careful observer could find no fault in her.[48] Mary was *beautiful,* secondly, in the *perfection of her outward appearance.* "The beauty of a woman cheereth the countenance of her husband, and a man desireth nothing more" (Ecclus. 36:24), for nothing so pleases a man as to see the chastity and physical integrity of his spouse, and these virtues Mary possessed in abundance, as is evident in her answer to the angel: "How shall this be done, because I know not man?" (Luke 1:34).[49] Mary was *beautiful,* thirdly, in the *sincerity of her affections.* "I know that thou art a beautiful woman. Say, therefore, I pray three, that thou art my sister" (Gen. 12:11,13), said Abram to his wife Sarai, since she had for him the sincerity of a chaste love. This kind of love the Virgin Mary had for God; hence in the Canticle she is called *sister* and *spouse:* "Thou hast wounded my heart, my sister, my spouse" (Cant. 4:9).[50] In order to stress this threefold beauty, the spouse in the Canticle is thrice called the *fairest of women.* In the first chapter: "If thou know not thyself, O fairest among women, go forth, and follow after the steps of the flocks" (Cant. 1:7); in the fifth chapter: "What manner of one is thy beloved of the beloved, O thou most beautiful among women?" (5:9), and again: "Whither is thy beloved gone, O thou most beautiful among women?" Herein is indicated the singular privilege of this threefold beauty, because of which Mary was the most beautiful of women, not with a vain beauty, but with true beauty, to which all spiritual women should aspire if they would be honorable in character or in their deeds and conduct, modest in outward appearance, and immaculately pure in the affections of their heart.[51]

The Blessed Virgin was likewise a *gracious* woman, for which reason she was prefigured by Esther, of whom it is said that "she appeared agreeable and amiable in the eyes of all" (Esth. 2:15) and that "she had favour and kindness before the king above all the women" (Esth. 2:17). To no

(48) "Fuit enim mulier *speciosa;* unde figuratur per Abigail; primi Regum vigesimo quinto: *Erat Abigail mulier prudentissima et speciosa. Speciosa* namque fuit Virgo Maria: primo, propter *honestatem actuum;* Iudith undecimo: *Non est talis mulier super terram in aspectu, in pulcritudine et in sensu verborum.* Erat enim adeo honesta in verbis et factis, ut a nullo posset in aliquo reprehendi." *Ibid.*

(49) "Secundo, propter *integritatem sensuum;* Ecclesiastici trigesimo sexto: *Species mulieris exhilarat faciem viri sui et super omnem concupiscentiam hominis superducit desiderium.* Nihil enim est adeo placitum viro, sicut videre castitatem et integritatem in uxore sua, quae plenaria fuit in Virgine Maria, secundum quod Lucae primo dixit Angelo: *Quomodo fiet istud, quoniam virum non cognosco." Ibid.*

(50) "Tertio, propter *sinceritatem affectuum;* Genesis duodecimo: *Novi, quod pulcra sis mulier; dic ergo, obsecro te, quod soror mea sis:* quando habet ad eum sinceritatem amoris casti, quem amorem habuit Virgo Maria ad Deum; ideo *soror* et *sponsa* dicitur in Canticis canticorum." *Ibid.*

(51) "Propter hanc triplicem pulcritudinem designandam in sponsa et in Virgine Maria Spiritus sancti instinctu sponsa in Canticis ter dicitur *pulcherrima mulierem.* Nam capite primo dicitur: *Si ignoras te, o pulcherrima inter mulieres* etc.; et quinto: *Qualis est dilectus tuus, o pulcherrima mulierum?* et in eodem iterum: Quo abiit dilectus tuus, o pulcherrima mulierum? In quo insinuatur huius triplicis pulcritudinis singulare privilegium, propter quod fuit speciosissima mulierum non pulcritudine vana, sed pulcritudine vera, ad quam debem conari omnes viri spirituales, ut sint honesti in moribus sive in actibus et gestibus, modesti in sensibus et immaculati in affectionibus interioribus." *Ibid.*, 712b, 713a.

other woman can these words be applied in a spiritual sense as truly and as appropriately as they are applied to Mary, for she was *gracious,* first, because she had grace *sufficient* for her needs. "The grace of a diligent woman shall delight her husband, and shall fat his bones" (Ecclus. 26:16). Mary had sufficient grace to please God and to practice all the virtues, to *fatten bones,* as it were, for through that grace, she always advanced from good to better.[52] Mary was *gracious,* secondly, because she was full of *surpassing* grace. Ecclesiasticus says: "A holy and shamefaced woman is grace upon grace" (26:19). The holiness of virginal innocence is the choicest grace, a grace in which the Virgin Mary was without a peer, in consequence of which, Christ thus addresses her: "My sister, my spouse, a garden enclosed, a garden enclosed, a fountain sealed up" (Cant. 4.12).[53] Mary was a *gracious* woman, thirdly, because she was full of superabundant grace. To her the angel said: "Hail, full of grace, the Lord is with thee. Blessed art thou among women" (Luke 1:28), and he added: "The Holy Ghost shall come upon thee" (Luke 1:35). Upon the Virgin already inundated with grace comes the Holy Ghost, so that rightly to her may be applied the words of the Proverb: "Many daughters have gathered together riches; thou hast surpassed them all" (Prov. 31:29), and the words of the Psalm: "Thou hast visited the earth, and hast plentifully watered it" (64:10).[54] Hence if we wish to obtain grace, there is no better plan than to go to her who is *full of grace* and rightly therefore called the "throne of grace," according to the words of St. Paul to the Hebrews: "Let us go therefore with confidence to the throne of grace, that we may obtain mercy and find grace in seasonable aid" (4:16). Surely, through no one can grace be better obtained than through her to whom the angel said: "Thou hast found grace with God" (Luke 1:30).[55]

Mary was, lastly, a *dutiful* woman, charitable, full of good offices towards all, like the sun ever shedding her mighty radiance upon the earth. There-

---

(52) "Fuit nihilominus beata Virgo mulier *gratiosa;* unde designata fuit per Esther, de qua (dicitur) Esther secundo, quod *omnium oculis gratiosa et amabilis videbatur;* unde et paulo post subditur, quod invenit *gratiam et misericordiam coram rege super omnes mulieres.* Hoc autem de nulla alia muliere ita sane et recte intelligi potest spiritualiter sicut de gloriosa Virgine, quae gratiosa fuit: primo, quia plena gratia *sufficiente;* Ecclesiastici vigesimo sexto: *Gratia mulieris sedulae delectabit virum suum et ossa illius impinguabit.* Sufficientem enim habuit gratiam ad placendum Deo et ad exercitium omnium virtutum sicut ad impinguationem ossium; profecit enim per gratiam illam semper de bono melius." *Ibid.,* 713a.

(53) "Secundo, quia plena gratia *praeeminente;* Ecclesiastici vigesimo sexto: *Gratia super gratiam, mulier sancta et pudorata.* Sanctitudo cum pudore virginali gratiam excellentem dicit quae in Virgine Maria praecellens fuit; Canticorum quarto: *Hortus conclusus, soror mea sponsa, hortus conclusus, fons signatus." Ibid.*

(54) "Tertio, quia plena gratia *superabundante:* Lucac primo: *Ave, gratia plena, Dominus tecum, benedicta tu in mulieribus; et post: Spiritus sanctus superveniet in te.* In tanta namque superabundantia gratiae Spiritus sanctus venit, ut merito ei possit dici illud Proverbiorum ultimo: *Multae filiae congregaverunt divitias; tu supergressa es* universas; et in Psalmo: *Visitasti terram et inebriasti eam." Ibid.*

(55) "Propter quod, si gratiam volumus obtinere, nullum est sanius consilium, quam ut eam accedamus, quae est *gratia plena,* et ideo *thronus gratiae* merito nuncupatur, secundum illud ad Hebraeos quarto: *Adeamus cum fiducia ad thronum gratiae eius, ut misericordiam consequamur et gratiam inveniamus in auxilio opportuno.* Per nullam enim potest gratia melius inveniri, quam per illam cui per Angelum dictum est: *Invenisti gratiam apud Deum." Ibid.*

fore she was prefigured by the Valiant Woman whom Solomon praised: "She hath risen in the night, and given a prey to her household, and victuals to her maidens" (Prov. 31:15). These words are rightly applied to the Virgin who in season and out of season intercedes in our behalf, as St. John says: "And the wine failing, the mother of Jesus saith to him: They have no wine. And Jesus saith to her: Woman, what is that to thee and to me?" (2:3, 4). In this incident is shown the exceedingly great readiness of Our Lady to render service and her solicitude for the human race.[56] Now Mary is full of good offices towards us, first, in *delivering us from evil,* as prophesied in the words which God spoke to the serpent in the Garden: "I will put enmities between thee and the woman; she shall crush thy head" (Gen. 3:15). Indeed, she crushed our adversary and delivered us from his power when "she destroyed all heresies in the whole world."[57] Mary is a *dutiful* woman, secondly, in *advancing us in good.* The Proverb says: "A wise woman buildeth her house, but the foolish will pull down with her hands that also which is built" (Prov. 14:1), which rightly is understood of Mary and Eve, for as Eve by her foolishness has pulled us down from good, so the Virgin Mary by her wisdom advances us in good by erecting a spiritual edifice, as it were.[58] Mary is a *dutiful* woman, thirdly, by *finishing in the best.* "A gracious woman shall find glory" (Prov. 11:16). Mary has found glory for herself and for others, because through her, the gate of heaven has been opened to us; through her God came down to us, so through her, we must go up to God.[59]

Thus does St. Bonaventure liken Our Lady to the sun "when it riseth to the world in the high places of God."[60] Like that glorious body shining high in the heavens, the Blessed Virgin, the Mirror of Justice, shines forth as the perfect reflection of her Divine Son. Her whole person is alight with the light of her Beloved, not with the mighty splendor of the Sun of Justice but with the blinding rays of that pure light softened to the silvery radiance of the

---

(56) "Fuit etiam postremo mulier *officiosa;* unde intelligitur per illam mulierem a Sapiente laudatam, Proverbiorum ultimo, de qua dicitur: *De nocte surrexit deditque praedam domesticis suis* etc. Hoc recte competit Virgini, quae non tantum opportune, sed etiam importune interpellat pro nobis, quod designatum fuit Ioannis secundo: *Deficiente vino, dicit Mater Iesu ad eum: Vinum non habent. Et dicit ei Iesus: Quid mihi et tibi est, mulier?* In quo insinuatur nimia officiositas et sollicitudo, quam beatissima Virgo habet pro genere humano." *Ibid.*, 713ab.

(57) "Est enim nobis officiosa: primo, *liberando* a malo, in cuius figura dicitur Genesis tertio ad serpentem: *Inimicitias ponam inter te et mulierem;* et post: *Ipsa conteret caput tuum.* Ipsa namque contrivit adversarium nostrum et nos liberavit ab eo, cum 'cunctas haereses interemit in universo mundo'." *Ibid.*, 713b.

(58) "Secundo, *promovendo* in bono; Proverbiorum decimo quarto: *Sapiens mulier aedificat domum suam; insipiens exstructam quoque manibus destruet;* quod recte intelligitur de Maria et Eva; sicut enim Eva sua insipientia nos deiecit a bono, sic Virgo Maria sua sapientia nos promovet in bono tanquam spirituali aedificio manum apponendo." *Ibid.*

(59) "Tertio, *consummando* in optimo; Proverbiorum undecimo: *Mulier gratiosa inveniet gloriam.* Ipsa namque invenit gloriam sibi et aliis, quia per ipsam aperta est nobis porta caeli; sicut enim per eam Deus ad nos descendit, sic oportet, nos per eam ad Dominum ascendamus." *Ibid.*

(60) "Ex praedictis igitur colligi potest, quod Virgo beata tanquam mulier perfecte et simpliciter bona similitudinem habet expressam ad solem in mundo orientem propter quadriformis proprietatis excellentissimam tripiicationem, hoc est propter duodecim privilegia excellentia, propter de qua dicitur: *Mulier amicta sole* etc., *et in capite eius corona stellarum duodecim;* in quo datur intelligi excellentia duodecim praedictarum praerogativarum, pro quibus non immerito Virgo comparatur *Soli oriente mundo in altissimis Dei.* Benedicta igitur et venerabilis sit Virgo Maria in aeternum. Amen." *Ibid.*

heart and soul of woman. The holiest and most womanly of all women, Mary shines with every prerogative of nature and of grace as the glory and exemplar of all womankind and as a light and guide in the imitation of her Son. She is the epitome of all dignity, of all virtue and holiness, of all beauty and sweetness and grace, of charity and service, of motherly solicitude for all. She is all women in one glorious woman, with a woman's charm and grace and beauty and fascination. "Virgo et mater admirabilis," Virgin and Mother in both body and spirit, she is the ideal and inspiration not only of nuns who have consecrated their virginity to God but also of mothers who in her and by her have received the mission to purify, enlighten, ennoble, and console the heart of man, and thus add their increase to the heavenly kingdom. As Mary brought forth the cornerstone of the great spiritual edifice which is the Church, so every mother must bring forth stones hewn from the great quarry of humanity and cut by discipline and self-restraint to fit the Cornerstone, which is Christ. As Mary brought forth from the virgin womb of her flesh the great Leader of our salvation, so every Christian mother is to bring forth not only from the womb of her flesh but from the womb of the baptismal font, valiant soldiers of Christ, their King, Who stands ready to reward the victors with golden crowns of everlasting peace and joy.

CONCLUSION

"There is a shame that bringeth sin,
And there is a shame that bringeth glory and grace" (Ecclus. 4:25).

Two women stand over and against each other in the scheme of the ages,—the one the cause of death, the other the cause of life to herself and the whole human race. The destiny of the First Woman, as planned by Almighty God, was a dazzling one. Surpassingly fair in body, immaculate in soul, she was to be the stainless fountain of a stainless race, the inexhaustible source of a stream of life both natural and supernatural. But Eve's dignity turned to a shame and the ignominy of her fall makes us forget the glory of her beginnings. Through pride and rebellion of soul, she initiated a fall which carried humanity towards the very abyss of eternal death and she who was to have become the mother of all the living became in very truth the mother of all the dead. But God brooks no intervention of His plans, no pause in the majestic movement of His designs. Beside the bowed and shamed figure of Eve, so beautiful in the freshness of her creation, there arose out of the ages yet to come the vision of another Woman who would gather to herself all the loveliness of womanhood and leave it infinitely more lovely by her coming. She would remove the stain and the reproach that dwelt with the name of Woman since the Fall and restore to her sex that primacy of innocence, that light of honor which it was to have by nature and in the designs of God. From the very seed of the First Mother, God fashioned a new fountain of supernatural life, surpassing in beauty that which had appeared on earth at the dawn of creation. Thus, Eve's shame turned to "glory and grace," for she was the instrument in begetting a race which would bear Mary, the Mother of the Redeemer. Once again the whole destiny of the human race rested in the hands of a Woman. This time she did not fail, but reversing the role of Eve and fully compensating for her weakness, she initiated the home flight by which humanity mounts peak by peak to the very throne of God.

When the little Hebrew maid, repeating the prophecy of Lia (Gen. 30:13), said "All generations shall call me blessed," she did not say too much, but hardly enough, for her praise was sung by the mouth of God Himself long before her birth when He announced her in Paradise as the Woman who would crush the serpent's head. The prophets sang of her in words of mystery; strange and lovely prototypes presaged her coming and since the lips of the Angel voiced her first homage, greetings more countless than the stars have re-echoed from her children throughout the world. Her sweet name resounds in the canticles of the Church; she is written into great literature, woven into gorgeous tapestries, and sculptured into purest marble. In every age and in every clime, endless petitions from a thousand shrines rise efficaciously to her Immaculate Heart which God Himself made deep and wide to mother all mankind.

All the world is Mary's. God had her in His mind and heart when He began to create it. When He made the bright and glorious sun, He intended it to serve as her gown. When He placed the stars in the firmament, He knew that twelve of the brightest would one day embellish her crown. And when He made the moon, the fitting symbol of Earth with her changes and vicissitudes, He was thinking of a footstool for the Queen. Mary is the Eternal Woman, timeless with the timelessness of God and of his Church. And when this world will have passed away, when her work as Mediatress will be finished and the last of her children will have entered Heaven's Gate, the Woman of Genesis, the Woman of Cana and of Calvary will reign on forever as the Woman of the Apocalypse, the Eve of the New Covenant, the glorious Queen of Heaven. Then with all the heavenly court and the nine choirs of Angels we shall bow down in reverence before the Woman vestured with the sun, the moon beneath her feet, and on her head a starry crown. All generations shall call her blessed. Before her throne will rise the endless chant: "Blessed art thou among women and blessed is the fruit of thy womb, Jesus." Blessed forever be thou, O Mary, and blessed forever be the fruit of thy womb, Jesus,—Jesus, the eternal Son of God Who with the chrism of His Godhead has forever anointed and ennobled our common humanity,—Jesus, the Eternal King Whom through all the blissful ages of eternity we shall adore with the profoundest homage that can be given to God alone, as truly man as He is truly God, as truly God as He is truly man, one of our race and blood Brother of us all.

BIBLIOGRAPHY

Ambrose, S., *In Lucam. 2.1,* t.15; *De Instit. Virg.,* t.16, Migne, P. L., Paris, 1879.

Aristotle, *Works of Aristotle* translated into English under the editorship of W. D. Ross, Oxford, Clarendon Press, 1931.

Augustine, S., *Opera Omnia,* Migne, P. L., Paris, 1879. t.32-44.

Bernard, S., *Super "Missus est"; In Vigilia nativ. Domini,* Migne, P. L., t.183.

Bonaventurae, S., *Opera Omnia* . . . edita studio et cura PP. Collegii S. Bonaventurae . . . anecdotis aucta, prologomenis, scholiis notisque illustrata, ad Claras Aquas (Quaracchi) ex typographia Collegii S. Bonaventurae, 1882-1902.

Chrysostom, S., *In Matthaeum Homil.* xxxii, t.56; *De stud. praesent.,* t.63; *De Virginitate,* t.64, Migne, P. G., Paris.

Cyprian, S., *De Unitate Ecclesiae,* t.4, Migne, P. L.

Gellius, Aulus, *Noctes Atticae* I, II, III, Loeb Classical Library, Harvard University Press: Cambridge, Mass.

Healy, Sister Emma Thérèse, *St. Bonaventure's De Reductione Artium ad Theologiam, A Commentary with an Introduction and Translation,* St. Anthony Guild Press: Paterson, N. J., 1939; second edition, Franciscan Institute, St. Bonaventure, N. Y., 1955.

Hugh of St. Victor, *De B. M. Virginitate,* t.176, Migne, P. L.

Jerome, S., *Ep. 22 ad Eustochium, Ep. 48 ad Pammachium,* t.22; *De Perpetua Virginitate,* t.23, Migne, P. L.

Meyer, Hans, *The Philosophy of St. Thomas* translated by Rev. Frederic Eckhoff, B. Herder Book Co.: St. Louis, Mo., 1944.

Migne, J. P., *Patrologiae cursus completus,* ser. Latina, Paris, 1879.

Pereira, O. F.M., B. Alves, *La Doctrine du Mariage selon Saint Augustin,* Paris, 1930.

Plato, *The Republic,* Loeb Classical Library, Harvard University Press: Cambridge, Mass.

Pohle-Preuss, *Christology; Mariology,* B. Herder Book Co.: St. Louis, Mo., 1930.

Roschini, G. M., *Mariologia,* Rome, 1947.

Scotus, John Duns, *Comment. in Quatuor Libros Sententiarum* edited by Vivès. *Reportata Parisiensia* edited by Vivès. *Joannis Duns Scoti Theologiae Marianae Elementa* edited by C. Balich, Sibenik in Jugoslavia, 1933. *Lectura Completa* edited by C. Balich.

Thomas Aquinas, S., *Summa Theologica,* Paris, Vivès, 1889: *The "Summa Theologica" of St. Thomas Aquinas* literally translated by Fathers of the English Dominican Province, second and revised edition, London, Burns Oates & Washbourne Ltd. Benziger Bros.: New York.

INDEX

Aaron, priesthood of, 161-162
Abigail, type of Mary, 179, 220, 264
Abraham or Abram, 126, 158, 265
Adam, principle of his species, 13-14
  prototype of Christ, 73-74, 233, 254-255
Advocate, title of, 252-253
  St. Anselm on, 253
  St. Bernard on, 253
Agatha, St., 134
Agnes, St., 134
Albert the Great, ix, 11
Alexander of Hales, ii, 12
Ambrose, St., 6, 65, 124, 163, 184, 193, 195
Angel, salutation by, 212-221
Annunciation, the, 171
Anselm, St., 211, 214, 253, 261
Aristotle, 9-12, 30, 79, 123, 132, 165
Ark of the covenant
  figure of Mary, 230, 245-246
Assumption, Mary's, 246-250
Athanasius, St., 6
Augustine, St., 7, 20, 74, 80, 86, 90, 93, 100-102, 120-121, 123, 126, 127-128, 147, 159, 162, 164, 176-177, 179, 189, 214-215
Aureole, the, 135-137

Bernard, St., 184, 190, 192, 193, 198, 199, 213, 216, 217, 218, 219, 228, 235, 253, 257, 259
Birth of Christ, the virginal, 184-186, 196-198
  St. Bernard on, 192, 198
Bonaventure, St., *passim*

Cause of our joy, 211-212, 234
Cecelia, St., 134, 189
Cervantes, 133
Chastity, conjugal, 89-93, virginal, 119-128
  St. Augustine on, 126, 127, 128
  St. Chrysostom on, 128
  Milton's praise of, 133
Chaucer, Geoffrey, 45
Christ, the Ideal Man, 52
  the Virgin, 119, 120
  virginal conception of, 173-178, 180-186
    Hugh of St. Victor on, 210
  virginal birth of, 191, 196-198, St. Bernard on, 198
  His relation to His Mother, 177-180
Chrysostom, St. John, 7, 46, 65, 128, 133, 164
Church, Holy Mother, St. Cyprian on, 71
  Bride of Christ, 71, 83, 107-108
  the Mystical Body of Christ, 71-73
  Virgin-Mother, 241
Circle, the, 74-75
"Closed Gate," 180-181, 184
  St. Ambrose on, 184
Comfort of the afflicted, 257, 259
Concupiscence, 33, 49
  Mary's immunity from, 160-161
"Corruptio optimi pessima," 50
  St. Gregory Nazianzen on, 50
Cyprian, St., 71

Damascene, St. John, 172, 174, 178, 239
Dante, 200, 201, 258
David, Mary of the house of, 161-162, 191-192, 201
  St. Augustine on, 192
  St. Bernard on, 192
Destruction, order of, 30
Dryden, John, 45

Elizabeth, St., 167, 171, 195, 222, 225
Esther, type of Mary, 205, 212, 216, 217, 249, 252, 253, 254, 258, 261, 265
Eve, creation of, 7-8
  sin of, 27-40
  punishment of, 41-45
  prototype of Mary, 209, 234, 240-241, 254-255

Fountain and river as symbols of Mary, 256-257, 261-262
Fullness of Mary's grace, 212-219
  St. Bernard on, 213, 217, 218, 257
  St. Jerome on, 217, 218, 257
  St. Thomas on, 213

Galen, 11-12
"Garden enclosed," 181-266
Gate of Heaven, 259-261, 267, 328, 338
Gate of the Temple, symbol of Mary, 181, 259-261
Grace, Mary's gifts of, 212-219
  St. Bernard on, 213, 216, 217, 218
Gregory of Nazianzen, St., 50
Gregory of Nyssa, 6, 159

Health of the sick, 257
Help of Christians, 254-257
Hippocrates, 11-12
House of Gold, 226-227
Hugh of St. Victor, 88-89, 94-95, 120-121, 188, 210

Incarnation, the plan of, 69-78
  St. Augustine on, 74
Intellect, active and passive, 21-24
  St. Bonaventure on, 21-24
  St. Thomas on, 21-24
Isaac as type of Christ, 158

Jahel, type of Mary, 219
Jerome, St., 124, 128, 129, 183, 190, 240, 257, 262, 265
Joseph, marriage of Mary and, 161-164, 187-194
  "a just man," 190-191
  virginity of, 190-191
    St. Bernard on, 190
    St. Jerome on, 190
  paternity of, 191-192
  witness to Mary's virginity, 192
Judith, 220, 247, 264
Justin, St., 162
Juvenal, 145

Lia, 159, 269
Lily of Christ, 138-154; cf. *Virgin*
Lombard, Peter, 17, 35, 85-86, 163, 164
Lucy, St., 134, 141

Man, creation of, 2-5
the head of woman, 14, 23-24
St. Bonaventure on, 14-15, 104-108
St. Thomas Aquinas on, 15, 105
Marriage, a natural institution, 82-83
Israelites' view of, 119, 159
of God with human race, 203
Christian, 79-109
definition of Peter Lombard, 87
definition of St. Bonaventure, 87
its symbolism, 83-85, 88-89, 94-95
Hugh of St. Victor on, 94-95
sacredness of, 90-93
St. Augustine on, 90, 93
its primary physical end, 7
its three qualities, 26, 95-99, 102
its nature and purpose, 87-101
St. Thomas Aquinas on, 101
Pope Pius XI on, 94
its threefold blessing, 100-103
St. Augustine on, 100-102
its reciprocal obligations, 104-108
its spheres of activity, 109-114
Aristotle on, 109
Plato on, 109
remedy against concupiscence, 83
St. Augustine, St. Bonaventure, Peter Lombard, St. Thomas Aquinas on, 85-86
essence of, 162-163, 164
St. Ambrose on, 163
St. Augustine, Peter Lombard and Hugh of St. Victor on, 163-164
St. Chrysostom on, 164
of Mary to Joseph, 161-164, 187-194
St. Augustine on, 189
Hugh of St. Victor on, 188-189
reasons for Mary's marriage, 192-194
St. Ambrose and St. Bernard on, 193
Mary, Blessed Virgin
the Ideal Woman, 157-168
the perfect virgin, 158-161
the perfect wife, 161-164
the perfect mother, 165-168, 194-198
the Virgin Mother of God, 169-202
her dignity, 168
Mother of Christ, 173-180
St. John Damascene on, 174, 178
Purification of, 183-184
Spouse of the Holy Ghost, 194-195
St. Ambrose on, 195
Bride Mother of Christ, 203-244
St. Bernard on, 204
St. Jerome on, 210
her humility, 196, 226
her purity, 224-226
a virtuous woman, 264
a beautiful woman, 264-265
a gracious woman, 265-266
a dutiful woman, 266-267
a valiant woman, 235, 238-241, 264
her death, 245
her assumption into heaven, 246-250
her enthronement, 250-251
her crowning as Queen, 251-252
the Eve of the New Covenant, 254-257, 270
Matter and form, 9, 17-19
Mediatress, Mary our, 252-254
St. Anselm on, 253
St. Bernard on, 257, 258-259
Meyer, Hans, ix, 10, 15, 105
Mirror of Justice, 227-228
Morning Star, 206-207, 258-259
Mother, Mary the perfect, 165-168, 194-198
Mother Inviolate, 180-187
Mother most chaste, 187-194
Mother most admirable, 194-198
St. Ambrose on, 195
St. Bernard on, 196-198
Mother of Our Creator, 198-200
Mother Undefiled, 214-215
Mother most pure, 224-226
Mother most amiable, 230-231
Mother of Our Redeemer, 233-238
cf. *Mary's spiritual motherhood,* 233-244
Mother of divine grace, 256-257
Mother most merciful, 252-253, 256, 257
Mother of Good Counsel, 258
Mother of the Mystical Body of Christ, 241-242
Motherhood, human, 165-166
Israelites' views of, 159
Aristotle's views of, 165, 166
spiritual, 233
Mary's physical, 173-179
St. Augustine on, 176-177, 178
Mary's spiritual, 233-244
St. Augustine on, 232
Mystical Rose, 200-202

Nazarites, 158, 159
Nestorius, 172, 176
Nicolas, Blessed, 47

Paradise, freedoms of, 27
Plato, 79
Pope Sixtus V, ix
Presentation of Jesus in temple, 183
Procreation, the human, 8-9
Aristotle's views on, 9-12
St. Bonaventure's views on, 10-13
St. Thomas Aquinas' views on, 9-12
woman's part in, 9-13
two schools of thought on, 11-12
Duns Scotus on, 12

Queen of All Saints, 246-252
Queen of Angels, 248-249, 250
Queen of Apostles, 243-244, 250
Queen of Confessors, 244, 250
Queen of Heaven, 250-252
Queen of Heaven and Earth, 245-268
Queen of Martyrs, 238-240, 250
Queen of Mercy, 253, 256
Queen of Patriarchs, 247, 250
Queen of Peace, 250
Queen of Prophets, 250
Queen of the Universe, 260
St. Anselm on, 260, 261
Queen of Virgins, 250

Rachel, 159
Rebecca, 159, 221
Reason, higher and lower, 21-23
Refuge of sinners, 254, 257
Resurrection of women, 80
St. Augustine on, 80
Ruth, type of Mary, 159, 220, 264

Sacrament, definition of, 85

INDEX

Sacrament of Baptism, 72
  of Matrimony, 87-115
  of Holy Orders, 103, 121
Sara or Sarai, type of Mary, 159, 167, 195, 204, 265
Scotus, Duns, 11, 12, 17, 174, footnote 8
Seat of Wisdom, 228-230
  St. Bernard on, 228
Serpent, the, 28, 29
Sexes, the corporal unity of the, 6
  distinction of the, 6-8
    views of St. Athanasius, St. Ambrose and St. Gregory of Nyssa on, 6
    St. Chrysostom on, 7
    St. Augustine on, 7, 20
  complements of each other, 18
    cf. *Intellect, active and passive*
  attraction of the, 18-19
  purpose of the difference in the, 6
  inequality of the, 13-15, 21-23
  moral and spiritual equality of the, 25-26, 31, 106-108
  nature and qualities of the, 23-25, 109-115
    Aristotle's views on, 109-110
    Plato's views on, 109
Sin, original, 39-40
  of Adam, 35-38
  of Eve, 35-38
    Peter Lombard on, 35
Singular Vessel of Devotion, 238-241
Sinlessness, Mary's, 214-215
  St. Augustine on, 214
Shakespeare, William, 133
Soul, the breath of God, 2
  the image of God, 3-5
  the creation of the, 7
  the, the form of the body, 19
  "imago creationis," 72-73
  "imago recreationis," 72-73
  individual differences in souls, 16-18
    St. Bonaventure, Duns Scotus, Peter Lombard and St. Thomas Aquinas on, 16-17
  infusion of Christ's, 176
Spiritual Vessel, 209-212
  St. Anselm on, 211
Sun, the symbol of Mary, 262-268

Thomas Aquinas, St., ix, 5, 9-12, 15, 17, 20, 21, 22, 85, 101, 105, 213
Tower of David, 254
Tower of Ivory, 253

Veneration, Mary's right to, 246-249
Vessel of election, Mary the, 205-206
Vessel of honor, 205-206, 209
Virgin, the Lily of Christ, 138-154
  her humility, 139
  her purity, 140-141
  Mary, the perfect, 158-161
  Holy Virgin of Virgins, 207-209
Virgin most faithful, 222-224
Virgin most powerful, 257-258
Virgin most prudent, 220-222
  St. Bernard on, 220
Virgin most renowned, 219-220
Virgin most venerable, 246-249
Virginity, its three aspects, 119-128
  the virtue of, 120-125
    St. Augustine on, 120, 121, 123
  the loss of, 124-125
    St. Jerome on, 124
  the glory of, 125, 128, 136-137
  state of, compared with state of Matrimony, 125-128
    St. Augustine, St. Chrysostom and St. Jerome on, 128
  excellence of, 129-134
  reward of, 135-137
    St. Jerome on, 129
  six advantages of, 142-153
    St. Augustine on, 147-148
  in the Old Law, 158-160
  Mary's physical, 180-187
  Mary's vow of, 158-161
  Mary's spiritual, 207-233

Widow, 53, 56-58
Wife, 53
  Mary, the perfect, 161-164, 187-194
    Peter Lombard on, 164
Woman, her formation from rib of Adam, 7-8, 13-15, 21-26
  her equality with man, 1-5, 79-81
    Peter Lombard on, 15
  her inequality with man, 13-15
  man's help-meet, 7-8, 15, 19-20
    cf. *Procreation, human*
  her part in human generation, 9-13, 165-166
  her physical nature, 6-15
    Aristotle on, 9-10, 79
    St. Thomas on, 10
  her psychological nature, 16-26, 40
    St. Thomas Aquinas on, 20-21
  her subjection to man, 106-107
  her part in the Fall, 27-40
  her punishment, 41-45
  St. Bonaventure's attitude toward, ix, 46-51
  St. Thomas' attitude toward, ix, 9-12, 20-21
  St. Chrysostom's opinion of, 46
  Christ's attitude toward, 52-65
  mission of, 53
  first to announce Christ's resurrection, 65
    St. Ambrose and St. Chrysostom on, 65
  in Christian marriage, 79-116
  the Valiant Woman, 113-114, 238-244, 264
    St. Bernard on, 235-236
Women, in Gospel stories, 53-65
  their faith, 54-56
  their devotion to Christ, 60-65
  their reward, 64-65
  the resurrection of, 80